Autocrats Can't Always Get What They Want

EMERGING DEMOCRACIES

Series Editors

Dan Slater is James Orin Murfin Professor of Political Science
and Director, Center for Emerging Democracies
University of Michigan

Pauline Jones is Professor of Political Science
and Edie N. Goldenberg Endowed Director,
Michigan in Washington Program, University of Michigan

---

*Struggles for Political Change in the Arab World: Regimes, Oppositions,
and External Actors after the Spring*
Lisa Blaydes, Amr Hamzawy, and Hesham Sallam, Editors

*Autocrats Can't Always Get What They Want: State Institutions and Autonomy
under Authoritarianism*
Nathan J. Brown, Steven D. Schaaf, Samer Anabtawi, and Julian G. Waller

Seeds of Mobilization: The Authoritarian Roots of South Korea's Democracy
Joan E. Cho

None of the Above: Protest Voting in Latin American Democracies
Mollie J. Cohen

The Troubling State of India's Democracy
Šumit Ganguly, Dinsha Mistree, and Larry Diamond, Editors

Lobbying the Autocrat: The Dynamics of Policy Advocacy in Nondemocracies
Max Grömping and Jessica C. Teets, Editors

Ghosts in the Neighborhood: Why Japan Is Haunted by Its Past and Germany Is Not
Walter F. Hatch

Making Sense of the Arab State
Steven Heydemann and Marc Lynch, Editors

*The Dictator's Dilemma at the Ballot Box: Electoral Manipulation,
Economic Maneuvering, and Political Order in Autocracies*
Masaaki Higashijima

*State Institutions, Civic Associations, and Identity Demands:
Regional Movements in Greater Southeast Asia*
Amy H. Liu and Joel Sawat Selway, Editors

Opposing Power: Building Opposition Alliances in Electoral Autocracies
Elvin Ong

A complete list of titles in the series can be found at www.press.umich.edu

Autocrats Can't Always Get What They Want

State Institutions and Autonomy under Authoritarianism

NATHAN J. BROWN
STEVEN D. SCHAAF
SAMER ANABTAWI
& JULIAN G. WALLER

UNIVERSITY OF MICHIGAN PRESS

ANN ARBOR

Copyright © 2024 by Nathan J. Brown, Steven D. Schaaf,
Samer Anabtawi, and Julian G. Waller
Some rights reserved

This work is licensed under a Creative Commons Attribution-NonCommercial 4.0 International License. *Note to users:* A Creative Commons license is only valid when it is applied by the person or entity that holds rights to the licensed work. Works may contain components (e.g., photographs, illustrations, or quotations) to which the rightsholder in the work cannot apply the license. It is ultimately your responsibility to independently evaluate the copyright status of any work or component part of a work you use, in light of your intended use. To view a copy of this license, visit http://creativecommons.org/licenses/by-nc/4.0/

For questions or permissions, please contact um.press.perms@umich.edu

Published in the United States of America by the
University of Michigan Press
Manufactured in the United States of America
Printed on acid-free paper
First published August 2024

A CIP catalog record for this book is available from the British Library.

Library of Congress Cataloging-in-Publication Data

Names: Brown, Nathan J., author. | Schaaf, Steven D., author. | Anabtawi, Samer, author. | Waller, Julian G., author. | Michigan Publishing (University of Michigan), publisher.
Title: Autocrats can't always get what they want : state institutions and autonomy under authoritarianism / Nathan J. Brown, Steven D. Schaaf, Samer Anabtawi & Julian G. Waller.
Other titles: Autocrats cannot always get what they want | Weiser Center for Emerging Democracies series.
Description: Ann Arbor [Michigan] : University of Michigan, 2024. | Series: Emerging democracies | Includes bibliographical references (pages 271–293) and index.
Identifiers: LCCN 2024013660 (print) | LCCN 2024013661 (ebook) | ISBN 9780472076970 (hardcover) | ISBN 9780472056972 (paperback) | ISBN 9780472904600 (ebook other)
Subjects: LCSH: Authoritarianism. | Dictatorship. | Public institutions—Management. | Autonomy.
Classification: LCC JC480 .B75 2024 (print) | LCC JC480 (ebook) | DDC 320.53—dc23/eng/20240418
LC record available at https://lccn.loc.gov/2024013660
LC ebook record available at https://lccn.loc.gov/2024013661

DOI: https://doi.org/10.3998/mpub.12761544

The University of Michigan Press's open access publishing program is made possible thanks to additional funding from the University of Michigan Office of the Provost and the generous support of contributing libraries.

Cover photograph: Presidential Address to the Federal Assembly, Gostiny Dvor, Moscow, February 21, 2023. Photograph by Maxim Blinov, RIA Novosti, courtesy of Kremlin.ru (CC-BY 4.0).

This book is dedicated to Amy Hawthorne, Harolene June Pickens, Diana Nassar, and Gordon and Joan Paille.

Contents

Acknowledgments	ix
1. Understanding Authoritarianism	1
2. Taking Some Parts of Authoritarian States Seriously, Sometimes	55
3. Constitutional Courts	89
4. Parliaments	135
5. Religious Establishments	187
6. Does Authoritarianism Make a Difference? No, but Democracy Does	243
Bibliography	271
Index	295

Acknowledgments

This book is the product of individual wrestling but collective collaboration. Each of us found ourselves delving into overlapping aspects of authoritarian governance as part of our scholarly work even though we focused on different structures (judiciaries, religious establishments, social movements, and parliaments). Our home discipline of political science had a lot of guidance to give on how to think about authoritarianism, but that guidance proved to be quite varied in how useful it was in the specific instances we encountered. We began by surveying what had been written with an eye to understanding not only our discipline's collective wisdom and ongoing divides but also its blind spots—ones we indeed found, but many of which were of surprisingly recent vintage.

The resulting book proceeded very much as a collaborative project as we read and researched together—all the while carrying on our independent work. Three of us were writing doctoral dissertations when we began this project, while a fourth had filed his dissertation long ago but was continuing empirical research on matters related to authoritarian governance. We consulted regularly with colleagues, who were supportive and helpful, sometimes through their encouragement, often through their doubts, and always through their suggestions of ways to refine, correct, or add to what we were saying. In particular, we express sincere gratitude to Isam Abdeen, Sultan Alamer, Celeste Arrington, Lucy Barnes, Brandon Bartels, Mark Berlin, Ingrid Creppel, Bruce Dickson, Veronika Fikfak, Lillian Frost, Stas Gorelik, Henry Hale, Adam Harris, Patrick Jory, Gabriel Kelly, Eric Kramon, Janet Lewis, Yonatan Lupu, Michael Miller, Kimberly Morgan, Rosalie Rubio, Sverrir Steinson, Anum Syed, Julie Thompson-Gomez, Lisa Vanhala, and Scott Williamson.

At the University of Michigan Press, we encountered a truly helpful review process and a distinctly helpful set of suggestions for refinements. Readers of this book should add their gratitude to ours for the guidance and help we received in improving its contents. We are thankful for the support provided by Dan Slater, the series editor; Elizabeth Demers, who oversaw the earlier stages of the project; and Haley Winkle, who helped push this project through to its conclusion.

CHAPTER I

Understanding Authoritarianism

Rebel General Alfredo, delivering his demands to mediator Joachim Messner to exchange his hostages for the president:

> "They won't give the President," Messner said.
> "That's who we came for."
> Messner sighed and nodded seriously. "Well, I came here on vacation. It seems that no one is going to get what they want."
> —Ann Patchett, *Bel Canto*

Egypt's president to the Shaykh of al-Azhar on the latter's reluctance to endorse changes in divorce procedures (January 2017):

> "You wear me out . . ."
> —President Abdel Fattah al-Sisi

Authoritarianism seems to be everywhere in the political world, but how do authoritarian systems work? We have learned a lot about how they begin and end, but how do they live and breathe in the meantime? Is an authoritarian system whatever an unaccountable ruler wants it to be, or do its rules, procedures, and institutions matter in ways unrelated to rulers' interests? We write this book in part to answer the question: If we wish to understand how authoritarian systems work, when should we look at the interests and intentions of those at the top and when should we look at the inner workings of the various parts of the state?

We answer that question by saying, "It depends." That response is far less banal than may initially appear, since we also write the book to explore what it depends on. Our objective is to understand when and under what sort of contexts the inner workings of authoritarian states matter. To this end, our inquiry investigates the conditions under which authoritarian state institutions (courts, legislatures, even religious establishments) develop autonomy over their own operations and in designing and pursuing their missions in sociopolitical life. Indeed, our view is that state institutions—and their varying degrees of autonomy from the whims of the ruling executive—often matter quite a bit when we think about the quotidian realities of authoritarian systems.

For many ordinary citizens, state officials, and even rulers, how state institutions work is self-evidently important. A spouse trapped in an abusive marriage is less likely to ask about the intention of the regime and more about how courts, police, and public social service providers have made policy over such issues. A judge dealing with a crushing load of cases likely wishes to know whether it is better to please a party apparatchik by acquitting his friends or, alternatively, a judicial superior by speedily plowing through case files in order to earn a promotion. A leader of the doctors' syndicate would certainly benefit from knowing whether to lobby the Ministry of Health, powerful local bosses, or parliament itself if she wishes to change licensing requirements.

Even dictators have such questions: President al-Sisi of Egypt has not been worried that the turbaned and learned Shaykh of al-Azhar might overthrow him, but he did try to get the Shaykh to toe the official line about terrorism, clamp down on problematic scholars, and support government policy initiatives—and the president failed on each count. Similarly, Russia's President Putin did not worry that the Constitutional Court was about to challenge his new (legally unnecessary) constitutional referendum in 2020, yet that same court was unmolested as it reasserted its own authority among the judicial organs of the Russian state and focused on enforcement follow-through by other state ministries at the same time.[1]

The variation in state institutional autonomy that we seek to explain is, thus, quite important; indeed, since most politics is not about regime change—and regime change is not a common thing—we are probing the sorts of politics that most people are concerned about most of the time.

Our question about how authoritarianism operates in the day-to-day and year-to-year tumble of politics does not assume that such systems

---

1. Alexei Trochev and Peter H. Solomon (2018), "Authoritarian Constitutionalism in Putin's Russia: A Pragmatic Constitutional Court in a Dual State," *Communist and Post-Communist Studies* 51 (3): 201–14.

always operate in the same way; surely they do not, nor should we expect them to. In the coming chapters, we show that when state bodies institutionalize themselves and forge linkages with other political actors, they are better equipped to realize a meaningful degree of autonomy over their internal affairs and may even be able to pursue their own sense of mission in politics. And we show how deeply these conditions vary—that authoritarian systems can be quite different in how much and in what ways their inner workings matter.

These claims cut against the grain of a sizeable corpus of recent scholarship, which often bypasses the variation that interests us and, when it does indeed notice it, explains that variation primarily in terms of the intentions of rulers or the stability that autonomous institutions can provide to a regime. This body of work most typically approaches authoritarianism *from the top down*; it takes authoritarian institutions seriously but also adopts a macrolevel view that focuses specifically on how institutions are perceived and utilized by autocrats seeking to maximize power and prolong their rule. Of course, an emerging literature on authoritarian institutions is now increasingly interested in exploring their activity *from the bottom up*, emphasizing how publics, political activists, and social movements either mobilize or eschew engagement with authoritarian state institutions when pursuing their agendas.

While both approaches have produced important insights, they reflect a shared view that authoritarian institutions matter primarily in terms of how they are deployed by forces outside the institutions in question, whose agency and interests receive the main analytical spotlight. The top-down approaches in particular explain and understand the role of institutions through ascribed *functionalist* logics—a characterization of an approach to political knowledge that privileges explanations for why a given institution exists and what it does based on assumptions of utility and usefulness to the ruler and regime. A court that delivers defeats to ministerial challenges from this vantage is thus explained as solving some principle-agent problem for the dictator, or a parliament whose committees seem unusually active is simply doing so because it is distributing rents or coordinating elites in a way that is helpful to the regime.

We agree that this approach has important (and enticingly parsimonious) explanatory power. And it sometimes works. But it has often been overstretched and too uniformly applied to provide a universally valid way to view authoritarian political systems. Functionalist logics are powerful yet sometimes fail in the details or require handwaving when something does not seem to make sense. If a state institution does something strange, we must just look harder for how it serves the ruler. Most dangerously, functionalism can result in a picture of an authoritarian system in which the chief mover of causal import is always the regime executive, with everything else in the polity's institutional ecosystem explained primarily as a function of their will, whim, and wish.

In this book, we choose to investigate authoritarianism *from the inside out* in order to make distinctions that better explain when and how authoritarian institutions can manage their own activity, develop and pursue their own political interests, and exhibit a distinctive agency that warrants independent consideration. We look within the sprawling body of the authoritarian state to better appreciate how its institutions operate and, further, to draw attention to the possibility that authoritarian institutions might serve themselves just as much as their political masters or public clienteles.

The point of departure in our project is conceptual. This introductory chapter explains why a new theoretical approach to authoritarian politics is not just warranted but necessary. Our task here is to examine why existing conceptions of authoritarianism so commonly seem to obscure the analysis of state institutions as autonomous entities, even though those entities can sometimes—but certainly not always—carry tremendous weight in policymaking and enforcement across the heterogeneous swathe of today's authoritarian countries.

We begin first by developing our account of how authoritarianism operates in broad strokes—and, specifically, by outlining our argument on the conditions that allow state institutions (the operating machinery of authoritarian politics) to achieve real autonomy when performing their roles. Second, we work to establish conceptual clarity by detailing how this book defines "authoritarianism" and "institutions," as well as by highlighting how the ways in which we fall in line with existing definitions (and why) are just as intellectually provocative as the ways in which we diverge. Third, we show why conducting institutional analysis in authoritarian systems has become so tricky and why there is a strong impulse (which we wish to resist but not fully abandon) to place much of the analytical spotlight on autocrats—as opposed to the institutions themselves. Finally, we explore how forging a new path forward will require renewing our efforts—and recovering some older efforts—to tease out the boundaries and distinctions among rulers, regimes, and states in authoritarian settings.

How Does Authoritarianism Work—for Those Who Work It?

Much of the current interest in authoritarian politics has inherited an intellectual genealogy taken from the quirks and interests of a scholarly community that grew very interested in democracy, democratization, and transitions in the late twentieth century. Scholars have since developed some very good tools to understand how long authoritarianism lasts and what happens when it breaks down. But these tools do not always lend themselves to good answers when our question shifts from explaining regime change and persistence to asking how authoritarian governance operates most of the time—the quotidian life of authoritarian rule that occupies the attention of most such regimes and the people they rule the vast majority of the time.

Our move to examine how authoritarian state institutions operate *from the inside out* is motivated by our own research—sometimes encountering systems run by "dictators" (who are indeed dictatorial) but where the inner workings often seemed to be beyond the reach or even interests of those whose will was supposed to apparently dictate policy. We have come across autocrats who found important levers of state power inaccessible or who mastered them so crudely that the machinery of the state backfired on them. We have met judges, bureaucrats, and midlevel officials who seemed to have some real sense of professional mission; those who advanced their careers not by toeing the regime's line but by currying favor with their colleagues or constituents; and enclaves within the state that seemed to carry on regardless of who was at the helm of the political system. And we have encountered groups of citizens who approach state structures whose officials did not always look to the top for guidance before deciding how to respond.

For some, the idea that authoritarian rulers or regimes (or those governed by them) are truly concerned with institutions—much less constrained by them—is improbable. But many others are rediscovering an older truth that authoritarianism and institutions are not always opposites. These scholars have begun to take state institutions quite seriously even when the regime controlling them is authoritarian. But much of this scholarly effort still falls back on the interests or intentions of autocrats, properly understood. It does so by uncovering ways in which authoritarian rulers and regimes can maintain themselves better if they tolerate some institutions (such as parliaments) and even allow some autonomy to critical parts of the state (such as judiciaries or even militaries).

This can be a very useful perspective, though it is quite top-down. But it risks falling into the trap of assuming that all institutional configurations serve the ruler, and the task of scholars is more broadly to find out when and how. More subtly, it can leave a great deal of intra-institutional variation among regimes unexplained: if, for instance, we discover that authoritarian regimes that allow parliaments survive longer, then why do some rulers avoid them? And why is there such tremendous variation among authoritarian countries in the roles that parliaments play?

Perhaps the explanation does not simply lie in the intentions or interests of the ruler or the regime. Any global answer to the question "Why do authoritarian rulers allow parliaments?," for instance, can subtly lead us away from such historical particularities. King George I did not create a parliament from whole cloth in order to help him solidify his succession to the throne, though it did so. The Hanoverians found parliament when they got there—and were able to use it. Other Georges in later years found that very same parliament to be much less useful, cooperative, or malleable, at least from their ruler-centric perspective. Yet in no sense could we call eighteenth-century England a democracy, nor should we stretch our definitions to Whiggishly make it a democracy-in-waiting.

The realization that authoritarian rulers can profit from institutions has gone a long way in reinforcing the scholarly tendency to adopt functionalist logics when studying authoritarian politics. To be specific, we use the term *functionalist* here primarily to mean the attempt to explain *attributes* of the system (such as autonomous judiciaries) by reference to the *purpose* or *role* they serve in maintaining the system. A closely related, if sometimes arguably distinct, usage of functionalism is to cast attributes of the system purely as functions of regime or ruler actions, intentions, or interests (with the distinction among these three often receding in importance).

That is, if judges are independent, it is because a ruler made them so, wanted them so, or has an interest in them being so. Functionalist logics are commonly associated with a unique way of asking research questions and framing puzzles that can sometimes get dangerous by baking in important pieces of their answers by assumption: Why, exactly, do *dictators create, establish, tolerate, or allow* this or that state institution? Why, perhaps, do *dictators permit* some state institutions to acquire autonomy? These logics, correspondingly, lead to a distinctly top-down way of answering those questions by virtue of assuming the "who" (dictators) and the "how" (executive creation or permission) behind variation in institutional structure ex ante.

A strict functionalist logic is one that posits that autocrats deliberately create state institutions to serve a specific purpose and that, once created, the institution does precisely that. A looser, and more nuanced, functionalist logic may refrain from assuming that autocrats create institutions and imbue them with their will (admittedly a reductionist treatment of complex historical processes) but would still ultimately arrive at the view that autocrats countenance an institution's existence because they find it useful in some way. Such views can sometimes allow that rulers make hard choices—tolerating some institutional autonomy even when it does not always align with their short-term goals—secure in the knowledge that the institution enjoying limited autonomy will ultimately serve the regime's survival or other long-term interests.

In both cases, we wind up explaining institutions by the needs of the system, the regime, or the ruler. So, when we look at authoritarian regimes throughout the world and see that those with parliaments last longer, we arrive at a retroactive understanding for why rulers would create them.

But, again, what if we are interested in variation among quite disparate systems that are all authoritarian? And what if we take a historical view and begin noticing that many regimes do not create but instead inherit their parliaments? And what if we wish to explore the changing role of a parliament over time, or over a given plenary session, or in a specific policy sphere, or in certain procedural prerogatives and activities?

A functionalist logic might get us somewhere in some instances, and this book will not dismiss any functionalist explanation out of hand. Instead, we are interested in when functionalism will help us, when it will not, and where else to look if systemic needs or ruler desires cannot help us analytically. A focus on history does not rule out ruler intentions or interests, but a historical institutionalist approach—which is what we follow in this book—can lead us to emphasize other neglected parts of a comprehensive explanation. This historical institutionalist framework allows us to make better sense of the low-level political chaos, awkwardly plural struggles, and bungling institutional confusion that is often more typical of authoritarian systems than a functionalist view easily allows.

Historical institutionalism is a framework approach that emphasizes how timing, sequences, and path dependence affect institutions and, in so doing, shape social, political, and economic behavior and change.[2] The his-

---

2. Sven Steinmo (2008), "Historical Institutionalism," in *Approaches and Methodologies in the Social Sciences: A Pluralist Perspective*, ed. Donatella Della Porta and Michael Keating (New York: Cambridge University Press).

torical institutionalist approach typically relies on inductive lessons from empirical case studies, and it is attuned to critical junctures and the political vagaries that have long-standing ramifications over time.

For our purposes, historical institutionalism provides a valuable corrective to the currently dominant theories of regime intentionality. It alerts us to emphasizing the contingent nature of social and political life and its foreseeable (and unforeseeable) knock-on effects. Our goal in applying a historical and institutionalist analysis is to maintain theoretical modesty; the approach lets us discover autocratic intentionality where it exists and releases us from being perturbed and theoretically confounded when such deductively presumed intentionality does not seem to explain empirical variation across country cases.

Suboptimal arrangements are everywhere in authoritarian politics, far more readily so than effective top-down direction. Weaving together the historical and institutionalist perspectives aids us considerably as we deal with the effects of institutional evolution, the lock-in of odd privileges and prerogatives, and the complicated layering of vying bureaucracies, competing fiefdoms, and crystalized societal and elite expectations about how things are and should be done.

In carrying out our empirical analysis, we will demonstrate that in authoritarian polities, political power—the capacity to set the agenda, decide on areas of authority, effectuate policy change, and act as the final arbiter over decisions and nondecisions—can often be more diffuse, haphazard, and contingent than much of the existing literature would lead us to believe. And we will also find linkages between state institutions and important social constituencies littered throughout the political system, though in varying ways and to varying degrees. Viewing authoritarianism primarily from the top can lead us to miss important dynamism below.

Looking beyond the strategies that authoritarian rulers use to maximize their power and survival, we aim to explain when—and how—state institutions separate from the autocratic executive matter under authoritarianism. When do authoritarian institutions acquire the capability to run their own affairs and set their own agendas—and to what degree? In which areas can state institutions wield influence independent of authoritarian rulers and regimes? Under what conditions will they actually engage in policymaking, influence decisions, provide interpretations on how to govern, resist overrule, or engage in distinct pursuits they develop on their own? And do they do so even when such actions may conflict with the ruler's or regime's core interests?

By probing these questions, we argue that state institutions in authoritarian systems are most capable of achieving *internal autonomy* (control over their own affairs and operation) and *mission autonomy* (influence over decision-making, zones of authority, and policy development) when:

- they maintain strong *linkages* to supportive constituencies vertically within society or horizontally across other elements of the state apparatus; and
- they enjoy a high degree of internal *institutionalization* in the form of stable processes that provide structural hierarchy, coherence, complexity, and adaptability.

Because we take a close look at particular cases and pursue an approach that relies heavily on history, we will show that different dimensions of autonomy emerge in a multiplicity of patterns that are often unique to the case, the time period, and the specific nature of the institution and thus vary considerably. But close historical study does not prevent generalization: we also argue that the variation can be most easily explained through reference to linkages with extra-institutional sources of power and processes of institutionalization that serve to strengthen the body overall.

In addition to an exploration of the institutional complexity inherent in how authoritarianism works, this book is an effort to clarify exactly when currently reigning theories and functionalist lenses hold well—and when they do not. And here, too, we will observe linkages and institutionalization to be important factors. As we discuss regarding scope conditions in chapter 2, functionalist logics are most empirically powerful when state institutions are poorly institutionalized and unlinked to non-regime audiences in the state and society.

In such circumstances, institutional activity is acutely dependent upon elite (dis)favor and more amenable to change in line with the goals of rulers and regime officials. Functionalist theories that emphasize regime interests are, thus, not one-size-fits-all tools as they are so commonly treated in contemporary scholarship. Instead, they become suitable tools for explaining ebbs and flows in institutional autonomy precisely when linkages and institutionalization are either absent or notably fragile.

In developing these arguments, we may be cutting against the grain of recent writings. But we are actually seeking to revive some of the insights of older writers on the politics of what we now call authoritarianism, who often took the institutional richness and structural diversity of authoritarian systems much more seriously and treated authoritarian institutions as more autonomous than recent scholarly writings. They were often more alert to ways in which important social groups were linked to official actors.

We proceed first by defining the term "authoritarianism" as it will be used throughout this project and by discussing why that particular usage is both conceptually and empirically meaningful. We then move to specify how we conceptualize authoritarian "institutions" as the object of our inquiry and, subsequently, to detail how the evolved scholarly understanding of authoritarian political systems both introduces and camouflages obstacles to fine-grained institutional analysis within those systems.

What Defines an "Authoritarian" System and Why It Matters

Authoritarian systems are not democratic—by definition—but the term "authoritarianism" originally indicated only a partial subset of nondemocratic regimes while other terms, such as "totalitarian" or "sultanistic" regimes, were initially set apart from authoritarian systems. While it has been forgotten by many, this tendency to define authoritarianism in contradistinction to a range of systems (and not just define it as nondemocracy) was quite explicit in much work—three decades ago, Philippe C. Schmitter and Terry Lynn Karl wrote of regime types: "Democratic is one; others are autocratic, authoritarian, despotic, dictatorial, tyrannical, totalitarian, absolutist, traditional, monarchic, oligarchic, plutocratic, aristocratic, and sultanistic." They referred readers to Juan Linz for his similarly "valiant attempt to make some sense out of this thicket of distinctions."[3]

In recent years, scholars have gradually evolved in their usage of the term by clear-cutting the thicket to the point that they now treat authoritarianism as an expansive residual category that encompasses all nondemocratic regimes. Much of this evolution has occurred without really acknowledging it as such—while "authoritarianism" began as something a bit more specific than "nondemocracy," that conceptual specificity has receded in most current understandings.

We do not fight the tide that has swept all nondemocracies into the authoritarian realm. But we wish to be conscious and explicit about the implications of doing so. In this book we will apply our argument to a diverse array of nondemocratic systems, and thus we do not resist this

---

3. Philippe C. Schmitter and Terry Lynn Karl (1991), "What Democracy Is . . . and Is Not," *Journal of Democracy* 2 (3): 75–88.

evolved definition and follow the practice of treating authoritarianism as a residual category. But we do not wish for the implications of this (otherwise often unacknowledged) choice to pass unnoticed. We will accept the residual definition for its undoubted utility. But we will simultaneously hold firmly to conceptual caution by working to insist that the residual definition should not lead us to overlook the great variations in the way authoritarianism works in practice and, in particular, the variation in the roles played by state institutions.

Our caution here is in reaction to the widespread trend toward overstretching the application of top-down and functionalist logics that was discussed above. Such top-down approaches can be quite warranted and fruitful in some cases (i.e., when analyzing state bodies with low linkages and institutionalization). But they also fall a bit too easily into implicit assumptions that describing a system as authoritarian tells us much of what we need to know about how it operates and, more to the point, that we can analyze and understand all of the institutional variation guided by a belief that whatever exists was created by and serves the interests of the ruler. Our response is to say, "Not so fast . . . sometimes yes, but sometimes no. It varies. Perhaps we need to take a closer look and make fewer underlying assumptions."

An authoritarian system is nondemocratic to be sure, but this does not mean that it is a system in which an unelected autocrat is in absolute control of the state apparatus. Of course, nobody would actually advance such a claim in its starkest forms. But scholars of authoritarian politics face a great need to make sense of a complicated political world, one further compounded by the fact that the term "authoritarianism" itself broadly encompasses most political systems that have ever existed in human history—indeed, all the very, very many ways to describe different varieties of nondemocracy. More than anything else, this tremendous scope and heterogeneity across political systems that we now define as "authoritarian" creates a great need for simplifying assumptions.

And given that simplifying assumptions are necessary, seeing dictators and autocratic regimes as controlling the system and molding it to suit their needs from the top down often seems like a good one. Leaning into this assumption, however, has significant ramifications for the inferences that we make about—and the way that we understand—authoritarian politics. Despite their enormous institutional diversity, scholars making this top-down assumption have generally, and almost unavoidably, come to approach authoritarian states as if they all operate according to an overarching logic of regime survival.[4] State and regime can thus be collapsed together and jointly understood through a straightforward exercise of probing an autocrat's needs and desires.

With this line of inquiry, theories in the field can fall into an unspoken view that authoritarian systems are roughly homologous at an essential level as much as they may vary in many particulars—headed by a dictatorial individual or collective, supported by a host of institutions (courts, parliaments, bureaucracies, armies, intelligence services, and so on), the existence and structure of which do vary but do so primarily because of acts of self-serving intelligent design by the dictator. Dictators do face dilemmas at times—they need an institution to be credible or to perform well, but they do not wish it to be able to ignore regime instructions or needs. On this view, authoritarian societies are treated uniformly—even if not deliberately—as systems where state institutions lack much independent relevance in policy and decision-making influence except when it is functional for the system or the ruler.

A general notion that dictators wield significant control over state institutions is often quite valid, but they may do so for a variety of motives or be short-sighted and make a number of mistakes. And even when dictators do mold institutions, we should not forget they rarely do so ex nihilo; most institutions evolve from the patrimony of an often distant and complicated inheritance.

The implicit assumptions that guide current efforts are thus not always wrong, but neither are they always right. As we will show throughout this book, they hold much better in some cases than others, and the criteria differentiating such cases are intimately related to institutional (mesolevel)—and not just systemic (macrolevel)—attributes that vary significantly within and across nondemocratic systems.

Moreover, expecting uniformity in the appropriateness of these top-down assumptions across authoritarian countries seems implausible, especially since we generally define an authoritarian system by what it is not, dumping the enormous range of nondemocratic polities together into one basket. We may not always be wrong to do so; there might indeed be things that all nondemocratic systems share. Simplifying assumptions can make generalization easier, but they have costs. And in recognition of these costs,

---

4. Bruce Bueno de Mesquita, Alastair Smith, Randolph M. Siverson, and James D. Morrow (2003), *The Logic of Political Survival* (Cambridge: MIT Press). Jennifer Gandhi and Adam Przeworski (2007), "Authoritarian Institutions and the Survival of Autocrats," *Comparative Political Studies* 40 (11): 1279–1301.

we believe that engaging in an exercise of conceptual humility may provide more avenues for insight than the tools and approaches that we have converged on in recent decades.

Through a range of historical case studies, this book aims to cultivate a deeper understanding of the structures conducting day-to-day politics within an authoritarian state—when and how state institutions begin to control their own affairs and pursue missions or interests that are distinct from those of an authoritarian executive. As noted above, our analysis is both historical and institutionalist in nature. To take historical processes and the internal, institutional context of a given polity seriously, we will adopt a fine-grained approach to charting the evolution of—and ebbs and flows in—institutional autonomy over time in each case. And in taking institutions seriously, we place a great emphasis on viewing institutional operations and activity from the inside; actions taken *by* a state institution and its personnel will be just as central to our discussion as decisions made *for* them by autocrats and their cliques.

To further clarify the scope of our investigation and the structures that occupy the focus of our empirical analysis, we now proceed to specify how this book conceptualizes the institutions that populate authoritarian systems cross-nationally.

Conceptualizing Authoritarian Institutions the Old-Fashioned Way

Political scientists use the term "institutions" in many ways, which differ according to not only the topics being studied but also the analytic approaches that scholars deploy. Some uses are very expansive, deployed especially by those who follow what has come to be termed "the new institutionalism," that is, "formal or informal procedures, routines, norms and conventions embedded into the organizational structure of the polity."[5] That usage is appropriate for some settings, but for our purposes we deliberately imply something much narrower since we are interested in formal and official bodies. When we write of "institutions" we are indicating concrete structures with clear boundaries: state organizations made up of groups of individuals that have some formal structure and bureaucracy (parliaments, political parties, courts, religious establishments, militaries, secret police forces, central banks, and the like). In this section we explain

---

5. Peter Hall and Rosemary Taylor (1996), "Political Science and the Three New Institutionalisms," *Political Studies* 44 (5): 938.

our choice, as our treatment of institutions owes more to Max Weber than to Douglass North.

Rational choice approaches that have arisen in the social sciences in the last few decades (with older antecedents) conceive of institutions in relation to a decision-making environment where actors behave strategically, defining them as "humanly devised constraints that shape human interaction"[6] or, more formally, "patterns of regularized behavior that reflect Pareto-optimal equilibria."[7] By virtue of this approach, institutions in rationalist perspectives are characterized foremost as "mitigating collective-action problems, particularly the commitment and enforcement problems" or, alternatively, as "the structural means by which political winners pursue their own interests."[8]

In the authoritarianism literature, this is the view of institutions that has grown most pervasive and understandably persuasive, as scholars disproportionately investigate institutions for their capacity to "alleviate commitment and monitoring problems,"[9] "solicit economic cooperation . . . [and] provide incentives for people to reveal their private information,"[10] or serve as "credible constraints" that facilitate power sharing and prolong regime survival.[11] We will see more below why we find that this definition can lead us to focus too heavily on the question of "why institutions emerge and are sustained" and skew us toward answering that question in terms of the functions that they perform.[12]

Alternative definitions of institutions have moved away from the structural functionalism that can be facilitated by the rationalist approach. Historical institutionalists, as noted above, define institutions as formal or informal procedures, routines, norms, and conventions—stressing that

---

6. Douglass North (1990), *Institutions, Institutional Change and Economic Performance* (New York: Cambridge University Press), 3.

7. Peter Hall (2010), "Historical Institutionalism in Rationalist and Sociological Perspective," in *Explaining Institutional Change: Ambiguity, Agency, and Power*, ed. James Mahoney and Kathleen Thelen (New York: Cambridge University Press), 204.

8. Terry Moe (1990), "Political Institutions: The Neglected Side of the Story," *Journal of Law, Economics and Organization* 6:213.

9. Carles Boix and Milan Svolik (2013), "The Foundations of Limited Authoritarian Government: Institutions, Commitment, and Power-Sharing in Dictatorships," *Journal of Politics* 75 (2): 300.

10. Gandhi and Przeworski (2007), 1281.

11. Joseph Wright (2008), "Do Authoritarian Institutions Constrain? How Legislatures Affect Economic Growth and Investment," *American Journal of Political Science* 52 (2): 322–43.

12. Kathleen Thelen (1999), "Historical Institutionalism in Comparative Politics," *Annual Review of Political Science* 2 (1): 369–404.

institutions do not just "provide strategically useful information, they also affect the very identities, self-images and preferences of the actors."[13] A slightly different version of this approach comes in the form of sociological institutionalism, which conceives of institutions as "models, schemas or scripts for behavior"[14] and emphasizes "the social and cognitive features of institutions rather than structural and constraining features."[15]

At first glance, the historical and sociological approaches present themselves as attractive models for conceptualizing authoritarian institutions—especially since our investigation shares the goal of allowing institutions to be much more than useful mechanisms for resolving collective action and coordination problems with defined logics already built in. Yet we find that the way both of the latter camps define institutions—as some combination of formal and informal rules, norms, conventions, routines, schemas, scripts, or cognitive templates—is both broader and more amorphous than the object of our inquiry, with the potential to obscure and generalize our targets of study overmuch.

When most people speak of state institutions, they tend to see the term in a more narrow, old-fashioned, and concrete sense. To update their usage, a state institution might be described as "anything with a .gov domain name." Fear of flippancy and perhaps a desire for historical depth lead us to avoid using that as a formal definition, but it gets closest to what we mean—and what is sometimes used in practice by scholars who focus on the state. The structures that we explore in this project are most conventionally referred to as "political institutions,"[16] at least in research on democratic and authoritarian regimes. These most commonly include legislatures, executives, cabinets and various agencies. Because we expand our set of institutions to other, less clearly political institutions like courts and religious establishments, we will refer to these bodies generically as "*state institutions*" instead.

---

13. Hall and Taylor (1996), 939.

14. Elizabeth Clemens and James Cook (1999), "Politics and Institutionalism: Explaining Durability and Change," *Annual Review of Sociology* 25:445.

15. Martha Finnemore (1996), "Norms, Culture, and World Politics: Insights from Sociology's Institutionalism," *International Organization* 50 (2): 326.

16. Typically, scholars use the term "political institutions" to indicate bodies that are in some way related to electoral politics—legislatures, executives, parties. This is true even in authoritarian systems, where elections by definition do not matter in the same way that they do in democracies. Because we investigate political institutions (parliaments) as well as institutions that are often (even if inappropriately) viewed as nonpolitical (courts, religious establishments), we group them together under the umbrella category of "state institutions."

So we are focusing on a narrower group of state "institutions" than others sometime do but spend some time on the definition here to avoid confusion. While we are largely writing in line with what has implicitly become standard practice in scholarship on authoritarian politics, it is far from standard in most work on institutionalism—whether rationalist, historical, or sociological. When situating our study in relation to the new institutionalism literature, it would certainly be more precise to refer to the structures that we investigate as state "*organizations*," which are differentiated from institutions by the fact that they are "made up of groups of individuals bound together by some common purpose to achieve certain objectives."[17] Yet, we opt to continue using the term state "institutions" for the sake of clarity, as many audiences will be more accustomed to viewing institutions as organizational structures, populated by actors and characterized by some formal bureaucracy (in this book, legislatures, constitutional courts, and state religious establishments) rather than as the less tangible alternative of norms, cognitive scripts, or routinized patterns of behavior.

Nevertheless, acknowledging the overlap between how we use the term "institutions" in this book and how other literatures use the term "organizations" is itself a valuable way to situate our concerns and goals alongside a well-established method of analysis. After all, we are not the first to question whether functionalist logics of organizational (or institutional) activity truly explain as much variation in political processes and outcomes as may appear. Two decades ago, Michael Barnett and Martha Finnemore, for instance, raised very similar issues when probing the limits of functionalism in scholarship on international organizations:

> Do international organizations really do what their creators intend them to do? . . . Most [existing] theories explain IO creation as a response to problems of incomplete information, transaction costs, and other barriers to Pareto efficiency. . . . Closer scrutiny would reveal that many IOs stray from the efficiency goals these theories impute and that many IOs exercise power autonomously in ways unintended and unanticipated by states at their creation.[18]

This approach bears a marked resemblance with our own. And that parallel should itself attract our interest, suggesting that political science

---

17. Douglas C. North (1994), "Economic Performance through Time," *American Economic Review* 84 (3): 361.

18. Michael Barnett and Martha Finnemore (1999), "The Politics, Power and Pathologies of International Organizations," *International Organization* 53 (4): 699–732.

research in many other settings, both international and domestic, follows the path that we wish to hasten our colleagues toward in this book. Scholars may begin by assuming that institutions are designed to serve—and do serve—a specific function. But they then find that motivations of the founders do not explain all of what institutions wind up doing. That is the path we have followed, and we write to invite others to join us.

By investigating when authoritarian state institutions can run their own affairs and pursue their own interests, we raise a persistent question of organizational politics, although in a different setting. And perhaps we should not be surprised to find that, even in authoritarian environments, we often reach a similar conclusion that institutions can exercise power autonomously, deviating from elite interests in unintended, unanticipated, and often frustrating ways. Frustrating for whom? Often for diverse actors who find that institutions seem not to serve their desired purposes. And that is the point.

New Barriers to Institutional Analysis: Authoritarianism as Seen from Above

Why do authoritarian institutions seem to defy easy study? In this section, we argue that the way the concept of authoritarianism has evolved in the social sciences has directed scholarly focus toward rulers and regimes and away from state institutions. To this end, we briefly trace the subtle conceptual shifts that inhibit what we believe are important lines of inquiry into how authoritarianism actually operates through institutions. In doing so, we consolidate our claims made earlier that "authoritarianism," in the simplified manner with which scholarship now plants its conceptual flag, holds both benefits and detractions—and that by acknowledging some of the forgotten understandings, we can recapture much of their value while still holding firm to the modern residual approach.

While much of our basic vocabulary about political structures (e.g., "democracy" and "dictatorship") can be traced back two millennia or more to the classical world, "authoritarian" is a relatively new term. When it was introduced in the nineteenth century, it tended to refer to an individual trait—a manner of behaving or a preference to pay great deference to existing authorities.[19] Bossiness more than state structure was at issue.

---

19. The idea of measuring an "authoritarian personality" in psychology and using it to understand macro-political structures and behavior spread with the influence of philosopher-psychologist Theodor Adorno and colleagues. T. W. Adorno, Else Frenkel-Brunswik, Daniel J. Levinson, and R. Nevitt Sanford (1950), *The Authoritarian Personality* (New York: Harper

It came to refer to entire political systems in the twentieth century (Hannah Arendt, e.g., made the connection between orders based on hierarchy and command and those based on liberty, reason, and persuasion) but only passed into common scholarly usage starting in the 1960s.[20] When the term was pushed into broader circulation, particularly by the work of Juan Linz, it referred to a family of political systems that existed not so much in counterpoint to democracy (though they were undemocratic) but explicitly as distinct from "totalitarianism."[21]

Originally, authoritarianism as a political system (or regime type) was defined specifically by virtue of its institutions and modes of exercising state power, not the identity of its rulers (unelected presidents, kings, generals, or otherwise). Linz noted different institutional variants of authoritarianism from the outset but observed that they all tended to lack the highly ideological and mobilizational aspects, among others, of totalitarianism—itself a distinct system (not yet a subtype of authoritarianism).

As interest in the category of totalitarianism declined and interest in democracy rose, Linz's particular approach to defining "authoritarianism" as just one form—among many—of nondemocracy faded in the literature. The term "authoritarian" rapidly expanded to encompass most political systems—and in some definitions, *all* political systems, including totalitarian ones—that shared an absence of democratically elected executives but otherwise diverged greatly in their institutional configurations. Words that had a very different meaning at other periods—"dictatorship" and "autocracy" most notably but also some others, such as "tyranny"—have now slid into each other, even being used interchangeably at times.

To give brief examples, in one influential article on authoritarian institutions, Jennifer Gandhi and Adam Przeworski use autocratic, authoritarian, dictatorial, and nondemocratic rule completely synonymously.[22] This is often explicit and deliberate by those who discard implicit elision for direct acknowledgment. Scott Gehlbach, Konstantin Sonin, and Milan W. Svolik state: "We use the terms dictatorship, autocracy, authoritarian

and Brothers). As that work lost its luster, political research on authoritarianism as a personality trait generally receded, though there has been some resurgence in recent years that in analysis tends to conflate political regime and personality, potentially further undermining conceptual utility for both fields.

20. Hannah Arendt (2005), "What Is Authority?" in *The Promise of Politics* (New York: Schocken). Essay originally published in 1954.

21. Most fully developed in Juan Linz (2000), *Authoritarian and Totalitarian Regimes* (Boulder: Lynne Rienner).

22. Gandhi and Przeworski (2007).

regime, and nondemocratic regime interchangeably."[23] Earlier, writing alone, Svolik stated with characteristic analytical clarity: "Dictatorship is a residual category that contains all countries that do not meet established criteria for democracy."[24] Przeworski, Alvarez, Cheibub, and Limongi were similarly explicit about this residual approach to defining authoritarianism in their pioneering analysis, *Democracy and Development*:

> We treat dictatorship simply as a residual category, perhaps better denominated as "not democracy." Our procedure is to establish rules that will disqualify a particular regime as democratic, without worrying about the nature of regimes eliminated in this manner.[25]

As a result of contemporary approaches to classification, other regime categories used in the past—oligarchy and absolutism, for instance—have largely disappeared and been folded into authoritarianism.

How, exactly, do we go about speaking of such a large group of political systems in one breath? The heterogeneity of the category has given rise to a need for capacious terminology, which risks paving over institutional differences and variation. Scholars have come to refer vaguely to authoritarian "regimes" (the term is used much more rarely in democratic systems) largely because of a need to indicate a set of individuals, groups, or structures in authority that does not comprise the entire state apparatus but that varies so much from one society to another that we cannot designate a specific structure (like a "cabinet," "executive branch," or "administration").[26] By using such terms, we bypass the need to name specific actors and institutions. We allow ourselves to speak of all authoritarian systems at once

---

23. Scott Gehlbach, Konstantin Sonin, and Milan W. Svolik (2016), "Formal Models of Nondemocratic Politics," *Annual Review of Political Science* 19:565–84.

24. Milan W. Svolik (2012), *The Politics of Authoritarian Rule* (New York: Cambridge University Press), 20.

25. Adam Przeworski, Michael E. Alvarez, José Antonio Cheibub, and Fernando Limongi (2000), *Democracy and Development: Political Institutions and Well-Being in the World, 1950–1990* (New York: Cambridge University Press), 18.

26. Our need for capacious vocabulary because of institutional heterogeneity extends beyond our reference to "regimes." E.g., some scholars have come to refer to a "selectorate" to vaguely designate those who have the capacity to choose leaders because the identity of those individuals or groups share so many different sets of characteristics across systems (they may be members of a party, an informal or social class–based elite, or have positions in various powerful state or non-state institutions). The use of the term suggests some very limited constraints on rulers but ones that are at best loosely institutionalized. See, e.g., Bueno de Mesquita et al. (2003).

despite their disparate institutional makeup and widely variable forms of internal power distribution and interaction.

This approach focuses our attention in sometimes fruitful directions, having inspired useful work on political parties, succession mechanisms, and parliaments in a vast array of systems. But it has costs. As a result of the conceptual shift toward broadly equating authoritarianism with nondemocracy, recent scholarship too commonly elides substantive engagement with older understandings of authoritarian politics that propelled much twentieth-century research and crafted insights on how different political systems worked with great nuance. This now neglected understanding is what we conceive to be a "Linzian" view of authoritarian systems, which differs from more modern analyses in recognizing these polities as much more complex, irreducible to macrolevel categorizations of individual rulers or ruling groups, and distinctive primarily by virtue of their internal institutions and organizing structures rather than simply their (un)electoral systems of executive selection. The Linzian approach to comparative classification used a paring knife, carving out more numerous and finer divisions between systems. Today's approach uses the cleaver, which lends itself quite well to making deep cuts to be sure—but also ones that are much cruder and less subtle.

This book advances a framework for recovering and reincorporating the Linzian approach in contemporary scholarship. The cleaver has often proved quite useful in making light work of heavy tasks, perhaps most notably through the proliferation of extensive cross-national datasets enabling the statistical analysis of different political systems over wide periods of time.[27] And this utility leads us to insist on retaining the modern and residual definition of authoritarianism (as nondemocracy) in our own analysis. Thus, while we do not attempt to revive Linz's initial—and much more specific—*definition* of authoritarianism, we do hope to draw the

---

27. See, e.g., Carles Boix, Michael K. Miller, and Sebastian Rosato (2013), "A Complete Data Set of Political Regimes, 1800–2007," *Comparative Political Studies* 46 (12): 1523–53; Barbara Geddes, Joseph Wright, and Erica Frantz (2014), "Autocratic Breakdown and Regime Transitions: A New Data Set," *Perspectives on Politics* 12 (2): 313–31; Monty G. Marshall and Ted Robert Gurr (2020), "Polity V: Political Regime Characteristics and Transitions, 1800–2018," *The Polity Project*; Michael Coppedge, John Gerring, Carl Henrik Knutsen, Staffan I. Lindberg, Jan Teorell, David Altman, Michael Bernhard, Agnes Cornell, M. Steven Fish, Lisa Gastaldi, Haakon Gjerløw, Adam Glynn, Sandra Grahn, Allen Hicken, Katrin Kinzelbach, Kyle L. Marquardt, Kelly McMann, Valeriya Mechkova, Pamela Paxton, Daniel Pemstein, Johannes von Römer, Brigitte Seim, Rachel Sigman, Svend-Erik Skaaning, Jeffrey Staton, Eitan Tzelgov, Luca Uberti, Yi-ting Wang, Tore Wig, and Daniel Ziblatt (2022), "V-Dem Codebook v12," *Varieties of Democracy (V-Dem) Project*.

field much closer back to Linz's *conception* of authoritarian politics as being heavily driven by internal institutional arrangements, pluralistic structures organizing state-society relations, and disparate modalities for exercising state authority.

The institutional arrangements that configure authoritarian governance are now much more variable than when Linz was writing half a century ago, back when the term "authoritarianism" had not yet absorbed—but was instead still conceptually distinguished from—alternative forms of nondemocracy like "sultanism" and "totalitarianism." Exploring the heterogeneous structure and operation of institutions inside the authoritarian state has, thus, only increased in importance. The empirical chapters of this book seek to breathe new life into the Linzian approach by recentering the analysis of institutions as paramount to crafting nuanced understandings of authoritarian systems from the inside out and not just from the top down. Before proceeding with that empirical effort, however, we first elaborate on why a more attuned—even if modified—Linzian perspective to authoritarian politics is in need of recovering and what exactly gets obscured from contemporary scholarship in the absence of this perspective.

For political scientists today, authoritarianism and its institutions are the opposite of pointillism in painting: scholars show individual elements of authoritarianism very clearly, but when we step back, it is not clear what the overall image adds up to.[28]

While the (blurry) focus is often on regimes, scholars sometimes move among levels of analysis in a way that makes it unclear whether the term "authoritarian" is describing the state, the regime, the ruler—or all three. We still encounter bossy and intolerant people who are said to have "authoritarian" personalities or tendencies, a throwback to the term's earlier usage as long as a century ago.[29] More recently, the individual attribute and the regime type have themselves sometimes become—perhaps unfortunately—conflated, as the "authoritarian" tendencies of populist leaders in the twenty-first century inspire concerns that they are undermining the entire democratic system due primarily to their personalities.[30]

---

28. This blurriness, of course, also has many roots in how authoritarianism is practiced in reality—as a game of using uncertainty to an autocracy's benefit. E.g., Andreas Schedler (2013, 6) argues that "competition under and over uncertainty [is] the driving force of politics under authoritarian rule."

29. For an example of a conscious move between regime type and personal attribute, see Christopher Sebastian Parker and Christopher C. Towler (2019), "Race and Authoritarianism in American Politics," *Annual Review of Political Science* 22:503–19.

30. Particularly notable has been the reaction to the election of Donald Trump as US

If we take the expansive view that authoritarianism comprises all non-democracies, we clearly need to distinguish varieties in the configuration of domestic state institutions. But we have no consensual language for distinguishing the many forms that authoritarianism can take, beyond simply pointing to the organizational characteristics of the ruler and of regime elites, often arriving at categories fairly inductively—by staring at them (especially their leaders) and then putting them in boxes according to what seems to stand out most obviously.[31] This leads us at times to miss how many institutional similarities authoritarian systems share but also how much they vary (and not just in their leadership)—and how much even the degree to which they are institutionalized varies.

So, yes, there continue to be earnest attempts to differentiate among authoritarian systems pursued by the emerging post-Linz generation of political scientists. But these attempts betray two flaws that restrict the ways in which researchers of authoritarian systems can deploy comparative institutional analysis. First, they are based more on an impressionistic sense of similarity than an explicit conceptual or even heuristic logic. We find here that the most succinct critique is delivered by Svolik:

> Most existing typologies fail to recognize that they implicitly collapse multiple, distinct conceptual dimensions of authoritarian politics into a single typology. . . . The resulting categories are neither mutually exclusive nor collectively exhaustive, and they require difficult classification judgments that weigh incommensurable aspects of authoritarian politics, thereby compromising the validity and reliability of empirical inferences based on them.[32]

Impressionistic as they are, prevailing classifications are not devoid of all theoretical grounding.

---

president. Some examples of this genre conceptually mixing theories of authoritarian personalities from psychology with implicit or explicit assumptions about threats to long-standing democracies include Taub (2016), https://www.vox.com/2016/3/1/11127424/trump-auth oritarianism; Linden (2017), https://theconversation.com/trumps-america-and-the-rise-of-the-authoritarian-personality-72770; and Gordon (2017), https://read.dukeupress.edu/boundary-2/article/44/2/31/6551/The-Authoritarian-Personality-Revisited-Reading

31. Barbara Geddes (1999), "What Do We Know about Democratization after Twenty Years?" *Annual Review of Political Science* 2 (1): 115–44. Barbara Geddes (2003), *Paradigms and Sand Castles: Theory Building and Research Design in Comparative Politics* (Ann Arbor: University of Michigan Press).

32. Svolik (2012), 21.

But this leads to the second problem: they assume that authoritarian regimes are to be classified primarily according to one top-down dimension: who is in charge? In one of the most influential typologies of authoritarian rule, Barbara Geddes identified four primary subtypes of authoritarianism: (1) military regimes, (2) personalist regimes, (3) one-party regimes, and (4) monarchies. Each category is defined exclusively by the nature of organizational authority and legitimacy that the individual or group at the apex of the political hierarchy holds.[33] This was refined in further work by Geddes and coauthors that would allow for hybrids that included party-military, party-personal, and military-personal categories. While more precise, this leads us only further into blurring the utility and distinction of such categorizations.[34]

Such typologies leave out elements that were seen as extremely important in earlier understandings of authoritarianism. Little attention is afforded to configurations of state institutions, much less the classic attributes that defined authoritarian political systems in the Linzian framework—limited pluralism as opposed to monism, depoliticization as opposed to mass mobilization, and the lack of a hegemonic ideology.[35] Scholars have increasingly begun to view politics in authoritarian societies chiefly according to *who* holds power at the top and not *how* power is exercised, structured, or channeled in institutions at the middle and the bottom of a political order.

Dictatorships of the left or the right, those that are redistributionist and those that preserve wealth for the dominant elite, those that pledge fealty to God, those that seek to edge out religion, those that claim to serve the proletariat, those that proclaim an ideology, those that eschew one, those that make judges their servants, those that allow for judicial autonomy, those that rule through bureaucracies, those that undermine them—all these differences became incidental. It is no wonder that such characteristics are thus explained—when they are noticed—as functions of who rules. Current classifications tend to rely on the actor or entity that exercises authority (military, individual, party) and sometimes the nature of its formal or informal structures (electoral authoritarianism, patrimonialism), but almost never do its values, ideas, norms, or policy outcomes enter into its perceived essence.

And, so, when we speak of "authoritarian institutions," we sometimes use the two halves of that term in a way that renders it an oxymoron. We

---

33. Geddes (1999).
34. Geddes, Wright, and Franz (2014).
35. Linz (2000).

probe the meaning of institutions in authoritarian contexts at times but treat them as epiphenomenal at others. We speak of modified or hybrid regimes without any conceptual or terminological consensus on what those might be, besides a general sense that they are authoritarian systems that are paradoxically populated by some seemingly "nonauthoritarian" institutions.[36]

Academe is not alone in its confusion. Even those who live under authoritarianism, who feel its effects or operate its mechanisms, give voice to ambiguities and contradictory claims. They speak not only of the dreary inevitability of authoritarian rule but also of the risks, fear, and uncertainty it brings. Key authoritarian personnel, when they write memoirs, seem to focus on short-term worries and rivalries rather than any explication of grand designs.[37] Those who operate under authoritarian conditions often claim that there are "red lines" for speech and action but then describe how such lines are blurry, tested, inconsistent, shifting, and often discovered only in practice.[38] They complain of the way in which authorities seem bound by no law other than their own whim—but also how punctilious attention to the law pushes much of policymaking and political activity outside of legal boundaries.

In documenting the conceptual fuzziness that has grown around the term "authoritarianism," we should notice an irony that it has led to a surprisingly uniform idea of how authoritarianism works. While authoritarianism is generally defined as an expansive residual category, the prevailing functionalist approach often leads to a very specific concept of regime that looks very much like what would have been called a "tyranny" in earlier centuries: a political regime in which state institutions are hollowed out by a ruler who is unbound by law or practice and, instead, uses political authority to serve only his own interest and will.[39] Again, Gehlbach, Sonin,

---

36. Moreover, recent work on authoritarianism tends to use the terms "hybrid," "electoral authoritarian," "competitive authoritarian," "semi-democracy," "semi-authoritarian," "illiberal democracy," and "inconsistent" regimes interchangeably; see, e.g., Larry Diamond (2002), "Thinking about Hybrid Regimes," *Journal of Democracy* 13 (2): 21–34; Andreas Schedler (2006), *Electoral Authoritarianism: The Dynamics of Unfree Competition* (Boulder: Lynne Rienner); Steven Levitsky and Lucan A. Way (2010), *Competitive Authoritarianism: Hybrid Regimes after the Cold War* (New York: Cambridge University Press).

37. Joseph Sassoon (2016), *Anatomy of Authoritarianism in the Arab Republics* (New York: Cambridge University Press).

38. Nathan J. Brown (2016), *Arguing Islam after the Revival of Arab Politics* (New York: Oxford University Press).

39. Roger Boesche (1993), "Aristotle's 'Science' of Tyranny," *History of Political Thought* 14 (1): 1–25. Aristotle, *Politics*, translated by C. D. C. Reeve (Indianapolis: Hackett), book V, chap. 11.

and Svolik help us by being clear and explicit: "A regime's ability to exercise powers beyond any constitutional constraints is often seen as the essence of dictatorship."[40] The word "temporarily" to qualify this exercise of power—one essential to earlier usages of "dictator"—has ended up on the cutting-room floor.[41]

Thus, modern scholarship tends to obscure the existence of state actors with any real autonomy unless autocrats bestow or permit it, as well as state institutions that perform any role that does not derive from the strategic interests of authoritarian rulers, let alone any possibility for even a modest authoritarian constitutionalism or structural boundary making in politics. Indeed, sometimes an authoritarian regime is defined almost precisely in such tyrannical terms.

Oddly, this much narrower and more specific image of authoritarianism has emerged from treating authoritarianism as a residual category for all nondemocracies, even though the leap from the residual (all nondemocracies) to the specific (systems where institutions principally serve the ruler) is rarely explicitly acknowledged. It is based, perhaps, on a democratic skepticism that any regime that does not answer directly to the people only serves its own interest and that any "exceptional" measures are likely to be permanent.

Implicitly, however, scholars do seem to be grappling with the side effects of conflating "authoritarianism" (as nondemocratic governance) with a system in which state institutions are either impotent or beholden to autocrats and regime elites. This struggle has given rise to an entire industry of research on "hybrid," "pseudo-democratic," "semi-authoritarian," or "electoral authoritarian" regimes—because such clear association of power with the commands of a singular ruler or close set of regime elites often fails to obtain, and quite obviously.

Such terms have proliferated as specialists, with increasing frequency, encountered state institutions that seemed (at least on the surface) to operate in ways that are not easily reducible to regime interests. These institutions have typically included elections,[42] multiparty legislatures,[43] mass

---

40. Gehlbach et al. (2016), 566.

41. John Ferejohn and Pasquale Pasquino (2004), "The Law of the Exception: A Typology of Emergency Powers," *International Journal of Constitutional Law* 2 (2): 210–39.

42. Diamond (2002).

43. Wright (2008). Jennifer Gandhi (2008), *Political Institutions under Dictatorship* (New York: Cambridge University Press).

parties,[44] and independent courts,[45] though the conceptual boundaries of a "hybrid" regime have also broadly (and quite ambiguously) subsumed more nebulous institutional configurations as well: "constitutional oligarchies," "exclusive republics," and "tutelary" theocratic or military regimes.[46] Once more, we see the plethora of adjectives and differentiable nouns returning to the study of nondemocracy in an increasingly extensive but still thinly conceptualized manner.

These various categories of "hybrid regimes" are all united by a belief that the political institutions scholars observe within them "do not reflect their true nature" as authoritarian systems.[47] The most concrete definitions of hybridity make this explicit:

> We can define a hybrid regime as a set of institutions that have been persistent, be they stable or unstable, for about a decade . . . characterized by the break-up of limited pluralism and forms of independent, autonomous participation, but the absence of . . . a minimal democracy.[48]

Treating systems in which state institutions have political relevance or autonomy as a distinct breed of authoritarian regime is now leading us to terminological cacophony. Scholars have found a need to create new regime categories, or to use various adjectives to qualify "authoritarianism," precisely because we have subtly blended the modern concept of authoritarianism with the classical concept of tyranny—creating an ideal type of rule by a single autocrat (or close-knit collective) where state institutions are epiphenomenal, reflect existing distributions of power, exist to serve elite interests, and promote regime survival.[49]

This conceptual architecture abandons the original meaning of authoritarianism as a subtype of nondemocracy with institutional structures dis-

---

44. Beatriz Magaloni and Ruth Kricheli (2010), "Political Order and One-Party Rule," *Annual Review of Political Science* 13:123–43.

45. Bruce Gilley (2010), "Democratic Enclaves in Authoritarian Regimes," *Democratization*, 17 (3): 402.

46. Levitsky and Way (2010), 14.

47. Michael K. Miller (2011), "Democratic Pieces: Hybrid Regimes, Electoral Authoritarianism, and Disaggregated Democracy" (PhD diss., Princeton University), 6.

48. Leonardo Morlino (2009), "Are There Hybrid Regimes? Or Are They Just an Optical Illusion?" *European Political Science Review* 1 (2): 282.

49. Schedler (2006). Leah Gilbert and Payman Mohseni (2011), "Beyond Authoritarianism: The Conceptualization of Hybrid Regimes," *Studies in Comparative International Development* 46 (3): 270–97.

tinct from those of totalitarianism, and it also hollows out its more modern meaning as a residual category encompassing the wide diversity of nondemocratic systems. It is this process of conceptual slippage that has—though tacitly and perhaps inadvertently—produced contemporary top-down conceptions of authoritarian politics. Furthermore, it has compounded the difficulty that scholars face in understanding authoritarian state institutions without looking at them primarily—and sometimes purely—from the perspective of a micromanaging and self-interested autocrat. Such a view has empirical merit in many cases, especially in our era of increasing simplification of the structural outlines that many authoritarian regimes now share. But it leads us into a set of inferential fallacies, to which we now turn to better recognize both how they emerge and what can be done to resist making them without prior empirical verification.

Rulers Can't Always Get What They Want

"Authoritarianism" encompasses not only various kinds of rulers—generals, kings, clerics, party stalwarts, apparatchiks, politicians, or lawyers—but also diverse organizational forms throughout its formal and informal structures. Neglected in much of the macro-regime tradition of contemporary scholarship, the agency of the middle and lower rungs of the authoritarian state—its officers, judges, bureaucrats, teachers, and clerks—can have important influence on the nature of policymaking and forms of institutional autonomy that may exist. Nondemocratic policy is not simply a matter of rulers who can say, "*L'état c'est moi—et le régime aussi.*" Institutions—and institutional evolution—should not always be allowed to fade into the background as distracting historical noise.

As noted at the outset, it is the urge to look cross-nationally among a variety of regimes (rather than intensively and historically at specific regimes) that helps lead many studies of authoritarian institutions to cluster around the question of why authoritarian regimes have institutions at all and to answer that question in terms of the function they serve for the ruler. For instance, Gandhi's study of authoritarian institutions begins with the puzzle, "If legislatures and parties are nothing but mere ornamentation, then *why would some dictators 'dress their windows?'*"[50] This question—which scholars continue to reiterate[51]—is framed from the viewpoint of a self-

---

50. Jennifer Gandhi (2008), "Dictatorial Institutions and Their Impact on Economic Growth," *European Journal of Sociology* 49 (1): 7.

51. Nathan M. Jensen, Edmund Malesky, and Stephen Weymouth (2014), "Unbundling

interested autocrat and implies that the ruler herself decides whether or not to create institutions. The assumptions baked into this approach leave very little room for an answer that avoids reducing the establishment of authoritarian parties and legislatures to ruler interests (which is exactly the conclusion that Gandhi reaches in her analysis).[52]

As we also observed at the outset, this functionalism flows in large part from a desire to explain how authoritarianism can last so long, which is a valuable question to be sure. Scholars have sought to ask why authoritarianism persists, when it fails, and what happens after it fails (and with a special interest in possibilities that it will give way to democracy). In the process, they have come across puzzling ways in which authoritarian systems develop seemingly democratic elements and have explained that finding by showing that such innovations can serve authoritarian ends. Independent courts help autocrats attract investment[53] and solve information problems.[54] Multiparty legislatures allow autocrats to promote inter-elite cooperation through co-optation or by reducing commitment problems,[55] manage societal discontent,[56] and even encourage economic growth.[57] And elections enable autocrats to distribute patronage,[58] signal regime dominance to the citizenry,[59] legitimize authority among both elites and masses,[60] and share power among elites.[61]

These are all useful insights that should be retained as we continue

---

the Relationship between Authoritarian Legislatures and Political Risk," *British Journal of Political Science* 44 (3): 655–84.

52. See Geddes (2003), chap. 2 on "how the questions you ask affect the answers you get."

53. Tamir Moustafa (2007), *The Struggle for Constitutional Power: Law, Politics, and Economic Development in Egypt* (New York: Cambridge University Press).

54. James Rosberg (1995), "The Rise of an Independent Judiciary in Egypt" (PhD diss., Massachusetts Institute of Technology). Randall Peerenboom (2002), *China's Long March to the Rule of Law* (New York: Cambridge University Press).

55. Gandhi (2008), *Political Institutions under Dictatorship*. Svolik (2012). Tyson L. Roberts (2015), "The Durability of Presidential and Parliament-Based Dictatorships," *Comparative Political Studies*, 48 (7): 915–48.

56. Dawn Brancati (2014), "Democratic Authoritarianism: Origins and Effects," *Annual Review of Political Science* 17:313–26.

57. Wright (2008).

58. Ellen Lust-Okar (2006), "Elections under Authoritarianism: Preliminary Lessons from Jordan," *Democratization* 13 (3): 456–71.

59. Beatriz Magaloni (2006), *Voting for Autocracy: Hegemonic Party Survival and Its Demise in Mexico* (New York: Cambridge University Press).

60. Lee Morgenbesser (2016), *Behind the Façade: Elections under Authoritarianism in Southeast Asia* (Albany: SUNY Press).

61. Boix and Svolik (2013).

to explore the workings of nondemocratic political systems. But they also reflect a distinctly elite- and ruler-centric vision of authoritarian politics that falls into a trap of monodominance and interest logics typified by classical tyranny. Most recent writings on authoritarianism still begin with a single autocrat (hence, the equation of authoritarianism with autocracy, tyranny, dictatorship, and other nondemocratic political forms) and view the system from the perspective of that individual or equivalent small, corporate group. The focus on elections (or their corruption or absence) leads attention away from other ways social groups can form linkages with parts of the society. Institutions come into being primarily to serve the purposes of the ruler. Characteristic of this trend, Beatriz Magaloni and Ruth Kricheli state that "autocrats are fundamentally interested in their own survival in power" as an opening to understanding why they construct certain institutions the way they do.[62]

The inclination to reduce all of nondemocratic politics to an autocrat's logic of survival[63] is so pervasive that it is often implicit even in works that take authoritarian institutions most seriously. One of the most recent influential works on authoritarian parliamentary bodies, Rory Truex's *Making Autocracy Work*, begins by addressing the "purpose" of a parliament very much in terms of the function it serves for an authoritarian regime and introduces the National People's Congress (NPC) in China in those terms. This work is not broad and cross-national but intensive—and it still eschews a historical approach. The actual origin, history, and evolution of the NPC is considered only much later in the book; and even that discussion centers on ruler motives.[64]

Contrast this with an approach that reversed this sequence (which is what we set out to do in this book), probing the workings of Chinese authoritarianism by first asking about the NPC's origins and then considering how it had evolved over the decades, perhaps partly (but not necessarily wholly) in response to regime actions and guidance. To be clear, both approaches hold promise for providing insight—and perhaps the case of China is uniquely unsuited to a nonfunctionalist approach in this instance;

---

62. See Magaloni and Kricheli (2010), 126. To be fair, the authors note the functionalism issue. And to be fairer still, Magaloni is widely known for her work on the Mexican system under the Institutional Revolutionary Party, one that went far beyond understanding Mexican politics as the projection of a single autocrat. See Magaloni (2006).

63. Bueno de Mesquita et al. (2003).

64. Rory Truex (2016), *Making Autocracy Work: Representation and Responsiveness in Modern China* (New York: Cambridge University Press).

our task here is to express discomfort with the way the former has come to seem so natural that it now edges out the latter.

In authoritarian political systems, a great deal of politics and institutional activity happens outside of—sometimes even in opposition to—the interests of rulers and regime elites. Under President Abdel Fattah al-Sisi, Egypt has an unabashedly authoritarian political system. But for President al-Sisi, holding the reins of the executive office does not always imply an ability to steer policy. In 2015, al-Sisi lashed out at al-Azhar University, the central node of Egypt's state-religion complex, for failing to deliver on the policy of "religious revolution" that he promised.[65] And later in 2017, the administrative courts moved to block al-Sisi's decision to transfer control of the Tiran and Sanafir Islands to a vital financial patron, Saudi Arabia.

These contests themselves left effects—the presidency bided its time with al-Azhar and sat out the battle but moved sharply to rein in the leadership of the administrative courts. The regime's authority—and its ability and willingness to redraw lines of authority—varies from one institution to another as well as over time. Could these decisions be reducible simply to calculations of managing the coordination of elites or assessing risks to regime survival? Perhaps, but only if we wish to gloss over the actual content of the decisions and simply state some post hoc logical justifications. And such an answer would tell us very little about the actually existing authoritarian politics in that country.

Rulers and regimes wrestle with state institutions to degrees and in ways that vary over place as well as across different bodies. The obstacles that authoritarian regimes encounter when devising and implementing policy are hardly unique to Egypt. In the 1950s and 1960s, the Soviet military resisted a series of reforms spearheaded by the ruling Communist Party, which proposed cutting the defense budget, reducing the size of the army, and enhancing the party's authority over internal military affairs.[66] As a part of the Lateran Pacts between Italy's fascist government and the Catholic Church, Benito Mussolini recognized the Church's independent authority over matters of education and matrimonial policy.[67] In China,

---

65. Nathan J. Brown and Katie Bentivoglio (2015), "Egypt's Resurgent Authoritarianism: It's a Way of Life," *Carnegie*, https://carnegieendowment.org/2014/10/09/egypt-s-resurgent-authoritarianism-it-s-way-of-life-pub-56877

66. Harold G. Skilling and Franklyn Griffiths (1971), *Interest Groups in Soviet Politics* (Princeton: Princeton University Press).

67. Leicester C. Webb (1958), *Church and State in Italy, 1947–1957* (Victoria: Melbourne University Press).

the Communist Party is often unable to implement state policy in rural areas, as local leaders and bureaucrats routinely ignore or mishandle policy programs devised by central party officials.[68] And throughout its tenure, Brazil's military government—despite the absence of truly democratic elections or genuine opposition parties—suffered a series of policy defeats by the National Congress, which rejected government-crafted bills related to taxes, public wages, and municipalities.[69] State institutions can be quite troublesome things to autocrats and in notably differentiable ways—and recognizing this fact is necessary to avoid the fallacy of overstating a ruler's or regime's control over the day-to-day operation of politics.

It is not merely cross-national variation that should concern us here; variation over time within the same political system should attract our attention as well. Prevailing images of authoritarianism give little room for institutional continuity and evolution. They minimize the role of decisions made for tactical rather than strategic reasons. And they frequently neglect the existence of political outcomes that do not follow a ruler's interests or are completely unintended consequences of regime actions.

To study German politics in the early twentieth century, Soviet politics under Brezhnev, Chinese politics in the 1980s, Japanese politics after the Meiji Restoration, or the Roman Empire after Augustus, an abstract view of the political system only in tyrannical terms would lead us to miss much of the politics. Even the current interest among students of authoritarianism on elections focuses so much on our assumptions about regime intentions that it often misses consequences. In this case, we can focus far too much effort on asking about the strategic logics of why regimes hold elections in the first place, which is why one of this book's authors has argued in regard to elections in the Middle East that this

> misstate[s] the way the question is posed by the participants who . . . largely accept and expect elections as a normal part of the political landscape. Both government and opposition in the Arab world show little sign of asking many questions about whether and why to hold elections, but instead think hard about how to use them.[70]

---

68. Kevin J. O'Brien and Lianjiang Li (2006), *Rightful Resistance in Rural China* (New York: Cambridge University Press), 28.

69. Scott W. Desposato (2001), "Legislative Politics in Authoritarian Brazil," *Legislative Studies Quarterly* 26 (2): 300–301.

70. Nathan J. Brown (2012), *When Victory Is Not an Option: Islamist Movements in Arab Politics* (Ithaca: Cornell University Press), 16.

The historical institutionalist approach that we advance throughout this book offers a means of stepping back from an overreliance on hard-and-fast assumptions about regime intentionality. Authoritarian politics and institutions change as much by accretion as by grand design. Autocrats are real, but they sometimes seem less like a master sorcerer and more like a sorcerer's apprentice.

Recovering Some Lost Meanings . . . but Leaving Others Buried

To clarify our conceptual thinking here, it can be helpful to try to recover some distinctions among political systems that we seem to have lost over time. In this section, we seek to restore interest in authoritarian institutions in a manner that moves beyond the top-down orientation and closer to approaching authoritarianism and its politics from the inside. And as soon will become clear, we use the word "restore" quite intentionally.

Political writings in the classical and early modern tradition made frequent use of classifications and typologies. While these varied from writer to writer, they tended to be based on two elements, one fairly familiar to current scholarship, the other partially lost. The first (and familiar) dimension was based on the number of people who ruled; terms in current usage like "monarchy," "autocracy," "oligarchy," "aristocracy," and "democracy" come directly from this understanding that political systems were to be understood in significant measure by how many people exercised authority or were integral to decision-making.[71]

But such usage reflected an understanding that the varying number of people were exercising political authority directly and personally rather than striving to steer and shape a complicated state apparatus. The complex institutional and bureaucratic machinery of the modern administrative state consequently has little echo in classical typologies. Of course, there were some offices to be staffed and some attention to how that might be done, though analyses were rudimentary and sometimes seem odd to current readers.

For example, classical understandings often cast selection of officers by lot as the most "democratic" due to its nature as a random sample of the population. (This sense of democracy has been lost in most areas except jury selection in a few societies.). Electing representatives was sometimes seen as democratically suspect since it naturally rewarded the wealthy who

---

71. Aristotle (1998).

could cultivate the skills necessary to win votes. Only the invention of the idea of representative government complicated, without completely negating, this picture by shifting the definition of the concept of democracy.[72] How various offices related to each other, the distinction between offices held by individuals and complex institutions, hierarchies of law—such matters, while they drew some attention when it came to devising arrangements in specific political systems, rarely influenced classical conceptualizations.[73]

The second, and far less familiar, dimension for classical typologies was explicitly normative, though it also had a heavily institutional (or at least structural) dimension: the purposes for which political authority is used or the standards (or, relatedly, the laws by which it is bound).[74] Regimes were categorized by asking questions about virtue and the common good. Those political systems that operated for a conception of the greater good and in accordance with laws and traditions were distinguished from those that used political authority for the benefit of the ruler, unbound by any such standards and making rules on an ad hoc basis depending on the interest or whim of those in power.[75]

A tyranny was not simply rule by what we would now call an autocrat but also rule by one who ruled for his personal benefit and without consideration for law and justice. By contrast, the term "dictator" tended to be used for officers who were unbound by law, but only on a temporary and emergency basis in pursuit of the public good. Hence, the classical terms "dictatorship" and "tyranny" were not synonyms as they are today but instead were defined in direct opposition to each other.[76] "Democracy," in contrast to its present largely positive image, operated under something of a dark normative cloud because majorities were often criticized as oper-

---

72. Bernard Manin (1997), *The Principles of Representative Government* (Cambridge: Cambridge University Press).

73. In attempting to cope with the significance of such developments, current theorists are driven to graft a bit of Weber onto such classical understandings (with terms like "patrimonialism" and "bureaucratic authoritarianism" entering the vocabulary).

74. Geoffrey C. Kellow and Neven Leddy (2016), *On Civic Republicanism: Ancient Lessons for Global Politics* (Toronto: University of Toronto Press).

75. Walter Nicgorski (1991), "Cicero's Focus: From the Best Regime to the Model Statesman," *Political Theory* 19 (2): 230–51.

76. Likewise, just rule by the few was called "aristocracy" and just rule by the one was called "monarchy," then seen as a normatively legitimate form of government. On monarchy, see, e.g., Clifford A. Bates Jr. (2002), *Aristotle's "Best Regime": Kingship, Democracy, and the Rule of Law* (Baton Rouge: LSU Press); and Richard Romeiro Oliveira (2019), "The Aristotelian Theory of Regimes and the Problem of Kingship in Politics III," *Trans/Form/Ação* 42 (2): 31–58.

ating in their own immediate interests and some seemed to follow popular whim rather than law. They were also seen as easily misled by demagoguery, thus giving way easily to tyranny and its malign tendencies of making public power serve private gain.

Democracy's virtuous form (or what we might call a democracy today but then seemed a different regime type), termed "polity" in translations of Aristotle, has remained something of an unclear puzzle for scholars on what it actually entailed.[77] Current references to "tyranny of the majority" are a vestigial reminder of the classical suspicion often directed against democratic governance. In a world in which the majority of citizens were seen as poor, short-sighted, and easily manipulated by promises of redistribution, democracy conjured far more fear than hope for many classical authors—a fear that gave the word "democracy" negative connotations as recently as the nineteenth century even among those whom we retrospectively identify as democrats.

It is easy to see what we have lost, forgotten, or discarded in this second normative dimension of classifying regimes. We will not go so far as to return to labeling political systems as good or bad. But we include normative elements in this book by exploring how state institutions can identify their own normative missions, push policies, and influence decisions in an effort to pursue them as they conceive them. We will take the ability of institutional actors to develop and pursue their own image of the common good as a significant variable to watch.

So we will work to bring a part of this second dimension back into our understanding. But before this restoration work, we pause to consider the three reasons why previous scholars have learned to distrust the normative dimension of regime classification.

First, there seems to be an unwritten convention of bracketing normative concerns, burying them, or mentioning them and then moving on. While a general, normative preference for democracy is marked in current scholarship, it is often implicit. Scholars aspiring to undertake empirical research are sometimes motivated by normative concerns— especially democracy, equality, and rule of law—but they typically prefer to avoid references to normative principles in their definitions. The implicit agreement of the vast majority of scholars with the norms and predilections of contemporary liberalism and its values allows for these

---

77. Kevin M. Cherry (2009), "The Problem of Polity: Political Participation and Aristotle's Best Regime," *Journal of Politics* 71 (4): 1406–21.

normative preferences to remain largely assumed and self-evident rather than explicitly stated.

Second, by using terms like "tyranny," "dictatorship," and "autocracy" interchangeably in the contemporary political world, by treating monarchies as a similar kind of system (with the difference only lying in modes of succession and oft sought but rarely seen constitutional limitations), by presuming that all ruling individuals or groups are motivated primarily by their power-hungry desire to retain authority, and by failing to distinguish between oligarchies and aristocracies, scholars seem to be analyzing politics informed by a hard-eared cynicism. Many simply do not trust leaders who claim to be governed by a higher standard or set of laws unless they see clear popular mechanisms that compel them to do so. The idea of authoritarian rule bound not by democratic procedure but by virtue and higher purposes seems unlikely in some writings and virtually oxymoronic in others. Even the idea of an autocrat bound by law—a strong classical antidote to tyranny—is difficult to conceive of today without that law originating through some kind of democratic oversight (with an undemocratic constitutionalism almost never appearing in scholarly writings).[78]

Third, the abandonment of the normative dimension to classifying regimes has been informed by another barely spoken but clear shift in interest in recent decades already discussed above: scholars are interested in authoritarian regimes primarily for how and when they emerge, how they reproduce themselves, and *especially* how and when they fall. Our own inquiry, by contrast, is more interested in how they operate on an ongoing basis, what decisions are made and how they come about, what policies end up being developed and implemented, and how state institutions and processes work.[79]

Thus, our current terminological confusion is based in part on scholarly usage of terms that were invented for a different set of conceptions

---

78. The Huntingtonian hope that single-party authoritarianism might be that rare virtuous form of nondemocracy for the developing states of the world has long since faded from the literature (Huntington [1965] and [1968]). At the same time, work on the benefits of the developmental state and cases of high-performing authoritarian rule in Singapore, South Korea, China, and Taiwan has continued, although seemingly regionally bound and sometimes referred to apologetically or with caveats to not take them as a model able to be emulated (Ortmann and Thompson [2016]; McFaul and Stoner-Weiss [2008]).

79. It is, therefore, no accident that only one classical term survives fairly intact for a specific kind of what we now lump together as authoritarian regimes: monarchy. Because that kind of a regime is understood to be defined by its succession mechanism, and thus by its own reproduction and empirically notable staying power, it retains some usefulness.

of the political world.[80] And they were built to describe different kinds of states that are now less representative of contemporary political orders. The modern bureaucratic state virtually requires that we try to understand how institutions can play some role in operating the machinery of decision-making, policy development, and implementation that extends beyond the purposes (typically quite narrow) of the rulers who invented them.[81]

When we use these ancient terms, therefore, we need to be far more conscious about what we are adopting and what we are leaving behind. For current purposes, we do not insist on restoring the full normative dimension to our understanding of political systems. But we do seek to separate—as the classical definition did—the question of how many rule (or who the ruler is) from how that rule is exercised. We do not wish to use our sense of "good" and "bad" or "public interested" and "selfish" as categorizing devices, but we do ask whether a regime is constrained by laws and institutions and, if so, which ones and how much. And that will lead us to explore whether institutions are able to define and pursue their own sense of mission or the public good that may be separate from those of the regime.

Might judges develop some sense that they have a higher task of applying the law and pursuing justice and not just in a corrupted form that categorically serves an autocrat's interests? Can parliamentarians acquire some concern for their own constituents, special regard for their own self-understood role in society, or a broader political agenda that extends beyond pure fealty to those at the apex of the executive? Do religious institutions in authoritarian systems anchor their actions or policies in a sense

---

80. Our current scholarly conceptions allow us to look beyond class as a social category; are based on a greater acceptance of difference; betray a more jaundiced view of those who claim to have a higher purpose in mind; are more able to distinguish between the people and the poor; and give us a greater ability to see those excluded from political community. But in the process, we have lost an ability to incorporate the purposes of political community (often reducing it to individual preferences); detect institutional politics in a nondemocratic setting; separate regime from ruler and state; and take ideology or moral norms seriously.

81. It is useful here to note that precise procedural and institutional arrangements, which now stand at the center of many of our understandings of how to classify political systems, were an attribute that interested classical authors but not an essential one. They were tools to help a system operate, to maintain it, and to make it just (or not) but not part of its essence—the classical categories were not phrased directly in institutional or procedural terms. This was understandable, with authority being exercised more directly by ruling individuals or bodies and the complex institutional apparatus of the modern state not in evidence. Hence, the vocabulary that we use to describe political systems was derived from not only a normative orientation that no longer prevails but also a fundamentally different understanding of how political systems operate.

of right and wrong that is not merely translated from regime instructions? If they do achieve some sense of autonomy in their mission, students of authoritarianism should take notice. We seek to explore when this happens and thus resist the unspoken tendency to define such possibilities out of viable existence.

How Are Democracies Different, and Which Differences Matter?

If we remove the implicit insistence that authoritarianism, despite its clear diversity, is inherently tyrannical in the classical sense, what really remains of our current understanding of authoritarianism, however, is something a bit clearer: *it is a political system in which executive authority is not in practice accountable, directly or indirectly, to any structure or process that is recognizably democratic in the modern sense.*[82]

By accepting this very recent understanding of "authoritarianism" as a residual category, we embrace the clear result that democracy and authoritarianism form a pair of mutually exhaustive categories. But this definition also means that we are focusing on a very specific conception of what about democracy interests us: electoral accountability of the executive through competitive voting with uncertain outcomes. And doing so not only allows a bit of analytical clarity but also allows us to understand how democracy might be different—and why (and to begin to suggest, as we will at the conclusion of this study, why it might not always be so).

Democracies are different not simply in allowing for a greater level of participation in governance but also because they can be approached as roughly homologous. This description of them seems odd, but it is firmly rooted in how we have come to understand the term. Let us explore what such a narrow and specific definition of democracy suggests.

If we wish to have an analytically sharp definition that can tell us whether a system is democratic or not but that remains agnostic in what other practices and values might be associated with it, it might be best to start with the succinct definition of democracy introduced by Adam Przeworski: a political system in which parties lose elections.[83] The converse of such a system is, in fact, precisely what residual conceptions of authori-

---

82. The "modern sense" of democratic accountability here refers to what has been called the "Schumpterian," "minimalist," or "procedural" conception of democracy in which such accountability is achieved foremost through a competitive electoral process.

83. Adam Przeworski (1991), *Democracy and the Market: Political and Economic Reforms in Eastern Europe and Latin America* (New York: Cambridge University Press), 10.

tarianism mean when using the term, though that meaning often gets buried or overlooked. Half a century ago, Samuel Huntington and Clement Moore wrote:

> Democracy exists where the principal leaders of a political system are selected by competitive elections in which the bulk of the population have the opportunity to participate. Authoritarian systems are non-democratic ones.[84]

Simply put, in a democracy there is no political party that can be assured victory. According to this definition, elections are a necessary but not sufficient condition for democracy—for democracy to exist, all parties that enter elections must be able to lose. Of course, the various good things associated with democracy—such as the full panoply of civil and political liberties, property rights, and the rule of law—can certainly play a role in ensuring that parties can organize and that they can win (and, more critically, lose), as the thicker, "polyarchy" model of democracy suggests.[85] But systems can also limit, define, or ignore some or all of these things and remain democracies if they keep competitive elections, as critics of democracy have always noted. They may be stupid or evil, illiberal or flawed, when they do so, but they are not necessarily undemocratic.

Przeworski's definition appears at first glance to recover democracy's original and core meaning—rule by the people. But, actually, it introduces two specific institutional requirements that are alien to classical conceptions: parties and the election of leaders. These requirements now seem natural, but they are really quite modern modifications of the term. Ancient democracies had neither formal parties nor elections. And they therefore look very unfamiliar.

Przeworski's definition, thus, implies a measure of homologous structure among modern democracies. Both authoritarian and democratic systems vary considerably among themselves. But democracies—as conceived in this way—have many other similar institutional features. They have executives, parliamentary chambers, parties, and elections. This is not true

---

84. Samuel Huntington and Clement Moore (1970), "Conclusion: Authoritarianism, Democracy, and One-Party Politics," in *Authoritarian Politics in Modern Society: The Dynamics of Established One-Party Systems*, ed. Samuel Huntington and Clement Moore (New York: Basic Books), 509.

85. Robert A. Dahl (1971), *Polyarchy: Participation and Opposition* (New Haven: Yale University Press).

by definition; but it is what has emerged through the historical experience of the last two hundred or so years. The struggle over establishing democracy (elections among parties with uncertain outcomes) was fought in most countries over how these various structures and mechanisms would relate to each other; the structures therefore are invested with great political significance. When we wish to compare democratic political systems, we have a ready-made list of specific institutions and procedures that draw our immediate attention—made indeed by decades of intense political struggles.

Our deeply ingrained cynicism about authoritarian politics should not be taken so far as to assume that the only mechanisms that matter are democratic ones, yet it easily slips into our analysis. Scholars of comparative politics regularly reach to explain authoritarian policymaking according to the basic common feature across authoritarian systems, the absence of democratic mechanisms and practices.[86] Hence, the field tends to approach authoritarian political systems as if they are as similar to each other as democratic ones—with "regime type," or basic, structural distinctions in the top echelon of ruling political elites, being the main source of variation explored by contemporary scholars.[87] But such an approach implies that manifold differences in the structure and operation of authoritarian state institutions below the top executive are epiphenomenal or uninteresting.

By drawing attention to how variation in authoritarian policymaking can be affected by differences in the form, operation, and influence of state institutions, we intend to challenge the scholarly tendency to treat authoritarian systems—or sometimes subtypes of authoritarian regimes—as roughly analogous entities. Of course, we do not mean to imply that authoritarian polities necessarily have weak institutions, betray a larger gap between formal and informal structures, or are unbound by rules. Empirically we may find that these are features of some or even many authoritarian systems, but they are not true by our definition. Indeed, we should expect great variation here—Libya in the late twentieth century and

---

86. Bueno de Mesquita et al. (2003), e.g., position the existence of democratic mechanisms—as reflected through a democratic polity's larger "winning coalition" size (W)—as the key force explaining variation in most policy outcomes across regimes: war/peace, political survival, corruption, economic growth, and the distribution of public versus private goods, broadly defined.

87. Geddes (1999) and (2003). Magaloni and Kricheli (2010). Axel Hadenius and Jan Teorell (2007), "Pathways from Authoritarianism," *Journal of Democracy* 18 (1): 143–57. Jessica Weeks (2012), "Strongmen and Straw Men: Authoritarian Regimes and the Initiation of International Conflict," *American Political Science Review* 106 (2): 326–47.

imperial Germany in the late nineteenth were extremely different on such dimensions. State institutions in authoritarian systems are a motley crew; while we find similarities across many cases, heterogeneity is more commonly the rule than the exception.

Recognizing the considerable diversity in authoritarian institutions—across cases and over time—is likely to prove both necessary and rewarding for comparative analysis. Indeed, implicit views regarding state institutions—their roles, structures, and relations to both political elites and societal constituencies—may be precisely what pushes scholars to view the difference between democracy and authoritarianism as profound.

In fact, we propose something of a curious, perhaps provocative mirror-image tendency. In democracies, political uncertainty is baked into the top levels of governance in the form of leadership transitions through repeated, regular, and competitive elections. At the lower and middle levels of public administration, however, we need not be committed Weberians to expect to find state institutions that have evolved to operate under diverse leaders (who harbor varied political interests and goals) and adapt to the requirement of conducting business in an environment of routinized leadership change.

For these reasons, state institutions in democracies, especially stable ones, tend to have higher degrees of institutionalization and stronger linkages to a broad array of actors rather than just the ruler or regime. While not present by definition, these institutional features seem so prevalent in practice that contemporary views of democracy tend to presuppose them, conflating the concept of "democracy" with existence of a functioning modern administrative state. Where the latter fails, we start throwing adjectives around again to describe the nature of rule and governance once more.[88]

Authoritarian systems, however, certainly can also adopt bureaucratic and institutional features associated with legal-rational authority and the modern administrative state.[89] The degree to which they do so varies considerably—as one should expect should happen when "authoritarianism" is a residual category. We should be highly alert to this variation.

Authoritarian systems that do not develop the mechanisms of legal-rational authority, or do so quite minimally, were initially viewed as a distinct category of political system that was something other than "authori-

---

88. David Collier and Steven Levitksy (1997), "Democracy with Adjectives: Conceptual Innovation in Comparative Research," *World Politics* 49 (3): 430–51.

89. Ernst Fraenkel (2017 [1941]), *The Dual State: A Contribution to the Theory of Dictatorship*. English edition (translated by Jens Meierhenrich) (New York: Oxford University Press).

tarian" (*patrimonialism*[90] in some writings and *sultanism*[91] in others). These alternative systems were defined precisely by the "blurring of the line between regime and state" and the virtual inseparability of ruler and state.[92] While the bulk of "sultanistic" regimes were nondemocratic, we should keep in mind that the vast majority of nondemocratic regimes were not themselves sultanistic. Moreover, the category of sultanism, while heavily associated with nondemocracy, was viewed as being applicable to some democratic systems as well; according to Chehabi and Linz it included the curious cases of "the rule of Eric Gairy in Grenada (1974–79) and that of the Bird family in Antigua" among others.[93]

The most critical difference between politics in democratic and authoritarian systems may not be the mere existence of elected versus unelected leaders (even though that is the defining difference). After all, many democratic leaders are acutely self-interested, seeking to maximize their power and perpetuate their rule just as much as any rational and self-serving autocrat. Instead, the most profound differences may result from variation in the nature of state institutions that so typically flows from the existence of competitive elections for senior positions in a modern administrative state. Democratic systems tend to develop in ways that foster higher levels of institutionalization, stronger linkages with societal constituencies, and a greater separation between rulers, regimes, and states. But this is not always the case; democracies can lack—and authoritarian systems can have—these sorts of institutional arrangements. We will come back to this line of argument and make it a focal concern in the concluding chapter, as we view its implications for comparative political research as being highly consequential.

Distinguishing among Authoritarian Rulers, Regimes, and States

We view authoritarianism as varying not simply in the character of its institutional arrangements but also in its degree of *structural differentiation*— the extent that rulers, regimes, and states are either interwoven or distin-

---

90. Max Weber (1978), *Economy and Society: An Outline of Interpretive Sociology* (Berkeley: University of California Press). Guenther Roth (1968), "Personal Rulership, Patrimonialism, and Empire-Building in the New States," *World Politics* 20 (2): 194–206.

91. Linz (2000).

92. Houchang E. Chehabi and Juan Linz (1998), *Sultanistic Regimes* (Baltimore: Johns Hopkins University Press), 10.

93. Chehabi and Linz (1998), 9.

guishable from one another.[94] When such differentiation is obscured or overlooked in comparative analysis, scholars can unconsciously confound different sources of political authority in authoritarian societies, by, for example, loosely using words (like the "ruler" and the "regime" or the "regime" and the "state") as if they are interchangeable or in practice fused together. Of course, distinctions among such terms are a staple of introductory political science courses. But actual usage—and empirical reality— sometimes does not follow such clear distinctions. Functionalism can collapse the lines among state, ruler, and regime. But by showing that state institutions can, in many circumstances, operate with significant autonomy from autocrats and regime elites, we will identify important forms of structural differentiation that exist—to varying degrees—even within patently authoritarian contexts.

In this way, attentiveness to *structural differentiation* will emerge as a key implication of our empirical analysis. If autocrats completely penetrate the state apparatus (a hallmark feature defining older conceptions of "sultanistic" or "neo-patrimonial" rule), structural differentiation between rulers and states is utterly lacking. And if a military junta or dominant party cadre fully co-opts or subordinates state institutions and their personnel (a goal to which most twentieth-century totalitarian and fascist leaders aspired), differentiation between regimes and states would similarly be quite minimal. But by recentering Linz's conception of "authoritarianism" as distinct from all of these systems through its attribute of limited pluralism, we are quickly reminded that nondemocratic rule does not necessarily obviate structural differentiation between rulers, regimes, and states. It most certainly can in some authoritarian settings, particularly when treated as an expansive residual category that now folds sultanistic, neo-patrimonial, fascist, and totalitarian systems into its conceptual ambit. But our exploration of institutional autonomy within authoritarian societies (so defined as "nondemocracies") will show that this is not always the case.

We should clarify here the level at which we undertake our analysis: we

---

94. The concept of structural differentiation is one that Huntington (1968) viewed as a core element of rational-legal authority, one cultivated through the process of political modernization. In an earlier work, Huntington (1966) more fully identified "structural differentiation" as being present when political authorities and functions are dispersed among distinct institutions or entities. Thus, a political system with low structural differentiation is one in which ruler, regime, and state are effectively fused and the political functions performed by each entity are not meaningfully distinguished or separable. See Samuel P. Huntington (1966), "Political Modernization: America vs. Europe," *World Politics* 18 (3): 378–414.

will focus on individual institutions (such as courts and legislatures) much more than the system as a whole. We seek to explain when such bodies are autonomous, but we do not aggregate upward to probe the overall level of autonomy of all state institutions in a specific system. It is not because the latter task is unimportant. Just the opposite. It is a central concern of scholarship, but we think we need to pause first and look at individual institutions to understand them better before proceeding to greater degrees of aggregation.

Throughout the empirical chapters, we illustrate that individual state institutions can be meaningfully autonomous (from rulers and regimes) in authoritarian systems. But such autonomy almost always varies across institutions within the same country—a judiciary may be insulated from an autocrat's interference, for instance, but a legislature or Ministry of Justice may be fully penetrated and beholden to that very same autocrat. Our mesolevel study of institutional autonomy in a range of cases will reveal that structural differentiation is possible, sometimes widespread, and also highly variable across authoritarian societies. It cannot simply be assumed away as a byproduct of today's common tendency to implicitly equate authoritarianism (as a residual category for all nondemocratic regimes) with tyranny (as a very specific structure of rule), as was discussed above.

We do not ourselves devise or employ any overall measure of *structural differentiation* at the systemic level. Comparative measurement efforts— such as the Polity Project, Freedom House, and Varieties of Democracy— reflect a great awareness among contemporary scholars that aggregating complex phenomenon within an authoritarian system into a single macrolevel variable (e.g., "executive constraints," "civil liberties," "rule of law," "pluralism," or "government effectiveness") can be both quite reductionist but also highly rewarding. While we do not undertake such aggregation ourselves, we hope to help those who do. And, thus, we do pause here to draw attention to structural differentiation at the level of the entire system, as we expect this factor to be highly relevant for readers who seek to apply our framework in their own macrolevel studies moving forward. By aggregating the degree of autonomy that all state institutions possess within a particular authoritarian polity, one may devise a macrolevel descriptive variable—a holistic assessment of how much the state apparatus is, in aggregate, meaningfully differentiable from the autocratic executive and the cadre of regime elites that surrounds them.

Conceptual Imprecision: Why Are "Regimes" So Slippery?

Indeed, those we follow were very much interested in the systemic level. Variation in structural differentiation was quite central—though in somewhat different ways—to the understanding of authoritarianism as crafted by Juan Linz, who was explicit in noting:

> We speak of authoritarian *regimes* rather than authoritarian *governments* to *indicate the relatively low specificity of political institutions*: they often penetrate the life of the society. . . . [But] in contrast to some analysts of totalitarianism, we speak of regimes rather than societies because the distinction between state and society is not fully obliterated even in the intentions of rulers.[95]

Given the sheer variability of its institutional arrangements, authoritarianism was appreciated as a system that made structural differentiation possible—but did not guarantee it. While systematic consideration of structural differentiation has receded in recent work, it has not been completely erased. Slater and Fenner, for instance, conceptualize the state as a system of institutions that are critically distinct from the autocrats and regime elites who monopolize executive power within a system: "The state [is] a kind of machinery that is linked but not reducible to the actors who operate it."[96] Developing this point in terms that align a great deal with our own historical and institutionalist approach, they further explain:

> Regime leaders are not usually the original architects of the states they operate. Drivers may customize, repair, or "soup up" their cars, but they rarely build them from scratch or convert them into something that dramatically outperforms the original model. State apparatuses are typically inherited rather than originally constructed by the regimes that run them.[97]

Here we see a clear, conceptual distinction made between regimes, their leaders, and their state apparatuses—one that is shaped more powerfully by

---

95. Linz (2000), 160–61; italic emphasis added.

96. Dan Slater and Sofia Fenner (2011), "State Power and Staying Power: Infrastructural Mechanisms and Authoritarian Durability," *Journal of International Affairs* 65 (1): 16.

97. Slater and Fenner (2011), 16.

"long-term historical forces"[98] than autocratic innovation or intentionality. Because this approach to taking structural differentiation seriously is one that we similarly aim to elevate in the authoritarianism literature, we must go a step further in our discussion of this factor to detail how rulers, regimes, and states ought to be distinguished conceptually. And we find considerable confusion here. We will first present the confusion—but then move immediately to use that confusion to our advantage.

In an often cited article, Philippe C. Schmitter and Terry Lynn Karl define "regime" in a manner that moves among system, rules, individuals, constitutions, and informality, which accurately reflects the range of current uses but simultaneously makes it difficult to tell what a regime is, what it is not, and how ruler and state fit within or without it as a concept:

> A regime or system of governance is an ensemble of patterns that determines the methods of access to the principal public offices; the characteristics of the actors admitted to or excluded from such access; the strategies that actors may use to gain access; and the rules that are followed in the making of publicly binding decisions. To work properly, the ensemble must be institutionalized, that is to say, the various patterns must be habitually known, practiced, and accepted by most, if not all, actors. Increasingly, the preferred mechanism of institutionalization is a written body of laws undergirded by a written constitution, though many enduring political norms can have an informal, prudential, or traditional basis.[99]

Beginning with this understanding of "regimes" in mind, we will conclude this introductory chapter with two claims about terminology that may seem odd at first but will prove both frank and helpful. First, while ruler and state are easy to define in formal terms, regime is more slippery because it is rarely used how it is formally defined. The formal definition generally refers to rules or regularities, but we will present and embrace the meaning that is actually attached to the term's usage in practice—the group of top political officials in an authoritarian system.

Second, distinguishing among state, ruler, and regime is often hard, especially in some authoritarian systems but not in others. And that dif-

---

98. Slater and Fenner (2011), 16.
99. Schmitter and Karl (1991), 76.

ficulty can be of great interest and lies at the center of this book as one of its primary contributions to macrolevel research on authoritarian politics. To that end, we will keep the variable prospects for structural differentiation in the back of our heads as we explore each state institution and each case presented in the book. Knowing when to talk about ruler, regime, and state at the macrolevel actually helps inform how we understand where mesolevel state institutions fit within the polity overall. Indeed, sometimes we will find strict delineation—bureaucrats versus politicians, where never the twain shall meet. In others, we will find elements of the "regime" properly speaking in these same state institutions, often as leader figures such as chief justices or parliamentary speakers and party leaders. And others will be curious mixes—but always with the potential for provocative differences in how these state institutions relate to ruler and regime in particular.

Ruler, State... and What We Really Mean by Regime

Ruler, state, and regime are used so frequently that a definitional discussion seems pedantic. We probe these terms not for mere pedantry, however, but for uncovering why "regime" in particular is something important to watch—but difficult to define.

Let us turn first to "ruler." The ruler, defined as the senior executive official in the political system, might be an individual or conceivably a very small group of key individuals exercising executive power at the highest level. It might even be an institution (perhaps a presidium, central committee, or junta) at the apex of the state or party. It is conceivable that the "ruler" might actually not formally occupy a state position—as with Libya's Mu`ammar al-Qadhdhafi, who came to abjure formal titles, or China's Mao Zedong, whose most significant formal positions lay in the Chinese Communist Party—as long as the individual or structure effectively exercises supreme executive authority. The odd and sometimes indistinct institutional arrangements characteristic of such systems should not lead us to spin our wheels in prolonged definitional deliberations but instead alert us that the nature and degree of institutionalization in such systems is itself distinctive (with Libya having a weak state and China one where a fairly strong state and quite strong party were fused).

A "state" is similarly not difficult to define; as a term in widespread use for a considerable period, there is an array of formal definitions to draw on. But in this study, we will consider the state in modified, Weberian fashion to be a public political authority with the capacity for the sole use of legitimate force and regulation within a given territory. It therefore includes any public body formally operating on the basis of that authority. In the modern era, the state tends to be quite sprawling, with executive and quasi-executive bureaucracies intermixed with explicitly political and judicial bodies as well as (sometimes) independent or otherwise distinct entities all nestled within its broad ambit.

The difficult term for scholars has always been "regime." And here we wish to frankly acknowledge what we suggested above: that we will use the term as it is actually most often used, not as it is formally defined (but rarely used). By "regime" we mean the set of top political officials of a nondemocratic system—broader than the ruler but consisting of those in top leadership, policy-making positions. These top political officials form the upper tier of political elites in a given polity and have meaningful political relevance but extend beyond the executive core itself.

Why do we define a "regime" as consisting of people rather than rules, norms, or practices? The term is indeed usually defined as the basic political rules. And if those rules are about electing leaders, few would hesitate to speak of a "democratic regime." But referring to regimes in democracies often stops there—about the only time it is used that way is when we refer to "regime type." And, even then, it is used very broadly to refer to democratic as opposed to authoritarian (as the two overarching "regime types"). It also refers to subtypes of authoritarian systems but never subtypes of democratic ones. One never hears of Canada's "Westminster regime" contrasted with Mexico's "presidential regime" or the Italian "multiparty regime" in contradistinction to the Japanese "dominant party regime." Thus, the actual definitions of regimes turn out not to be bypassed for democracies.

For authoritarian systems scholars ostensibly look immediately to the governing system, institutions, and rules (formal or informal) generally based on a fairly capacious strategy of including all relevant features that one could think of. For instance, David Collier and Fernando Cardoso referred to *regime* as

> the formal and informal structure of governmental roles and processes. The regime thus includes such things as the method of selection of the government (election, coup, selection process within the military, etc.), formal and informal mechanisms of representation, and patterns of representation.[100]

---

100. See the glossary in David Collier, ed. (1979), *The New Authoritarianism in Latin America* (Princeton: Princeton University Press), 402–3.

More succinctly, Barbara Geddes has referred to regime as "sets of formal and informal rules and procedures for selecting national leaders and policies."[101]

But what, then, is *not* the regime? In practice, scholars move quickly from a vague reference to rules and institutions to governing elites—broader than the "ruler," generally, but defined more by authority than any specific set of positions. Geddes later more frankly refines the definition to mean a "leadership group," that is "the small group that actually makes the most important decisions,"[102] a change in part to distinguish from selectorate theory, which suggests a minimum winning coalition that is unlikely to actually be active in influencing policy as a decision-making subset.[103] We applaud such frankness, since that is how scholars usually use the term "regime," and we intend to follow it.

Why does regime actually refer largely to authoritarian contexts, whereas democracies are often free from having their leadership groups defined as "regimes"? And why does it really mean leadership group in such a system more than formal or informal rules?

The first question is almost never explicitly addressed, but the pattern is striking. France has had a "Fourth Republic" and a period of Gaullist rule but generally only a Vichy regime; the Nazi regime followed the Weimar Republic and was succeeded by the Federal Republic (at least for those who wish to find an alternative to the "Third Reich").

How do we justify such a surrender to what might seem like sloppy and inconsistent usage? The frank definition of regime and its deployment in authoritarian contexts more than democratic ones are not so much sloppy as they are a response to the need to undertake comparative analysis. Defining democracy and authoritarianism the way we have means that most modern democracies are fairly homologous. They differ, of course, but it is fairly easy to identify specific, politically relevant structures filled with elites at regular intervals through competitive elections that can be easily compared (such as "cabinets," "governments," or "administrations"). We do not need a vague category to refer to the leadership group because we have specific places to look and we know which ones they are.

But since authoritarianism is a residual category, the wide range of authoritarian systems varies much more considerably in how much—and which—institutions possess political significance. We therefore reach for

---

101. Geddes (1999), 16.
102. Geddes, Wright, and Franz (2014), 315.
103. Bueno de Mesquita et al. (2003).

a term that seems to suggest the group of individuals or institutions that "matter" while allowing the precise individuals or institutions to vary according to the system.

In common usage, commentators, even scholars, frequently (even usually) refer to a regime by using the personal name of the ruler—the Franco regime, the Marcos regime, the al-Qadhdhafi regime, and so on. Even when scholars use a slightly less personal term to refer to a regime—such as the "bureaucratic authoritarian regime" in Argentina—and allow for a regime to survive its namesake (a complication that arose, e.g., when referring to the continued "Salazar regime" in Portugal after Salazar's death) or even allow a personnel interlude in the state's highest office (the Medvedev period might be seen as part of an ongoing Putin regime), many seem to use the term to mean something far less ambitious than the entire political or constitutional order.[104] And it is not surprising that they do so, again because of the diversity of authoritarian regimes. To describe regimes only by formal rules (or even informal ones) would make comparative analysis difficult; to name them by who is running them is far easier.

As a result, when most scholars speak of a "regime," they may speak abstractly as if they are referring to rules and institutions, but they generally more concretely mean to indicate a stable group of top political officials and perhaps the economic, media, and military elites closely associated with them, governing in an authoritarian setting. Hence, a major change in senior officials—or in where they come from—would be a regime change in an authoritarian system. (If it occurred in a democracy, we would call it an election in which the opposition wins.)

In this study, we will bow to what has emerged as informal practice, though it is rarely recognized as such, and refer to "regime" collectively as the senior decision-makers in a state governed by an authoritarian manner. This definition makes the "regime" close to the authoritarian equivalent of "administration" in American usage or "government" in parliamentary systems.

Of course, in this book we will at times wish to refer to the entire political system and not merely just the top officials. And at such points we will use that term by referring to the "system," meaning what might also be called the constitutional order (a term that we will generally avoid primarily because it is not always clear if the user intends to refer to a written doc-

---

104. With the National Assembly and constitutional system suspended, the Vichy regime did not even know what to call itself, settling on the "French State" as opposed to the preceding "French Republic."

ument or to the basic rules of the system whether or not they are included in a formal constitution). As we have noted, the "system" so conceived is often very difficult to specify in practice, and we will not place much analytical weight on it.

We will therefore refer to authoritarianism in several guises, generally specifying the level at which we are applying the term: an authoritarian ruler (unaccountable in any democratic manner), regime (set of key, senior elites operating without any democratic accountability), state (public political authorities at all levels operating without democratic accountability), or system (a "constitutional" order that may lack any such electoral oversight mechanism).

But being clear on what we mean by a regime does not always make it easy to distinguish between a "regime" on the one hand and a "ruler" or "state" on the other. That does not frustrate us; it fascinates us.

Making a Virtue Out of Necessity: Can They Be Distinguished in Practice?

While scholars should be more cognizant of the specific actors and institutions being referred to by the terms "ruler," "regime" and "state," we should also pause to take note of the frequent difficulty of distinguishing among them. Indeed, after having clarified the definitions we will use, we should explain that the confusion is not all the fault of scholars. In some cases, these terms are difficult to distinguish, but in others they are not. That fact alone is worthy of our attention. Thus, we should investigate not simply *how* but also *when* researchers ought to distinguish among the ruler, the regime, and the state in authoritarian societies. Scholarly confusion is not merely based on fuzzy thinking; sometimes it stems from a rather fuzzy reality, one that our definitions should highlight rather than obscure.

In some places, the state apparatus is virtually an extension of the person or the household of the ruler. Indeed, as noted above, it was such systems that the terms "patrimonialism" and "sultanism"[105] were invented to describe. Such arrangements render state institutions incapable of pursuing any mission or interests other than those defined by the top executive officials. State institutions similarly lack autonomy in highly totalitarian regimes, where membership in various state institutions is contingent upon allegiance to a certain ideology or association with a strictly controlled, totalizing, and mobilization-oriented ruling party.

---

105. Chehabi and Linz (1998).

Conversely, the distinction between regime and state is much more pronounced in a system in which state institutions are less penetrated by the regime—that is, where institutions like the judiciary, various bureaucratic actors and offices, and central banks show some degree of separation from political elites and, thus, a capacity for autonomously defining their own mission and interests. Reality is not always muddy. Another way to get a sense of the state/regime distinction is to probe the degree to which various state institutions are able to pose persuasively as strong but neutral and outside of politics. For example, while in Putin's Russia bureaucratic entities like the Central Electoral Commission or the Ministry of Finance are understood as tools of regime interest and elite state capitalist corruption, the governance of the Central Bank remains strongly identified as technocratic, trustworthy, and independent—a perception widely held by media and political actors who at the same time can quite truthfully emphasize the personalist, authoritarian system they live in more broadly.

In short, we can understand the variations among authoritarian systems in part according to *how much* ruler, regime, and state are distinguishable. Sometimes it is hard to detect the dividing lines. Hard cases may make bad law, but we will use them here to help us make good scholarly analysis. When analytical distinctions among ruler, regime, and state are difficult to make, we do not need to abandon them but sometimes show greater interest in what that difficulty tells us. In being alert to the *degree* to which these distinctions are helpful, the extent of differentiation among ruler, regime, and state will underlie much of our analysis.

The Plan of the Book

By clarifying our conceptual vocabulary—through both defining and tracing the evolving meanings underpinning terms like "institutions," "authoritarianism," "democracy," "rulers," "regimes," and "states"—we aimed to better contextualize and specify the objects and scope of our inquiry. In what follows, we will deploy the concepts that we have devised, revised, adopted, or otherwise recovered in this chapter to examine the conditions under which state institutions are capable of developing autonomy in authoritarian political environments.

In chapter 2, we present a theory of authoritarian state autonomy, beginning by delineating two distinct forms of institutional autonomy as our outcomes of interest. The first is *internal autonomy*, or the extent that state institutions are able to effectively control their own affairs and administration.

Second, we explore *mission autonomy*, or the capacity for state institutions to pursue their own senses of mission in some area of public policy or decision-making influence. This chapter proceeds to explicate two factors that enable authoritarian institutions to develop internal and mission autonomy: (1) high levels of institutionalization in the form of structural hierarchy, coherence, complexity, and adaptability; and (2) strong linkages to supportive constituencies in society or allies elsewhere within the state apparatus.

We begin our empirical analysis of authoritarian state institutions in chapter 3, turning to constitutional courts. Constitutional courts are highly specific institutions, are easily identifiable, and occupy particular spaces within the broader matrix of political life. Generally impotent in terms of executing their own decisions and often restricted in their focus (and sometimes marginal for many political actors) because of their technical nature, constitutional courts can sometimes operate at the whim of the regime yet sometimes are able to emerge as significant, if often ultimately corralled, institutions able to deviate from the regime's desires.

We thus investigate this curious variation in some detail: it is an ideal way to begin our probe of how far functionalist logics can bring us and where they are likely to mislead. The chapter offers a paired comparison of constitutional courts in Egypt and Palestine. By contrasting the establishment and historical evolution of these judicial bodies, we show that institutionalization and linkages have fostered varying levels of autonomy in the Egyptian Supreme Constitutional Court over time, whereas the absence of these factors have left the Palestinian Supreme Constitutional Court as a fairly impotent body in which functionalist theorizing brings more explanatory value.

Chapter 4 proceeds to analyze parliaments, beginning with a historical analysis of how these legislative institutions have evolved across the diversity of authoritarian regimes over time. This chapter allows us to expand our analysis from the previous one by examining a more variegated set of bodies. Actually, while parliaments vary from one system to another, they do so much less than they used to. We chart a sharp historical convergence toward an oddly powerful set of homologous institutional configurations and structures across such bodies. The outcome of this isomorphic tendency has been the development of a vast array of authoritarian parliaments with a considerable set of formal, though latent, powers to use if they ever get the nerve: legislative obstruction, ministerial interpolation, rights to bill initiative, budgetary authority, cabinet responsibility, and votes of no confidence.

It is easy to answer the question of why authoritarian regimes invent parliaments: they don't. We show how parliaments, unlike many constitutional courts, are usually inherited by authoritarian regimes, sometimes having roots in the distant past, so regimes most often remold and manage rather than invent them. Parliaments allow us to probe the meaning of autonomy a bit more deeply—the degree to which it emerges but also when it expresses itself less by articulating a clear vision and more by obstructing the regime or forcing it to adapt. And they allow us to probe linkages a bit more—both within the state and with social actors—because they are more broadly embedded in society and politics than constitutional courts.

Authoritarian parliaments are often treated as meek entities—until they suddenly become vexing headaches to authoritarian rulers and their plans. The chapter then proceeds to analyze the Russian State Duma and Kuwaiti Majlis al-Umma to assess when—and whether—authoritarian legislatures actually ever use these powers to pursue internal and mission autonomy in practice.

In Russia, waxing and waning institutionalization pushed forward by mild or ambitious parliamentary leadership over time accounts for significant variation in the Duma's capacity for internal autonomy, while its mission autonomy has remained largely nonexistent and ill-defined. In Kuwait, we find that the Majlis al-Umma's degree of internal and mission autonomy is directly related to its strong linkages to various public constituencies that have shifted over time. These linkages have allowed the Majlis to engage in a negative, contrarian form of mission autonomy—halting government action and frustrating regime initiatives—rather than pursuing a positive sense of its own mission in public policy. Moreover, we conclude that because the Kuwaiti Majlis enjoys a high degree of adaptability and coherence, but very minimal levels of complexity and hierarchy, the body is able to use its powers to intervene widely in politics—but never in a sustained or well-organized way, which leads its interventions to be gawkish and haphazard.

Chapter 5 concludes our empirical analysis with an investigation of religious establishments and state religious institutions in imperial and Nazi Germany, Saudi Arabia, Egypt, and Thailand. We use this diverse set of cases to better identify the types of institutionalization and linkages that matter—and how they matter—in the development of institutional and mission autonomy. The German cases highlight a specific importance for institutionalization in the forms of hierarchy, coherence, and complexity and, further, show that linkages to public constituencies become less effective when those constituencies are themselves supportive of the ruler or regime.

In Egypt and Saudi Arabia, we show that institutionalization and linkages to a broad population of believers facilitated religious establishments' pursuit of internal and mission autonomy. But we also observe an important distinction involving the extent to which linkages were either folded into the state or forced into networks of operation outside of the public sphere. Finally, our analysis of the religious establishment in Thailand shows that linkages are less effective in promoting institutional autonomy when they are established primarily with disorganized and localized groups of religious actors and organizations; that enduring linkages between a state religious establishment and a previously deposed regime often place internal autonomy in the crosshairs; and that incoherence and the destabilization of hierarchies within the religious establishment precludes the pursuit of mission autonomy.

We will conclude in the final chapter by revisiting many of the ideas that we have explicated thus far, placing a particular emphasis on analyzing how implicit preconceptions of the modern administrative state commonly (often for good reason) spill into our understanding of democratic and authoritarian regimes. And we will show that these preconceptions—and the distinct institutional configurations that they implicate—are often doing much of the work in explaining variation in policy-making process and outcomes across a diverse array of political systems.

Consequently, the core distinction between democratic and authoritarian politics may not always involve political elites (elected or unelected) or ruling organizations (dominant parties, militaries, bureaucracies, monarchies, etc.) but rather may lie in the way that democracies tend to encourage a greater degree of separation between rulers, regimes, and states. They thereby, often provide more favorable political environments for state institutions to become institutionalized and develop strong independent linkages to both public and private constituencies. Of course, these characteristics do not always emerge in democratic systems, nor are they always absent from authoritarian systems. Reality is often much messier than our conceptual categories for political regimes portray it to be. We expect that recognizing, and embracing, that messiness rather than defining it out of existence will open fruitful avenues of research on democratic and authoritarian politics.

CHAPTER 2

Taking Some Parts of Authoritarian States Seriously, Sometimes

The problem is that as we have developed ever more sophisticated comparative statics we have inadvertently built scientific models that are out of sync with the way the world actually works.
—Sven Steinmo, *The Evolution of Modern States: Sweden, Japan, and the United States*

Functionalist accounts of state institutions in authoritarian regimes, while elegant and powerful, are very often unsatisfactory—and for the very same reason that they are so elegant and powerful. Simplifying assumptions about intentions, leaders, and institutions push complicating possibilities to the margins. And sometimes those need to be at the center rather than the margin of our attention. Such was the argument of the previous chapter. We offer this chapter as an attempt to move beyond these observations and develop a useful framework to ask other questions about institutions that top-down and functionalist logics tend to obscure. Here we seek to provide a theory of institutional autonomy under authoritarianism in a way that addresses two specific problems.

First, if autocrats are all similarly assumed to devise and mold state institutions in ways that promote their power and survival, what explains the tremendous differences across authoritarian institutions that we observe in practice, both over time and cross-nationally? Why, for instance, do some regimes discover a strategic use for autonomous constitutional courts, others for pliant ones, and others go without them entirely? Why do some autocrats find it functional to consolidate dominant parties, others to break them apart, and others to eschew party politics altogether? And why do we find autonomy in some institutions but not others at the very same time, when elite or mass pressures on autocrats do not vary? To answer that such considerable institutional variation within and across authoritarian systems is simply the result of rational calculations based in the interests of the rulers and a clear-eyed understanding of the tools at their disposal seems unlikely, to say the least.

Second, functionalist explanations of authoritarian politics and institutional activity frequently seem quite implausible—which, in our view, hints that they need to be used more sparingly and strategically rather than deployed indiscriminately. These explanations suggest that regimes build institutions almost as they like, allowing at best that such institutions, once formed to serve a regime, might then operate in unintended ways (a party created for one purpose may not always serve that purpose, or a court may go off the rails at times). We have already asserted that simplification for the sake of analysis and generalizable statements can lead to looking past historical details to broad global trends. Our approach, enriched by insights from historical institutionalism and a deep appreciation of context and time, leads us to suspect that this simplification may be less benign than it appears. It is likely that autocrats try and steer state institutions toward their own ends, but it is unlikely that such steering will always explain much of what they do, and it should certainly not form the base of our modeling assumptions. Most of all, authoritarian institutions, states, and societies are all exceptionally diverse in these regards, in no small part because we clump so very many polities within the residual category of authoritarianism.

In short, contemporary understandings of authoritarian institutions tend to make a number of simplifying assumptions, though often unconsciously: that institutions are very malleable, that rulers are the ones who shape them, that the shaping can be explained by the ruler's desire to maintain power, and that rulers do a pretty good job at strategizing how to mold state structures. In the previous chapter, we argued that the problem with top-down and functionalist theories of authoritarianism is not that they are false but that they vary considerably in how much they are true. Such varying levels of truth risk overshadowing the many other ways in which authoritarian politics takes place, both from the bottom up and from the inside. The regulation of the construction of houses of worship, the way disputes between landlord and tenant are adjudicated, the ways in which citizens in a rural province draw parliamentary attention to their irrigation needs—all these are deeply political topics, but the outcomes, and the structures for producing those outcomes, are not chiefly about regime maintenance. The daily life of autocracy is far more banal than pronouncements about the manic survival-prepping of such regimes would lead us to believe.

How, then, can we better account for the great variation in the degree to which different rulers and regimes—all of them authoritarian—actually drive decision-making and policy direction across cases, over time, and in different issue areas? If explanations based on ruler intentions and strategies differ so much in their helpfulness, what other factors should we consider?

We contend that a greater emphasis on the independent effects of sometimes autonomous or unshackled state institutions is necessary to understand widespread variation in the fundamental nature of authoritarian politics. Most institutions that operate under authoritarian conditions predate existing regimes. They are founded at particular moments to be sure, but sometimes those moments lie decades or even centuries in the past. New regimes often write new constitutions, for instance, but the best predictor of what is included in a country's constitution is what was in its old one.[1] Constitutional courts are relatively new innovations, yet their structures are highly isomorphic across states, and they have seemingly become de rigueur parts of most states' institutional fabric over the last half century—whether an autocrat would like them or not. Parliaments are some of the oldest institutional fixtures found worldwide, even in utterly authoritarian regimes, and their accumulated weight of ages and the historical evolution of their privileges and prerogatives can hang as a frustrating, latent power even with regimes dismissive of popular assemblies. Meanwhile, religious establishments run the gamut of ancient lineage and modern artifice, usually in a complicated mess of old practices and bodies set within newer, only semi-rationalized structures and, quite uniquely, sometimes formally influenced by transnational ties that lie beyond a given autocracy's remit.

While it is important to examine *why* dictators do and do not allow state institutions to constrain their political authority,[2] we should not mistake answers about ruler and regime motivations as always accounting

---

1. Zachary Elkins, Tom Ginsburg, and James Melton (2009), *The Endurance of National Constitutions* (New York: Cambridge University Press).
2. Milan W. Svolik (2012), *The Politics of Authoritarian Rule* (New York: Cambridge University Press).

for institutional activity and outcomes. There are, to be sure, occasional moments of court closure, parliamentary prorogation, or anticlerical disestablishment. But many such moments tend to be short-lived. They are often the result of regime fits of pique that rarely last long and even more rarely cause total disjuncture from a past institutional heritage. More often than not, they simply give birth to a new layer of institutional development. Real moments of grand institutional design by autocrats pursuing a clear functional interest, especially ones that occur ex nihilo, are really quite unusual—even if they have rightly been a major focus of study for many scholars.

In authoritarian societies, the ruler or regime might be the source of political authority in some areas of policy but not in others. Indeed, macrolevel logics of regime survival are unlikely to inform routine policy decisions or to automatically overcome entrenched institutional interests inherited from prior times, invested with their own legitimacies, or protected by powerful constituencies within the state or outside of it. Thus, our inquiry turns to explore state institutions from the inside as part of an effort to treat them seriously as locations where autonomy from the fiat directives of the ruler may be found.

For instance, authority over questions of religious policy—often affecting marriage, divorce, contraception, education, and public morality—frequently resides more in religious institutions (which can be linked to, distinct from, recognized by, or wholly part of the state) than it does in the regime. Such a distinction may transcend the party- or junta-based nature of a given regime, according to today's fashionable typologies. Egypt's forthright religious establishment resides in a nominally military-dominated authoritarian regime, while Russia's resurgent Orthodox Church successfully frames the moral policy agenda of the regime through institutional lobbying in parliament and elsewhere alongside a powerful media apparatus, all within a highly personalist polity—yet both would be more similar to each other than the moribund religious institutions in party-based Syria or Venezuela, where we might expect more regime interest in providing such bodies some extra leeway under institutional logics of survival. Moreover, state institutions are frequently unwilling or unable to translate regime directives into public policy. Illustrating this point, the literature on principal-agent problems between regime and bureaucracy[3] indicates that, even in authoritarian systems, state institutions often

---

3. James Rosberg (1995), "The Rise of an Independent Judiciary in Egypt" (PhD diss.,

mismanage, obstruct, and redirect the top-down transmission of political authority from the regime to the body politic.[4]

Though we may identify authoritarian political systems by the absence of a common trait—free and fair electoral mechanisms for selecting executive officeholders—we must still resist the temptation to treat authoritarian polities as homogenous when, in fact, they differ greatly in how state institutions are structured, how they operate, and how they relate to both the ruler and the regime. Rather than assuming that this basic common denominator across authoritarian polities is the driving force behind domestic policy, we should instead recognize the degree of variation in autonomy within and across authoritarian systems, both in the structure of state institutions and in the extent to which these institutions can be separated from rulers and regimes.

Our belief is that current understandings of authoritarian politics have overemphasized the connection between rulers, regimes, and political decision-making, such that we need to bring the diversity of organizations and bodies (and potential confusion) that is the state back in. Taking the state to be a collection of disparate public institutions, we seek to understand when those institutions can gain autonomy, under what conditions they exercise that autonomy, and in what ways they do so. In the process, we will have to trade a degree of the elegance and parsimony built into older theories in exchange for greater precision, contextualization, and richness.

Because we aim to be clear, we will turn first to defining what we mean by institutional autonomy and exploring how we will know it when we find it. In the first section, our analysis will pay particular attention to institutional autonomy at two different levels: (1) *internal autonomy*, or the capacity for institutions to run their own affairs and set their own agendas; and (2) *mission autonomy*, or the ability for various institutions to define their own purposes and wield influence independent of rulers and regimes in certain areas of public policy, decision-making, and political life.

We will then turn to the second part of the chapter, in which we probe what kinds of factors might be relevant in explaining when and how inter-

---

Massachusetts Institute of Technology). Mathew D. McCubbins and Thomas Schwartz (1984), "Congressional Oversight Overlooked: Police Patrols versus Fire Alarms," *American Journal of Political Science* 28 (1): 165–79. Tom Ginsburg (2008), "Administrative Law and the Judicial Control of Agents," in *Rule by Law: The Politics of Courts in Authoritarian Regimes*, ed. Tom Ginsburg and Tamir Moustafa (New York: Cambridge University Press).

4. Kevin J. O'Brien and Lianjiang Li (2006), *Rightful Resistance in Rural China* (New York: Cambridge University Press).

nal and mission autonomy arise. We suspect that accretion, accident, and institutional agency are as much a part of the explanation as regime intention and functional need. Evolution, and not merely intelligent design, is at work. That is, we believe the role of time and the weight of history are critical and cannot be unbundled from the politics of an authoritarian regime, even many years later. But we seek to go beyond remarking on complexity to considering what factors are likely to be most influential when explaining variation in institutional autonomy. In recovering a measure of theoretical parsimony, our approach will home in on two: how much a structure is *linked* to other state bodies, societal constituencies, or even international actors; and how much it is *institutionalized* in terms of its own adaptability, coherence, hierarchy, and complexity. The second section, thus, defines and theorizes these factors in relation to potential alternative explanations. The third section will then address the degree of differentiation between state and regime independently because, while not part of our explanation, it will always be lurking in the shadows and sometimes come into the foreground. We wish to be explicit on why we think that differentiation is important and why we must pay attention to the way it varies.

The fourth section concludes by explaining how we will utilize the empirical chapters of this book when using historical and contemporary case studies to trace the workings of each factor. Our aim is not to develop a formal causal model but to refine our explanation for institutional autonomy by considering a diverse range of actual experiences. As we noted in chapter 1, our inquiry investigates three kinds of institutions—constitutional courts, parliaments, and religious establishments—to explore how linkages and institutionalization work in practice under authoritarian conditions. By analyzing such distinct institutions in a series of comparative case studies, we aim to develop a more nuanced understanding of authoritarian politics from the inside, one that emphasizes the politics as much as the authoritarianism.

What Exactly Do We Mean by Institutional Autonomy?

We are interested in explaining the various ways in which authoritarian political systems work in their day-to-day lives, turning the focus away from regime collapses or heroic efforts to survive crisis. We argue that major aspects of the life of an authoritarian system are determined in significant part by the nature and degree of autonomy that individual state institutions exercise. And that leads us to probe when, how, and how much state institutions can develop autonomy across the heterogeneous mess of non-democracies worldwide. We explicitly recognize that autonomy means different things in different contexts and can be expressed to varying degrees and in different ways—this context-specific nuancing will form the bulk of our discussion in later empirical chapters. Yet, before that exploration, we begin here by defining the two forms of institutional autonomy that we take as our primary outcome of interest throughout the rest of the book.

First, we will examine variation in *internal autonomy*: the degree to which state institutions make decisions about their internal structure, personnel, and allocation of resources according to their own procedures or whether they can only make such decisions in a manner that reflects the will or interests of the regime. When assessing internal autonomy, notable questions include whether a state institution hires its own staff and promotes, disciplines, or terminates them according to its own discretion or procedures; has internal mechanisms for selecting (and retaining) its own leaders; controls its own internal budget allocations; sets its own rules (formal or informal) guiding how it operates in practice; manages its own internal agenda; or interacts with other state institutions as a procedural equal, among other points of interest.

To add some empirical flavor to this conceptualization, Spain's judiciary in the Franco period provides a useful example of an authoritarian institution with meaningful internal autonomy, albeit with minimal political influence. The judiciary itself selected and trained new judges, and judges could not be removed before they reached the compulsory age of retirement (seventy years old).[5] While it would be wrong to say that the Spanish judiciary of that authoritarian period had political independence or was able to contest the regime's goals and views, the judiciary was able to maintain an internal sense of authority within its specific, limited institutional remit, which both provided it distinct power in the broader complex of Spanish institutional politics and would impact how the regime underwent its own transition from power in later years. Telling the tale of the Spanish judiciary as a functionalist account of intentional regime safeguarding and preparation for an uncertain future quite seriously mistakes the banality of authoritarian institutional life for grand logics and all-knowing strategy.

In a very different political and institutional setting, Ken Opalo observes significant levels of internal autonomy for the Kenyan parliament (Bunge)

---

5. Jose J. Toharia (1975), "Judicial Independence in an Authoritarian Regime: The Case of Contemporary Spain," *Law and Society Review* 9 (3): 475–96.

under its era of one-party authoritarian rule. Its members were selected through "reasonably competitive" (though still undemocratic) single-party elections, it enjoyed great operational independence regarding its budget and internal procedural rules, and it was hardly a rubber stamp, even if it lacked the ability to legislate whatever outcomes it wished (or could pass by majority). Bills were forced to work their way through formal legislative channels, were pressed to receive significant input from members of parliament (MPs), and could face procedural delays that might cause them to "die slow deaths in committee" or result in formal amendment or rejection.[6] That the regime would generally get its way and could muscle the parliament to do what it was told misses the complexity and internal autonomy of the parliament, which despite its overall tertiary political status found itself with procedural privileges and internal mechanisms that were respected and honored and could in modest ways shape the passage of bills.

If state institutions enjoy internal autonomy, we will find that rulers and regimes have little ability to interfere in their operation and internal affairs—in-house decisions are made in-house. Of course, achieving high levels of internal autonomy does not necessarily mean that an institution has strong influence over political processes and outcomes that unfold outside of its walls. Nor does it mean that such autonomy is guaranteed to last forever.

That brings us to the second form of autonomy we are interested in: *mission autonomy*, or the extent to which state institutions can articulate, advocate for, and pursue positions on policy issues, political decision-making, or implementation that may be distinct from those that are advanced or favored by the regime. As we discussed in the previous chapter, few studies of authoritarian institutions focus on the purposes that power is brought to serve or on the ability of those within such institutions to coalesce around what they see as just or good. We believe such issues—the intersection of norms and power—need more attention because they vary in important ways. Mission autonomy goes beyond institutions defending themselves, their operations, budgets, jurisdiction, or personnel. It more broadly involves the ability to independently define a sense of mission and purpose and to pursue it. This does not require an institution to be successful in all (or even any) of its mission, just that it be able to define and actively work for specific policy goals—and perhaps even hold some conception of the common good.

---

6. Ken Ochieng' Opalo (2019), *Legislative Development in Africa: Politics and Postcolonial Legacies* (New York: Cambridge University Press), 194.

Taking Some Parts of Authoritarian States Seriously, Sometimes · 63

As a rather provocative example, the Ugandan parliament demonstrated an infamous capacity for mission autonomy by passing with great effort the 2014 Anti-Homosexuality Act, which made homosexuality a criminal offence subject to life imprisonment—all despite objections from President Yoweri Museveni and considerable opprobrium from the international community.[7] This effort to criminalize homosexuality had been a project of ambitious MPs since the mid-2000s and had been repeatedly buried by a regime eager to avoid annoying important international donors that disapproved of illiberal domestic policies. That it required the Ugandan constitutional court to nullify the law—a curious example of constitutional checks in action, all under a clearly authoritarian system—suggests a much more complicated political picture than simple ruler-oriented frameworks allow us. In a similar way, the Brazilian Congress displayed signs of mission autonomy in the late 1960s by blocking a number of economic initiatives that, despite being supported by the military regime, it found to be unsuitable.[8] That both parliaments would ultimately lose these battles—Uganda by constitutional means and Brazil by regime efforts to repack the congress with more pliant loyalists—only furthers the relevance of viewing state institutions through a lens of autonomy and unexpected divergence from regime interest rather than instrumental utility.

Moving out of the parliamentary arena, we see forms of mission autonomy deeper in history as well. The Soviet military exhibited its own form of mission autonomy by throwing its support behind Nikita Khrushchev, rather than Georgy Malenkov, in the succession struggle that unfolded after Stalin's death. This decision was partly driven by Malenkov's intention to shift investment toward consumer goods and away from heavy industry, which Soviet military officers viewed as threatening "the foundations of the socialist economy"[9] and deprioritizing the sector of the economy most critical to the defense industry.[10] Here, the clearly held sense of purpose and interest of the military as an institutional whole provided justification for a serious incursion into the high-stakes politics of a party-based regime.

Additional examples of authoritarian institutions pursuing their own

---

7. Paul Johnson (2015), "Making Unjust Law: The Parliament of Uganda and the Anti-Homosexuality Act 2014," *Parliamentary Affairs* 68 (4): 709–36.

8. Scott W. Desposato (2001), "Legislative Politics in Authoritarian Brazil," *Legislative Studies Quarterly* 26 (2): 300.

9. Colonel I. N. Nenakhov, *Voennaia mysl'* (official publication of the General Staff), no. 10, October 1953.

10. Roman Kolkowicz (1985), *The Soviet Military and the Communist Party* (Boulder: Westview Press), 107–9.

interests or conceptions of the common good are abundant: Saudi Arabia's religious police enforcing their own views of morality in public space; Egyptian judges overturning executive acts that they consider to be unjust or, alternatively, as jeopardizing national sovereignty;[11] Chinese bureaucratic agencies adopting distinct organizational missions and distorting the upward flow of information so that they can pursue their own interests rather than party-mandated activities;[12] and discussions within military establishments that identify and articulate motivations for coups launched years down the road (e.g., among Thai officers in the 1920s and within the Egyptian military academy in the 1930s).[13] All of these bespeak a fractious tendency among state institutions across and within authoritarian regimes worldwide, one that variations in autonomy at the unit level best captures.

Specific institutional goals or conceptions of the common (or particularistic) good might change, of course. When we encounter parliaments, for instance, we will analyze an institution where preferences vary considerably according to the composition of its membership over time—those MPs will not see the parliament's role the same way as time goes on, let alone conceive of a broader mission in an identical way (perhaps despite our idealized vision of the responsible statesmen or legislator, this rarely happens even in the most virtuous and incorruptible democracies). Constitutional courts, on the other hand, have memberships that are less changeable and more narrowly cast in a very particular sociopolitical stratum. And the culture of judges is quite distinct, with cross-national variations across legal cultures, but often with recognizably similar (if very general) views on the public good and normative importance of law. But with the concept of mission autonomy, we are interested in whether institutions operate as if they have a vital public role to play and can change their own policy preferences based on choices made within—rather than made for—the institution. Before proceeding to define and conceptualize factors that we expect will help us explain variation in institutional autonomy, both internal and mission, we should advance three observations that will be useful for our empirical inquiries.

First, the waters will sometimes get muddied when assessing mission autonomy, though due to muddy realities rather than conceptual slippage.

---

11. For a notable example, see the Tiran and Sanafir Islands case.

12. Kenneth Lieberthal and Michel Oksenberg (1988), *Policy Making in China: Leaders, Structures and Processes* (Princeton: Princeton University Press), 16–23.

13. Samuel Huntington (1968), *Political Order in Changing Societies* (New Haven: Yale University Press), 204.

In the clearest cases, we will observe mission autonomy when state institutions pursue goals that directly conflict with those of the regime. In other cases, institutions may develop a sense of mission or set of goals to which rulers and regimes are ambivalent or uncaring. And in the most difficult cases, state institutions may willingly choose to pursue missions that align with those of political elites—as Lisa Hilbink has observed in her analysis of the Chilean judiciary.[14] Mission autonomy can take on many forms across many contexts, which means we will need to search for its presence or absence in various ways. It might manifest as an institution pursuing a distinct policy on matters the regime views as technical or unimportant. It might render an institution useless to the regime because of its slow and ponderous decision-making or independent value for measured and thorough deliberation—like a court that rarely rules against regime wishes but takes years to ponder before offering judicious support and therefore cannot be called upon when needed. It might allow an institution to develop and pursue a political vision that annoys the regime but does not seem alarming. Or it might even put forward visions that pose an existential threat to the regime.

Second, we will generally view mission autonomy as being predicated on internal autonomy—though we do not include this in our definition of the concept. An institution that cannot command itself is unlikely to be able to define, much less pursue, a mission separate from that of the regime. But to avoid paving over meaningful variation in the operation of authoritarian institutions, we only stipulate that internal autonomy is a highly favorable—but not a per se necessary—condition for mission autonomy. Exceptions are certainly possible, even if infrequent. For instance, institutions that are heavily policed by the regime may harbor their own policy goals or missions but pursue them surreptitiously—or place them in temporary dormancy—to avoid soliciting active regime interference in their affairs. Moreover, state institutions are themselves not monolithic actors; the co-optation and control of an institution's leadership indicates a lack of internal autonomy, but this does not preclude the possibility of mission autonomy on the part of its rank-and-file membership, such as in our analysis of religious establishments whose lesser clerical classes hold quite clear views of their role in society, despite institutional restrictions from above. And, in some cases, mission autonomy—especially if exercised

---

14. Lisa Hilbink (2007), *Judges beyond Politics in Democracy and Dictatorship: Lessons from Chile* (New York: Cambridge University Press).

in a way that a regime deems threatening—might be precisely the thing that precipitates the abrogation of internal autonomy. Those who stick out their necks too far risk decapitation—a tradeoff that often is remarked in studies of judiciaries and in franker conversations with senior judges.

Finally, we treat internal and mission autonomy as features that vary over time, polity, and institution. This means that there are many cases in which both kinds of autonomy will be extremely low, and such state institutions are more likely to be clear pawns of regime will.

It is relevant to note that in many ways our approach to institutional autonomy parallels, and is inspired by, the broad tradition of neo-institutionalist political science.[15] Although we position our inquiry foremost in the historical institutionalist camp, it is not our desire to do so in a pure orthodox manner. While the historical institutional framework will prove highly informative in our analysis, we aim to advance it primarily as a framework—one quite useful for guiding our inquiry—and not as a dogma.

Our inductive analysis and insistence on taking slow-moving processes of historical evolution seriously share much with historical institutionalist perspectives, and this makes engagement with the historical institutionalist framework rewarding and profitable. We believe that there is a strong merit in viewing institutional capacity, powers, and experience as being influenced by path-dependent (but not immutable) features of agglomeration and accretion. The temporal dimension to these processes has a powerful impact on the toolkits and realms of behavior that actors utilize or steer clear of as they navigate the troubled waters of authoritarian politics.

So how do time and temporality fit into our analysis? As we set out to trace the autonomy of state institutions, we deliberately chose a fairly balanced sample of newly designed bodies as well as older ones. As a result, we are able to explore how, with the passage of time, institutions often become deeply rooted, stickier, more complex, and less malleable than they were at the moment of their inception. But as our inductive analysis shows, taking temporal processes seriously need not lead us to a teleological view that the capacity for institutional autonomy progressively and linearly increases as time goes on. Path dependence is real, but it is by no means deterministic. Linkages and processes of institutionalization can expand and entrench themselves as state institutions endure over the years, but they may also in some cases recede, be gradually eroded, or even be swiftly disrupted in periods of crisis or regime change.

---

15. Peter Hall and Rosemary Taylor (1996), "Political Science and the Three New Institutionalisms," *Political Studies* 44 (5): 936–57.

Taking Some Parts of Authoritarian States Seriously, Sometimes · 67

We will similarly emphasize the role of historical contingency, of unintended consequences, and of the ubiquity of short-term and tactical thinking as fundamental to understanding the day-to-day life of authoritarian institutional politics, as well as how they have evolved or devolved over time. Our reliance on a stricter definition of the term "institution," while remaining deeply skeptical of reading ruler intentionality into observed autonomy, means our approach remains distinct from but closely tied to the historical institutionalist approach.[16]

We also likely differ from much historical institutionalist work by relying a bit less on concepts such as path dependence, ever-increasing returns (in this case to autonomy), or classic patterns of endogenous change via layering, conversion, drift, and erosion.[17] These patterns of institutional development are indeed powerful in many cases, and we do use them, but perhaps with a greater insistence that their applicability is a concern to discover. We wish above all to avoid assuming specific trajectories of institutional growth ex ante.[18] Achieving institutional autonomy under authoritarianism often requires perpetually traveling a bumpy path that involves switchbacks and diminutions, or odd spheres of political life where an institution's autonomy remains high while in other areas that same institution is utterly neutered for a time or forever. Our point here is to be humble about the patterns we find. Just as every political order is subject to decay and decline,[19] every autonomous institution in authoritarian regimes may be resilient, or it may be submerged—and we cannot always rely on a single model or historical trajectory to tell us when or why. We believe that focusing on the linkages that the body (and its membership) has with society and with other parts of the state as well as its own internal investments in institutionalization is a promising endeavor. And in this way, we hope to better track the vagaries and confounding muddle of institutional autonomy that we actually see present within and across autocracies.

To that end, our inductive case studies will look to develop accounts

---

16. Kathleen Thelen (1999), "Historical Institutionalism in Comparative Politics," *Annual Review of Political Science* 2 (1): 369–404.

17. See Paul Pierson (2000), "Increasing Returns, Path Dependence, and the Study of Politics," *American Political Science Review* 94 (2): 251–67; Raghu Garud, Arun Kumaraswamy, and Peter Karnøe (2010), "Path Dependence or Path Creation?" *Journal of Management Studies* 47 (4): 760–74; and Paul A. David (2001), "Path Dependence, Its Critics and the Quest for 'h=Historical Economics,'" in *Evolution and Path Dependence in Economic Ideas: Past and Present*, ed. Pierre Garrouste and Stavros Ioannides (Cheltenham: Edward Elgar).

18. Giovanni Capoccia (2016), "When Do Institutions 'Bite'? Historical Institutionalism and the Politics of Institutional Change," *Comparative Political Studies* 49 (8): 1095–1127.

19. Huntington (1968). Francis Fukuyama (2014), *Political Order and Political Decay: From the Industrial Revolution to the Globalization of Democracy* (New York: Macmillan).

of institutional autonomy in its ebbs and flows that allow for historicity and privilege an open view on outcomes over any preference for universal logics.[20] Thus, our approach draws heavily from historical institutionalism and its emphases, but we do so in a pragmatic way—given the clear methodological parallels—but do not strictly treat canonical features of that research agenda (e.g., its definition of "institutions") as doctrine.

Two of our core state institutions studied—constitutional courts and parliaments—in fact have aspects that quite well illustrate this principle. Constitutional courts have been promoted starting in the twentieth century with a very particular organizational structure and relation to other parts of the state and should be just as good potential cases for path-dependent trends of gradual assertion as they are for functionalist models of tactical co-optation. Yet we find a far more mixed picture, of gains and losses and overwhelming political frustration that fits neither picture convincingly. In parliaments, we indeed note the curious homogeneity of structures across autocracies today yet find both a basic stickiness (a point for historical institutionalism) and absurdly varying actual autonomy within case (a point against it). Both of these findings strongly imply that more proximate institutional features existing somewhat stably in society (*linkage*) or across an institution's continuity (*institutionalization*) may have greater purchase than always assuming strategic intention or being too laden with implications of slow-moving teleology.

As is clear, our primary concern is with scaling far back the overwhelming reliance on functionalist logics in contemporary academic research on authoritarian politics. While these logics are not always unwarranted, we view the literature's disproportionate reliance on them as a troublesome development for contemporary scholarship. Functionalist assumptions have accumulated in such a way that they now burden the vastly diverse and heterogenous residual category that is authoritarian regimes with strong assumptions of tyrannical control and justification by systemic nature. Overzealous appliers of path dependence, institutional layering, or sociological institutional meaning making are far harder to come by, but we still wish to avoid that potential misstep as well. Given all this, we explicate our two primary independent variables below, conceptualizing them at the mesolevel as more appropriate for truly assessing the nature of institutional life and political dynamics under authoritarianism. We further discuss how

---

20. John R. Hall (2007), "Historicity and Sociohistorical," *The Sage Handbook of Social Science Methodology*, ed. William Outhwaite and Stephen P. Turner (Thousand Oaks: Sage).

attentiveness to these variables will shed light on scope conditions that determine when functionalist approaches to authoritarian institutions are most—and least—likely to offer productive methods of inquiry.

Linkages and *Institutionalization*, or How Should We Characterize Individual State Institutions?

So what explains variation in levels of internal and mission autonomy? This section outlines the core argument that we will flesh out further through each empirical chapter: that authoritarian institutions are more likely to develop both forms of autonomy when (1) they enjoy strong *linkages* to groups that can protect them, offer them support, or provide powerful constituencies for them; and (2) they are highly *institutionalized* and therefore harder for regimes to bend, manipulate, or control. We should note that these two factors both exist at the mesolevel; they are attributes of an individual institution itself, not the broader regime or political system. Further below, we will draw as well on a third factor associated with institutional autonomy initially introduced in the previous chapter: *structural differentiation*. As a macrolevel characteristic, it is an attribute of the political system as a whole, capturing the extent to which the ruler, regime, and state are distinguishable in a given society. We will not work this into our explanation directly, as it is situated at a higher level of analysis and is reflexive of—but not a causal factor producing—institutional autonomy throughout the state apparatus in aggregate. But, as we explained earlier, we are interested in positioning our study in dialogue with the multitude of long-standing efforts to explore variation across authoritarian systems at the country level. So we will highlight structural differentiation as a factor that we can illuminate from our findings. Before moving to conceptualize and theorize each factor, we must first be explicit about the inferences we aim to produce when analyzing how and why linkages and institutionalization matter for authoritarian institutions.

First, our empirical inquiry is not designed to generate a formal model or test a definitive explanation according to the rigorous assumptions of causal inference. Here, we intend to work explicitly from a position of induction. We aim to highlight linkages and institutionalization as key factors among others that are especially helpful in explaining variation in institutional autonomy, that travel well across the considerable diversity of authoritarian systems, and that will therefore redirect our attention to fruitful areas based on a sounder understanding of the various ways authoritarianism actually operates as well as the various institutional arrangements and outcomes it produces. We proceed in this chapter somewhat abstractly, outlining our theory for why we expect that linkages and institutionalization warrant greater consideration in research on authoritarian institutions, a set of expectations derived from close case knowledge and inductive theorizing. We then move in the rest of the book to probe this theory in detail, analyzing these factors through a series of case studies, both to assess their usefulness and to refine our understanding of their effects over time and cross-nationally. All the while, we seek to charitably assess when a functionalist explanation may work perfectly well—and when such an attempt fails to do so.

Second, although we eschew explicit tests of causality, we do seek to provide evidence that institutional autonomy is systematically more likely when conditions of institutionalization and linkage are present—that is, we believe our assessments lend themselves to a probabilistic account of variation in autonomy. But in order to assess institutional autonomy in diverse cases and under disparate historical conditions, our empirical chapters do not advance a tight and explicitly causal research design. The insights that we produce in this book are made through context-rich historical process tracing within cases over time, paired comparisons across cases, and multiple within-case comparisons assessing empirical congruence or divergence across different settings.[21]

Accordingly, we will more modestly view the inferences that we derive as being correlational or observational in nature, where contextually relevant empirical detail is key in understanding variation, while firming up a patterned way to think about authoritarian institutional politics. Yet plausible evidence of causality will indeed emerge from our analysis, particularly through our emphasis on antecedent conditions, sequencing, and evolution in institutional development. This emphasis will move us to relax prevailing assumptions that institutions are designed by autocrats at specific moments to serve specific functions and instead to consistently explore a number of historically attuned questions. We will thus repeatedly ask what the political environment looked like when the institution first emerged; whether institutional structures were either created or inherited by rulers or regimes; when and how linkages and institutionalization intensify or

---

21. Stephen Van Evera (2015), *Guide to Methods for Students of Political Science* (Ithaca: Cornell University Press). Jason Seawright and John Gerring (2008), "Case Selection Techniques in Case Study Research: A Menu of Qualitative and Quantitative Options," *Political Research Quarterly* 61 (2): 294–308.

recede over time; whether institutional attributes are sticky or malleable; when institutional attributes change, how they change, and who (if anyone) changed them deliberately; and whether institutions were granted autonomy from willing autocrats, wrested autonomy from reluctant autocrats, or enjoyed autonomy long beforehand and afterward maintained or lost it. This brings us now to the two mesolevel factors that we expect are driving much of the variation in levels of internal and mission autonomy that authoritarian state institutions acquire: *linkages* and *institutionalization*.

Conceptualizing Linkages

We conceptualize linkages as incorporating vertical ties between a given state institution and public constituencies and groups in society; horizontal ties with other institutions or powerful actors in the state apparatus; and ties with international actors that can be vertical or horizontal depending on the specific nature of the relationship in each case and may be mutual and reciprocal, patron-client, central-peripheral, and so on.

Thus, linkages can develop on one of three levels, though combinations are certainly possible. First, there might be vertical linkages to the broader society: authoritarian parliaments and their memberships can cultivate independent ties to regional, popular, or powerful sectoral constituencies that they represent; courts can acquire ties to supportive human rights organizations or bar associations; religious establishments can be linked to large populations of believers or religious civil society organizations. Second, there can be horizontal linkages between a given institution and other parts of the state apparatus that are not routed through the regime: parliaments might gather information from expert state bodies or contain MPs with particularly close personal ties to supportive figures in the security services, judiciary, or executive ministries; ministries of education might resort to a state-sanctioned religious authority in developing a catechism for students; religious establishments might develop direct relationships with powerful state actors who ascribe to their creed or faith or even have the religious loyalty of partisans in the parliament; judges might be part of a broader state legal complex including the ministry of justice, the public prosecution, and attorneys general.[22] Finally, there may also be linkages at the international level: experts in a specific field might forge bonds

---

22. Terence C. Halliday and Lucien Karpik (1997), *Lawyers and the Rise of Western Political Liberalism: Europe and North America from the Eighteenth to Twentieth Centuries* (New York: Oxford University Press).

with their colleagues in other countries in developing a set of professional standards; interparliamentary plenary bodies, reciprocal party friendship agreements, and mutual, regular "fact-finding" exchanges may strengthen ties between MPs in different countries as well as foster ideological innovation and policy concept diffusion; religious institutions recognized by—or incorporated into—the state may have organizational ties to transnational religious entities (such as the Roman Catholic Church or the Ecumenical Patriarchate of Constantinople); technical ministries in developing countries (such as those for housing and public works, water and energy, agriculture, or urban planning) may cultivate independent ties to international donor agencies who work with them directly in implementing projects.

With the concept of linkages, we aim to draw attention to how state institutions, even in authoritarian societies, may not solely represent the autocratic executive but can also directly enmesh themselves within support networks (societal, state, or international) and cultivate direct ties of their own, not just those that flow through rulers and regimes. Linkages may emerge through repeated interaction between an institution and other state or international actors, sometimes producing a sense of mutual interest and collegiality. They may form because the institution has developed its own reputation for reliability, critical expertise, or astuteness in solving important problems. In other cases, state institutions may deliberately cultivate alliances with different constituencies (public or private) for strategic purposes.

The way that linkages form for institutions with societally representational features, most notably parliaments, will often be particularly distinctive in this way. Single-member district and other constituency-oriented electoral systems can more directly facilitate ties between individual MPs and regional social constituencies in ways unmediated by a regime-controlled party or bureaucratic apparatus. Ideological affinity may greatly strengthen linkages between conservative or neoliberal deputies and powerful business groups—likewise for subaltern ethnic groups and their co-ethnic parliamentarians or left-liberals and educated, urban constituencies. Parliaments may publicly introduce or amend legislation to increase budgets or administrative discretion for state allies they seek to court, even if those proposals are ultimately vetoed by the autocratic executive. Religious institutions similarly have unique ways of cultivating linkages by directly embedding themselves in the lives of their adherents. Religious establishments can have strong impacts on the daily life of people through their social functions as the legitimate presiders over baptisms, weddings, and burials, through proselytization, the collection of alms, or the provision of charity and even welfare services. Some religious establishments have important hands in the health-care field or in education, and many are major parts of organizing the manifold local social and community activities that the average person experiences regularly.

Clearly, linkages can take different forms in different contexts. This heterogeneity will prove quite useful in our comparative analysis of authoritarian state institutions. The linkages that we observe will sometimes be informal, particularly those generated through collegiality, via reputation, or by ideological affinity. But, in many cases, linkages emerge precisely because state institutions follow formal legal procedures in a manner that gives them an effective partnership or constituency: judges must routinely interact with bar associations in performing their official duties; religious establishments charged with educating the public will create alumni networks in the process; parliaments whose MPs are the main point of contact for citizens when faced with the mysterious and sometimes damaging decisions from an unaccountable regime will often find themselves needing to articulate those interests—and therefore gain those constituencies' favor in later days—in their institutional role. Linkage can breed further linkage, and the successful connections and goodwill engendered in the past can have important impact on the future of a given state institution's autonomy in the future.

We expect that when *linkages* exist, they facilitate the acquisition of internal and mission autonomy by authoritarian state institutions through their mobilizational capacity, their deterrent capacity, and their transformational capacity. Beginning with mobilization, we posit that societal, state, or international constituencies that share ties with a state institution can often come to view its activities as valuable, venerable, or even indispensable. Such constituencies may mobilize to persuade political elites of the institution's importance, lobby them to maintain and expand its role in political life, or defend the institution against regime attempts to subordinate it. In terms of deterrence, even if linked constituencies and groups will not mobilize in defense of a state institution, rulers and regimes simply believing that they might can still significantly increase the expected costs of interfering in that institution's internal affairs or obstructing its self-perceived mission. Last, a transformational effect can work by shifting the way that institutional actors and personnel perceive their own position vis-à-vis the regime. Instead of conceiving of themselves purely as subordinates of the regime, institutions with strong linkages may come to view themselves as wielding leverage against regime elites, as part of broader professional networks or as representatives of a discrete community (narrow or broad, international or domestic). This shift in mindset can profoundly affect the missions that state institutions adopt for themselves, the way they navigate relationships with rulers or regimes, and the way they operate in the political realm.

Conceptualizing Institutionalization

Linkages matter in the development of internal and mission autonomy, but they are not determinative, nor are they all that matters. Even the strongest ties between constituency and state institution may mean little if there is no stable, organizational capacity undergirding it. We now proceed to theorize the second mesolevel factor that we will use to explain variation in institutional autonomy: *institutionalization*, a term often used by scholars, though one unhappily without a fixed definition—and given the various meanings of "institution," such a fixed definition is unlikely to arise. We wish to explain modestly how we will use the term for the purposes of this book—and to explain that we will thus focus on the degree of adaptability, complexity, coherence, and hierarchy that characterize the specific state body being examined. To explain why and how this conception fits with those of others, a brief detour into the nuances of the term will be helpful.

Political scientists often use the term "institutionalization" in a way that relates not to specific state institutions but rather to the regime or the political system as a whole. Alfred Stepan treats institutionalization synonymously with regime consolidation;[23] Barbara Geddes uses the concept to indicate systems of rule by a party or other formal organization rather than by an individual;[24] others use institutionalization to denote systems in which autocrats organize and exercise their power through formal state institutions (i.e., legislatures, bureaucracies) rather than in a direct and personal manner.[25] While such ways of conceptualizing institutionalization have proven quite productive, we mean to use the term in a way that more

---

23. Alfred Stepan (1978), *The State and Society: Peru in Comparative Perspective* (Princeton: Princeton University Press).

24. Barbara Geddes (1999), "Authoritarian Breakdown: Empirical Test of a Game Theoretic Argument," paper presented at the annual meeting of the American Political Science Association, Atlanta.

25. Thomas Pepinsky (2013), "The Institutional Turn in Comparative Authoritarianism," *British Journal of Political Science* 44 (3): 631–53. Dan Slater (2003), "Iron Cage in an Iron Fist: Authoritarian Institutions and the Personalization of Power in Malaysia," *Comparative Politics* 36 (1): 81–101.

specifically captures mesolevel variation in the structure and features of state institutions that we feel to be valuable and necessary, even if it runs counter to other usages.

Scott Mainwaring's analysis of party systems moves us a step in this direction, defining institutionalization as the process by which "an organization becomes well established and widely known, if not universally accepted."[26] But for our purposes, this definition is still a bit too amorphous, as it does not direct us to specific features that make an institution "established." Seeking more precision, we turn to Samuel Huntington's *Political Order in Changing Societies*, a seminal work that emphasized the importance of institutionalization to stable authoritarian government. Huntington used the term to specifically refer to an institution's degree of "adaptability, complexity, autonomy, and coherence."[27] Three of those elements work quite well for our inquiry (we will exclude "autonomy" since it would make our argument circular, a potential problem we will explore in a moment). Along the same lines and in a more expansive and fully Weberian vein, Eva Bellin writes that

> institutionalization invokes the constellation of qualities that Weber used to distinguish bureaucracies from patrimonially driven organizations. An institutionalized coercive apparatus is one that is rule-governed, predictable, and meritocratic. It has established paths of career advancement and recruitment; promotion is based on performance, not politics; there is a clear delineation between the public and private that forbids predatory behavior vis-à-vis society; and discipline is maintained through the inculcation of a service ethic and strict enforcement of a merit-based hierarchy.[28]

Bellin's full set of criteria is likely more than we need; we can imagine, for instance, highly institutionalized bodies that are not strictly meritocratic; they might be nepotistic within their own ranks without undercutting their institutionalized status—the Egyptian and Jordanian judiciaries, for instance, regularly favor sons of sitting judges for new appointments. Yet, where it counts, these judicial entities are also clearly institutional-

---

26. Scott Mainwaring (1998), "Party Systems in the Third Wave," *Journal of Democracy* 9 (3): 68.

27. Huntington (1968), 12.

28. Eva Bellin (2004), "The Robustness of Authoritarianism in the Middle East: Exceptionalism in Comparative Perspective," *Comparative Politics* 36 (2): 145.

ized, providing structure and organizational heft far beyond what nepotism might otherwise suggest. We will thus use Huntington's simpler definition, such that institutionalization is determined by the adaptive capacities, complex and detailed organizational patterns, and inherent coherence within a given state institution. But we cite Bellin (and refer back to Weber) precisely because both are attempting to identify the same kind of distinction that we are—when state institutions have features that enable them to acquire stability and firmly consolidate themselves within a given political environment.

Let us turn to each of the three elements included in our definition of institutionalization (as well as introduce a fourth, hierarchy).

The first, *adaptability*, is not the same as malleability if that means that others outside the institution can shape it to their will. Instead, it represents whether an institution can adapt itself to new circumstances, has demonstrated a capacity to weather challenges that emerge in its environment, has developed a set of responses or procedures to deal with a wide variety of problems, and is capable of finding new roles for itself in social and political life as society changes and old roles become obsolete.[29] In the empirical chapters, we will see an institution's adaptability operate particularly in instances of regime change, throughout advancing stages of state building and development, and during crises that threaten the institution directly—in some ways, high adaptability means a capacity for creativity under pressure by a beset-upon state institution. We anticipate that institutional adaptability facilitates the pursuit of internal and mission autonomy by enabling state institutions to roll with the punches. Highly adaptable state institutions will continue finding a niche for themselves as regime goals—and even regimes themselves—change; they will better deal with rulers or regimes that attempt to rein them in through new mechanisms; and they will shift how they pursue their missions in innovative ways when faced with new circumstances and challenges.

Second, *complexity* indicates the presence of extensive and interconnected internal procedures guiding institutional activity as well as advanced specialization and professionalization within the institution. Additionally, complex institutions are those that play a multitude of roles in society and are characterized by a "multiplication of organizational subunits . . . and differentiation of separate types of subunits."[30] We posit that institutional complexity promotes internal and mission autonomy by making an institu-

---

29. Huntington (1968), 13–15.
30. Huntington (1968), 18.

tion's operational structures much more difficult for rulers or regimes to navigate and control; by making it costlier for rulers and regimes to replace experienced and specialized personnel with loyalists; by providing state institutions more opportunities to defend their prerogatives or put forward their own agendas in multiple arenas; and by making regimes reliant on the institution's continued operation in a variety of sectors and, thus, fearful of a work stoppage and reluctant to dissolve it or undercut its effectiveness. In this way, functionalism can be a double-edged sword; the more functional a state institution is for rulers and regimes—or the greater scope of functions it performs—the less replaceable it is, the better positioned it is to entrench its operation, and the more capable it is to make modest deviations away from elite interests and toward its own interests without retribution.

Third, *coherence* refers to an institution's ability to maintain unity and keep its officials, members, and subunits acting in concert. Institutions are incoherent when they exhibit a high degree of internal fragmentation, infighting, and discoordination. We expect that coherent institutions have a greater ability to achieve internal and mission autonomy because they are capable of operating as a unified pressure group when asserting their interests against the regime or defending their turf from regime incursions. Similarly, coherent institutions will be less susceptible to regime subordination through a divide-and-conquer strategy, whereby opportunistic members are selectively co-opted and elevated to leadership posts precisely because they are willing to forsake loyalty to the institution and its mission in exchange for personal benefit. Finally, coherence is also at work when otherwise discordant elements of a state institution can adhere to a singular conception of their and their institution's role—regardless of whether they act on it. A state institution with a coherent self-understanding will aid in it working toward its own internal autonomy as well as comfort with testing the bounds of its capabilities.

A final element that in some ways straddles both complexity and coherence, and that we believe deserves independent consideration despite its absence in the Huntingtonian conception of institutionalization, is that of *hierarchy*—as clear chains of authority within an institution can greatly affect degrees of internal coordination and unity. Within complex institutions, different segments of the body may develop in different ways, acquire their own interests and views of the world, or find distinct ways of perceiving and pursuing the institution's overall mission.[31] Institutions that

---

31. Michael N. Barnett and Martha Finnemore (1999), "The Politics, Power and Pathologies of International Organizations," *International Organization* 53 (4): 724.

are organized hierarchically can minimize such sources of incoherence, both by clearly identifying leaders authorized to articulate the institution's mission and by giving those leaders "effective capacity to recognize cooperation and defection and to reward and punish them accordingly."[32] In the empirical chapters, we will pay much attention to the hierarchy component of institutionalization, anticipating that hierarchies can pose unique, sometimes disparate, effects for institutional autonomy. When institutional elites are co-opted by the regime, for instance, hierarchic control affords those elites more tools for compelling rank-and-file personnel to follow regime interests. But, in many cases, an institution's leaders may not be regime loyalists—perhaps because their expertise (and not regime fealty) elevated them through the ranks, perhaps because they attained their posts before the current regime took power, or perhaps because their own ambitions make them clear-eyed in seeing the promising potential powers of the state institution that they now control. In such instances, institutional hierarchy can be a powerful coordination device that enables institutional leaders to mobilize members in lockstep to pursue a mission that they identify as crucial or, alternatively, to ward off regime attempts at interference in internal affairs.

To explicitly situate the concept of institutionalization at the mesolevel, we should be clear in pointing out that adaptability, complexity, coherence, and hierarchy are all characteristics of organizations. As we mentioned above, the term "institutionalization" has sometimes been positioned at the macrolevel and used to characterize the political system in aggregate (by Huntington himself, most famously). We do not use it in that sense, but our conceptualization does share parallels with how Alfred Stepan deployed institutionalization on the macrolevel as an analogue for regime consolidation.[33] We too intend the concept of institutionalization to evoke images of consolidation, though for discrete state institutions rather than regimes. A high degree of institutionalization maps onto consolidation specifically by making state institutions more difficult for autocrats to reform, reshape, subdue, or control at whim.

Even while we do not conceptualize institutionalization at the macrolevel, its usage in that way by other scholars of political regimes may be relevant to our first factor, linkages. We anticipate that a political landscape populated by other strong institutions will likely be more conducive to the

---

32. Slater (2003), 83.
33. Stepan (1978).

formation of linkages—that is, there will be allies and powerful voices to link up with. Thus, linkages and institutionalization may sometimes reinforce each other—for instance, in environments with what are sometimes called nonexecutive "veto players."[34] Although useful, we avoid this term, as many of the institutions we consider achieve their influence not by holding an absolute veto but by being able to shape outcomes. Formal veto capability—among our state institutions of choice sometimes found in parliaments and sometimes in courts—is an element of system-level structure, not what we mean when we want to look at state institutions themselves.

Alert readers may worry here that we are falling into a trap. Are we saying that autonomous institutions come about when institutions have autonomy? No—we are explicitly excluding autonomy itself from our definitions of linkages and institutionalization, though we will certainly need to be careful to avoid circularity in our empirical inquiry. An autonomous state institution is defined by its actions—its effectiveness at commanding its own internal business or actually promoting its external power—not by characterizations of its connections to extra-institutional constituencies or the patterns of its organization itself. But while we are not coming too close to circularity for comfort, there is something in this fear that we may need to pay attention to and even embrace. Being attuned to the risk of circularity alerts us to the temporal nature of the processes that interest us. The level of institutional autonomy at a particular time is a function not only of regime needs but also of past levels of autonomy. Informally, history matters. In more formal terms, if we were analyzing institutional autonomy using statistical models rather than historical case studies, we would likely need to account for a nontrivial amount of autocorrelation, whereby past values of the outcome influence subsequent values.[35] We will address this issue in our process tracing analysis by being attentive to developments that indicate when autonomy is a self-reinforcing phenomenon and when it is not. Institutions characterized by strong linkages and strong institutionalization, for instance, are well equipped to cultivate autonomy,

---

34. George Tsebelis (1995), "Decision Making in Political Systems: Veto Players in Presidentialism, Parliamentarism, Multicameralism and Multipartyism," *British Journal of Political Science* 25 (3): 289–325. Yonatan Lupu (2015), "Legislative Veto Players and the Effects on International Human Rights Agreements," *American Journal of Political Science* 59 (3): 578–94.

35. John R. Oneal and Bruce Russett (1997), "The Classical Liberals Were Right: Democracy, Interdependence, and Conflict, 1950–1985," *International Studies Quarterly* 41 (2): 283. Nathaniel Beck, Jonathan N. Katz, and Richard Tucker (1998), "Taking Time Seriously: Time-Series-Cross-Sectional Analysis with a Binary Dependent Variable," *American Journal of Political Science* 42 (4): 1260–88.

and they might strive to use what autonomy they do acquire to continue building more. It might also be possible for them to use their autonomy to establish new linkages, push for increasing levels of institutionalization, or gradually transform internal autonomy into mission autonomy over time.

But if the past matters, it can be also remade. Regimes inherit state structures, but they can sometimes remold them—and history can matter in that way as well. A regime that comes into power or that faces a major crisis might learn from history how not to repeat a mistake. It might even move to reduce the autonomy of an institution it found operating in a way inimical to its interest or agenda, perhaps by stunting or reversing its institutionalization or decoupling it from linkages in society. But regimes might also miscalculate or find that yesterday's solution is causing today's problems. On the part of state institutions, it is true that some autonomy can enable or encourage efforts to develop greater autonomy—but that can also lead to overreach. An institution that sticks out its neck too far at one moment may find that the regime chops off its head at the next. In our empirical analysis, we will show that regimes (and institutions) can make their own history but not as they please. They make it not under self-selected circumstances but under already existing circumstances—given and transmitted from the past.

Linkages and Institutionalization as Scope Conditions for the Utility of Functionalist Theorizing

While linkages and institutionalization will provide the core of our account for variation in institutional autonomy under authoritarianism, we must also remain alert to potential alternative explanations. We have positioned our theory in contrast to functionalist logics of institutional development not just as a framing device or a stylistic effort to construe an expeditious strawman but rather because the main group of alternative explanations for institutional autonomy under authoritarianism fall into a basket of what we broadly refer to as "top-down functionalism." This basket incorporates any account for the presence or absence of institutional autonomy that derives its explanation by reference to the interests and actions of autocrats—most typically in pursuit of power maximization, regime stabilization, or political survival.

Profound insights have been produced by analyzing how authoritarian institutions are perceived, used, and structured by calculating rulers and regime elites. Crippling state institutions' capacity for autonomous activity can serve autocrats' interests in fostering obedience throughout the state apparatus and supplying a regime "with the 'infrastructural power' necessary to implement its command."[36] But letting out the leash and allowing state institutions to acquire autonomy can also be functional for autocrats seeking to consolidate or prolong their rule by facilitating elite coordination,[37] promoting regime legitimation,[38] attracting foreign investment,[39] and broadly "improving autocrats' abilities to share power and control the public more effectively."[40] Sometimes, the structure, activity, and autonomy of state institutions are indeed well understood by looking from the top down through the lens of regime interests.

Our empirical chapters will take functionalist logics quite seriously, and they will be especially attentive to *when* these logics demand serious and independent consideration. Our aim is not to push scholars to completely discard functionalist theories of authoritarian autonomy outright but instead to be more cognizant of contextual factors that signal when functionalism is most—and least—applicable. In many instances, our case studies indeed provide evidence that variation in institutional autonomy is driven by the actions and interests of autocrats as they pursue regime stabilization and seek to consolidate their rule. But it is important to note that we find top-down and functionalist accounts to be most powerful precisely when linkages and institutionalization are lacking, temporarily disrupted, or otherwise weak.

In this way, linkages and institutionalization emerge as scope conditions determining when scholars are—and are not—on sure footing when they pursue efforts to explain institutional autonomy by referencing functionalist and regime-centric logics. Scope conditions are clauses restricting the applicability of the relationship stated in the hypothesis and specify circumstances under which the relationship expressed in a hypothesis is expected to hold true.[41] A scope condition creates a conditional concept

---

36. Slater (2003), 82.

37. Carles Boix and Milan Svolik (2013), "The Foundations of Limited Authoritarian Government: Institutions, Commitment and Power-Sharing in Dictatorships," *Journal of Politics* 75 (2): 300–316.

38. Jothie Rajah (2011), "Punishing Bodies, Securing the Nation: How Rule of Law Can Legitimate the Urbane Authoritarian State," *Law and Social Inquiry* 36 (4): 945–70.

39. Tamir Moustafa (2007), *The Struggle for Constitutional Power: Law, Politics, and Economic Development in Egypt* (New York: Cambridge University Press).

40. Scott Williamson and Beatriz Magaloni (2020), "Legislatures and Policy Making in Authoritarian Regimes," *Comparative Political Studies* 53 (9): 1526.

41. Martha Foschi (1997), "On Scope Conditions," *Small Group Research* 28 (4): 535–55.

to which the theory applies, like "in democracies" or "under conditions of very low institutionalization"—this limits the applicability of a given theory and provides greater context to which cases and times we should expect the theory to apply.

When *linkages* to state and societal constituencies are lacking, institutions have less of a support base that can be mobilized to fend off a ruler's or regime's attempts to interfere in their affairs. And when *institutionalization* is low, the internal wherewithal and resources needed to operate with either indifference or opposition to an autocrat's interests are themselves quite limited. Accordingly, functionalist explanations for how state institutions operate in authoritarian contexts are most appropriate when linkages and institutionalization are low but, conversely, least appropriate when linkages and institutionalization are high. Persistently scrutinizing these two mesolevel variables is, thus, a critical first step to identifying the merits of macrolevel theorizing.

It is, however, important to note that while theoretical discussions on scope conditions are often framed in deterministic language ("if X is present then A, if not then B"), we find a need for greater nuance than such a categorical approach allows. Linkage and institutionalization are not binary features that either fully exist or are entirely absent. Instead, they vary a great deal as a matter of degree. For this reason, our treatment of linkage and institutionalization as factors that condition the usefulness of functionalist theories should also, in an effort to avoid any deterministic sense of overconfidence, be understood as a gradational argument that falls along a continuum. The more linkage and institutionalization we observe for particular authoritarian state institutions, the less functionalist logics that emphasize top-down regime interests will apply. Conversely, as we observe less linkage and institutionalization along the continuum, functionalist theorizing will acquire more explanatory power.

Yet even when functionalism does help, we also find that regime attempts to promote or inhibit institutional autonomy rarely produce stable outcomes. Macrolevel theorizing based on regime needs or intentions has a solid basis when linkage and institutionalization are weak, but its utility is neither unlimited nor uniform over time. Autocrats most typically seek to restructure a state institution or reorient its activity for short-term and tactical (as opposed to strategic) reasons. In some cases, they fail to achieve their goals—particularly when linkages and institutionalization later develop and become more pronounced. In other cases, autocrats achieve their goals in the short term but inadvertently introduce dynamics that affect medium- and long-term variation in institutional autonomy in unforeseen and unintended ways. Much like our own theory of linkages and institutionalization, alternative explanations for variation in institutional autonomy that rely upon top-down and functionalist logics are best understood in a way that is both historically rooted and temporally variable.

With these observations in mind, we now turn to a key feature of the political environment that affects state institutions' pursuit of internal and mission autonomy—the extent of differentiation between state and regime. This is a macrolevel attribute of authoritarian systems, one that strongly influences the circumstances under which regimes and state institutions operate. As is the case with many macrolevel features of political systems, we will see that such differentiation tends to emerge or fade quite gradually over time through an accumulation of different processes, some of which are deliberate and directed while others are more or less incidental. In this way, we most directly bring in concepts of evolution and the slow accretion of powers, distinctions, and authorities that are so often missing in functionalist accounts.

Structural Differentiation:
Exploring Autonomy's Bounds from a Bird's-Eye View

We argue that the degree to which rulers, regimes, and states are distinguishable in a given system reflects the overall development of internal and mission autonomy for state institutions within a given polity. We have been speaking of the level of "institutionalization" thus far only as a characteristic of individual state bodies (mesolevel). But as we noted earlier, there is a general level of institutionalization for a political system as a whole (macrolevel) that can be quite informative to cross-national research that takes the country as its unit of analysis, particularly statistical studies that extend their scope to all authoritarian countries—and sometimes all countries, including democratic ones—throughout the world.

Some countries have very elaborate state apparatuses that are clearly differentiated from senior executive positions. There are procedures, chains of command, and divisions of responsibility that are both clear and stable over time. The other extreme is when such features of political life are absent or wholly unstable—whatever institutional coherence exists operates at the day-to-day direction of the ruler or regime. Systems on both extremes can be wholly authoritarian, but they operate in different ways. Indeed, as we saw in the previous chapter, the very concept of "regime" is often used precisely because the ruling group's structure, nature, and relation to the "state" vary so greatly across various authoritarian systems that applying any clearer terminology proves elusive.

We believe that the overall level of what we will call *structural differentiation* matters a great deal for the operation of authoritarian politics. In political systems that lack differentiation, the regime will completely penetrate the state apparatus such that it is difficult (perhaps even inappropriate) to refer to ruler, regime, and state as separate entities. For systems with a high degree of differentiation, however, the state apparatus exists as an entity that is distinguishable from the ruler and regime—and this state structure often predates regime emergence, organizes itself in a way that is largely detached from ebbs and flows in key regime programs over time, and endures even after regimes fall.

Authoritarian rulers and regime elites might still attempt (successfully or unsuccessfully) to guide, control, or restrict state activity, thereby eliminating the autonomy of state institutions and reducing the overall level of structural differentiation in a system. The key difference, however, is that when differentiation is high, neither the ruler nor the regime *is* the state (and rulers would have to confess, "L'état *n'est pas* moi; I just work here"). In highly differentiated political systems, the regime might control or command the state in some critical or politically salient areas, but the two entities are still not one in the same. Of course, the degree of structural differentiation exists along a continuum, and those rulers with a moderate degree of separation from their states might make the more middling announcement, "L'état est moi, en parte; I am the captain of this ship, and some of the crew even listen to me."

If a large number of fairly autonomous state institutions arise, that may translate to the macrolevel by indicating a fairly high level of differentiation between state and regime. It seems likely that state institutions in the same system can have a kind of effect on each other; a subordinated religious establishment, for instance, may desire autonomy from the regime and find help in this effort by an already autonomous judiciary issuing verdicts on the clergy's behalf.

But we do not explore such possibilities systematically at the system-level here. Our causal exploration in this book is focused on the mesolevel of analysis, specifically probing historical and cross-national variation in the attributes of discrete state institutions.

Selecting State Institutions:
Where Are We Going to Look to Assess Autonomy?

Thus far, we have defined the factors that promote institutional autonomy fairly broadly, hoping to deploy them to help us probe the way authoritarianism works and to improve our understanding of it. But if these concepts are broad, they manifest themselves quite subtly in many different settings. We have therefore chosen to focus the bulk of our empirical analysis on authoritarian systems that we know well (generally in the Arab world and Central and Eastern Europe), more comfortable in our ability to detect when the broad brushstrokes of functionalism are likely to obscure the real workings of authoritarian politics in critical ways. But we do not restrict ourselves to such places and work to complement our understanding by wading into cases where we are less sure of our footing but are persuaded that what we may lose in nuance we will gain in insight.

We begin by looking to explain how and when internal and mission autonomy can arise even in an unlikely place: constitutional courts. Constitutional courts are favorable cases for functionalist explanations of institutional activity for several reasons: they are generally created at discreet points in time; they have a clear legal and constitutional mandate that is drawn up by an existing regime; their role in constitutional adjudication and interpretation draws them into issues that are likely to be critical to regimes; they are small, easily identifiable structures whose membership is quite finite; and they generally hold no real ability to enforce their own decisions.

In our chapter on constitutional courts, we show how both the Egyptian and the Palestinian constitutional courts were created in remarkably similar circumstances. In both cases, regimes faced crises involving succession, their own control over the state apparatus, and power struggles within. In both cases, regimes created a court for short-term tactical reasons and designed that court to serve their needs. In the Egyptian case, the court evolved in a more autonomous direction, first achieving a degree of internal autonomy and then subsequently developing some mission autonomy. When it did so, the court provoked regime reactions and attempts to rein it in, targeting especially its internal autonomy. Those attempts were episodic and clumsy but were sometimes effective.

We also discover the importance of courts developing linkages and institutionalization that allow them to secure their positions, making regime attempts to reshape them clumsier and more costly. In the Palestinian case, we see what happens when such linkages and levels of institutionalization are missing, leading to a much more pliant body despite a convoluted process of creation. Moreover, our paired comparison of constitutional courts in Egypt and Palestine reveals that institutions with a similar formal structure can have vastly different prospects for maintaining internal and mission autonomy based on the degree to which a meaningful degree of differentiation exists within the political system—while both regimes exhibit highly personalist tendencies, state and regime are much more clearly differentiable in Egypt than in Palestine, to the latter's detriment.

From this chapter, then, we develop our major themes and ideas: we begin to explore linkages and institutionalization. We also encounter some other themes: regime tactical thinking and the role of unintended consequences; the ebb and flow of autonomy or the necessity to understand autonomy as something that varies over time; and the way in which internal autonomy is a necessary, but not sufficient, condition for mission autonomy.

We then move in the next two chapters to far more complicated cases that are selected to allow us to probe these ideas more fully. The Egyptian and Palestinian courts alert us to the importance of time, to the downsides of tactical thinking, and to the potential for having to deal with unintended consequences, but courts also are highly specialized bodies with quite elite and distinct roles in a polity. To better explore the vagaries of linkage and institutionalization, we move to more amorphous and broadly empowered state institutions. We first turn to parliaments, as they allow us to look closely at longer patterns of institutional development and how these inheritances can matter even when such bodies sometimes seem the perfect example of do-nothing, even pitiable, institutions.

As parliaments are the most glaringly political state institutions, they are often quite bound and restricted by regimes that wish for domestic tranquility, but they are also often the most heavily endowed with powers and potentiality. This juxtaposition makes any gains to autonomy particularly felt and meaningful, if sometimes a bit quixotic in the final result. We approach authoritarian parliaments in three ways: showing the long histories of such bodies in authoritarianism that have over time evolved into common patterns of constitutional position that now provide significant, latent powers to such assemblies in the modern era; tracing the desultory patterns of internal autonomy in the Russian parliament by way of tendentious institutionalization largely decoupled from linkage to the broader society; and showing the considerable importance of societal linkages in the Kuwaiti parliament that have both maintained its internal autonomy and crafted a frustrating form of mission autonomy that has caused no end of trouble for the regime over many decades. We develop further what institutionalization and linkage actually look like on the ground and place them within an institutional context whose origins and contours can quickly diverge from the perfect desires of a regime—even when the regime had previously developed them.

Armed with a more nuanced sense of our basic themes, we then proceed to scrutinize state religious establishments, by far the most heterogeneous and understudied institutional aspect of authoritarian regimes today. This is not a common place to study such regimes, and that is precisely why we choose it. When Juan Linz introduced the concept of authoritarianism, he actually pointed to the role of religious institutions—in his case the Catholic Church—as a feature distinguishing it from totalitarianism. For Linz, Francoist Spain was unique because it respected the autonomy of social institutions like the Church far more than its totalitarian contemporaries, which could not countenance any such autonomous social organizations. We feel that Linz's observation of a special, institutional relationship between religious establishment and a historical authoritarian regime is far more generalizable than scholarship has thus far appreciated—even here we will find a broad range of variation worth exploring.

Religious structures often straddle the state-society divide, so they are a particularly good vantage point for us to probe linkages to societal constituencies. They are also institutionally complex, often with different attached or semi-attached structures that can include educational institutions, charitable arms, houses of worship, and centers of theological thought scattered both within and without the state. While constitutional courts are quite specific in their structure and parliaments are increasingly similar in their broad privileges and prerogatives, religious establishments are decidedly not, giving us a much wider array of formal institutional arrangements to study. And we will encounter a great deal of diversity not only in the institutions and their arrangements but also in how linkages and institutionalization operate. Linkages are critical but sometimes inchoate or working at cross-purposes, and institutionalization occurs in some ways that may seem odd at first glance. Finally, we show that state religious establishments' prospects for internal and mission autonomy are quite particularly related to the overall level of state/regime differentiation at the macrolevel, both over time and across cases.

Previewing Our Closing Provocations, or Is It the Authoritarianism That Really Matters Here?

Armed with these more focused studies, we will have a much better understanding of when authoritarian institutions matter. But that will force us at the end to return to the oddity that we opened with—the ultimately residual quality to our working category of authoritarianism. Does removing democratic accountability really matter so much for these state institutions? Is that really what makes these institutions' behavior and potential acts of autonomy distinct?

Defining authoritarianism as nondemocracy as we have done—and examining authoritarian institutions in that context—tilts us very subtly toward the banal yet profound view that authoritarian institutions can be different from democratic ones. But even this banality might not be vague enough. The fact is that they may not always be. It is noteworthy that an institutional turn in three distinct areas—American political development, advanced industrial democracies, and authoritarianism—all have begun to explore approaches based on historical institutionalism, punctuated equilibrium, and path dependency about the same time, but without much cross-fertilization. Writings in the first two areas focus on democracies, but they are striking for how infrequently they advance explanations in terms of electoral outcomes or even direct democratic oversight. Many analyses of authoritarianism begin with the explicit assumption that autocratic rulers are motivated by a desire to retain power. But so are most governing parties in democracies—but no analyses of democratic states start from the assumption that all institutions chiefly reflect that priority.

We need to be open to the possibility that the logic of political survival explains only a limited amount about institutional structures or policy outcomes in either authoritarian or democratic systems.[42] And if that is the case, authoritarianism and its institutions might be less distinctive beasts than we have presumed.

We will return to consider the importance of the distinction in the final chapter.

---

42. December Green and Laura Luehrmann (2016), *Contentious Politics in Brazil and China: Beyond Regime Change* (Boulder: Westview Press).

CHAPTER 3

Constitutional Courts

There can be no doubt that behind all the pronouncements of this court, and in my case, behind the arrest and today's inquiry, there exists an extensive organization. An organization that not only engages corrupt guards, inane inspectors, and examining magistrates who are at best mediocre, but that supports as well a system of judges of all ranks, including the highest, with their inevitable, innumerable entourage of assistants, scribes, gendarmes, and other aides, perhaps even hangmen. . . . And the purpose of this extensive organization, gentlemen? It consists of arresting innocent people and introducing senseless proceedings against them, which for the most part, as in my case, go nowhere.

—Franz Kafka, *The Trial: A New Translation Based on the Restored Text*

The image of constitutional courts that prevails in writings on authoritarianism is anything but Kafkaesque. Rather than seeming extensive, incompetent, labyrinthine, puzzling, and pointless, they are generally portrayed to be useful tools that regimes summon to serve their own self-interested ends.

We may find that is sometimes the case. But sometimes it is not, and it is that variation we wish to probe. So we will not start by assuming that courts must serve the regime's purpose and then divining what that purpose might be. Instead, we leave the matter open and ask: when can judicial institutions—specifically constitutional courts—achieve autonomy in authoritarian systems?

The setting of a constitutional court nestled within an authoritarian system is an ideal place to test our intuitions, noted in the prior chapter, about the roles that *linkages* and *institutionalization* play in achieving and maintaining institutional autonomy. After noting the key features, and critical limits, of constitutional courts as apex judicial institutions and then assessing what linkage and institutionalization mean in a court context, we develop our theory empirically by examining the founding and operation of two particular, and similarly structured, constitutional courts in Egypt and Palestine. These courts lend themselves well to a juxtaposition of initial intention and subsequent institutional endowment. Egypt's Supreme Constitutional Court (SCC) was intentionally established by an authoritarian regime in the 1970s to be denuded of autonomy and even to sideline elements of the judiciary that showed meek autonomy in the past. And Palestine's Constitutional Court was established in a protracted political struggle over the 2000s in which institutional autonomy was very much a central question and a core intention of several actors.

These two cases allow for a fruitful controlled comparison of judicial institutions. In terms of formal structure, Palestine's Constitutional Court began as a nearly identical replica of the Constitutional Court that Egypt had established decades earlier. Indeed, the 2003 Draft Law for Palestine's Constitutional Court resembles a copied and pasted version (with minor tinkering) of Egypt's own 1979 Supreme Constitutional Court Law, with both legal frameworks being analogous on court jurisdiction, judicial appointments, judges' rights and authorities, the internal hierarchy among judges, and court procedures.[1] The two laws are so similar that in a classroom setting, it would be an obvious case of plagiarism by the authors of Palestine's 2003 Draft Law. In the real-world political setting, however, it is instead a clear-cut case of institutional diffusion in the design of judicial systems.[2]

As we detail in our historical analysis, Palestine's 2003 Draft Law was amended over time before its Constitutional Court was ultimately established in 2016. But the body's Egyptian roots remained apparent even in the final draft. The political circumstances surrounding each constitutional court's creation in 1979 and 2016, respectively, were also broadly comparable. Both courts were established by authoritarian executives who were seeking to bolster their own control over the state judicial apparatus at critical moments and who found themselves relying upon very similar

---

1. The practice of borrowing laws from Egypt, Jordan, Ottoman legislation, and even the Israeli military is common practice in the Palestinian judiciary, which finds its institutional roots in these various legal frameworks.

2. Thomas Ambrosio and Jakob Tolstrup (2019), "How Do We Tell Authoritarian Diffusion from Illusion? Exploring Methodological Issues of Qualitative Research on Authoritarian Diffusion," *Quality and Quantity* 53 (6): 2741–63.

institutional structures to pursue this goal. These commonalities allow us to develop a paired comparison of historical trajectories that broadly controls for institutional design and formal structure in our explanation of judicial autonomy. Starting conditions for constitutional courts in Egypt and Palestine were highly similar, but the outcomes yielded from these two roughly homologous institutional frameworks diverged a great deal in practice. We argue that such divergences, particularly with respect to institutional autonomy, are best explained by differences in each court's degree of linkages and institutionalization.

Our historical analysis of Egypt and Palestine will show that the creators' intentions for constitutional courts were achieved in both cases but for only a short period—indeed, it seems that intentionality has often had little bearing on the actual lives of these judicial bodies over time. It is linkages and institutionalization that matter most, not regime intentions. Judges on Egypt's SCC have been quite able to use critical linkages to supportive groups and increasing institutionalization to realize varying levels of internal and mission autonomy over time. Meanwhile, their judicial colleagues in Palestine, who preside over a court with a paucity of linkages beyond the regime proper and severely lacking institutionalization, have so far been unable to do so.

In tracing these bifurcating processes—a strikingly similar pair of judicial structures with opposite fates—we will discover that functionalist logics emphasizing regime goals and strategies can be quite useful, at least in the short term, for explaining the negative case of how courts might lack autonomy and serve authoritarian regimes (which they sometimes in fact do). Yet, in this observation there is a puzzle: initial intention and subsequent autonomy are poorly, and quite unevenly, related. It does not seem to be the case that constitutional courts necessarily do a good job of solving, as opposed to causing, long-term problems for authoritarian regimes. Indeed, our findings on constitutional courts will highlight short-term, ad hoc decision-making and unintended outcomes much more than farsighted intelligent design by autocrats.

The cases we have chosen illustrate three key insights critical for our understanding of institutional autonomy and its generation under authoritarian conditions. First, most autocrats do create constitutional courts with a function in mind. Sometimes that function is a controlled sort of autocratic legalism.[3] Other times it is truly to create a squib of an institution, a

---

3. Annabel Ipsen (2020), "Repeat Players, the Law, and Social Change: Redefining the Boundaries of Environmental and Labor Governance through Preemptive and Authoritarian Legality," *Law and Society Review* 54 (2): 201–32. Peter H. Solomon Jr. (2010), "Authoritarian

formal placeholder whose position is fully disempowered.[4] But as creative as authoritarian rulers may be in their initial founding acts for constitutional courts, the extent to which they get what they want is conditional on the court's linkages to powerful actors outside the regime and on the degree of institutionalization that the court itself can build.

Second, functionalist arguments carry a lot of explanatory power *when* those two conditions are lacking, as is the case in Palestine. But if linkages to powerful actors outside of the regime develop or if a court grows more institutionalized over time as it has become in Egypt, these arguments fit poorly, as constitutional courts will often emerge as regular, if intermittent, obstacles in the rulers' way.

We connect these insights together in a third observation: the creation of an institution and its evolution need to be understood differently. The Egyptian court was created to serve regime needs; it still found the ability to strike out on its own. The Palestinian court was incubated by actors who wished to hem in the regime, but it was ultimately hatched by those who found ways to prevent it from doing so.

Why Constitutional Courts? Friendly Turf for Functionalist Logics

We start on the terrain of constitutional courts in an effort to address the primary competing explanation we set ourselves against: that of a top-down, regime-centric functionalism. If there is any institution where authoritarian regimes are likely to ensure that their interests are served, it is in bodies that issue binding interpretations of the constitution. The stakes are high (interpretation of the basic legal framework); the institution's members are few and fairly isolated from the rest of the regime (and thus seemingly easy to dominate); and they act by way of abstruse procedures that would seem easy to manipulate.

If we can find autonomy in these unfriendly circumstances, it will establish the plausibility of our argument.

For our purposes, constitutional courts have the added benefit of being uniquely well suited to analysis through historical case studies and process

---

Legality and Informal Practices: Judges, Lawyers, and the State in Russia and China," *Communist and Post-Communist Studies* 43 (4): 351–62.

4. Melissa Crouch (2020), "Pre-Emptive Constitution Making: Authoritarian Constitutionalism and the Military in Myanmar," *Law and Society Review* 54 (2): 487–515. Nick Cheeseman (2015), *Opposing the Rule of Law: How Myanmar's Courts Make Law and Order* (New York: Cambridge University Press).

Constitutional Courts · 93

tracing. Unlike religious establishments, some of them millennia old, and parliaments, also often rooted in practices of a society's poorly remembered past, constitutional courts are generally consciously created at a specific point in time—Austria was a pioneer in forming a body whose role was to review legislation on a constitutional basis.[5] All other constitutional courts were built within the past hundred years.[6] The founding of a constitutional court generally requires a clear legal text creating a body to adjudicate fundamental disputes about the constitutional order. Whoever creates such a body seems likely to know what they are doing and, surely, to have some purpose or function in mind. And they are unlikely to wish to lose control of their creation. The original Austrian constitutional court, which fell victim to fascism, serves as a reminder of how vulnerable these institutions are.[7] Such vulnerability leads observers to believe that autonomous behavior within such bodies is highly risky and thus unlikely. Others have noted about courts in general that there is "a long-standing presumption among many political scientists that courts in authoritarian regimes serve as mere pawns of their rulers."[8]

But if this sort of functionalism drives much analysis, nuance is creeping in—though in a way that still (and quite tautologically) retains functionalism to explain both subservient courts and more independent ones. Discovering autonomous courts in authoritarian settings has led scholars of comparative judicial politics to make innovative arguments, but ones that also preserve an assumption that autocrats' intentions dictate the evolution of independent judicial bodies.[9] Plausible explanations for why autocrats strategically allow courts to become autonomous have proliferated: they are seen to delegate, police, reassure, or gain legitimacy not simply by cre-

---

5. Hans Kelsen (1942), "Judicial Review of Legislation: A Comparative Study of the Austrian and the American Constitution," *Journal of Politics* 4 (2): 183–200.

6. Francisco Ramos (2006), "The Establishment of Constitutional Courts: A Study of 128 Democratic Constitutions," *Review of Law and Economics* 2 (1): 103–35.

7. Torbjörn Vallinder (1994), "The Judicialization of Politics—A World-Wide Phenomenon: Introduction," *International Political Science Review* 15 (2): 91–99. John Ferejohn (2002), "Judicializing Politics, Politicizing Law," *Law and Contemporary Problems* 65 (3): 41–68.

8. Tom Ginsburg and Tamir Moustafa (2008), *Rule by Law: The Politics of Courts in Authoritarian Regimes* (New York: Cambridge University Press), 1.

9. Nathan J. Brown (1997), *The Rule of Law in the Arab World: Courts in Egypt and the Gulf* (New York: Cambridge University Press). Gretchen Helmke (2002), "The Logic of Strategic Defection: Court-Executive Relations in Argentina under Dictatorship and Democracy," *American Political Science Review* 96 (2): 291–303. Jodi Finkel (2008), *Judicial Reform as Political Insurance: Argentina, Peru and Mexico in the 1990s* (Notre Dame: University of Notre Dame Press). Lisa Hilbink (2012), "The Origins of Positive Judicial Independence," *World Politics* 64 (4): 587–621.

ating a constitutional court but by letting out its leash a little.[10] And let us briefly explore this functionalist approach more thoroughly, since we are assessing it as an alternative explanation (and will find it sometimes useful, when *linkages* and *institutionalization* are lacking).

Powerful courts are viewed as aiding autocrats by facilitating social control,[11] legalizing repression,[12] promoting state centralization,[13] implementing unpopular policies, or overturning popular policies that have grown too costly.[14] Thus, enhancing the autonomy of the judiciary in general—or constitutional courts specifically—is typically depicted by scholars as something that is consciously done in pursuit of a grander function or interest: bolstering international legitimacy,[15] increasing domestic support for the regime,[16] attracting foreign investment,[17] promoting markets and expediting economic development,[18] strengthening administra-

---

10. Fiona Shen-Bay (2018), "Strategies of Repression: Judicial and Extrajudicial Methods of Autocratic Survival," *World Politics* 70 (3): 321–57. Jaqueline M. Sievert (2018), "The Case for Courts: Resolving Information Problems in Authoritarian Regimes," *Journal of Peace Research* 55 (6): 774–86. Michael Albertus and Victor Menaldo (2012), "Dictators as Founding Fathers: The Role of Constitutions under Autocracy," *Economics and Politics* 24 (3): 279–306.

11. Martin Shapiro (1981), *Courts: A Comparative and Political Analysis* (Chicago: University of Chicago Press).

12. Anthony W. Pereira (2005), *Political (In)justice: Authoritarianism and the Rule of Law in Brazil, Chile, and Argentina* (Pittsburgh: University of Pittsburgh Press).

13. Brown (1997).

14. Ran Hirschl (2008), "The Judicialization of Mega-Politics and the Rise of Political Courts," *Annual Review of Political Science* 11:93–118. Georg Vanberg (2008), "Establishing and Maintaining Judicial Independence," in *The Oxford Handbook of Law and Politics*, ed. Gregory A. Caldeira, R. Daniel Kelemen, and Keith E. Whittington (New York: Oxford University Press).

15. Susan Whiting (2017), "Authoritarian 'Rule of Law' and Regime Legitimacy," *Comparative Political Studies* 50 (14): 1907–40. Tom Ginsburg and Alberto Simpser (2014), "Introduction," in *Constitutions in Authoritarian Regimes*, ed. Tom Ginsburg and Alberto Simpser (New York: Cambridge University Press). David Law and Mila Versteeg (2014), "Constitutional Variation among Strains of Authoritarianism," in *Constitutions in Authoritarian Regimes*, ed. Tom Ginsburg and Alberto Simpser (New York: Cambridge University Press).

16. Iza Ding and Jeffrey Javed (2021), "The Autocrat's Moral-Legal Dilemma: Popular Morality and Legal Institutions in China," *Comparative Political Studies* 54 (6): 989–1022. Tom Ginsburg (2003), *Judicial Review in New Democracies: Constitutional Courts in Asian Cases* (Cambridge: Cambridge University Press). Jothie Rajah (2012), *Authoritarian Rule of Law: Legislation, Discourse and Legitimacy in Singapore* (New York: Cambridge University Press).

17. Tamir Moustafa (2007), "Mobilizing the Law in an Authoritarian State: The Legal Complex in Contemporary Egypt," in *Fighting for Political Freedom: Comparative Studies of the Legal Complex and Political Liberalism*, ed. Terence C. Halliday, Lucien Karpik, and Malcom Feeley (London: Bloomsbury).

18. Mary E. Gallagher (2017), *Authoritarian Legality in China: Law, Workers, and the State*

tive oversight,[19] promoting elite coordination,[20] and establishing political "insurance policies" and other guarantees in the case of losing power.[21]

Some of these conclusions are well documented in particular cases, yet extrapolating to a general argument has two problems. First, it becomes significantly harder to explain—or even allow for—variation in judicial autonomy. If independent courts provide such overtly desirable benefits to autocrats, it is unclear why they are established in some systems but not tolerated in others. Second, it becomes a bit too easy to fall into a trap of explaining judgments that are convenient and those that are inconvenient for the regime as equally serving some kind of long-term regime interest. Most fundamentally, the prevailing functionalism betrays a strong tendency to assume causes (and even intentions) from observed effects.

In what follows, we show that the coexistence of authoritarian rule and judicial autonomy is only sometimes as perplexing as it seems to outside observers.[22] By comparing constitutional courts that emerged under similar circumstances in Egypt and Palestine, we argue that the development of autonomous constitutional courts is directly associated with two key variables situated outside the ambit of authoritarian regimes: (1) *linkages* to supportive constituencies within the state and society at-large and (2) the degree of *institutionalization* for the judiciary as a corporate body and set of legal institutions.

In short, top-down theories of judicial autonomy that emphasize regime interests and intended functions are warranted in some instances but not others. Institutional autonomy is not a direct product of regime design, and much variation in internal and mission autonomy for constitutional courts is not reducible to simple changes in autocrats' intentions, political goals, or regime maintenance strategies.

(New York: Cambridge University Press). Lynette Chua and Stacia L. Haynie (2016), "Judicial Review of Executive Power in the Singaporean Context, 1965–2012," *Journal of Law and Courts* 4 (1): 43–64.

19. Rosberg (1995).

20. Robert Barros (2002), *Constitutionalism and Dictatorship: Pinochet, the Junta, and the 1980 Constitution* (New York: Cambridge University Press).

21. Finkel (2008). Brad Epperly (2016), "Political Competition and De Facto Judicial Independence in Non-Democracies," *European Journal of Political Research* 56 (2): 279–300.

22. Steven D. Schaaf (2021), "Contentious Politics in the Courthouse: Law as a Tool for Resisting Authoritarian States in the Middle East," *Law and Society Review* 55 (1): 139–76. Steven D. Schaaf (2022), "When Do Courts Constrain the Authoritarian State? Judicial Decision-Making in Jordan and Palestine," *Comparative Politics* 54 (2): 375–99.

The Argument: Linkages, Institutionalization, and Judicial Autonomy

Our comparison of constitutional courts in Egypt and Palestine will illustrate how variation in judicial linkages and degrees of institutionalization permits for widely different levels of internal and mission autonomy. And this observation helps clarify when, exactly, functionalist logics are likely to be most useful to retain when explaining the degrees of autonomy achieved by authoritarian institutions. When linkages are weak and institutionalization is low, autocrats' interests and regime survival strategies become more powerful determinants of the presence—or absence—of institutional autonomy.

Constitutional courts in Egypt and Palestine were created by their respective regimes at specific points in time and for similar reasons—as devices to maintain control of the judiciary during a political crisis tinged with succession issues and to place constitutional disputes in the hands of reliable judicial figures. Yet, while the Egyptian court evolved in surprising directions that have generated considerable, if temporally varying, internal and mission autonomy for the body, its Palestinian counterpart has remained incapable of distancing itself from the regime's grasp. Given the similarity of regime intentions and formal court structures in each case, understanding such divergence in outcomes requires incorporating contextual factors that determine what kind of constitutional courts ultimately emerged, how they operate, and how they evolved over time.

We first argue that by developing linkages with powerful groups in society, such as legal communities, intellectual or professional elites, human rights groups, media outlets, unions, or social movements, constitutional courts become better equipped to assert and protect their autonomy from authoritarian regimes.[23] Similarly, judicial actors who cultivate independent linkages to supportive international and domestic constituencies have access to resources that can be wielded to deter regimes from targeting the integrity of constitutional courts.[24] Equally important are linkages to other institutions within the state (militaries, bureaucracies, and other elite allies),[25] which pressure and restrain the regime's efforts to shape the judi-

---

23. Brandon L. Bartels and Eric Kramon (2020), "Does Public Support for Judicial Power Depend on Who Is in Power? Testing a Theory of Partisan Alignment in Africa," *American Journal of Political Science* 114 (1): 144–63.

24. Zahid Shahab Ahmed and Maria J. Stephan (2010), "Fighting for the Rule of Law: Civil Resistance and the Lawyer's Movement in Pakistan," *Democratization* 17 (3): 492–513.

25. Jian Xu (2020), "The Role of Corporate Political Connections in Commercial Law-

cial sphere. And for scholars who are most focused on macro- or systemic questions, we note that such linkages to other state actors are themselves most feasible in settings with a greater overall degree of structural differentiation (i.e., clearer separations between ruler, regime, and state) at the country level.

Our analysis of linkages will draw upon—and seek to expand—a growing body of sociolegal research that stresses the role of judges' "audiences," allies, and "support structures."[26] Even in authoritarian systems, these constituencies allow for methods of "off-bench resistance" against interference from political actors in judicial affairs.[27] And judges are not "passively reliant" on these support structures; they exhibit a meaningful degree of agency in building and strengthening societal, state, and international linkages.[28]

In addition to linkages, the second key factor producing variation in constitutional courts' autonomy is the degree of institutionalization in the judiciary—its complexity, coherence, adaptability, and hierarchy. Here, we are interested in how complex the institutional infrastructure is and how deeply rooted constitutional courts are in the political landscape. Coherence within the court itself reflects strongly on judges' ability to articulate a sense of mission, to develop a corporate identity that guides the court in setting its own agenda, and to ensure a regularized, internal hierarchy separate from the personnel tendencies of the regime. We find that such professionalization is more prevalent when the judicial establishment (prior to formal constitutional court formation) predates the regime of the day.

How will we know that such a specialized court enjoys autonomy? In the judicial sphere, we will look for instances in which judges wield influence on policy matters in accordance with views that differ from those of the regime (i.e., *mission autonomy*). Mission autonomy appears when judges issue rulings that either (1) ambitiously conform to a professional ideal

---

suits: Evidence from Chinese Courts," *Comparative Political Studies* 53 (14): 2321–58. Yuhua Wang (2018), "Relative Capture: Quasi-Experimental Evidence from the Chinese Judiciary," *Comparative Political Studies* 51 (8): 1012–41.

26. Yasser Kureshi (2021), "When Judges Defy Dictators: An Audience-Based Framework to Explain the Emergence of Judicial Assertiveness Against Authoritarian Regimes," *Comparative Politics* 53 (2): 233–57.

27. Alexei Trochev and Rachel Ellett (2014), "Judges and Their Allies: Rethinking Judicial Autonomy through the Prism of Off-Bench Resistance," *Journal of Law and Courts* 2 (1): 67–91.

28. David Landau (2018), "Courts and Support Structures: Beyond the Classic Narrative," in *Comparative Judicial Review*, ed. Erin F. Delaney and Rosalind Dixon (Cheltenham: Edward Elgar).

that seeks to uphold the rule of law or to maintain the integrity of the legal profession or (2) more parochially, move policy practices and outcomes closer to their own corporate or ideological interests, whether in the legal, economic, political, or social domains.[29]

Less ambitiously, perhaps, the fingerprints of constitutional courts and judges may not be evident in national politics, but they appear in how the judiciary manages to dictate its own affairs and defend the interests of its personnel from outsider encroachment (i.e., *internal autonomy*).

By adopting a consciously historical lens in our analysis, we will more clearly see that such forms of institutional autonomy do not develop in a linear fashion. Often, the backlash that results from autonomous activity on the part of courts prompts regimes to clip their wings and step in to limit what they deem to be patterns of "problematic" behavior. One step forward can result in two backward. Courts sometimes stick out their necks—sometimes so far that their heads ultimately come to rest on the chopping block.

A Controlled Comparison of Divergent Courts: Egypt and Palestine

There is a reason that we begin this study by examining a very similar structure of constitutional courts in Egypt and Palestine (with one heavily modeled on the other). While both bodies operate in different political settings, they share many common features. The use of paired comparisons has become widespread in political science generally and judicial politics in particular because it allows descriptive depth while maintaining analytical control.[30] Most countries have judicial or quasi-judicial bodies to rule on constitutional disputes, but in these two cases we have an uncannily similar pair.

The two constitutional courts were created by authoritarian executives with a similar goal: consolidating their own control over the broader judicial system by creating a body at its apex that they sought to control. And similar institutional frameworks were ascribed to constitutional courts in pursuit of this goal, primarily because the authors of Palestinian legislation

---

29. Onur Bakiner (2020), "Endogenous Sources of Judicial Power: Parapolitics and the Supreme Court of Colombia," *Comparative Politics* 52 (4): 603–24.

30. Sidney Tarrow (2010), "The Strategy of Paired Comparison: Toward a Theory of Practice," *Comparative Political Studies* 43 (2): 230–59. Rachel M. Gisselquist (2014), "Paired Comparison and Theory Development: Considerations for Case Selection," *PS: Political Science and Politics* 47 (2): 477–84. Celeste L. Arrington (2019), "Hiding in Plain Sight: Pseudonymity and Participation in Legal Mobilization," *Comparative Political Studies* 52 (2): 310–41.

for a constitutional court essentially began by (1) importing Egypt's 1979 SCC Law; (2) modeling it almost identically; and then (3) adapting that law's details to reflect the Palestinian context in ways that were generally more semantic than substantive.

By comparing a similar court in two systems that have a limited number of differences—and whose differences are readily identifiable—we can very clearly home in on the variation both in the context (i.e., degrees of linkage and institutionalization) and in the outcome (i.e., institutional autonomy). This allows us to explore cause and effect and match our claims against alternative explanations. Egypt and Palestine both have widely similar judicial systems that are rooted in a history of Ottoman rule, British oversight, and even considerable direct influence (of Egypt on Palestinian laws, judicial structures, and legal training). Combined with the divergence in the outcome that we study, the similar characteristics of these systems are strong enough—both influenced by precolonial, colonial, and postcolonial regime experiences—that the two cases are particularly well suited for this type of controlled comparative analysis. Because autocrats' intentions, institutional design choices, and the structure of surrounding legal institutions are broadly comparable in both cases, we must look to other factors to explain the divergent trajectories in each constitutional court's degrees of internal and mission autonomy.

Of course, the differences between the two cases, especially with regard to full political sovereignty of the respective states (with Palestine trying very hard to act like a sovereign entity but very often failing), should not be far from our minds. As it turns out, that difference is an important contextual factor, but the immediate explanation for such very different courts lies much more in linkage and institutionalization.

The Egyptian and Palestinian constitutional courts were unusually similar in institutional structure, political circumstances surrounding their emergence, and the concerns motivating autocrats to establish them. But they arose in states that were quite different. Both Egypt and the Palestinian National Authority (PNA) were led by authoritarian regimes. Yet, the Egyptian state was far more institutionalized, and it enjoyed historically greater separation from ruling executives and their regime cliques. Egypt's judiciary also had a stronger sense of corporate identity, more tools of institutional authority, deeper historical roots, and even some potential allies. The PNA was not even a full state, built its court on weak and internally fragmented judicial foundations, and inserted a new institutional actor into a setting where it would have no allies outside of the regime—as the Palestinian regime itself never had much structural differentiation from any of the various organs comprising its administrative state apparatus.

Egypt's Supreme Constitutional Court was created over the course of a decade through events that took place in three key years: 1969, 1971, and 1979. And its structure was significantly reshaped in 2000, 2011, 2012, and 2019. In all seven instances, autocrats acted with short-term motivations—there were specific constitutional questions, portentous legal disputes, or immediate political struggles that motivated these changes. But in all cases, each change had unintended consequences down the road. The Egyptian SCC's bold rulings—especially pronounced in the 1980s and 1990s but with occasional recurrences since then, most markedly in 2012—were an effect of judicial autonomy, professionalism, institutionalization, and linkages to state and societal actors far more than simply regime interests. Egypt's constitutional court was formed by a regime trying to control the rest of the judiciary, making its creation seem to be a function of regime needs. But the new institution found for itself an ability to carve out an independent voice and issue rulings that caused a series of headaches for that same regime and for successive rulers. While the Egyptian regime has been able to react and mold the court, it has acted slowly and with tools that are at best clumsy, often with unforeseen medium- and long-term effects.

The Palestinian case diverges from Egypt's success quite notably. The PNA was founded in 1994 to rule Palestinians in the West Bank and Gaza in matters where Palestinians were granted political autonomy under supposedly interim agreements with Israel. Many of its state-like institutions (such as the presidency itself) were new, untested, malleable, and in practice extensions of the ruling party (Fatah). The courts were themselves much older (with roots far deeper than those of the PNA), but they had been weak, sidelined in previous decades, and plagued by internal factionalism among the judges themselves.[31] These judicial institutions had various historical and legal origins (Ottoman, Egyptian, Jordanian, and Israeli) that had never been knitted together effectively and produced an overall low level of institutionalization and persistent incoherence within the judicial establishment as a whole.

The rise of influential state and societal allies in favor of an independent judiciary briefly paved a viable path for a liberal and independent constitutional court in Palestine. But linkages to those allies were critically dis-

---

31. Schaaf (2022).

rupted by the time the body was finally created. Palestine's Supreme Constitutional Court was shaped in a series of steps in which legislation was drafted, the court was mentioned in a constitution (or Basic Law) of 2002, and it was granted a legislative basis (2006), but it did not actually form until much later (2016). As with Egypt, each step was taken by the regime for tactical reasons having to do with pressing but short-term political rivalries, concerns about some litigation, and worries that existing judicial actors were not sufficiently pliant. But while the Egyptian SCC emerged in a context in which the judiciary had developed its own agenda, corporate identity, and many potential allies, Palestine's judiciary had little such institutional roots and a weak corporate identity. Its level of autonomy, thus, fluctuated with the waxing and waning of its ultimately temporary, and feeble, allies. Unlike in Egypt, few consequences were unintended; in the Palestinian case, poor institutionalization and weak linkages render regime-centric functionalism empirically sound as an explanation for the SCC's (quite minimal) autonomy.

Egypt

The Egyptian SCC's jurisprudence, as well as its very existence, has attracted considerable attention especially since the 1990s.[32] The dominant explanation among scholars for its establishment was most recently summarized by Tamir Moustafa, who drew from a functionalist logic in positing that "authoritarian regimes sometimes establish autonomous judicial institutions to address the pathologies endemic in many of their states" and endorsed the idea that "by establishing an independent court, the government benefited from increased investment, a larger tax base, and long-term political viability."[33] This account is plausible and seems, at first glance, to fit the facts: Egypt's rulers moved to construct the court and to attract foreign investment at about the same time. And the SCC did seem to push political redlines until it finally crossed them, after which it had its wings clipped. Such is the enticing and parsimonious logic of top-down

---

32. Brown (1997). Moustafa (2007). Bruce K. Rutherford (1999), *The Struggle for Constitutionalism in Egypt: Understanding the Obstacles to Democratic Transition in the Arab World* (New Haven: Yale University Press). Kevin Boyle and Adel Omar Sherif (1996), *Human Rights and Democracy: The Role of the Supreme Constitutional Court of Egypt* (London: Kluwer Law International). Nathalie Bernard-Maugiron (2008), *Judges and Political Reform in Egypt* (Cairo: American University in Cairo Press).

33. Moustafa (2007), 236.

explanations that fit a narrative of regime interests to explain the broad institutional dynamics of the Egyptian SCC.

We follow much of Moustafa's account, especially guided by the attention he pays to what we term "linkages." But a closer examination of the chronology suggests that this account is sometimes helpful but still betrays several problems by sometimes overstating—and even misstating—the role of regime interests at one key moment: the formation of the court in 1979. Unintended consequences are very much part of the story of the SCC—as Moustafa shows for the court's evolution but we believe was true from the very beginning. Of course, the regime and its interests still mattered: Its leaders came to feel that the SCC had become a headache and did clip its wings. But the Egyptian SCC seems to have a cyclical sense to its autonomy and has tended to not stay quiet after scholars have pronounced it thoroughly tamed.

The Egyptian SCC: From Short-Term Solution to Part of the Ecosystem

The Egyptian SCC was created not by a regime seeking to give credible commitments to economic elites but by a regime unchallenged by opposition in society but still uncertain of its ability to control the state—with long-standing structural differentiation between ruling officials and state bodies giving good reason for this sense of uncertainty. That regime formed the SCC not to assure investors that it would observe the rule of law but to bring elite, already existing judges more under its control. While the regime had a clear function for the SCC in mind (using it to control the broader judicial establishment), it largely failed because the judiciary already had sufficient institutionalization and corporate identity to succeed in planting the seeds of autonomy within this new, executive-oriented judicial structure. The Egyptian regime's focus on co-opting an already cohesive section of elite society meant that the process that built the Egyptian SCC simply baked in a powerful linkage into what would evolve into a constitutionally empowered institution.

In this sense, functionalist logics provide a great deal of leverage in explaining the origins of the Egyptian SCC, but they quickly falter when our interest shifts to explaining its subsequent development and particularly its acquisition of internal and mission autonomy at later dates. It is tempting to ask *why* the Egyptian regime decided to transform this body—created to obey the president and serve his unique socialist ideology—into a judicial actor that did the opposite in the 1980s and 1990s. But that question is deeply misleading in the Egyptian case, and the answer is that it never made such a decision. While the regime did indeed back off the desire to micromanage most judicial outcomes in the 1970s, Egypt's rulers did not have strong reason to suspect the actions they took would have the effects that they did. There is little evidence of intentionality on the part of the regime—just the opposite is more commonly the case.

The bulk of Egypt's modern judicial system was built and institutionalized in a series of steps in the second half of the nineteenth and the first half of the twentieth centuries, generally on a civil law model. By the mid-twentieth century, the judicial framework had developed a high level of institutionalization, producing a system of courts that was centralized and hierarchical—one that allowed some hallmarks of autonomy from the executive branch. Judges had developed a strong degree of institutionalization through their sense of cohesive, corporate identity, augmented by informal social and familial networks. "Judicial families" tended to send a regular stream of members into the judiciary, creating intergenerational linkages. Judges shared common education in a small number of law schools, providing for close socialization among peers, and entered the judicial corps generally within a few years of finishing university education. Career paths were shaped by decisions made by bodies dominated by senior judges; the principle of seniority shaped career advancement. And judicial institutionalization was further formalized by the existence of a Judges Club, where judges could discuss matters of professional concern and collectively formulate a coherent sense of professional mission in a social, yet corporate setting.

While sensitive political cases were not often handled in these courts for the first half of the twentieth century, the courts could be bold on occasion. Indeed, even the judicial review of the constitutionality of legislation was established initially not by construction of a specialized constitutional court but by judicial action in the 1940s. In that period, the country's administrative courts, established to adjudicate cases in which a state actor was a party, successfully asserted (in a way roughly analogous to the well-known story of *Marbury v. Madison* in the United States) the principle that they could effectively cancel legislated acts that violated the constitution. Such authority was rarely used but existed as a latent and tentatively accepted judicial power—one the courts claimed for themselves rather than had bestowed upon them by the regime.

Even when a single-party, authoritarian system was built in the 1950s and 1960s, the judiciary was largely untouched (after an initial purge of the administrative courts). But the regime did inscribe authoritarian measures deeply into the Egyptian legal framework and built special security courts and quasi-judicial bodies under its direct control for sensitive political cases when it found the judiciary either too slow or unreliable—the suppression of the Muslim Brotherhood and the purging of old regime politicians being notable instances of this. In this way, Egypt retained a judiciary with considerable authority on paper and some autonomy in practice, but without an ability or willingness to constrain the regime in any serious way.

In 1969, Egypt's leaders suddenly decided that was no longer enough. Motivated likely by the public emergence of critical judges who were using the Judges Club as a platform and shaken by popular protest and the suggestion of fissures within the regime, Egypt's president Gamal `Abd al-Nasir issued a series of decrees in 1969 collectively referred to as "the massacre of the judiciary."[34] He dismissed over two hundred judicial personnel, placed the judiciary under a new structure headed by the president, and created a new "Supreme Court"—the body that eventually became the SCC—with the explicit purpose (enshrined in an "explanatory note" that accompanied the decree) of ensuring that the courts followed the regime's official ideology (in this case, socialism) even if legal texts had not yet been updated to match ideological goals:

> It has become clear in many cases that the judgments of the judiciary are not able to join the march of development which has occurred in social and economic relations; this is a result of the inadequacy of legislation or a result of interpretations unsuitable for the new relations. . . . The independence of the judge is not a characteristic the society bestows on him; rather it is established in the interests of justice and the people.[35]

The Supreme Court was placed at the apex of the judicial system and given the task, among others, of judicial review of the constitutionality of legislation. With judges appointed directly by the president for three-year terms, its explicit purpose was to make sure the regular courts followed the policy directions and desires set out by the executive no matter what the law actually said. In this way, the sinews of the SCC were initially shaped to a large extent by top-down regime interests, functionalist logics, and strategies for sustaining a system of executive-dominated authoritarian rule.

---

34. Brown (1997).

35. `Abd Allah Imam (1976), *Madbahat al-qada* [The Massacre of the Judiciary] (Cairo: Maktabat Madbuli), 136.

In 1971, Egypt was given a new constitution that did address judicial matters. Perhaps mindful that establishing a supreme court with constitutional authority by emergency presidential decree was anomalous, the new document provided for the body, renaming it the "Supreme Constitutional Court" but leaving its other details to ordinary legislation (with the existing Supreme Court continuing to operate in accordance with the 1969 decree law until that legislation was written). The document did enshrine some of the steps taken in 1969, such as the presidentially headed body overseeing the judiciary as well as the commitment to socialism, but it backed away from total subjugation of the judiciary. What was at stake seemed less liberalization in any political, much less economic, sense and more a rejiggering of the state apparatus by a regime that was itself being reconfigured in significant ways.

In 1970, 'Abd al-Nasir died, and his successor, Anwar al-Sadat, found his presidency hemmed in by what he referred to as "centers of power"— state and party institutions headed by potential rivals, themselves readily distinguishable from, and ostensibly hostile to, the new ruler. In 1971, Sadat purged many of these rivals; later that year, a new constitution scaled back the authority of some of the institutions they had headed. The single regime party was retained for a few years (but eventually dismantled), and clearer (though still fairly ambiguous) legal guarantees were given that made unfettered executive actions more difficult. Some of these steps, such as a constitutional clause holding individual officials criminally accountable if they failed to enforce court orders, ultimately relied on judicial actors, thus ensuring a continued place for the developing judicial hierarchy.

The result was a new system of bureaucratic authoritarianism, emerging in the 1970s and fully blossoming in the 1980s and 1990s (under al-Sadat's successor, Husni Mubarak), in which the presidency operated through its domination and management of institutions that otherwise worked somewhat separately from each other. The governing party, multiple security agencies, military bodies, mass media, various bureaucracies, officially chartered professional associations, trade and professional unions, key judicial structures, local government, and various segments of the bureaucracy had some autonomy within their own realm; structural differentiation was controlled and tamed but not eliminated. These state bodies were each headed by a figure selected by and loyal to the president, and that figure was able to demonstrate his or her usefulness not simply to the presidency but also to the sector in question by lobbying the presidency for favors (jurisdiction, perquisites, salary, and legislation).

This was a system that generally served the regime well on a daily basis but was not always easy to manage (and that produced state institutions that had some capacity to define their own corporate interests and act on their own). Even when that system did function, it did not always do so smoothly. Sometimes constituencies (such as organized labor or professional associations) would demand more than the presidency was willing to give; sometimes autonomy could protect dissident voices; and sometimes the heads of each institution could use the lack of oversight to pursue sectoral (or even personal and individual) interests at the expense of those of the regime or the society.

In this way, the judiciary was brought back within the fold from the early 1970s onward—as one state institution among many others granted limited internal autonomy but placed under watchful general oversight. Most judges dismissed in 1969 were reinstated; each judicial actor was given some autonomy in matters of hiring, promotion, and budgeting; and judges were given higher salaries and other perquisites, perhaps to assuage their sense of grievance and to co-opt their leaders. The regime retained tools to oversee judicial bodies (generally through the Ministry of Justice and the appointment of key officials like the attorney general) and to avoid them when necessary (through emergency rule and special courts); it also invented some new ones (such as the Socialist Public Prosecutor, a body that could pursue regime enemies using vaguely defined legal authority). In this way, the regime sought to limit mission autonomy by promoting institutional complexity and hierarchy that stood outside the remit of the SCC as a peak institution. The overall result was a judiciary that became progressively more institutionalized and could generally perform administrative oversight through enforcing legislation but that was also unlikely to confront the regime directly without putting itself at risk—and would lose such a confrontation in the unlikely event it chose that path.

This internal restructuring seemed largely political in nature; the SCC envisioned in the 1971 constitution would certainly have had little impetus pushing it in a liberalizing political direction, much less an economic one. The private sector generally and investors specifically were given few guarantees in the constitution. There was some general language about respecting property rights, but those clauses (Articles 34–36) had little meaning without clear legislation that was at best slow in coming.[36] More strikingly,

---

36. E.g., Article 35 provided that "nationalization shall not be allowed except for considerations of public interest, in accordance with a law and subject to compensation." See the translation: https://static1.squarespace.com/static/554109b8e4b0269a2d77e01d/t/5554

they were undermined by a whole series of other clauses providing for socialism, leveling of incomes, worker participation, and the role of the public sector. And indeed, the Supreme Court—as it was called until a full law providing for its structure and operation was promulgated in 1979— was not characterized by either political or economic boldness. When the SCC eventually moved against socialism, it had to toss out entire constitutional clauses as irrelevant or outdated. That it would eventually do so could hardly have been foreseen when the court was first created.

What, then, allowed the SCC to acquire sometimes impressive levels of internal and mission autonomy? It is the judges themselves, the structure of the authoritarian state, and benign neglect by the regime that provide a more persuasive explanation for these developments than regime needs or intentions.

The legislation creating the SCC (law 48 of 1979) was handed over to drafters—most of whom came out of a legal profession scarred by the massacre of the judiciary and some of whom were suspicious of the Supreme Court as it had been constructed then. They wished to build a court that was not set apart from the rest of the judiciary and that had clear independence from the executive. But they lost in both efforts. What they got— though there is no evidence anybody realized it at the time—was a law that did not prevent these goals. It kept the SCC safely under presidential control over the short term but made subtle shifts that, over time, gradually allowed regime domination to decline and be replaced by further increasing levels of institutionalization.

The 1979 law, as written, transferred the existing judges on the Supreme Court to the new body; allowed the chief justice to be appointed by the president of the republic; and allowed the president to select new justices from two names, one forwarded by the SCC's General Assembly (consisting largely of the existing justices, all at that point direct presidential appointees) and a second by the SCC's chief justice (himself, of course, a presidential appointee). From a regime perspective, it seemed like a suitable way to entrench the supine Supreme Court, not launch the court in a new direction. From reading the text of this law, it seems apparent that if (and when) an autonomous SCC later emerged, it was not a function of regime intention. It certainly offered little indication to those who were paying attention that an autonomous court was being promised

a9e2e4b0277cbe1604b0/1431611874992/Egypt+1971+Constitution+as+amended+2007.pdf (accessed 27 November 2019).

by the regime; even if it did emerge, the 1971 constitution gave it blunt tools at best to press for political liberalization and even fewer tools to push for economic liberalization. Even so, the provisions of the SCC law and prevailing practices allowed a powerful and autonomous SCC to develop slowly without changing the law itself.

*Whose Court Is It Anyway? Cycles of Seizing
and Losing Institutional Autonomy*

The jurisprudence of Egypt's SCC, especially but not exclusively in the 1990s, was remarkable for its boldness as it issued a number of verdicts that indicated a meaningful degree of mission autonomy: the court moved against parliamentary election laws on four occasions (1987, 1990, 2000, and 2012), forcing the dissolution of parliament on three of those occasions. It took Egypt's qualified constitutional language on political rights and used it to strike down laws hampering press freedom and political parties. It ruled against the country's nongovernmental organization (NGO) law, it mandated more neutral electoral administration, and it took bold steps defending private property. To extrapolate these insights beyond the institution itself and to the broader system level, the SCC began to act as a vanguard protecting structural differentiation within a variety of state and societal institutions outside of the legal sector proper.

The SCC's audacity was not unlimited in scope (it tended to shy away from some security-oriented cases such as those involving the military or the police) or in time (beginning in the early 2000s until the uprising of 2011 it was a far more quiescent body). And it has also once more lost its gumption with the consolidation of a new post-2013 authoritarian order.

In order to understand the boldness of the SCC, we turn to the laws that govern its operation and underscore how the law of the court allowed (but hardly encouraged) certain norms to evolve within this body rather quickly. While the constitutional position of the court since its establishment in the 1979 law has been central, its powers have been intermittently latent or activated and in many ways rely on fragile processes of institutionalization that have typified the court's evolution, its strengths, and its weaknesses.

Informal norms that facilitated institutionalization, particularly in the forms of hierarchy and coherence, have been central to the court's achievement of significant internal autonomy. Quite early in the court's institutional history, a tradition was established in which the president simply selected the most senior SCC judge as chief justice and then the chief justice and General Assembly would settle on a single name for a new member to join, allowing the president a choice of exactly one when appointing new members. The tradition was established when the justices were holdovers from the SCC's origin as a handpicked presidential body, likely without anyone in the presidency worried about the long-term implications. But in practice (though not in law or in any commitment to anyone), the combination made for a de facto self-perpetuating body. After reviewing some of the SCC's landmark rulings, Brown notes that

> vacancies in the Egyptian Supreme Constitutional Court are filled by the current judges of the Court (who forward their choice to the president for the formal appointment), making the Court self-perpetuating, unlike any supreme or constitutional court in the world. The procedure, adopted in 1979, was followed by the series of bold decisions mentioned above.[37]

Anchored in a strongly corporate judiciary with an active memory of greater autonomy, allowed to develop in its own direction, given (if only by custom) a self-perpetuating status, and presented with opportunities by legal activists who sought to use the court to pursue their reform visions, the SCC began to evolve in its own direction in the 1980s. In addition to asserting and protecting its own internal autonomy, the court developed a noticeably distinct sense of mission autonomy as well. In time, it would move in a market-liberal ideological direction, simply ignoring many of the socialist commitments in the Egyptian constitution.

The irony of this shift could not have been anticipated by those who had set up the court, given that it completely subverted the initial ideological commitments made in the 1971 constitution (even as amended within a decade to back slightly away from socialism). In one of its landmark rulings, the SCC essentially said that constitutional jurisprudence could not be bound by outmoded ideological commitments no longer appropriate for the country—a method of reasoning remarkably similar to the one that designers of the court back in 1969 wished it to follow to pursue socialism despite the letter of law but that now was used to abandon it.[38]

---

37. Nathan J. Brown (2002), *Constitutions in a Nonconstitutional World: Arab Basic Laws and the Prospects for Accountable Government* (Albany: SUNY Press), 151.

38. Nabil Abdel Fattah (2008), "The Political Role of the Egyptian Judiciary," in *Judges and Political Reform in Egypt*, ed. Nathalie Bernard-Maugiron (Cairo: American University of Cairo Press).

In taking such steps, the SCC was able to pursue a distinct sense of mission aided very much by the vertical linkages in society that it had forged. Here legal mobilization was key—the way in which various NGOs and advocacy groups, themselves rooted in a strong legal community, found ways to ensure the court's autonomy and act as powerful cheerleaders and legitimizers of the institution. Linkages throughout Egyptian civil society multiplied especially in the 1990s, alongside the proliferation of human rights organizations (HROs) that were staffed by cause lawyers and funded largely by international donors. And those linkages empowered the Egyptian SCC by cobbling together a societal constituency with compelling motives to support and defend the court's authority.

The ability to achieve even limited success in constitutional litigation gave Egyptian HROs a vested interest in the SCC's continued operation and autonomy. Turning his analysis away from regime interests and toward societal linkages to a broader "legal complex," Moustafa observes that the Egyptian human rights movement institutionalized efforts to promote and protect the SCC's autonomy from regime interference—most formally by establishing organizations like the Arab Centre for the Independence of the Judiciary and the Legal Profession to lobby on the judiciary's behalf and establish ties with international organizations that could pressure the Egyptian regime to respect judicial autonomy.[39] And when the Mubarak regime in 1998 moved to curtail the SCC's jurisdiction (and by extension the scope of policy areas where it could exercise its mission autonomy), societal constituencies that had become linked to the court in previous years—NGOs, opposition parties, the lawyers' syndicate—quickly came to its defense.[40]

Linkages between the SCC and societal constituencies fostered a mutual usefulness and delivered benefits that flowed in both directions. Some HROs very explicitly began to incorporate legal contention in the SCC as a core strategy for pursuing their political objectives, a notable example being the Center for Human Rights Legal Aid establishing a special constitutional litigation unit that selectively supported cases in the regular courts based on their potential to later be referred upward to the SCC.[41]

That process of regular courts referring cases to the SCC brings us to a less visible set of linkages that proved every bit as powerful, ones that

---

39. Moustafa (2007), 201.

40. Moustafa (2007), 206–7.

41. Mona El-Ghobashy (2006), "Taming Leviathan: Constitutionalist Contention in Contemporary Egypt" (PhD diss., Columbia University), 180.

actually allowed these critical societal linkages to operate in the service of internal and mission autonomy: horizontal linkages to other parts of the state legal apparatus. This had an important base in the justiciability prerogatives of the court. Nonofficial actors could not resort directly to the SCC but had to do so through a concrete legal dispute in which they had material legal interest. As with many specialized constitutional courts, this meant that an active body would require that other judicial actors be willing to fill its docket.

If a case before a court (generally an administrative, civil, criminal, or personal status court) raised a constitutional issue, the judges on that court would refer it to the SCC. In short, an SCC without strong linkages to other judicial bodies would have been unable to operate or pursue any sense of mission, and legal mobilization would have found no traction. Moreover, the SCC tended to recruit new members from other judicial bodies or from individuals from families with strong judicial traditions, thus strengthening the cross-institutional ties with familial and professional accentuation.

When the regime finally began to realize the monster that it had allowed to emerge, it took steps to rein in the SCC, appointing a series of more reliable chief justices more clearly aligned with its wishes. Some have seen this as reason to describe the SCC as having "lost" autonomy[42] and as "transformed from the most promising avenue for political reform to a weapon in the hands of the regime to constrain the regular judiciary and sideline political opponents."[43]

This is largely accurate but not the end of the story. The combination of judicial and legal activism had indeed made the SCC annoying to the regime in the 1980s and 1990s. And it was able to steer the court uncertainly in a more pliant direction. But the regime never subdued it fully.

When Awad al-Morr, the chief justice who presided over the SCC during its boldest period and a public advocate for a more liberal economic and political order, stepped down as chief justice in 1999, the presidency first extracted concessions in return for following the unwritten norm of seniority before designating his successor and then abandoned that norm altogether, appointing a series of chief justices who were more closely tied to the presidency. Judicial figures whose careers showed them close to the regime or weak and pliant were found to head the body. But the SCC still

---

42. Moustafa (2007), 208.
43. Moustafa (2007), 218.

retained some corporate identity; its mission autonomy did not vanish but rather went into dormancy and was poised to reemerge and express itself fully when presidential micromanagement receded. And that step occurred in February 2011 when Hosni Mubarak was forced to resign and the military high command (the Supreme Council of the Armed Forces, or SCAF) temporarily assumed presidential authority.

In 2011, the SCC rushed to write its long-standing internal autonomy into law, with its unique self-perpetuation prerogative firmly at the center. The military junta temporarily governing (almost certainly mindful that the presidency might be won by an unreliable figure and anxious to protect state institutions from any new president's grasp) accepted an SCC-drafted text to make the SCC self-perpetuating by statute. At the time, it was not merely the SCC but also the state religious establishment and the military that received such protection. Enshrining structural differentiation and boundaries between such bodies and ruling political elites was viewed as a necessity, largely because the SCAF did not know exactly who those elites would be in the postrevolutionary environment—but it suspected that the most likely candidates (i.e., members of the Muslim Brotherhood) could not be trusted with control over legal and religious institutions.

The newly powerful SCC quickly used its significant constitutional position to protect itself and guard its internal autonomy further—it dissolved the parliament when deputies began discussing changing the statute the SCC had won from the SCAF. The court could feel confident in moving into the political breach in part because of its long-developed linkages to powerful elite constituencies—the judicial establishment and elite families that undergirded it, as well as fellow state institutions seeking similar treatment. Its significant coherence and adaptability as an institutionalized body made this confidence actualized quite quickly, reacting to the chaos of revolutionary ferment with alacrity and some skill. In the years following Egypt's 2011 revolution, linkages and institutionalization were key in facilitating the SCC's efforts to expand its own autonomy in the post-Mubarak political system. The extent of authority that the SCC came to wield, however, would ultimately have negative consequences for the court down the road.

The SCC's use of its authority to undermine the parliament particularly unnerved the Muslim Brotherhood, which had won a plurality of seats and then subsequently took the presidency; and the Brotherhood began to move slowly against the court. It began with organizing demonstrations that surrounded the court building and effectively shuttered the body temporarily and then continued by moving to pass a constitutional provision (in a constitution adopted by referendum in December 2012 under Brotherhood leadership) forcing the retirement of the most outspoken anti-Brotherhood justices.

The SCC seemed poised to use its new autonomy as an institutional bulwark against the presidency—not out of principle but specifically, in this case, because the Brotherhood held it. Not only did the court move against the parliament in 2012, but it dug in its feet on matters large and small. In the latter regard, it symbolically insisted that the newly elected president of Egypt, Muhammad Morsi of the Brotherhood, come to the SCC building to be sworn into office. More significantly, the court entertained challenges of all kinds to the emerging order. While it had little time to rule on most of these, it positioned itself to step carefully but still bravely. In June 2013, for instance, it restricted the president's authorities during a state of emergency by judiciously resurrecting a case that had slumbered on its docket for two decades.

But if the SCC was one of many state institutions wishing to defy the Brotherhood-held presidency, it was not clear what it could do and indeed showed some signs of tactical hesitation until July 2013 when a collection of state institutions and political actors formed to overthrow the president. When the coalition triumphed, the SCC lent its own chief justice as interim president.[44]

The post-2013 regime has gradually showed an ability to turn the SCC into a subservient instrument in a manner that might have marveled those who initially created it. The chief justice/interim president served while a new constitution was drafted (technically, a systematic amendment of the one pushed through by the Brotherhood during its brief period of leadership), lending an air of state neutrality to a process that resulted in a new regime dominated by the military and the security apparatus. And when that regime began to consolidate itself under the leadership of Field Marshall `Abd al-Fattah al-Sisi (after his election as president in 2014), the SCC again showed signs of tactical hesitation. While critical cases were often referred to the SCC, the justices deferred rulings, clearly unsure of their standing with the new regime and opting for caution during the period of uncertainty following Egypt's political transition.

---

44. Nathan J. Brown and Julian G. Waller (2016), "Constitutional Courts and Political Uncertainty: Constitutional Ruptures and the Rule of Judges," *International Journal of Constitutional Law* 14 (4): 817–50.

But rulings by other courts—chiefly administrative and criminal courts—that inconvenienced the regime provoked an effort to reverse the autonomy that the SCC had achieved in 2011. A contemporaneous crackdown on legal advocacy and human rights NGOs—forcibly closing or freezing the funds of some and arresting the directors and employees of others—meant that constituencies in Egyptian civil society linked to the SCC were on the backfoot as well and in no position to come to the judiciary's defense this time around. With its linkages hemmed in and handicapped in this way, the SCC found itself in a weakened position. The constitution was amended in 2019 to restore to the president some discretion in selecting the SCC's chief justice and other members—one that he immediately used to tap a candidate with less seniority than the one who had been in line for succession; in 2022 President al-Sisi reached far down the seniority ladder in search of a pliable figure. And two former chief justices who had led the SCC as it was brought into line were each granted a speakership in the two houses of parliament. Perhaps the final step in the body's subordination came when the president—claiming to act on the recommendation of the justices themselves—appointed the chief judge of the military courts, Brigadier Salah al-Ruwayni, to a seat on the bench. The move was unmistakably bold but also was pushed through with an air of embarrassed timidity by the president; the appointment decree and state press coverage, for instance, listed al-Ruwayni under his patronymic rather than family name—with the former sometimes used in Egypt for various reasons but in this case likely meant to keep the identity of the new justice away from the news and the public.

Overall, our story is a bit less clear than one in which the regime created the SCC, strategically gave it autonomy when doing so would serve the function of delivering political and economic benefits, and then reined the SCC in when it went too far in other areas. Judges, political activists, international actors, and other societal constituencies linked to the SCC played significant roles in affecting variation in the degree of internal and mission autonomy that the Egyptian SCC acquired over time. Moreover, regime actions were guided not simply by long-term strategies but more often by short-term challenges and annoyances: splits within its top ranks, the possibilities of popular protest, and the potential actions of cantankerous senior judges. At other times, the regime did not act and was simply unable or unwilling to do so. Key figures were often uninterested in what SCC justices were doing either because they seemed reliable (into the 1980s) or because they were careening from one crisis to the next (in 2011–13). And when regime leaders were interested, they found that they had a series of crude tools to confront, undermine, and tame the court, the use of which had their own unintended consequences.

Dropping a body like the SCC into a highly institutionalized, centralized, and authoritarian system—but one with a strong history of corporate judicial identity and characterized by fiefdoms and pockets of activism—led to the result of an SCC that could be a nuisance or a support for the regime in different ways and at different times in a manner that was hardly planned or amenable to any but the crudest attempts to steer.

When the court achieved significant levels of internal autonomy, it was accomplished informally as a result of increasingly strong levels of institutionalization developing within the judicial establishment—and later formally as the court entrenched itself as an integral (albeit tenacious) part of the Egyptian state apparatus. Horizontal linkages to allied agencies and actors within that state apparatus, in addition to vertical linkages to societal constituencies, allowed the court to exercise a formidable degree of mission autonomy over political, economic, and social issues at times.

The Egyptian regime, of course, was not passive—it took shots aiming to curtail judicial autonomy when the SCC seemed to overreach, some of which landed while others were deflected by the institutionalized and societally linked body. Significant blows to the SCC's internal and mission autonomy have been delivered in recent years, as a new regime seeks to consolidate its position as a heavy striker in the ring of Egyptian politics. But the SCC itself has accumulated half a century of experience as an adaptable rope-a-dope fighter, one that picks its exchanges carefully and has demonstrated a unique skill in weathering punches and allowing adversaries to tire themselves out as the court becomes more sure of its own footing. The SCC certainly appears to be on the ropes now as it faces a powerful and determined opponent, but its historical record of endurance should caution observers against declaring that it has been defeated prematurely. By taking an expansive view and analyzing the history of the SCC's evolution, its institutionalization, and its cyclical struggles with the regime, we suggest that institutional endurance has a unique value that should not be understated:

> [Muhammad] Ali admitted he was concerned about [George] Foreman, saying he was "too big" and "too strong." Remembering a photo

he had taken of Ali sparring . . . George [Kalinsky] said: "Why don't you try something like that? Sort of a dope on the ropes, letting Foreman swing away but, like in the picture, hit nothing but air?"[45]

Palestine

Perhaps if the Egyptian case reveals the shortcomings of top-down and regime-centric explanations, the overall narrative surrounding the creation and operation of a constitutional court in Palestine serves as a cautionary tale for us not to abandon functionalist logics altogether. In this instance, the regime found itself in dire need of immediate solutions to a host of rising challenges that ranged from internal rivalry to a potential succession crisis and a judiciary that seemed unreliable in delivering the regime decisive victories on critical issues. The regime's response was to establish a constitutional court to suit its interests in addressing these challenges—or rather to take a court structure that had already been designed in Palestinian draft laws modeled on Egypt's 1979 law for the SCC and, subsequently, tailor that structure to fit developing regime needs. And it got exactly what it wanted.[46]

This ultimately successful creation rested on a protracted and convoluted process of drafting and negotiation that itself casts doubt on the idea that autocrats can simply summon courts from whole cloth to deal with their problems. Indeed, in some ways the history of the Palestinian court is a reverse of the Egyptian history. In Palestine, the court was nurtured by many friends; following the path of its creation is a complex tale involving many political actors, some quite critical of the regime. But as in Egypt, the Palestinian SCC was ultimately established in a fit of presidential pique and designed with the goal of serving regime interests. But the Palestinian court was shorn of all of its linkages before it was allowed to begin operation, unlike the Egyptian court, which slowly achieved them long after its birth. Compared to Egypt's presidents in the twentieth century, the Palestinian leadership was much more successful in actually building the pliant court that it wanted. This was hardly a simple matter, and it entailed over a decade of political quarreling; but having finally achieved its goal in 2016, the Palestinian regime acquired a court that simply did anything that it wanted.

---

45. Angelo Dundee and Bert Sugar (2008), *My View from the Corner: A Life in Boxing* (New York: McGraw Hill), 191.

46. This section draws from research conducted by two authors (Anabtawi and Brown). Full version of the background history for Palestinian constitutional development can be found in Nathan J. Brown (2003), *Palestinian Politics after the Oslo Accords: Resuming Arab Palestine* (Berkeley: University of California Press), chapter 3.

Ultimately Palestine's SCC has served the regime's needs. But we will complicate the smooth, regime-centric narrative of the Palestinian court's founding by engaging in a process-tracing account of the protracted and intermittent drafting of the court's founding law, ending in the court's effects on Palestinian politics over a decade and a half later. This story highlights the importance of antecedent conditions and historical legacies, and it shows significant temporal variation in the regime's ability to design (and tamper with) the function, jurisdiction, and internal operation of a Palestinian constitutional court throughout the creation phase.

In the early stages, linkages between Palestine's judicial establishment and powerful state actors (notably the Palestinian Legislative Council) as well as societal organizations (NGOs, legal and political activists, human rights organizations) significantly undercut the regime's ability to construct a Supreme Constitutional Court that it could control and use to its own benefit. The regime was unable to get the court that it wanted between 1994 and 2005, though it was successful in the backup tactic of delaying the court's formal establishment under such unfavorable (in the sense of being too liberal) conditions. But a tumultuous, short-term crisis that ensued after Hamas won parliamentary elections in 2006 threatened the Palestinian regime, state, and societal legal complex alike. The fallout from this crisis disrupted the sustained pressure that liberal constituencies had previously leveraged to check executive fiat in designing Palestine's Supreme Constitutional Court.

As we will see, this disruption of linkages at a key historical moment— combined with the low degree of institutionalization in the Palestinian judiciary as a whole—is what created a distinctive political environment in which regime interests and functionalist logics become especially pronounced in dictating the consistently low levels of internal and mission autonomy that we observe for the Palestinian SCC.

While the history of Palestine's Supreme Constitutional Court is admittedly less lengthy than in Egypt, the body has been no less consequential in shaping the political system as a whole. Within just three years of operation, the Palestinian SCC has issued rulings that have helped the executive crack down on political rivals, dissolve the legislature altogether, and restructure the judicial branch entirely. While the court critically lacks autonomy and has indeed proved quite functional for the regime, our analysis will show that these outcomes were hardly inevitable and cannot be adequately explained without careful attention on the role of historical contingency as well as sustained political struggles (between regime, state, and society) over the nature of the SCC.

The Creation of a Liberal Court, in Theory (1994–2005)

The Palestinian Authority (PA), established in 1994 after the Oslo Accords were signed, embarked on a project of institution building by working to unify a slew of institutional structures founded and developed under various eras: Ottoman, Jordanian, British, and Israeli military rule. The PA's provisional constitution, the Basic Law of 2002, provided for a constitutional court and detailed in brief a vision for its mandate, but its actual foundation would take considerable time.

The first effort to establish a constitutional court under the PA was not driven by the regime. Just the opposite is the case. While the regime would seek to mold the court's proposed structure to align with its own interests, it was actors outside the PA's central leadership group who first appealed for a constitutional court to be established at the outset. The Palestinian SCC's genesis (as a prospective institution, though not its eventual establishment as a formal body years later) can be traced back to the efforts of domestic and international reformers to contain the powers of the PA leader, Yasser Arafat. To rein in Arafat's prerogative rule as president, those reformers endeavored to engineer a series of institutional shifts in the political system, which included calling for new judicial institutions.

The initial interest in introducing a constitutional court arose within the halls of the Palestinian Legislative Council (PLC) at a time of heightened jurisdictional tensions between the parliament and the PA cabinet, headed by Arafat. The parliament, which had been repeatedly sidelined by the presidency, contained influential deputies who grew disgruntled with the fusion of ruler (then, Arafat), regime (centered around the top brass of the Palestinian Liberation Organization and elites within the ruling Fatah party), and state in most other areas of public life (security and defense, as well as most state ministries at the executive and bureaucratic levels). Those deputies thought that a powerful and independent constitutional court would safeguard the parliament's legislative powers and hold an executive that seemed to do whatever it pleased accountable to clear laws and procedures.

Growing parliamentary interest in the creation of a constitutional court coincided with pressures in the same direction by international backers of the PA. The regime's tactical response was to acquiesce to these reforms by introducing a draft law that would establish a constitutional court as provided for in Palestine's Basic Law. It believed that if it could emulate the Egyptian SCC in structure, the regime would be able to use it as a powerful tool of the executive while denying a future in which it served as a counterweight that allied with the legislature. With this in mind, the executive branch took the first step in 2003 by introducing a draft law that was highly amenable to an authoritarian vision putting forward a near-exact replica of Egypt's 1979 constitutional court law before the PLC.[47]

The law they proposed would not have provided for internal autonomy; after all, the Egyptian court first achieved its autonomy not through legislative text but through strong linkages to state and societal actors as well as long-standing institutionalization in the Egyptian judicial apparatus. When it came to appointment and confirmation, the regime's proposed law placed both of those processes squarely in the hands of the executive and denied the parliament any role in them. The proposed law did not put a limit on the number of constitutional court judges able to be named either, which would leave the door open for the regime to appoint additional judges at any time in order to change the balance and leaning of the court. A court whose membership was so easily manipulatable by the regime would make achieving any degree of internal or mission autonomy quite difficult, given the little daylight between the executive and the court proper.

At the same time, reform-oriented MPs saw the constitutional court bill before them as an opportunity that they could use. In fact, how this bill evolved next showed the regime's blind spots and miscalculations. The period in which the bill entered the PLC was marked by both internal and external pressure for political reform. Using the amending powers of the legislature, parliamentary reformers introduced a new version of a constitutional court law[48] that would actually check the authority of the executive branch and consolidate the parliament's role in the political system. They believed that a strong and autonomous court could serve parliamentary interests and uphold the legislature's authority when confronted with executive overreach in the future.

This modified version of the draft law introduced in 2006 included concrete changes to the jurisdiction of the court, its structure, the confirmation of its judges, and the means of bringing a case to the court. These ambitious changes were meant to consolidate the parliament's role in Palestinian governance by ensuring a high degree of separation between the three branches of government and imposing executive accountability. Not only that, but the changes set out to plant the seeds for a court that was autonomous, both internally and in pursuing a mission of administering justice and resolving fundamental political disputes that persistently cropped up in the nascent Palestinian National Authority.

---

47. First draft bill of the law of the Supreme Constitutional Court, the PLC (2003).

48. Second draft bill of the law of the Supreme Constitutional Court, number 133, the PLC (2005).

More importantly, the effort to push forward such liberal amending legislation was an attempt by the PLC to separate itself from the regime by effectively taking power away from a president who had consistently marginalized it at every possible turn. This is clear in their amended draft that capped the membership of the court, making it difficult for the president to periodically influence its outcomes through expanding its membership. In addition, the amended draft required nominated judges to be confirmed by the PLC with a two-thirds majority vote. Such a step would have significantly hindered the president's ability to fuse the SCC with the executive branch by ensuring the appointment of loyal judges.

The parliament's own draft similarly expanded the SCC's jurisdiction by explicitly granting it oversight authority over "presidential and ministerial decrees and decisions," powers to adjudicate the "loss of legal capacity" by the president, to take punitive measures against the president, and to take appeal cases from individuals aggrieved by the actions of the president of the Palestinian National Authority, the Council of Ministers, any minister, or any governor violating constitutional regulations, freedoms, sanctities, or rights.

The PLC even included in the law of the SCC a provision that would give the SCC jurisdiction to adjudicate jurisdictional conflicts between the president and the prime minister, a key concern for parliamentary deputies at the time. The regime had never foreseen these items when it had embarked on the process of building the foundation for a constitutional court—indeed, the post of prime minister itself was a new one.

The regime and ambitious reformers became deadlocked, both trying to make incremental modifications to the court's law in order to alter the function of the body that would emerge from it. In this way, we observe that linkages to powerful constituencies who supported the idea of an autonomous constitutional court mattered a great deal, even before the court itself was ultimately established. Most critically, vertical linkages to key international donors and human rights organizations, as well as horizontal ones to a critical state institution—the parliament—meant that a number of influential actors were in favor and actively lobbying on behalf of an empowered court structure for their own instrumental purposes.

The result was a victory, albeit a temporary one, for those who envisioned a liberal and autonomous constitutional court as well as the constituencies behind them. The heavily modified SCC law was approved by the PLC toward the end of 2005, the same year Mahmoud Abbas was elected to replace Yasser Arafat as president. Under continuous and significant pressure from the European Union, the United States, and domestic state and societal constituencies seeking to introduce political reform, Abbas did not object to the second draft of the bill and proceeded to sign into law what could have been the most autonomous constitutional court in the Arab world.

But in a remarkable turn of events, the regime clumsily stumbled through a series of trial-and-error ruses aimed at reshaping the law to reflect its changing priorities just as it was further losing its grip on the parliament. Functionalist logics had clearly emerged to rally against a prospective legal framework that sought to endow the SCC with autonomy from the regime. But to most observers, the form that they took would have more closely resembled a half-baked, and increasingly petulant, tantrum than any sophisticated strategy of grand institutional design.

The first surprise came when readers of the law in the *Official Gazette* discovered a quite substantive difference between the bill that President Abbas signed and the one the PLC had approved and forwarded to him. The one he signed reverted to the language of the first draft on the issue of judicial appointments, no longer requiring the PLC's confirmation of presidential appointments to the SCC. This discrepancy—plainly illegal and easily found out—resulted in public outcry criticizing the regime for failing to follow the constitutional process.[49]

Facing public pressure from legal observers and the parliament,[50] the regime scrambled to save face and remedy the situation by claiming that a "bureaucratic error" had led the president to sign a wrong version of the SCC law.[51] Abbas then stubbornly notified the PLC that he was withdrawing his signature from the law altogether. This step had no legal precedent or justification, but it was effective in the secondary effort of delaying the Palestinian SCC's establishment under unfavorable conditions when constituencies advocating for a liberal body were mobilized in strength. By withdrawing his signature from the previously ratified (and surreptitiously amended) 2006 law, Mahmoud Abbas gave regime interests another bite at the apple; the president quickly revisited the law yet another time and demanded a laundry list of self-serving amendments before he would consider signing it again.

---

49. Isam Abdeen, letter to the editor, *Al-Quds*, January 2, 2006.

50. Isam Abdeen to Adnan Amr, Letter from the PLC to the President's office, January 3, 2006.

51. President Mahmoud Abbas to Rawhi Fattouh, Letter from the President to the Head of the PLC, January 23, 2006.

President Abbas suggested multiple edits to the 2006 draft law that aimed at preventing the SCC from developing internal or mission autonomy. Chief among them was a provision granting him exclusive control over the appointment process. He also instructed the parliament to delete entirely all clauses that gave the SCC jurisdiction over presidential and ministerial decrees or the authority to take punitive measures against the president. The letter also demanded the removal of a clause that allowed the SCC to examine appeal cases by individuals whose constitutional rights were violated by the government, and he wanted the court's ability to adjudicate jurisdictional conflicts between the president and prime minister taken away. In essence, Abbas sought a second chance at relitigating most of the major changes that the parliament had inserted during the initial amendment process. All of this would guarantee the regime a court that would be structurally bound to full subservience.

But why did the president demand such bold changes when he had just recently lost a battle with the PLC on these same points and acquiesced to a much more autonomous and powerful court? The president's request came two days prior to the first parliamentary elections in a decade, when the Islamist opposition movement Hamas appeared to be gaining momentum and rapidly outpacing his ruling party, Fatah, which had dominated the PLC thus far. The president most likely feared that a strong and autonomous SCC would become an imminent threat not just to his own authority but also to his party's monopoly on political power if Hamas won the parliament and prime ministership. A Hamas-controlled PLC endowed with authority to appoint constitutional court judges would have been especially threatening to Fatah partisans, within both the legislature and the executive. This threat created a momentary convergence of interests between the president and the PLC, as mutual opposition to Hamas temporarily overshadowed their own inter-institutional battles for authority within the Palestinian political system.

Moreover, the Palestinian judiciary was historically a poorly institutionalized and divided entity, particularly at its top echelons—with separate bodies and judges operating in the West Bank and Gaza. And the prospects of unifying the judicial apparatus under the singular leadership of a constitutional court meant that appointments to this new body would be especially contentious. The president likely understood that PLC deputies, growing fearful that their party may soon lose power to Hamas, may have suddenly become more amenable to the slashing of their own edits to the constitutional court law in a manner that aligned more closely with his vision. In this regard, President Abbas seems to have gotten fairly lucky—not in the respect that an Islamist opposition movement contesting his authority was gaining political traction but rather in finding that influential state, societal, and international actors had grown sufficiently apprehensive at the prospects of Hamas achieving power that they were willing to accept, and further empower, the president as an "enemy of their enemy." State actors, namely those in the legislature, who previously sought greater—and legally protected—degrees of structural differentiation from the ruler quickly muted their concerns and fell in line to back Abbas's centralization of authority instead. And international donors, similarly concerned with the prospect of Hamas attaining empowered parliamentary authority in Palestine, backed off on their efforts to lobby for meaningful judicial oversight of the executive in this period.

Indeed, Hamas's victory in the PLC elections on January 2006 flipped over the table. The Islamist party won a large majority of the new PLC seats. But before the incoming Hamas parliament took the constitutional oath, the outgoing one exploited an article in the interim constitution extending the mandate of sitting deputies until their replacements are sworn in to hold a "farewell session" five days before the newly elected parliament was inaugurated. The outgoing deputies—growing fearful of their incoming rivals and no longer interested in empowering a parliament or a judiciary over the executive—went on to pass legislation that would weaken the next parliament and strengthen the Fatah president, Mahmoud Abbas. The most notable decision that took place in that session was the approval of Abbas's amendments to the law of the SCC, which came into force in early 2006. Facing the threat of a Hamas opposition party in power, the outgoing parliament made sweeping changes that ended the prospects of an autonomous judiciary and a robust legislature for years to come.

A swiftly shifting political landscape, thus, fundamentally changed the primary cleavages of institutional Palestinian politics—and with the constitutional court regrettably at the center of them. Tussles between the executive and the legislature, alongside linkages with influential donor states and organizations, had initially provided an opening to craft a more structurally autonomous court. The rise of Islamism as a political force, however, united the executive and the outgoing legislature as it was deemed an existential threat to the party that had controlled both (and was also greatly favored over Hamas by the international community). On its way out the door, the legislature abandoned its ambitious reform agenda and neutered the court's latent constitutional capacity and autonomy from the executive in an effort to preempt its capture by their Islamist opponents.

All of the key international and domestic constituencies lobbying for an autonomous Palestinian SCC in the early 2000s abruptly shifted gears when Hamas emerged as a viable political party poised to take control of the PLC in 2006. The proposal to establish a constitutional court, which was previously forced upon the Palestinian president and regime rather than desired by them, went into dormancy as the SCC's proponents silenced their demands and pressures on the executive to create the court ceased. In the end, the political system soon fractured so completely that the SCC was basically forgotten for a decade before it was actually formed by an authoritarian president who, facing new short-term crises, found that he needed some judicial business done in a hurry. As occurred with the establishment of Egypt's SCC in the late 1970s, it was Palestine's authoritarian executive perceiving a functional interest in creating a constitutional court that drove its eventual establishment as a formal and acting state body in 2016.

Deinstitutionalization and the Eventual Establishment of the SCC

After a year of divided rule in Palestine between a Fatah president and a Hamas-led PLC, a brief civil war between the two sides resulted in Fatah and the presidency controlling the West Bank, while Gaza was left to Hamas and a rump parliament. That split allowed Abbas to claim lawmaking authority under the Basic Law's provisions for decree legislation in the absence of a parliament—an authority he still exercises as of this writing. In the period that followed the split, the president issued nearly three times as many laws as the PLC had in its entire first term (1996–2006), while Gaza's parliament under Hamas issued just as many new laws as the PLC had before the split.

The de facto result of the state division between the West Bank and Gaza was the freezing of all parliamentary activity and the fusion of legislative and executive powers in the hands of the president. In the absence of presidential or parliamentary elections that could invigorate pluralistic life within the institutions of the PA, the judicial branch—fragmented as it was—stood as the last potential source for accountability and the rule of law vis-à-vis a regime whose control over the state increased by the day.

Even despite the lack of a functioning constitutional court, the broader judiciary had—at times—issued rulings that reversed or undermined the president's decrees, notably in two key cases: one dealing with Abbas's main political rival, Mohammad Dahlan, and a second holding that Abbas's judicial appointments did not conform with the Law of the Judicial Authority. Such rulings were disturbing, and they augured poorly for a regime faced by episodic protests and finding recourse to repression.

Lawyers and legal activists in Palestine could also sometimes strategically exploit institutional incoherence and ideological divisions within Palestine's High Court; they strategically tried to ensure that lawsuits against PA officials were adjudicated by the panel of judges with a reputation for independence and concern with the rule of law, as opposed to a second panel of judges widely believed to be more sympathetic to the regime.[52] Elites within Fatah, chiefly the president himself, were deeply frustrated by the capacity for the regular courts to defy regime interests without being reined in by the High Court or the Supreme Judicial Council. This revealed an immediate problem to the regime, leading it to scorn the extent—though fairly minimal compared to Egypt—to which judicial authority was insulated from regime control.[53]

With an aging president and constitutional provisions for succession that risked handing executive authority to Islamist opponents who still formally controlled the legislature, the regime needed a consistently reliable judicial actor to do its bidding and issue binding interpretations that supported its actions. Forming and controlling a new SCC seemed like a solution to brewing concerns about the unreliable judiciary and uncertainty regarding its allegiances in the event of a future succession struggle.

In 2014, Abbas revived the long-hibernating constitutional court law and promulgated it unilaterally by decree. But before doing so, he also inserted five key amendments to further undermine the independence of the SCC and consolidate the executive's control over its proceedings. The amendments removed the cap on the number of judges, marginalized the role of the judiciary-led Supreme Judicial Council in the appointment process, and required the SCC to seek the approval of the president in deciding the court's internal operating procedures and bylaws. Criticism from political activists and civil society organizations in Palestine was sufficiently fierce to hold off implementation for two years.

---

52. Interview with Palestinian legal activist, July 30, 2017.
53. Interview with Palestinian cabinet minister, August 1, 2017.

During this period, the regime and the broader Palestinian judiciary went to battle with one another—thus further justifying the need for a compliant constitutional court in the regime's eye. An attempt to insert a regime loyalist as head of the nominating body for all judges (the Supreme Judicial Council) provoked strong reaction, was overcome by the judicial establishment only with considerable difficulty, and engendered further bad blood between the judiciary and the regime proper.[54] As the judiciary proved itself unwilling to fully submit to regime control, President Abbas launched a renewed effort to establish a politically pliant court at the apex of the judicial hierarchy, issuing a 2016 decree mandating the formation of the new Supreme Constitutional Court. In this way, the Palestinian SCC's actual emergence as an official institution has much in common with the origins of the similar body in Egypt; both were brought into being by authoritarian executives seeking to shore up their own control over the broader state judicial apparatus.

The judges Mahmoud Abbas chose to serve on Palestine's SCC were sworn in within forty-eight hours—and the body was promptly packed with Fatah loyalists. In a move that was striking if only for its bluntness, Abbas parachuted in as chief justice a little-known figure teaching in Morocco who had penned an inflammatory opinion piece in 2013 stating that Palestine's Basic Law was not a "constitutional" document but one that could be amended like any other law, that there existed an absolute presidential authority to make laws, and that MPs could have their parliamentary immunity stripped while the PLC was not in session.[55] Legal activists and civil society organizations, which were totally cut out of the process of establishing the new SCC, quickly found the new body to be completely antagonistic to their goals of pursuing liberal reforms and political accountability. Accordingly, societal opposition to the court—as opposed to linkages with that court—became the norm in Palestine. Some scattered efforts of resistance emerged from within the Palestinian legal community; at least one lawsuit was filed that aimed to overturn the presidential decree establishing the SCC on the basis of procedural violations. Unlike the early 2000s battles over this constitutional court, such efforts at resisting executive domination of the SCC failed to gain traction this time around, lacking any meaningful social mobilization, linkages to interested international parties, or powerful state allies capable of pushing them onward.

The protracted story behind the establishment of the SCC in this case

---

54. Schaaf (2022).

55. Muhammad El-Haj Kacem (March 29, 2013), "Stripping MP Dahlan of His Immunity Is a Sound Legal Procedure," *Al-Sabah*.

demonstrates that the origin of the court had little to do with regime interests or authoritarian design at first, which fits poorly with functionalist logics that explain how specialized courts emerge in authoritarian systems from the top down. The 2000s-era battles over a formally autonomous constitutional court were ones that pitted different political bodies against one another, not a preplanned solution to commitment or regime management problems.

At the outset, linkages to the parliament and to the international community helped solidify the most "liberal" version of the court on paper, which was abandoned in the changing political landscape of a rising Islamist political threat that disrupted those linkages and led the actors who initially supported an autonomous SCC to do an about-face. And, ultimately, the court's final creation—some fourteen years after it had been given a formal place in the PA's constitutional makeup—did in fact reflect logics of regime need, partly the result of a subsequent failure to reinvigorate linkages to constituencies supporting the judiciary in society or among other branches of the state.

A Court on a Short Leash: The Utility of Functionalist Logics

As a result of the fashion in which the Palestinian SCC was established and its packing with regime-loyal judges in 2016, the court lacked any supporters or allies outside of the president's inner circle. Specifically, from 2016 onward, the court's operation and work actually were a function of regime intentions and desires—in its short life, the SCC has not followed its Egyptian counterpart's path. It has no semblance of either institutional or mission autonomy.

Indeed, if anything, the SCC has burned its bridges with possible allies. The SCC has been almost universally denounced by the Palestinian legal community, and judges in other parts of the Palestinian judicial system view it with hostility and contempt. This court is seen as a creature of the regime and simultaneously isolated from other constituencies (official and unofficial) within Palestine. On top of this, the new SCC is the epitome of a noninstitutionalized judicial structure in very fundamental ways. As of this writing, it currently lacks its own building, instead obscurely operating out of an unused floor in the Civil Pension Bureau. It has only a skeletal administrative and clerical staff. The judges themselves are widely viewed as inexperienced within the judicial profession. One SCC judge explained this by noting that "the SCC is still a nascent body. . . . We are just now learning how to formulate our verdicts because our experience in this subject is very minimal."[56] Another SCC judge was especially critical of the body's low level of institutionalization:

> The reality is that the SCC was established without any infrastructure. . . . I was consulted two days before the President issued his decision to appoint me to the court, and I agreed. . . . If I had understood the reality of SCC at the time, I would not have agreed. I would not have agreed to my nomination.[57]

Given the SCC's low level of institutionalization and lack of any supportive constituencies outside of the executive branch, we should find it no surprise that the SCC in its early years of operation has acted rather quickly to support the president in the key cases it has so far taken. Between 2016 and 2019, the SCC issued twelve interpretations and forty decisions on constitutional appeals. Cases were often adjudicated so hastily that the court would issue follow-up decisions on a particular case contradicting its own previous rulings. Legal observers attribute some of these inconsistencies to the judges' lack of institutional and constitutional expertise. Nonetheless, the court did not in any of those fifty-two decisions issue rulings that undermined the interests of the regime—a quick review of its jurisprudence confirms its general subjugation and deference to regime interests.

The first case the SCC adjudicated following its establishment was one in which other judicial bodies had ruled against the president's decree to strip Abbas's main rival of his parliamentary immunity. This case may have even been the driving force behind the timing of the court's establishment in 2016. Once a top leader in the president's own party, Mohammad Dahlan was ousted from Fatah's Central Committee in 2011. In order to place Dahlan on trial for corruption, Abbas issued a decree depriving him of parliamentary immunity—something only the parliament could do according to the Basic Law. The regime claimed that the four-year term of the PLC had already expired and that it was therefore within the purview of the president to strip MPs of their immunity. Dahlan's lawyers challenged the constitutionality of the presidential decree. This question went to the High Court (which exercised jurisdiction over constitutional disputes because the SCC had not yet been formed), which handed the president a victory

---

56. Interview with Palestinian Supreme Constitutional Court judge, July 26, 2017.
57. Interview with Palestinian Supreme Constitutional Court judge, August 9, 2017.

by allowing a corruption trial in a criminal court to go forward. But the criminal court trying Dahlan upheld his immunity in a ruling that later was affirmed on appeal, further complicating the regime's ability to use official legal channels to repress and subdue its adversaries.

The establishment of the SCC allowed the case to follow the regime's preferred course: the matter of parliamentary immunity was almost immediately brought to its attention, and the SCC offered a legal interpretation of the laws governing parliamentary immunity,[58] affirming that the president's decree stripping Dahlan's immunity did not violate the constitution. The decision, however, still stressed that the PLC continued to enjoy its legal mandate per the Basic Law until a new parliament was officially sworn in—an opinion that the SCC would later reverse by the end of 2018. Shortly following this ruling, the Anti-Corruption Court sentenced Abbas's top rival in absentia to three years imprisonment and imposed a $16 million fine on embezzlement charges. The regime also used this precedent to strip five prominent (and often dissenting) Fatah members of their parliamentary immunity as well.

Aside from faithfully resolving internal rivalries to the favor of the presidency, the SCC was used to deliver a powerful message to the judiciary itself. In one key instance where the High Court ruled against the legality of the president's judicial appointments to the Supreme Judicial Council on a procedural basis, the SCC acted within hours to offer a constitutional interpretation upholding Abbas's decree against the ruling of the High Court. The SCC signaled in this decision not only that it was supreme over the judicial establishment but that it was also ready to step in should activist judges in the regular courts dare to undermine regime interests in their verdicts.

Of course, the SCC did not immediately bring the regular courts, notably the High Court, in line as the regime intended; dissension among regular court judges continued, even though it was greatly stifled. Some of the High Court's members rejected the SCC's legitimacy as an institution and interpreted its mandate to resolve constitutional disputes narrowly, in a way that did not encompass cases on the High Court's docket that raised statutory, as opposed to constitutional, questions. These judges were keenly aware that subjugation to the SCC was tantamount to subjugation to the regime, and they were loath to resign the minimal degree of internal

---

58. Ali Sawafta, "The Palestinian Supreme Constitutional Court Empowers Abbas to Revoke MPs Immunity," *Reuters*, November 6, 2016, https://www.reuters.com/article/palestine-ah-idARAKBN1310Z2

autonomy that the High Court did possess—though objections were now most commonly vocalized behind closed doors. When a High Court judge (and member of the Supreme Judicial Council) began to dissent publicly, a gag order was imposed on judges by the head of the Supreme Judicial Council, effectively silencing judges who attempted to deploy methods of "off-bench resistance."

Although judges who opposed the SCC's authority over the judicial establishment were prevented from publicly vocalizing their concerns, many of them still continued to adjudicate cases, at least until President Abbas moved to totally reconfigure the judicial establishment in 2019. But even before such steps were taken, the creation of the SCC significantly undercut the High Court's ability to impose legal oversight on the regime. From 2016 onward, many lawyers and legal activists grew unwilling to challenge executive violations in court, fearing that even if they did win, the SCC would just find a reason to step in and reverse their success.[59] In this way, the creation of the SCC inhibited legal mobilization against the Palestinian Authority even while many judges in the regular courts still rejected their new subordinate status.

With the regular judiciary supplanted and subdued, albeit not fully acquiescent, President Abbas began petitioning the SCC for measures that would dramatically shift the balance of power between Palestine's three branches of government in his favor. In December 2018, and at the request of the regime, the SCC issued a constitutional interpretation ordering the dissolution of the PLC,[60] which had not convened in over a decade. The decision went against the SCC's previous ruling, but it also explicitly went against the Basic Law's actual text, which says that a sitting parliament's mandate extended until the new deputies are officially sworn in.

The court's opinion was that this last provision could only be applicable if a new parliament was elected in a regularly scheduled election. Disbanding the PLC in the absence of any potential for new elections meant a further consolidation of executive power over the political system and ensured that the Hamas PLC speaker would no longer be next in line in the event of a presidential vacancy.

---

59. Interviews with Palestinian legal activists (July 18, 2017, and July 30, 2017). Also see annual reports issued by the Jerusalem Legal Aid Center in 2016 and 2017.

60. Samer Anabtawi and Nathan Brown (January 18, 2019), "Why Mahmoud Abbas Dissolved the Palestinian Parliament—and What It Means for the Future," *Washington Post Monkey Cage*, https://www.washingtonpost.com/news/monkey-cage/wp/2019/01/18/heres-what-the-dissolution-of-the-legislative-council-means-for-the-future-of-palestinian-governance/

Within seven months of dissolving the PLC and enjoying the constitutional stamp of the SCC, President Abbas moved forward in using his decree power to reform the decaying and polarized Supreme Judicial Council and retailor its internal procedures by issuing two consecutive decrees. The first, Decree 16/2019, lowered the mandatory retirement age for all judges to sixty. The second and more wide reaching, Decree 17/2019, ordered the total dissolution of the Supreme Judicial Council, all committees of the High Court, and the Court of Appeals. The decree further mandated the formation of a transitional Supreme Judicial Council tasked with reforming and restructuring the entire judicial apparatus.

This transitional body was broadly authorized to reestablish all court committees as well as to make recommendations regarding removal of individual judges, force them into early retirement, or reassign them if doing so was deemed vaguely to "affect the reputation" and the "integrity" of the judiciary or the public's trust. Finally, the decree instructed the newly formed transitional Supreme Judicial Council to begin preparing modifications to the Law of the Judicial Authority of 2002.

The effects of these decrees were immediately clear: nothing less than a purge that effectuated the regime's goal of bringing the regular courts in line. The decrees ended the tenure of fifty-two judges (including all thirty-five from the High Court) and sent them to retirement—roughly a quarter of all sitting judges. The decrees were thus described by legal activists as a "massacre of the judiciary" on par with the same named event in Egyptian judicial history. Many judges chose to call on the president directly to reverse course, though roughly sixteen judges chose to appeal the decrees before the SCC despite its pro-regime record.

And the SCC replied with two seemingly contradictory rulings almost simultaneously. The first appeared to give the regime a defeat when it struck down the president's first decree, reinstating all fifty-two judges who were sent to early retirement. But the second upheld the president's second decree, which allowed the president to dissolve judicial bodies, remove judges, and form a transitional judicial council to radically reconfigure the judicial establishment. This second decision not only gave the president all the structural changes he had made to subordinate the judiciary; it also undermined the first decision since it upheld the president's authority to remove judges arbitrarily based on the recommendation of the transitional Supreme Judicial Council. And within just three days of this SCC ruling, nineteen of the reinstated judges were simply removed once again on the basis of Decree 17/2019.

The rulings of the SCC, along with a series of presidential decrees modifying core Palestinian institutions (such as a new social security law and a cybercrime law), have piled on in the absence of potential veto players outside the executive. Fatah's main rival, Hamas, lacks political currency in the West Bank, other PLO factions are merely symbolic opposition, and civil society watchdogs have lost much of their influence among donor fatigue and international forces giving up on reforms in Palestine and the peace process.

It is precisely in this political context, where defendants of autonomous enclaves within the PA have faded, that the regime sought to consolidate and complete the centralization of power around the executive. The gradual death of the legislature and the decay of a judicial establishment that was poorly institutionalized from the start paved the path for unchecked regime dominance over Palestinian state institutions. The Palestinian SCC thus serves as a warning to courts that fail to establish linkages to societal actors or to find allies among other state institutions, all the while dealing with insufficient resources, under-capacity, and little institutional sense of self. Neither internal nor mission autonomy is ever guaranteed under authoritarianism, and failing to find strengths outside of the regime proper can have desultory effects.

Conclusion: Autonomy (Sometimes) in an Unlikely Setting

Through its exploration of constitutional courts in Egypt and Palestine, this chapter has assessed when functionalist accounts of institutional activity do and do not hold, and it has fleshed out conditions in which other factors are needed to explain variation in the levels of institutional autonomy (internal and mission) that we observe in practice. We conclude that higher degrees of linkages and institutionalization enjoyed by constitutional courts enhance their capacity for achieving autonomy from authoritarian regimes. But when linkages and institutionalization are lacking, as in the case of the Palestinian SCC, functionalist logics are apt to carry more explanatory weight.

In Egypt, the meaningful degree of structural differentiation between regime and state in the political system provided more fertile soil for institutional autonomy to take root. In this context, the Egyptian SCC was able to gradually develop strong horizontal linkages to the broader judicial establishment and state apparatus, in addition to vertical linkages with legal advocacy groups and human rights NGOs in Egyptian society. A particularly important linkage of convenience emerged between the SCC and the military in the crisis juncture that followed the 2011 revolution, which created an opening for the SCC to secure firm protections of its institutional autonomy in the post-revolution constitution—but proved a double-edged sword since the post-2013 political crackdown meant that the alliance with the military exposed the court when its other backers in society were circumscribed. Finally, we also found that the Egyptian SCC was highly institutionalized, particularly in terms of coherence (within the court itself in addition to the surrounding judicial establishment being a deeply corporate and professionalized institution), complexity in the institutional structure of the Egyptian judiciary and the deep roots with which it has entrenched itself in the state, and the high level of adaptability it had displayed in rolling with the punches in the boxing fight that is Egyptian politics—sometimes finding itself hit squarely in the jaw but rarely staying down for long and always avoiding a knockout punch.

In Palestine, we initially observed budding linkages in the creation phase of the SCC (both to the parliament and to the international actors who cared about cultivating judicial autonomy and establishing firm checks on executive authority) but found that those linkages were shattered after Hamas's victory in the 2006 elections. With a rising Islamist political threat, the PLC and international actors both quickly adopted a defensive posture against Hamas and were more willing to grant concessions to President Abbas. Supportive state, societal, and international constituencies quickly grew less concerned with constraining executive authority than with preventing Hamas from gaining influence within the Palestinian state, and as a result, they were willing to allow the low degree of structural differentiation in Palestine to lapse yet even lower in order to ensure that a reliable (even if authoritarian) executive figure kept control of the reins of Palestinian politics. Consequently, the Palestinian SCC law was redrafted hastily, without consultation or input from other actors (whether in the international community or in civil society) in a way that linked the court very explicitly to the presidency and isolated it as a pariah in Palestine's legal and judicial community.

The Palestinian SCC was formally created before any infrastructure for the court was put in place (offices, staff, established operating procedures, judges with constitutional expertise), meaning that the SCC suffered from a severe lack of institutionalization off the bat—it fundamentally lacked institutional complexity, internal coherence (except to the extent that all judges were similarly handpicked by President Abbas), capacity for adaptability when confronting new challenges (as the court was even ill-equipped to confront the everyday task of adjudication that it was formally tasked with), and an internal sense of hierarchy (there was a chief judge to be sure, but that position was nowhere near as meaningful as in Egypt, where a long history of professional and corporate culture in the judiciary and collegial norms among judges lent it weight).

This context, in which the Palestinian SCC lacked independent linkages to state or societal constituencies and was poorly institutionalized (to the extent it was institutionalized at all), is what created an environment in which internal and mission autonomy were fundamentally lacking; and this is what drives us to conclude that a functionalist approach to authoritarian institutions works particularly well in the Palestinian case.

Through paired comparison of the Egyptian and Palestinian SCCs, we have seen how linkages and institutionalization can help foster internal and mission autonomy for authoritarian constitutional courts while their absence can debilitate the prospects for institutional autonomy.

The paired comparison shows how the Egyptian SCC has issued many controversial rulings and made many political judgments, some of which may have been miscalculations. But if it made political or legal misjudgments, they were its own mistakes. By contrast, the Palestinian judiciary resembles Mr. Stevens, the butler who reflects on his service to a British aristocrat who strongly favored appeasement of Germany in the 1930s in *The Remains of the Day*: "I can't even say I made my own mistakes. Really—one has to ask oneself—what dignity is there in that?"[61]

---

61. Kazuo Ishiguro (1989), *The Remains of the Day* (New York: Random House), 211.

CHAPTER 4

Parliaments

All would be well if everything said in the Duma remained within
its walls. Every word spoken, however, comes out in the next day's
papers, which are avidly read by everybody. In many places the
population is getting restive again. They are beginning to talk
about the land once more and are waiting to see what the Duma is
going to say on the question. I am getting telegrams from everywhere, petitioning me to order a dissolution, but it is too early for
that. One must let them do something manifestly stupid or mean,
and then—slap! And they [the Duma] are gone!

—Tsar Nicholas II, letter to his mother, the Dowager Empress,
March 29, 1907

Parliaments are endowed with extensive formal powers, even in most
authoritarian systems, yet they often fail to use them. Their strength on
paper, in terms of constitutional prerogatives and status as an independent
political branch, juxtaposes oddly with undeniably timid political practice.
Officially empowered legislative bodies—with obviously political tasks and
symbolism baked into their structure—should be a most likely case for
autonomous lawmaking, strident debate, political dissension, and power
politics even within the confines of authoritarian rule. Yet, we all know very
well that this rarely seems to be the case.

Although authoritarian parliaments do not live up to the institutional
promise of their formal powers, scholars have grown increasingly reticent
to dismiss them outright. It is true that some still maintain the old cliché
of the useless "rubber stamp," and some parliaments certainly deserve this
label. Even so, the sweeping use of this image is receding as researchers

now seek to better understand how authoritarian parliaments may aid, support, and bolster autocrats' goals or regime maintenance more broadly.[1]

But is supporting the regime a sufficient explanation for the existence and day-to-day activity of authoritarian parliaments? We do not deny that some parliaments can be rubber stamps[2] or serve general functions of regime maintenance. But that only strengthens our urge to explore variation—why some enjoy more autonomy over their operations and even develop a distinct sense of mission, while others do not.

This chapter argues that parliaments can realize *internal autonomy* to the degree that they have strong linkages and institutionalization. *Mission autonomy*, by contrast, is much harder for parliaments to achieve; and when it arises, it tends to be decidedly negative (manifesting through vetoes or obstructionism rather than a positive program). While we share the literature's interest in studying parliaments that are useful or threatening to autocrats, we are especially fascinated by those that are just plain annoying. To clarify how our theoretical framework applies to legislative assemblies, it is important to note that our core concepts (linkage, institutionalization, autonomy) operate through parliamentary realities in three distinctive ways.

First, the varying roles, interests, and coherence of political parties can either undermine or emphasize parliament as a locus for politics. While parties may litigate or be tied to religious officials, they are not central to our understanding of courts or religious establishments. But when we look at parliaments, parties are one of the first things we see (and when they are weak or absent, we notice it right away). Second, having an unstable churn of individual deputies over time makes parliaments' activity rely heavily on ambitious individuals and forthright leaders. Third, parliaments are marked in the way they combine formal stability and continuity in their constitutional prerogatives and relative

---

1. Milan W. Svolik (2012), *The Politics of Authoritarian Rule* (New York: Cambridge University Press). Jennifer Gandhi (2008), *Political Institutions under Dictatorship* (New York: Cambridge University Press). Ora John Reuter and Graeme B. Robertson (2015), "Legislatures, Cooptation, and Social Protest in Contemporary Authoritarian Regimes," *Journal of Politics* 77 (1): 235–48. Carles Boix and Milan W. Svolik (2013), "The Foundations of Limited Authoritarian Government: Institutions, Commitment, and Power-Sharing in Dictatorships," *Journal of Politics* 75 (2): 300–316. Joseph Wright and Abel Escribà-Folch (2012), "Authoritarian Institutions and Regime Survival: Transitions to Democracy and Subsequent Autocracy," *British Journal of Political Science* 42 (2): 283–309.

2. Barbara Geddes, Joseph Wright, and Erica Frantz (2018), *How Dictatorships Work: Power, Personalization and Collapse* (New York: Cambridge University Press), 137.

forms of institutionalization, with tremendous variability in the degree and nature of their linkages to social groups.

We therefore proceed to analyze authoritarian parliaments in five steps. The first section explains why these bodies must be examined in ways that move beyond prominent functionalist assumptions.

In the second section, we describe how autonomy, institutionalization, and linkage look in the distinctive context of parliamentary bodies. When identifying mission autonomy, for instance, we are not solely looking for a courageous or noble form of parliamentarism. The long-standing frustration among autocrats is that parliaments are simply a theater of pompous, corrupt, and venal politicians.[3] This image is not simply a figment of autocratic imaginations; it is often shared by publics, observers, and even parliamentarians themselves.[4] An authoritarian parliament with mission autonomy often acts more as a veto holder or hurdle rather than a venue for incubating a normative direction for governance. And this matters conceptually; a parliament of cats can be dysfunctional in all kinds of ways, but it can also realize impressive autonomy.

The third section empirically probes the history of parliaments in authoritarian systems. We show that parliaments are far more common participants in the authoritarian ecosystem than is usually acknowledged. Here we emphasize the evolutionary trajectory of parliaments as formerly quite diverse yet now increasingly isomorphic in structure, constitutional privilege, and procedural tools. And structural differentiation plays an important role in this evolutionary convergence, through which the varying assemblies built by monarchs, dictators, and oligarchies of past eras transformed into bodies with significant latent powers that most autocrats must manage today. This historical analysis will help elucidate how institutionalization and linkage relate to parliamentary autonomy in a broad, comparative perspective.

The fourth and fifth sections turn to a paired comparison of two more recently constructed parliaments operating in authoritarian settings. Our first case, the Russian State Duma under Vladimir Putin's long tenure, is generally deprived of linkage with society. Relying then on processes of institutionalization alone, the Duma exemplifies the common reality of authoritarian parliaments that have been largely deprived of air but, when

---

3. Philipp Köker (2020), "Why Dictators Veto: Legislation, Legitimation, and Control in Kazakhstan and Russia," *Democratization* 27 (2): 204–23.

4. Lisa Blaydes (2010), *Elections and Distributive Politics in Mubarak's Egypt* (New York: Cambridge University Press).

chanced to hold ambitious actors, can be roused to assert autonomy in unexpected ways.

Even more vibrantly, our second case is the sometimes raucous Kuwaiti parliament, which finds itself with thick vertical linkages to societal constituencies that provide a strong support base. But those same linkages have also forced MPs to career into crisis and division regularly, sometimes making cats seem like herd animals by comparison. While its institutionalization remains mixed, the Kuwaiti parliament possesses a toolbox of procedural privileges sufficient to advance mission autonomy. And here, it clearly illustrates the negative face of mission autonomy—one that offers frustration and annoyance above all. This forces us to reconcile our beliefs in the ostensible good of an autonomous parliament with a reality that autonomy does not always mean more virtuous or laudable politics. Bringing the political back into the authoritarian parliamentary chamber means that politics is back, not that agreement or collaboration, let alone progress, is guaranteed.

Parliaments, Authoritarianism, and Untenable Assumptions

We begin by pushing against questions that have become so salient that they still capture the analytical focus of much recent scholarship: *why* do parliaments exist in authoritarian systems, and how might these bodies benefit regimes that are unaccountable to democratic procedures?[5] We maintain that these questions are satisfactorily answered elsewhere[6] but remain somewhat beside the point for our inquiry because they pack in assumptions that parliaments are anomalies to be explained in nondemocracies and that they are consciously created to serve autocratic ends. Instead, we wish to address a second question: *when* are parliaments able to achieve autonomy, and *what* does that autonomy actually look like in practice?

Much research investigating these institutions posits that parliaments are brought into existence to solve some specific problem for an autocrat,

---

5. Gandhi (2008). Jennifer Gandhi and Adam Przeworski (2007), "Authoritarian Institutions and the Survival of Autocrats," *Comparative Political Studies* 49 (1): 3–30. Joseph Wright (2008), "Do Authoritarian Institutions Constrain? How Legislatures Affect Economic Growth and Investment," *American Journal of Political Science* 52 (2): 322–43.

6. For a detailed review of such work, see Scott Williamson and Beatriz Magaloni (2020), "Legislatures and Policy Making in Authoritarian Regimes," *Comparative Political Studies* 53 (9): 1515–43.

one usually exemplified in game theoretic language of coordination and commitment, payoffs and equilibria.[7] Sometimes patronage and management of the opposition are also involved.[8] The workings of the institution itself seem to capture less attention; a parliament is generally understood in terms of its presumed function for regime maintenance (why do rulers bother with one; they must have a reason!).[9] We therefore slip into a tendency to view authoritarian parliaments primarily as bodies that can soak up discontent, promote regime coordination, assuage allies, and on occasion provide a mechanical balance or check that is, at the end of the day, a useful function to the regime overall.[10] Yet, for those less reflexively attuned to the functions that parliaments serve for authoritarian regimes, the question of what the founders of a parliament were thinking is both difficult to answer and perhaps a bit odd.

It is difficult because parliaments are often far older creations than the background assumptions of functionalist design imply. And it is unlikely that we can explain what parliaments do over long periods of authoritarian rule simply by pointing to a logic that existed at one place in time in a long bygone era.

Asking why autocrats build parliaments is an odd question as well because it assumes there is something unusual about authoritarian assemblies. But most parliaments, especially the hoariest democratic ones, are a residue of a decidedly authoritarian past. Indeed, most parliaments predate democracy. Many Latin American legislatures were established by colonial-era independence movements that usually installed oligarchies and autocracies, not democracies. African assemblies are mostly the inheritance of authoritarian structures from the late colonial era. And a fully democratic Europe is the broad reality of no more than the last few decades and no longer—but many of the continent's parliaments trace their histories back centuries.

Furthermore, new regimes frequently settle in with a parliament remaining in place (or quickly reconvened as extraordinary measures give

---

7. Svolik 2012. Scott Gehlbach, Konstantin Sonin, and Milan W. Svolik (2016), "Formal Models of Nondemocratic Politics," *Annual Review of Political Science* 19:565–84.

8. Ellen Lust-Okar (2006), "Elections under Authoritarianism: Preliminary Lessons from Jordan," *Democratization* 13 (3): 456–71.

9. Alejandro Bonvecchi and Emilia Simison (2017), "Legislative Institutions and Performance in Authoritarian Regimes," *Comparative Politics* 49 (4): 521–44.

10. Gandhi and Przeworksi (2007). Jennifer Gandhi, Ben Noble, and Milan Svolik (2020), "Legislatures and Legislative Politics without Democracy," *Comparative Political Studies* 53 (9): 1359–79. Joan Timoneda (2020), "Institutions and Signals: How Dictators Consolidate Power in Times of Crisis," *Comparative Politics* 53 (1): 49–68.

way to the resumption of routine governance), as we have seen in Egypt, Malaysia, Zimbabwe, and elsewhere in just the last decade. A functionalist explanation might be that parliaments serve irreplaceable legitimation roles in some kind of dictator's playbook.[11] Yet that is quite a lot to hang on an institution that is otherwise viewed so cynically, not least by populations themselves.

Far better to leave our assumptions at the door and worry less about why a ruler may have decided to create, or beneficently allow the continued existence of, a parliament. In most cases from the nineteenth to the twenty-first centuries, parliaments *simply exist*, and regimes must deal with them in one way or another. Many try to leash them, as in many Central Asian countries,[12] or manipulate legislative chamber rules to thwart oppositional policy initiatives.[13] Some communist countries structurally bind their parliaments with paralleled party institutions, leading to quiescence as in China or deigning to suffer needling as in Vietnam.[14] Some countries let them run freer but attempt with varying success to manage their activity tactically, as in monarchies like Jordan and Morocco.[15] A few manage the occasional temporary closure, such as in Thailand periodically.[16] But very few country studies suggest a true, easy freedom to just cast aside a parliament, or to brutally crush one, outside of extreme circumstances beyond the realm of daily politics.

While the discipline has moved on from a dismissive view of all authoritarian parliaments as damp squibs filled with yes-men,[17] it remains largely

---

11. Scott Williamson (2021), "Elections, Legitimacy, and Compliance in Authoritarian Regimes: Evidence from the Arab World," *Democratization* 28 (8): 1483–504.

12. Esther Somfalvy (2020), *Parliamentary Representation in Central Asia: MPs Between Representing Their Voters and Serving an Authoritarian Regime* (Milton Park, UK: Routledge).

13. Regine Smyth, William Bianco, and Kwan Nok Chan (2019), "Legislative Rules in Electoral Authoritarian Regimes: The Case of Hong Kong's Legislative Council," *Journal of Politics* 81 (3): 892–905.

14. Edmund Malesky and Paul Schuler (2010), "Nodding or Needling: Analyzing Delegate Responsiveness in an Authoritarian Parliament," *American Political Science Review* 104 (3): 482–502.

15. Janine A. Clark (2006), "The Conditions of Islamist Moderation: Unpacking Cross-Ideological Cooperation in Jordan," *International Journal of Middle East Studies* 38 (4): 539–60.

16. Kevin Hewison (2007), "Constitutions, Regimes and Power in Thailand," *Democratization* 14 (5): 928–45.

17. Xiabo Lü, Mingxing Liu, and Feiyue Li (2020), "Policy Coalition Building in an Authoritarian Legislature: Evidence from China's National Assemblies (1983–2007)," *Comparative Political Studies* 53 (9): 1380–416. Ben Noble and Ekaterina Schulmann (2018), "Not Just a Rubber Stamp: Parliament and Lawmaking," in *The New Autocracy: Information, Politics, and Policy in Putin's Russia*, ed. Daniel Triesman (Washington, DC: Brookings Institution Press).

wedded to a view of parliaments as toolboxes containing various solutions to regime troubles.[18] Our view contends, rather, that parliaments are often simply institutional givens, relics of a distant past, and ones that are difficult to dislodge; they are just part of the floor plan of a regime's structural house. That they sometimes prove helpful and sometimes dysfunctional is due far more to their own gradual institutionalization and their linkages to societal constituencies.

What Does Parliamentary Autonomy Look Like, and Where Does It Come From?

Rather than asking why parliaments are created or exist, we investigate how they operate, how much autonomy they achieve, and under what circumstances. This section sets the stage by teasing out how our conceptions of autonomy, institutionalization, and linkage manifest in such uniquely political institutions.

While bill crafting and speechmaking may be the best-known qualities of modern parliaments, democratic or authoritarian, a great deal of parliamentary work is concerned in more day-to-day scrutiny, oversight, and the internal management of legislative agendas and budgetary structures.[19] The internal autonomy of authoritarian parliaments, thus, hinges on the body's ability to police its own members, decide its own operating procedures, and provide its own investigative, oversight, research, and assessment mechanisms.

Parliaments with internal autonomy often have significant protections and benefits for individual deputies as well. Parliamentary seats can confer discretionary budgets and immunity from prosecution. This makes the office valuable to businessmen and other elites who often encounter questionable situations, especially in authoritarian systems where restrictions on speech, corruption, and clientelism can be common problems.[20]

---

18. Gandhi, Noble, and Svolik (2020). Ben Noble (2020), "Authoritarian Amendments: Legislative Institutions as Intra-Executive Constraints in Post-Soviet Russia," *Comparative Political Studies* 53 (9): 1417–54. Paul Schuler (2020), "Position Taking or Position Ducking? A Theory of Public Debate in Single Party Legislatures," *Comparative Political Studies* 53 (9): 1493–524. Nam Kyu Kim and Jun Koga Sudduth (2021), "Political Institutions and Coups in Dictatorships," *Comparative Political Studies* 54 (9): 1597–628.

19. Joachim Wehner (2006), "Assessing the Power of the Purse: An Index of Legislative Budget Institutions," *Political Studies* 54 (6): 767–85.

20. Elena Semenova (2012), "Patterns of Parliamentary Representation and Careers in Ukraine: 1990–2007," *East European Politics and Societies* 26 (3): 538–60. Simon Wigley (2003),

But here we come to an odd aspect of parliamentary autonomy: it may be expressed not by the body's ability to act coherently but by allowing individual members a field to operate independently of regime wishes in ways that seem unruly and selfish to regime and observers alike. And that means the form that mission autonomy in parliaments takes tends to be trickier to analyze. The most obvious way a parliament can show mission autonomy is by forming a coherent legislative agenda independent of regime wishes, but that is a tall standard. Even in many democratic systems, after all, executive support from a parliamentary majority is a constitutional necessity. We will therefore need to be alert to more subtle signs of mission autonomy.

In highly controlled authoritarian parliaments, the mission is clear and hardly autonomous: to serve and remain "politically subservient to the executive or the regime party."[21] But for every loyal Turkmen or Cuban deputy, there are parliamentarians that egg on policy contestation or elite factionalism and even link with a tolerated opposition. We must therefore see mission autonomy more as a willingness to assert prerogatives—often with obstructive or frustrating outcomes that engender little happiness in any corners.

Given all this, we wish to draw attention to four of the more public paper powers that the vast majority of parliaments—authoritarian or otherwise—hold and are often a part of many notable expressions of mission autonomy. Indeed, legislation crafting is not always the sine qua non of parliamentary activity.[22]

First among all, *interpellation* is one of the most common forms of autonomous activity that authoritarian parliaments can summon. The parliamentary privilege—wielded by individual deputies or party blocs—of forcing government officials to account for their actions in person to the legislative plenary or a committee is both a politically symbolic and an effectively scrutinizing tactic.[23] Unfriendly interpellation can embarrass executive officials, force unwelcome policy clarifications, and even cause

---

"Parliamentary Immunity: Protecting Democracy or Protecting Corruption?" *Journal of Political Philosophy* 11 (1): 23–40.

21. Gandhi, Noble, and Svolik (2020), 1364.

22. Svitlana Chernykh, David Doyle, and Timothy J. Power (2017), "Measuring Legislative Power: An Expert Reweighting of the Fish-Kroenig Parliamentary Powers Index," *Legislative Studies Quarterly* 42 (2): 295–320. Eric Kerrouche (2006), "The French Assemblée Nationale: The Case of a Weak Legislature?" *Journal of Legislative Studies* 12 (3–4): 336–65.

23. Matti Wiberg (1995), "Parliamentary Questioning: Control by Communication," in *Parliaments and Majority Rule in Western Europe*, ed. Herbert Döring (Frankfurt: Campus).

autocrats to doubt the capabilities of their own ministerial agents.[24] Malaysian parliamentarians have been quite effective in using this tool, even causing regime confrontations by overloading the government with hostile questioning. And our case study of the Kuwaiti parliament shows interpellation to be a repeated favorite of the fractious deputy corpus, which has brought down powerful figures including members of the ruling family.

Second, *procedural obstruction* tactics form the backbone of even further regime frustrations. From filibusters to quorum-denial tactics, the name of the game here has always been delay, embarrassment, and symbolic contestation.[25] The Ukrainian parliament under Viktor Yanukovych saw repeated plenary disruption, causing raucous scenes that comically undermined regime efforts at communicating a sense of national unity and stability. Plenary fisticuffs from the Turkish parliament under Erdogan to the Peruvian Congress under Fujimori; quorum-denial attempts in Iraq, Ethiopia, Cameroon, and Hong Kong; and speaking filibusters from midcentury South Korea to nineteenth-century Habsburg Austria are all additional examples. Our case of the Russian State Duma likewise found itself faced with disruptive "Italian strikes," local parlance for quorum-denial tactics, in 2012 during a larger period of political disturbance.

Third, in a very different way, autonomy can be expressed through exuberant, *active amendment* or *law proposition* by loyalists that may or may not be welcome to the regime.[26] This is a far more constructive form of mission autonomy, often taken by deputies seeking to make a name for themselves. From excited Pentecostal Ugandan deputies pushing an internationally embarrassing bill criminalizing homosexuality to Russian deputies suggesting returning the title of tsar to the head of state, there can be considerable efflorescence of lawmaking and law amending among MPs well within the remit of regime loyalty. This form of active parliamentary loyalism is only negative in its overexcitedness (moral laws in particular are

---

24. Miklós Sebők, Csaba Molnár, and Bálint György Kubik (2017), "Exercising Control and Gathering Information: The Functions of Interpellations in Hungary (1990–2014)," *Journal of Legislative Studies* 23 (4): 465–83. Hironori Yamamoto (2007), *Tools for Parliamentary Oversight: A Comparative Study of 88 National Parliaments* (Geneva: Inter-Parliamentary Union).

25. Rory Treux (2020), "Authoritarian Gridlock? Understanding Delay in the Chinese Legislative System," *Comparative Political Studies* 53 (9): 1455–92. Lauren C. Bell (2018), "Obstruction in Parliaments: A Cross-National Perspective," *Journal of Legislative Studies* 24 (4): 499–525. Gregory J. Wawro and Eric Schickler (2010), "Legislative Obstructionism," *Annual Review of Political Science* 13:297–319.

26. Gerrit Krol (2021), "Amending Legislatures in Authoritarian Regimes: Power Sharing in Post-Soviet Eurasia," *Democratization* 28 (3): 562–82.

touchy) but otherwise is yet another way in which legislators make themselves felt in broader regime politics.

Fourth, autonomy can manifest through the *dismissal* or *veto* of executive-sponsored bills. In recent years we have seen this in Uganda when faced with constitutional changes that would have undone term limits for the autocrat as well as in Venezuela when opposition forces sought to undo the "Bolivarian revolution." In many cases, parliamentary vetoes are quixotic and short-lived. Yet the fact that an attempt at autonomy was made is perhaps all the more striking, given these seriously unconducive institutional environments.

Institutionalization and Linkages in a Parliamentary Setting

Using our Huntingtonian framework, institutionalization in a parliament is reflected in its adaptability, complexity, hierarchy, and coherence. Long-lasting parliaments are adaptable as regimes face divergent crises, the rise of new elites, and perhaps even the threat of collapse. Parliaments that have resilient structures supporting more complex arrangements of interests have the capacity to intervene in a wider set of issues. Similarly, hierarchical institutions may better coordinate their activities.[27] Coherence—likely the most difficult task for their ever-changing memberships—allows for more concerted effort, be it by oppositions pursuing change or by assertive loyalists promoting their own interests.

What is distinct about an authoritarian parliament is that it occupies the odd place of being the most societally linked institution in an authoritarian regime that otherwise does not rely on truly broad, sustained public accountability to survive. Linkages between individual deputies or blocs to social constituencies can and do develop in authoritarian systems,[28] and such linkages may sometimes even serve to "threaten dictatorial rule rather than insulate it."[29] Particularly in countries with higher overall levels of structural differentiation (between rulers, regimes, and the state apparatus), horizontal linkages between parliaments and other state bodies can also be abundant. A ministry knowing that a certain group of deputies is

---

27. Thomas Diefenbach (2013), *Hierarchy and Organisation: Toward a General Theory of Hierarchical Social Systems* (Milton Park, UK: Routledge).

28. Marwa Shalaby and Abdullah Aydogan (2020), "Elite-Citizen Linkages and Issue Congruency under Competitive Authoritarianism," *Parliamentary Affairs* 73 (1): 66–88.

29. Ae Sil Woo and Courtenay R. Conrad (2019), "The Differential Effects of 'Democratic' Institutions on Dissent in Dictatorships," *Journal of Politics* 81 (2): 456–70.

reliable can mean a great deal, while members of the military or judiciary who trust parliamentary figures can go a long way to resolving information and coordination problems.[30] A convenient alliance between the parliament and other state institutions can make regimes reluctant to target these bodies, which might not be the case if that body was the only sticking point in an otherwise structurally undifferentiated system.

Yet vertical linkages with public constituencies are far more common, given the electoral connection that usually exists even in highly restrictive contexts.[31] Societal linkages tend to establish around co-ethnic groups, socioeconomic classes, regional publics, religious communities, businesses, and civil society organizations.[32] Such linkages are not universal realities, nor are they constant over time.

To grapple with such complexities, we reorient our study and begin with an empirical analysis investigating the evolution of parliamentary bodies in global perspective. Before adding detail with our case studies of Russia and Kuwait, we will trace the trajectory of parliaments over time and highlight the accumulation of a surprising number of powerful (if often latent) prerogatives among most parliaments throughout the world. By starting our empirical discussion with the wider history of representative assemblies, we are able to emphasize useful continuities: from classical Mediterranean civilization, to medieval pluralism, to the coherence and significant institutional isomorphism across parliaments over the last two centuries. Our aim here is to demystify the muddled relationship between representative bodies and authoritarianism, showing their respective histories to be much more intertwined than conventional wisdoms might suggest.

Assemblies, Diets, and Parliaments:
Historical Analysis of a Deep Authoritarian Legacy

When we view parliaments purely as elected bodies that write laws and practice some degree of executive oversight, we capture their current paper purpose almost everywhere they now exist but also erase much of their his-

---

30. Noble (2020).

31. Michaela Collord (2021), "Pressuring MPs to Act: Parliament, Organized Interests and Policymaking in Uganda and Tanzania," *Democratization* 28 (4): 723–41.

32. Didier Ruedin (2009), "Ethnic Group Representation in a Cross-National Comparison," *Journal of Legislative Studies* 15 (4): 335–54. David Judge (1998), "Parliament and Interest Representation," in *Parliament and Pressure Politics*, ed. Michael Rush (New York: Oxford University Press).

tory. At their founding, many parliaments had none of these characteristics and developed them only through bouts of contentious struggle. Although revisiting an extensive history of how legislative institutions evolved may seem to be a departure from a study focused on contemporary authoritarian regimes, we believe that a better empirical understanding of the evolution of parliaments—almost always under authoritarian rule until the great waves of democratization—is vital for two reasons.

First, we seek to show the exceedingly diverse origins of authoritarian parliaments and their under-remarked but seemingly inexorable trajectory of convergence toward the similar set of assemblies that are ubiquitous today. It does us little good to say that modern parliaments are oddly alike in their makeup without assessing why and how they became so. Our discussion below explains a great deal of why modern authoritarian regimes often have such strangely empowered parliamentary bodies lying within their bounds and existing as a latent institutional threat.[33]

Second, we wish to expand our historical understanding of autonomy in authoritarian parliaments to better probe diversity in their behavior. In fact, we will discover that some of the more seemingly idiosyncratic or anomalous activities of modern authoritarian parliaments have quite an old family resemblance to regimes predating modern social science's usual scope conditions.

To that end, it benefits our inquiry to focus not only on the "helpfulness" or "functionality" of authoritarian parliaments but also on their potential for dysfunction and vexing troublesomeness, which is far more commonly historically and critically underemphasized in research on authoritarianism today. Representative bodies have long been the bane of efficient and rational autocratic governance, yet they have lived on and continue to do so. Contextual explication will lift away much of this strangeness that underlies this observation.

New Parliament, Same as the Old Parliament

At the opening of this chapter, we referred to parliaments and legislatures interchangeably, an elision that may escape notice for many readers unless we draw attention to it. This is due to an often unremarked convergence of institutional forms among manifold kinds of assemblies, consultative struc-

---

33. Felix Wiebrecht (2021), "Between Elites and Opposition: Legislatures' Strength in Authoritarian Regimes," *Democratization* 28 (6): 1075–94.

Parliaments · 147

tures, representative gatherings, and lawmaking bodies throughout the last millennium. If we look backward, we quickly see that not all assemblies are popular or representative; not all legislate; and not all legislative bodies are even elected. Yet they all inform the ways in which modern authoritarian parliaments operate and dance around the strictures of autocratic desires.

What we may generically term "popular assemblies" have existed in a wide array of forms from at least the era of classical Greece onward. Tribal Germany and Afghanistan knew assemblies of some kind. Varying forms of context-specific assemblies under autocratic rule have been quite common across the centuries, especially in Europe and the broader Mediterranean world.

The classical Greek tradition that gives political theory much of its basic vocabulary included several forms of rule that required the regular meeting of peers in a formal assembly, ranging from the idealized civic "polity" to "aristocratic" rule based on collecting the most virtuous men together for the good of the state.[34] Republican Rome famously offered a form of exclusionary rule by urban, oligarchic families in a decision-making body as the key institutional focal point for centuries.[35] Even under the autocracy of the Caesars—a seminal form of authoritarianism that gave us the term "Caesarism" to describe plebiscitary dictatorship—senatorial assemblies occasionally asserted themselves to voice elite discontent with imperial policy.[36]

Representative assemblies were a part of the Germanic tribal tradition as acclamatory sites for acknowledging leadership and consenting to major elite decisions.[37] As feudal states accumulated power in the early medieval period, a wide variety of European polities found themselves regularly

---

34. Plato (1943), *Plato's The Republic* (New York: Basic Books).

35. Karl J. Hölkeskamp (2010), *Reconstructing the Roman Republic: An Ancient Political Culture and Modern Research* (Princeton: Princeton University Press). Alexander Yakobson (2010), "Traditional Political Culture and the People's Role in the Roman Republic," *Historia: Zeitschrift für Alte Geschichte* 59 (3): 282–302. Eric M. Orlin (2002), *Temples, Religion, and Politics in the Roman Republic* (Leiden, Netherlands: Brill). Olivier Hekster (2015), *Emperors and Ancestors: Roman Rulers and the Constraints of Tradition* (New York: Oxford University Press).

36. Alexander Yakobson (2012), "Political Rhetoric in China and in Imperial Rome: The Persuader, the Ruler, the Audience," *Extrême-Orient Extrême-Occident* 34:195–204. John Bagnell Bury (2014), *The Constitution of the Later Roman Empire* (New York: Cambridge University Press).

37. Andrew T. Young (2015), "From Caesar to Tacitus: Changes in Early Germanic Governance circa 50 BC–50 AD," *Public Choice* 164 (3–4): 357–78. Chris Wickham (2017), "Consensus and Assemblies in the Romano-Germanic Kingdoms: A Comparative Approach," *Vorträge und Forschungen* 82:389–426.

summoning elite assemblies and institutionalizing those meetings into permanent bodies.[38] Courts of rabbis known as Sanhedrin took on judicial and oversight roles in ancient Israel. Zoroastrian Mehestan Assemblies in the Parthian Empire brought clan and religious figures of importance together, most notably for succession difficulties. Consultative organs in various Middle Eastern polities acted in a similar fashion to Germanic and early feudal assemblies to discuss, acclaim, and accept elite decisions.

In many cases, these bodies metamorphized from intermittent gatherings to regular, standing councils tasked with adjudicating claims of sovereignty and legal responsibility.[39] The density and power of urban and proto-industrial centers were the primary drivers of rising parliamentary power vis-à-vis the sovereign, one that would develop into an essentially modern understanding of the structural place of legislatures by the nineteenth century.[40] And yet we must stress that all of this remained fundamentally authoritarian according to prevailing definitions of the term. Even so, proto-parliaments thrived in such an era.

The tendency toward a fissiparous patchwork of feudal warlords, noble claimants, and high fiscal requirements for taxes in Europe brought collective assemblies to a more formal institutional plane.[41] Those premodern parliaments, when effective, were defined by their peculiarly high linkage to feudal notables, urban oligarchs, or representatives of key social organizations like the Catholic Church or trade guilds. While their powers were often less institutionalized and contingent on the balance of military, monetary, or societally necessary forces at a given time, they remained stable parts of the authoritarian ecosystem.

This trajectory of assemblies and diets as part of medieval and early

---

38. Jan Luiten Van Zanden, Eltjo Buringh, and Maarten Bosker (2012), "The Rise and Decline of European Parliaments, 1188–1789," *Economic History Review* 65 (3): 835–61. David Stasavage (2010), "When Distance Mattered: Geographic Scale and the Development of European Representative Assemblies," *American Political Science Review* 104 (4): 625–43. Michael Graves (2014), *The Parliaments of Early Modern Europe: 1400–1700* (Milton Park, UK: Routledge. Wim P. Blockmans (1978), "A Typology of Representative Institutions in Late Medieval Europe," *Journal of Medieval History* 4 (2): 189–215.

39. Duncan Hardy (2018), *Associative Political Culture in the Holy Roman Empire: Upper Germany, 1346–1521* (New York: Oxford University Press).

40. Scott F. Abramson and Carles Boix (2019), "Endogenous Parliaments: The Domestic and International Roots of Long-Term Economic Growth and Executive Constraints in Europe," *International Organization* 73 (4): 793–837.

41. Gary W. Cox (2017), "Political Institutions, Economic Liberty, and the Great Divergence," *Journal of Economic History* 77 (3): 724–55. Walter Scheidel (2019), *Escape from Rome: The Failure of Empire and the Road to Prosperity* (Princeton: Princeton University Press).

modern authoritarian rule reached a pinnacle in Great Britain, where a permanently gathering parliament assumed greater roles in governance and critically took control of financial powers by the eighteenth century.[42] The collapse of absolutist, ancien régime states, beginning with the French Revolution, put the transformation of older assemblies into full parliamentary and legislative bodies firmly in the minds of nineteenth-century rulers, reformers, and revolutionaries from then on.[43] Nation-states born after the midpoint of the nineteenth century—whether democratic or authoritarian—almost always instituted such legislative bodies in their constitutions, sometimes building upon preexisting assemblies and sometimes inventing new ones.

Authoritarianism and Parliamentarism in Coexistence

Parliaments have continued to be an integral feature of authoritarian states in the modern era. Oddly enough, the rise of parliamentarism[44] in Europe was seen by practitioners at the time as explicitly opposed or generally unsuited for mass democracy.[45] Carl Schmitt's philosophy of authoritarian politics, for instance, treated parliamentary institutions as both distinct and completely antithetical to democracy.[46] This curious and long-standing antidemocratic view of parliaments is instructive as we seek analogs to the overwhelming presence of parliaments in modern authoritarian systems. Indeed, the rise of parliaments, as well as the older history of assemblies working alongside thoroughly authoritarian rule, gives us a longer genealogy that underlines the natural compatibility of these odd bodies with nondemocratic rulers and regimes.

---

42. Douglass C. North and Barry R. Weingast (1989), "Constitutions and Commitment: The Evolution of Institutions Governing Public Choice in Seventeenth-Century England," *Journal of Economic History* 49 (4): 803–32. Daron Acemoglu and James A. Robinson (2006), *Economic Origins of Dictatorship and Democracy* (New York: Cambridge University Press).

43. Susan Scarrow (2006), "The Nineteenth-Century Origins of Modern Political Parties: The Unwanted Emergence of Party-Based Politics," in *Handbook of Party Politics*, ed. Richard S. Katz and William Crotty (Thousand Oaks: Sage).

44. That is, the transformation of many European states' political systems into ones in which the legislative assembly was formally the most powerful actor among all state institutions, where high-ranking ministers sat inside the legislature, and under which there was a system of competing political parties.

45. William Selinger (2019), *Parliamentarism: From Burke to Weber* (New York: Cambridge University Press).

46. Carl Schmitt (1926), *Die geistesgeschichtliche Lage des heutigen Parlamentarismus* (München and Leipzig: Duncker & Humblot). This antidemocratic view of parliaments must be read with Schmitt's Nazi Party affiliation in mind.

The union of parliamentary bodies and authoritarian rule in the first generations of our modern world was no accident. The proliferation of new classes in European society—bourgeois merchants, educated elites, and reactionary church figures—found the authoritarian regimes of the nineteenth and early twentieth centuries unwilling to supply them places in governing institutions, so representation in parliaments became attractive. Such actors wanted a political voice, but they also wished to leave many others out in the cold. Many monarchs grudgingly accepted parliaments to corral otherwise explosive forces into contained fora.[47]

Co-optation and the inclusion of sociopolitical divisions in representative assemblies became a problem for monarchs to manage, with the alternative being a system closed to such voices—and perhaps rendered brittle by such heavy exclusion. This stage in the evolution of parliamentary institutions can in fact be understood in broadly functionalist terms, at least until the bodies quickly outran the intentions of their creators. Regimes and rulers bargained with important groups; those bargains were then encoded in the rules for selecting parliamentary deputies as well as institutionalizing their authority.

The outcome was not simply a function of regime intent. Indeed, many of the authoritarian parliaments of that era were particularly notable for their dysfunction and the trouble they caused to unaccountable monarchs and ministers as well as the frustration they gave to many hopeful actors seeing them as avenues of change. Parliaments sitting under the authoritarian regimes of pre–World War I Europe were often fractious, obstructionist, and self-regarding—not a far cry from many electoral authoritarian regimes today. They were constantly pushing for more autonomy, more powers to review budgets, to interpellate or impeach ministers, to elect the government, even to constrain monarchical authority. Party oppositions demanded time to speak, denounce, and represent, while pro-government factions wanted to show their worth and loyalty, gaining privileges for themselves and the institution they ran while doing so.

To be bold in our claims, the nineteenth-century model of obstreperous authoritarian parliaments fits exceedingly well with instances of parliamentary autonomy and annoyance that we observe in the twenty-first century. The saga of the unaccountable monarch versus the institutionalizing parliament of the nineteenth century even holds parallels to many presiden-

---

47. Lothar A. Höbelt (1986), "The Delegations: Preliminary Sketch of a Semi-Parliamentary Institution," *Parliaments, Estates and Representation* 6 (2): 149–54.

Parliaments · 151

tialist authoritarian regimes today. In both, parliaments have found themselves fighting or acquiescing to rule by executives constitutionally distinct and distant from themselves yet close enough to strike at it nonetheless.[48] And in this legacy, we see the distant seeds of structural differentiation between state parliamentary bodies and authoritarian rulers plant roots.

The twentieth century was quite destructively instructive for parliamentary studies in Europe: instead of abolishing the powers of parliaments, new authoritarian ideologies found creativity in developing single- and dominant-party systems to occupy legislative chambers. The new solution to the problem of feckless obstructionism and divisive debate that had plagued authoritarian parliaments of the prior era was technologically directed theater. Here, again, we find that functionalist logics have significant empirical traction in many cases, particularly where parliaments maintained a great deal of their formal power but were strategically managed by regimes through extreme party organization and discipline.

But for every acclamatory and propagandistic body in the ideal typical fascist or Communist mold, there were several that flirted with genuine, corporatist representation within nested and interlocking legislative institutions.[49] This was tried in a variety of ways across Europe and Latin America as different countries experimented with parliamentary sections or whole institutional chambers populated by—and with direct linkages to—farmers, industrial workers, business owners, educators, mothers, and many other social groups.[50] Moreover, the failure of German and Italian fascism, alongside the single-party systems that had arisen in the Baltics and Poland, undermined many of the institutional arrangements that had led to twentieth-century understandings of the "rubber-stamp" legislature.[51]

---

48. José Antonio Cheibub (2007), *Presidentialism, Parliamentarism, and Democracy* (New York: Cambridge University Press). Huang-Ting Yan (2020), "Does the Constitution Matter? Semi-Presidentialism and the Origin of Hegemonic Personalist Regimes," *International Political Science Review* 41 (3): 365–84.

49. António Costa Pinto, ed. (2017), *Corporatism and Fascism: The Corporatist Wave in Europe* (Milton Park, UK: Taylor & Francis). Alexander De Grand (1991), "Cracks in the Facade: The Failure of Fascist Totalitarianism in Italy 1935–9," *European History Quarterly* 21 (4): 515–35.

50. Perhaps most famously, Mussolini's Chamber of Fasces and Corporations, inaugurated in 1939 as a means to appease rising discontent, included, as separate corporate categories of representation, schools, civil servants, disabled veterans, nondisabled veterans, Olympic committee members, the National Opera, artists, and workers (and Albanian Fascists specifically), among others and alongside Italian Fascist Party members proper.

51. Rein Taagepera (1974), "Civic Culture and Authoritarianism in the Baltic States, 1930–1940," *East European Quarterly* 7 (4): 407–12. Vytas Stanley Vardys (1974), "The Baltic States in Search of Their Own Political Systems," *East European Quarterly* 7 (4): 399–406.

Of course, it is undeniable that the reputation and autonomy of parliaments reached a nadir in the immediate post–World War II period, as many of the era's dictatorships sought to avoid or dominate them entirely, often with short-term success but also frequently with longer-term failures. The impression of abject subordination, however unevenly it applied to real parliamentary bodies, was enough to obscure from scholars the way in which authoritarianism historically incorporated a wide range of experiences with parliamentary institutions.

Trajectories of Modern Authoritarian Parliaments: (Re)Converging on Common Wisdoms

While authoritarian parliaments were still surprisingly widespread in the twentieth century, they were often weak. And they were weak at a time when many scholars were formulating their ideas about authoritarianism. Despite the existence of representative assemblies with manifold formats and autonomy in a wide variety of authoritarian regimes over the centuries, the first and second generations of postwar political science were characterized by a comparative lack of active nondemocratic parliaments. The limited number of viable authoritarian parliaments in the mid-twentieth century—perhaps an idiosyncrasy of the postwar period—veiled the near ubiquity of often assertive parliaments as part and parcel of authoritarian governance. Even at the height of single-party systems, parliaments were usually still present—just eerily quiet. This momentary quietude meant that parliaments ended up being consigned to the margins of authoritarian politics by some of the most influential scholars of the period.

Communist regimes, while building peoples' congresses and supreme soviets into their institutional architecture in the 1930s and 1940s, also helped spread the image of authoritarian parliaments as simple rubber stamps by systematically undermining their political role through the remarkable innovation of the monolithic party state.[52] Juntas seizing power in Latin America, sub-Saharan Africa, and the Mediterranean basin sometimes prorogued parliaments for extended periods of time, seeing them as part of the problem of social pluralism and discontent, not the solution as in days of old.[53] And aspiring dominant-party or single-party regimes

---

52. J. Arch Getty (1991), "State and Society under Stalin: Constitutions and Elections in the 1930s," *Slavic Review* 50 (1): 18–35.

53. Michael L. Mezey (1983), "The Functions of Legislatures in the Third World," *Legisla-*

of the postcolonial, nationalist variety often tried their hand at reducing legacy legislatures into mere bureaucratic bodies or advisory councils.[54]

The marginalization of authoritarian parliaments in much twentieth-century scholarship has an empirical and context-specific justification, but it also led scholars to miss the very curious path of convergence in form that all parliaments have seen in the last half century. While a German tribal leader of the first century might have found the procedures, structure, and customs of the Roman Senate totally unfamiliar; yet a Japanese MP today would likely face only a language barrier to understand what happens on the floor of the Jordanian parliament. Interpellation, procedural rules for plenary debates, committee hearings, voting mechanisms, and procedures for recording minutes all fall within narrow bounds today. This emergent, modern model has been quite stable, despite the sizeable differences among the various parliamentary and proto-parliamentary bodies discussed above.

The homologous nature of parliaments goes beyond procedures. Largely gone (or surviving only in vestigial form) are the hereditary chambers, the restricted franchises, the curious corporatist curiae, and the sectoral interest chambers. Instead, we now see a singular format with a few optional bits that can sometimes be mixed and matched in different settings: unicameral or bicameral chambers; constitutional power to accept, reject, or modify budgets; rights of bill initiation and bill amendment; powers of ministerial interpellation, and confidence and no-confidence powers regarding ministers and a prime ministerial office (should it exist); and significant salaries, privileges, and criminal immunity benefits to parliamentarians.

And the modern model's constituent elements provide significant latent formal abilities, which are now almost generic aspects of most extant parliaments and provide them considerable constitutional centrality and potential for autonomous activity, even when not activated or actualized. Thus, most modern authoritarian states do not create, but simply live with, parliamentary institutions, ones generally gifted to them by recent or ancient history with formal powers and prerogatives that can be quite impressive when used.

---

tive Studies Quarterly 8 (4): 511–50. Stephen G. Xydis (1974), "Coups and Countercoups in Greece, 1967–1973 (with postscript)," *Political Science Quarterly* 89 (3): 507–38.

54. Raymond F. Hopkins (1979), "The Influence of the Legislature on Development Strategy: The Case of Kenya and Tanzania," in *Legislatures and Development*, ed. Joel Smith and Lloyd D. Musolf (Durham: Duke University Press). B. S. Sharma (1965), "Parliamentary Government in Uganda," *International Studies* 7 (3): 448–56.

But they are rarely used to the fullest—and sometimes are used little at all. This is what draws our attention.

Moving to Specific Cases

While a glance at history reveals how ubiquitous and unpuzzling the presence of parliaments is in authoritarian contexts, we still require a careful empirical examination to trace how these bodies gain and lose autonomy across cases and over time. We thus turn to two case studies in order to more closely scrutinize how patterns of institutionalization and linkage affect the degrees of internal and mission autonomy achieved by authoritarian parliaments.

Looking first to Russia and the three-decade-old State Duma, we find a moderately institutionalized parliamentary body with weak linkages to society and a subservient relationship to other state organs. This has led it to stay quiescent for the first half of its lifespan under Vladimir Putin's long authoritarian tenure. Mission autonomy has been almost entirely absent, with a singular (and instructive) exception of surprising obstruction in the early 2010s.

Yet the Duma's internal autonomy has varied more widely. Long deprived of creative leadership, recent cohorts of parliamentary officers and striving parliamentarians have grabbed on to the extant, if dusty, powers of the body and have sought to go about strengthening aspects of its internal institutional makeup. The modern Duma remains subservient and loyalist to the increasingly personalized executive of Putin's regime, but it has also made efforts to increase its own internal autonomy and achieve new bureaucratic, if not political, victories.

A second case, the Kuwaiti National Assembly, provides a notable alternative that highlights the power of strong (and broadening) linkages to public constituencies despite considerable downward pressure by the unaccountable Kuwaiti amir and a regime that is monarchical at its core. Although the National Assembly was suspended twice for overeager activity that was perceived to be a fundamental threat to the royal regime, its critical links to powerful societal groups, its significant latent endowment of parliamentary powers, and its central place in Kuwaiti national identity have always returned the institution to its role in prominent politics.

Most interestingly, the disruptive and dynamic nature of the Kuwaiti parliament does not simply reflect logics of autocratic co-optation but suggests a clear but uneven evolutionary trajectory generally toward norms of greater activity, scrutiny, and sense of self. The assembly has grown to assume a clear role in Kuwait's authoritarian political system. With moderate institutionalization derived from its important formal powers and a coherent overarching sense of membership (if not coherent factional interests), Kuwaiti MPs' high linkage to very different segments of society mean that the parliament's mission autonomy can grow quite strong. Yet this remains a negative form of mission autonomy, creating a fractious and active parliament noted more for the obstructive frustration it can inflict than its ability to pursue a positive sense of political or institutional vision.

The Russian State Duma: Decay, Sclerosis, and Bureaucratizing Institutionalization

We turn to our first case study to explore especially the role that *institutionalization*—and lack thereof—plays in the maintenance and development of institutional autonomy for authoritarian parliaments.[55] Tracing the often disheartening ebbs and flows of internal and mission autonomy in the Russian parliament's lower house, the State Duma (Gosudarstvennaya Duma), we find a state institution that has never fully risen to the occasion as a bastion for forming and expressing the will of the people or in charting its own careful destiny within authoritarian confines. Indeed, one constant has been a sense of its irritating distance from daily concerns.

The desultory state of the Duma's mission autonomy for much of the Putin era reflects an underlying and profound failure to develop linkages with social groups and the mass public. At the system level, a key reason for this failure is the low overall degree of structural differentiation, which isolates much of Russian society from a state apparatus that appears to be little more than an extension of the authoritarian executive. Russia is marked in the tremendous degree to which the reigning personalist autocrat erodes boundaries between ruler, regime, and state through strong-

---

55. The material in this section is based in part on research conducted by one of the authors (Waller) in the Russian Federation in 2012 and 2016-2017. In this regard, see Julian G. Waller (2023), "Mimicking the Mad Printer: Legislating Illiberalism in Post-Soviet Eurasia," *Problems of Post-Communism* 70 (3): 225–40; Julian G. Waller (2022), *Beyond the Rubber-Stamp: Essays on Parliamentary Bodies Under Authoritarianism*, PhD diss., George Washington University; and Julian G. Waller (2021), "Elites and Institutions in the Russian Thermidor: Regime Instrumentalism, Entrepreneurial Signaling, and Inherent Illiberalism," *Journal of Illiberalism Studies* 1 (1): 1–23.

arm and patronage tactics used to pack the state apparatus and central leadership group with cronies loyal to Putin (as an individual) above all else.[56]

We will, thus, observe how fluctuation in the Duma's autonomy has occurred within a relatively narrow range—one that is bounded by consistently feeble linkages between the parliament and broader society but with stronger linkages to other state bodies (themselves hardly insulated from the ruler) developing over time as the parliament has become further embedded in the authoritarian ecosystem of the Putin regime.

Yet even in the absence of strong societal linkages, the Russian parliament has still varied considerably in the degree to which it attracts public attention, generally as a function of changes in its internal autonomy. Those changes are evidenced today in a greater centrality in the lawmaking and approving process, a reassertion of formal, symbolic prerogatives vis-à-vis the government, and a hierarchical internal structure headed by a small group of fairly ambitious elites willing to make a name for themselves within the body—at least for the time being. Furthermore, when moments of notable mission autonomy have cropped up within the Duma, as they did in the 2012–16 parliamentary term to the great embarrassment and frustration of the regime, it was due to the interaction of moderate institutionalization with furtive attempts by ambitious MPs to harness and channel what few linkages did exist.

We argue in this section that variation in autonomy for the Russian parliament can be largely explained by dynamics of de- and reinstitutionalization on the part of the body itself, set against the backdrop of latent structural powers derived from the Duma's fairly recent construction along the lines of the standard convergence model of an empowered parliament. In fact, we use this case to illustrate situations when functionalist logics can have great merit, such as during the period of deinstitutionalization in the early and mid-2000s—a finding that aligns much with expectations that functionalism is most appropriate when linkage and institutionalization are weak.

We do not claim the Russian parliament to be an exemplar of energetic parliamentarism or consolidated authority but rather one whose operation and internal autonomy has varied, especially influenced by changing levels of institutionalization—a humble model that is in many ways quite common among contemporary authoritarian parliaments. By tracing how the

---

56. Steven M. Fish (2017), "The Kremlin Emboldened: What Is Putinism?" *Journal of Democracy* 28 (4): 61–75.

Duma has found some internal autonomy in odd pursuits of self-discipline and symbolic positioning, as well as short moments of frustrating mission autonomy, we will see both the promise and the pitfall of such bodies.

The Placeholder Parliament: Deinstitutionalizing the Duma

While many authoritarian parliaments have long pedigrees that have survived the turmoil of multiple regimes, the Russian experience entails a far sharper break from past practice. Built using a variation on the standard, modern parliamentary model, the Russian State Duma was consciously created in 1993 and has kept the same general format since then. Its predecessor chamber from the Soviet period, the Supreme Soviet, was specifically eschewed as institutional inheritance: its uncertainly vast yet rarely exercised constitutional powers; its classic communist layer-cake structure; and its long-standing membership were all unwelcome during the years of political transition. The reliance instead on French constitutional norms seemed more promising (notably to President Yeltsin, who saw only conflict with the Soviet-inherited body) and indeed gave the new parliament important latent institutional powers, ones that would be used frequently in the 1990s but then recede into the distance as forgotten memories of autonomy with the rise of the Putin regime in the 2000s.

The political regime in the Russian Federation has been nondemocratic for most of its post-Soviet history. Despite this, a good deal of institutional pluralism existed during the chaotic transition from communist rule in the 1990s. Russia initially carried over the political institutions of the Soviet constitution and the Gorbachev-era efforts at reforming that system. This institutional endowment, however, would only survive two years of tense, post-collapse politics before succumbing to crisis and being fundamentally reshaped—a sharp organizational break from the past that would provide much of the formal structure of Russian political institutions unto the present day.

The constitutional crisis in 1993 ultimately led to the abrogation of short-lived attempts at establishing structural differentiation between regime and state after the dissolution of the USSR; the Soviet-era constitutional court and legislature were shuttered, and full political power was seized by the Russian presidency, which then wrote a new constitution. This constitution provided for a legislature modeled on that of the French Fifth Republic, with legislative powers invested in both presidency and parliament as well as a prime minister responsible to the parliament but chosen by the president. While this constitution gave notable powers to the presidency, the new parliament remained a considerable thorn in the side of the government and held new authorities over the premiership that would become particularly troublesome. In addition, the assembly had all the standard privileges of a modern parliament, including deputy immunity, rights of legislative initiative, interpellation, and somewhat weak forms of no-confidence votes, as well as frameworks to develop committee structures, party blocs, and the like.[57]

In this way, the rapid turn from structural differentiation did not necessarily produce a concomitant lack of institutionalization in the new parliament—which instead was endowed with the standard, isomorphic procedural prerogatives that most parliaments (democratic and authoritarian) have enjoyed since the twentieth century. Over the course of the 1990s, the Duma consistently denied the government stable governing majorities, and communist-led oppositions to executive initiative were frequent.[58] By the late 1990s, the parliament even achieved moderate successes in forcing changes in government policy using threats of no-confidence votes in 1995 and 1997.[59] The chaotic, democratic parliament of the 1990s was often bemoaned as weak and ineffective, but it still possessed significant internal and mission autonomy, due to hectic but significant linkage with a diverse and ideologically pluralist post-Soviet society and steadily increasing processes of institutionalization in its latent prerogatives and privileges.[60]

The chaos and political instability of the 1990s, however, gave way in time to a period of increasing authoritarianism following the accession of Vladimir Putin to the presidency—which can undoubtedly be described using functionalist logics of elite consolidation and coordination. This period in the early and mid-2000s was characterized by a careful strategy of taming the once-fractious parliament. In line with broader efforts at recentralization around Putin's chosen clique of powerbrokers in the

---

57. Steven S. Smith and Thomas F. Remington (2001), *The Politics of Institutional Choice: The Formation of the Russian State Duma* (Princeton: Princeton University Press).

58. Jana Kunicova and Thomas Frederick Remington (2008), "Mandates, Parties and Dissent: Effect of Electoral Rules on Parliamentary Party Cohesion in the Russian State Duma, 1994—2003," *Party Politics* 14 (5): 555–74. Vladimir Gel'man (2005), "Political Opposition in Russia: A Dying Species?" *Post-Soviet Affairs* 21 (3): 226–46.

59. Tiffany A. Troxel (2003), *Parliamentary Power in Russia, 1994–2001* (London: Palgrave Macmillan).

60. Moshe Haspel, Thomas F. Remington, and Steven S. Smith (1998), "Electoral Institutions and Party Cohesion in the Russian Duma," *Journal of Politics* 60 (2): 417–39. Iulia Shevchenko and Grigorii V. Golosov (2001), "Legislative Activism of Russian Duma Deputies, 1996–1999," *Europe-Asia Studies* 53 (2): 239–61.

Kremlin, the Duma was hamstrung through a series of electoral laws that essentially eliminated independents and uncooperative opposition political parties from its chambers by 2007. Most importantly, the consolidation of parliamentarians (as well as regional elites) around a single dominant party started in 2001 with the merger of two competing "pro-presidential" parties—Edinstvo and Fatherland-All Russia—into the regime's chosen United Russia.[61] While this significantly boosted the coherence of MP action in the Duma over this period, the unified pro-presidential party was thoroughly captured by—and, in practice, not meaningfully differentiable from—the authoritarian executive.

No longer did MPs have such easy and direct links to their own constituencies; their linkages now ran through the president's party, which was largely built from the top down much in line with what functionalist logics of institutional development would lead us to expect.[62] On the one hand, top-down explanations for the consolidation and diminution of the Duma reveal themselves to be quite persuasive. On the other hand, we must note that these efforts first required explicitly undermining the electoral linkages that had previously empowered a class of fairly independent MPs as well as a growing sense of party identification among a subset of the population.[63]

In the broadest sense, little formally changed in the Duma's institutional structure. The body of the early Putin era retained its considerable procedural powers from the liberal democratic constitution that had been adopted in 1993. These powers allowed for considerable flexibility in how it organized its internal structures, as well as constitutional powers of no confidence, bill initiation, and ministerial interpellation. Over the decade of activity in the 1990s, as noted above, the parliament had engaged in a degree of impressive institutionalization, crafting a structure of parliamentary factions that proportionally interlocked with a complex series of legislative committees.

Most importantly, it perfected an internal body known as the Duma Council, whose membership consisted of legislative leaders (the speaker

---

61. Henry E. Hale (2005), *Why Not Parties in Russia? Democracy, Federalism, and the State* (New York: Cambridge University Press). Vladimir Gel'man (2008), "Party Politics in Russia: From Competition to Hierarchy," *Europe-Asia Studies* 60 (6): 913–30. Ora John Reuter (2017), *The Origins of Dominant Parties: Building Authoritarian Institutions in Post-Soviet Russia* (New York: Cambridge University Press).

62. Reuter (2017).

63. Hale (2005); Frank C. Thames Jr. (2001), "Legislative Voting Behaviour in the Russian Duma: Understanding the Effect of Mandate," *Europe-Asia Studies* 53 (6): 869–84.

and his deputies) as well as recognized faction heads. This body essentially set the legislative and working agenda of the parliament and was a key means by which the multiparty chaos of the 1990s pluralist Duma stayed organized.[64] In our terms, the Duma's institutionalization had proceeded to a fairly advanced stage regarding its own hierarchy and complexity but simultaneously had its coherence first undermined by hyper-pluralist politics and then effectively hollowed out by the takeover of the loyalist United Russia party. Further, the Duma's institutional adaptability was only partially tested, with the result being that it was somewhat too liable to stumble and fold when pushed on the backfoot.

These same internal workings proved to be a tempting target for the new administration. Parliamentary institutionalization loomed as an obstacle to the goal of authoritarian consolidation, but only by peeking into the inner workings could one understand how the body's autonomy was being undermined. Plans to undercut the parliament were masterminded and executed largely by Presidential Chief of Staff Vladislav Surkov.[65] His primary aim was to ensure a politically pliant parliament that would not get in the way of executive policy goals. The chosen method was developing the unitary party vehicle of United Russia that would physically dominate the parliamentary chamber simply by numbers and ensure that hierarchical discipline in the assembly emanated not from legislative interests but from the executive directly. By 2003, the party had been elected to a popular majority that was then augmented by defection from other parties and non-affiliated deputies and transformed into a constitutional supermajority.[66]

The vast reach of United Russia undercut parliamentary power not only by ensuring that a pro-regime voice would drown out all others but also by swallowing up the complicated institutionalized procedures of the legislature into simple roll-call voting where the only acceptable choice was "yes." The Duma Council, which had been so important because it

---

64. Thomas F. Remington and Steven S. Smith (1998), "Theories of Legislative Institutions and the Organization of the Russian Duma," *American Journal of Political Science* 42 (2): 545–72.

65. Philipp Casula (2013), "Sovereign Democracy, Populism, and Depoliticization in Russia: Power and Discourse during Putin's First Presidency," *Problems of Post-Communism* 60 (3): 3–15. Regina Smyth, Anna Lowry, and Brandon Wilkening (2007), "Engineering Victory: Institutional Reform, Informal Institutions, and the Formation of a Hegemonic Party Regime in the Russian Federation," *Post-Soviet Affairs* 23 (2): 118–37.

66. Thomas F. Remington (2006), "Presidential Support in the Russian State Duma," *Legislative Studies Quarterly* 31 (1): 5–32.

included a variety of differing factional interests each with differing agendas to promote, shrunk considerably and became sclerotic. The power of agenda setting largely fell back solely to the Speaker, who only allowed bills from the executive or those agreed to by the government ahead of time. Insofar as policymaking even entered the new, authoritarian parliamentary world, it was only in the executive-dominated "zero-reading" process and occurred before anything was even admitted to the parliament itself.[67] By the mid-2000s, the Duma had been safely removed from the realm of politics, with its Speaker even claiming once that "the Duma is not a place for discussion."[68]

The State Duma of the 2000s had been cowed by the executive and cut off from electoral linkages through increasingly uncompetitive elections. But, more importantly, it had fallen backward in terms of its institutionalization. The complex hierarchy of decision-making actors from the Speakership to the Duma Council to the committee chairmen had largely been flattened to just the Speaker and his staff. As the agenda was stuffed with executive-promoted bills, there was less need for the adaptability inherent in the Duma's previously fine-tuned internal organization. And there was also a high rate of turnover of MPs in these years—a consequence in part of seeing the job as a stepping stone to later executive appointment, further reflecting the overall lack of structural differentiation between the autocratic executive and leading state institutions. This meant that procedural knowledge and institutional know-how were now poorly retained within the Duma's ranks.[69] Concerted regime efforts succeeded in undermining the Duma's institutionalization, and the body's autonomy suffered dramatically as a consequence.

This period was widely characterized in Russian media and among political actors as a time of rubber-stamp mediocrity. Any sense of internal or mission autonomy by individual legislators or the body as a whole was broadly snuffed out. There could only be subservience before the regime and the carrots it offered to loyalists, nothing more. The surviving parliamentary parties outside United Russia—all of whom relied on shadow

---

67. Ekaterina Schulmann (2014), "Legislation as a Political Process" (PhD diss., Russian Presidential Academy of National Economy and Public Administration).

68. See Yuri Zarakhovich, "Russians Protest Putin's Rule," *Time*, http://content.time.com/time/world/article/0,8599,1595828,00.html

69. Anton Shirikov (2021), "Who Gets Ahead in Authoritarian Parliaments? The Case of the Russian State Duma," *Journal of Legislative Studies* 28 (4): 554–77.

Kremlin funds and largesse to maintain their organizations—quietly toed the regime line for multiple elections. United Russia itself dominated the chamber from 2003 onward, and in a period of high rent opportunities, economic growth, and genuine regime popularity there was little reason for parliamentarians to engage in bargaining or other activity through formal legislative means.[70] Legislators even routinely complained they had little to do and often failed to even show up to plenary sessions.

The regime party and parliament Speaker Boris Gryzlov of that era kept a tight lid on expressions of dissent or any unwelcome activities that might provide negative PR. This was a quixotic effort, as the reputation of the Duma in society plummeted. An institution having no mission autonomy and filled with increasingly disgruntled and lackadaisical MPs could not hide from public opinion, even in the controlled media environment of mid-2000s Russia. Minimal opportunities to present bills or gain control of parliamentary committees, as well as perpetual rumors of significant funds supplied by the Kremlin to faux opposition parties, fueled widespread suspicions of their co-opted nature. The fact that MPs were regularly seen driving around Moscow in six-figure German cars did not help with the efforts to resuscitate societal linkages, nor did the whiffs of criminal scandal or exploitation of parliamentary immunity that occasionally surfaced in the public eye.

A further change occurred in 2007, when the electoral system shifted from half proportional representation and half single-member districts to fully proportional representation. Seen as a measure to undercut the few remaining liberal MPs who kept getting elected in district seats, it also had the added benefit to the regime of eliminating small parties by raising the PR electoral threshold to 7 percent. This thoroughly consolidated the authoritarian party system around United Russia, but at the price of undermining the Duma's few remaining linkages with society. The lack of geographic representation diminished already declining efforts at constituency service, and the surviving political parties were all de facto paid for by Kremlin slush funds that were then disbursed to MPs on the party lists. This centralized system ensured loyalty to the regime but eviscerated ties to the rest of society—and even to the business, industrial, and regional elites who had been important linkages for parliamentarians in the late 1990s and early 2000s.[71]

---

70. Richard Sakwa (2010), *The Crisis of Russian Democracy: The Dual State, Factionalism and the Medvedev Succession* (New York: Cambridge University Press).

71. Hale (2005).

Revving the Parliamentary Engine and Reviving an Authoritarian Parliament

On the eve of anti-regime protests in 2011, the Duma was thus deinstitutionalizing and rapidly losing what linkages it still had to public and sectoral constituencies. Opposition catalyzed by the seeming arrogance of then-president Dmitri Medvedev and then prime minister Vladimir Putin in "castling," or presenting their pact to swap political positions as a fait accompli, precipitated a mass protest movement in Russian society. The campaign was focused around a strategy of voting for "anyone but United Russia."[72] Activists argued that although none of the opposition parties were independent of the Kremlin in truth, diminishing the electoral return for the ruling regime party would send a strong message and perhaps increase the level of political competition in the parliament.

This campaign proved exceedingly effective, even despite significant electoral fraud, and United Russia achieved only a bare majority in parliamentary seats, not even reaching 50 percent in the official popular vote.[73] There was a significant increase in the size of the opposition parliamentary parties, which set off extreme uncertainty over the stability of the political regime as a whole. During this period, the parliament became a disruptive forum for sincere and vehement political action. For the first two months of the Duma's Sixth Convocation in early 2012, the new parliament saw opposition parties become highly active, speaking out against regime policies (that they had only just voted in favor of a year prior), forcing increased debate and deliberation into the chamber, and even using quorum-denying obstruction tactics to force concessions from the parliamentary majority.[74]

Although the Duma was far less institutionalized than it had been at the start of the millennium, a sudden uptick in linkages to angry, protest-minded constituencies provided the push needed to exercise the parliament's long-disused potential for mission autonomy. Although opposition party leaders began to get cold feet by the end of February 2012, parliamentary obstruction in various forms continued into the summer, taken up by parties that very briefly saw constituency linkage as an attractive alternative to submission to the executive.

This was a major change in parliamentary strategy for the previously

---

72. Regina Smyth (2014), "The Putin Factor: Personalism, Protest, and Regime Stability in Russia," *Politics and Policy* 42 (4): 567–92.

73. Graeme Gill (2012), "The Decline of a Dominant Party and the Destabilization of Electoral Authoritarianism?" *Post-Soviet Affairs* 28 (4): 449–71.

74. Waller (2022).

quiet opposition, and it provoked intense interest in legislative affairs for those brief months. Importantly, the regime had not fallen, nor did it look liable to do so. In fact, many noted the impractical nature of these efforts to exert influence from within the Duma, given the presumed strength of the authoritarian executive. And yet leaders who in prior years had stated that they would run for president, but still make sure to vote for Vladimir Putin, were now engaging in obstructionist tactics and demanding extensive procedural votes and debates on new cabinet ministers. Significant election reforms were hurriedly proposed due to the strength of the protest movement and the pressure from the Duma, including the return of gubernatorial elections and a notable reduction in the hurdles to register political parties.[75]

In this moment of regime weakness, with the increase in the parliamentary weight of political parties that were not the regime's party of choice, the Duma burst forth in action. The particular goals of the activist MPs are very illustrative for our purposes and showed considerable focus in strengthening internal autonomy specifically: increasing the procedural power of MPs and committees; promoting the diffusion of power by lowering future barriers to entry for more political parties; and even simply allowing more MP speaking time for each piece of legislation. In essence, the riotous parliament of a few chaotic months was seeking to regain some of its latent internal powers that had atrophied in the previous decade of Putinism. In this way, we observe a noteworthy relationship between the rise of parliamentary linkages (to newly mobilizing anti-regime constituencies) and the concomitant rise of internal autonomy within the State Duma.

Regime Reconsolidation and Bureaucratic Institutionalization by the Ambitious

The Kremlin ultimately proved successful in marginalizing the anti-regime protest movement of this period, flexing its muscles through media, legal harassment, and a vast mobilizational effort during the March 2012 presidential election that saw the return of Vladimir Putin to the presidency. Party leaders were bribed with significant amounts of money as well as promises of extra seats in the upper house and in various governors' offices.

---

75. Grigorii V. Golosov (2012), "The 2012 Political Reform in Russia: The Interplay of Liberalizing Concessions and Authoritarian Corrections," *Problems of Post-Communism* 59 (6): 3–14.

With a vengeance, the uncertainty of 2011–12 was gone, and the Kremlin refocused its efforts through a concentrated campaign designed to isolate urban liberals from the rest of the country. This so-called conservative turn was widely castigated by the international community but proved to be surprisingly popular among much of the population.[76]

Given expectations from prior years of parliamentary quiescence and with the resumption of the regime's firm, authoritarian control, the change in the nature and role of the State Duma after the chaos of early 2012 was remarkable. A raft of illiberal and repressive laws was passed, ranging from a "foreign agents" law restricting NGOs to further strengthening of the powers of the security services.

Parliamentarians could still show an independent streak, but the most significant initiatives no longer went in an opposition direction. Perhaps the highlight of this period was a series of moral laws passed with alacrity, banning "homosexual propaganda," "insulting the feelings of religious believers," and other measures. Interestingly, most of these laws (with the exception of anti-protest bills) were written and sponsored by legislators from parties outside United Russia. In the case of the homosexual propaganda legislation, which proved to draw considerable domestic and international attention, the sponsoring legislator was from the political party A Just Russia—which had previously led the charge on countering the regime as late as 2012. Not only that, but she had done so as the brand-new head of the Committee on Family, Women, and Children's Affairs, which had not previously engaged in active policymaking or had a legacy of a strong, hands-on approach to legislative business.[77]

The increased procedural opportunities afforded to the three "opposition" parties in the parliament due to their plenary and committee numbers meant that enterprising legislators had new opportunities to increase the autonomy of the parliament, even if they were no longer acting as representatives of the protest movement. The spike in legislator-sponsored bills was notable in 2013 and 2014 compared to prior years, but what stood out especially was the highly controversial nature of many of them—leading media to dub the parliament a "Mad Printer" for its entirely unexpected legislative activity, its provocative and creative choice of issue areas to argue about, and its embarrassing incompetence at bill drafting. Submitting

---

76. Marlene Laruelle (2013), "Conservatism as the Kremlin's New Toolkit: An Ideology at the Lowest Cost," *Russian Analytical Digest* 138 (8): 2–4.

77. Julian G. Waller (2023), "Mimicking the Mad Printer: Legislating Illiberalism in Post-Soviet Eurasia," *Problems of Post-Communism* 70 (3): 225–40.

explicitly conservative and reactionary laws was seen by the most ambitious and worried legislators as a means to show publicly their own loyalty to the new ideological direction of the regime and to take advantage of the opportunity to advance themselves through greater name recognition.[78]

This new period of active policymaking by the Duma would not last past this strange post-protest, post-public repression period. New parliamentary elections held in September 2016 brought a massive supermajority to United Russia—on par with the election victory of 2003—and a new Speaker. Former presidential chief of staff Vyacheslav Volodin's new position as Duma Speaker was considered a demotion away from the autocratic center, and structural conditions suggested the Duma would revert to its rubber-stamping role.[79] The overwhelming dominance of United Russia left fewer procedural options for opposition parties regarding committee positions, and many ambitious deputies had left the Duma for the upper chamber—a prime example of the success that publicity-gaining actions in the plenary could bring to individual MPs.

Volodin's tenure as Speaker did not result in a return to rote rubber-stamping but rather was defined by bureaucratic turf wars with other elements of the Russian state. Volodin's push for internal reforms was framed as a series of measures to improve the quality of the infamous "Mad Printer": to enforce plenary attendance by inactive MPs; to mandate strict constituency visit schedules that limited attempts to expand linkage outside of official district ties; to resist the use of Duma deputies as formal submitters of bills written in ministries; to attempt to further curtail controversial moral or other grandstanding legislation; and to return certain lifestyle privileges to Duma MPs.[80] In essence, Volodin pursued strict hierarchy at the cost of procedural adaptability and deputy privilege, while pushing for greater "rational" coherence among MPs and the party system. In so doing, he sought to raise the Duma's internal autonomy, but only in ways that benefited the chamber at large, not the particularistic autonomy of its MPs. His allergy to allowing MPs to visit their own constituencies outside of strict, bureaucratic formats suggests strongly that independent linkages—and therefore efforts to cultivate support for mission autonomy—were

---

78. Waller (2023); Waller (2021).

79. Atsushi Ogushi (2017), "Weakened Machine Politics and the Consolidation of a Populist Regime: Contextualization of the 2016 Duma Election," *Russian Politics* 2 (3): 287–306.

80. Ben Noble (2019), "Volodin's Duma: Cabinet 2.0," *RIDDLE Russia*. David Szakonyi (2017), "New Rules, New Members, Same Results? A Look at the New Russian Duma," *Kennan Cable* 22.

decidedly off the table, while internal autonomy was seen as having benefits by itself even among staunch regime loyalists.

One example of this focus on internal autonomy was the repeated demand by the Speaker that the Duma be treated with bureaucratic respect by other ministries and agencies. Ministries were threatened repeatedly in an effort to halt the tradition of secretly giving deputies ministry-drafted bills to submit, thus bypassing proper channels of bureaucratic scrutiny.[81] And Volodin even directly threatened the Ministry of Economic Development for failing to properly report information on development funds, insisting on the parliament's "right" to such information. Thus, while putting the proverbial parliamentary whips on for individual members of the legislature, Volodin was quick to raise the relative bureaucratic stature of the parliament vis-à-vis other institutions.

Additionally, the Duma Apparat—the internal research and logistics arm of the legislature—became increasingly involved itself in vetting bills in order to avoid relying entirely on review by government ministries. The new Speaker thus pursued a careful increase in internal autonomy for the parliament through the institutionalization of hierarchy and coherence among its membership, while avoiding all hints at renewing linkage with society or granting procedural tools useable by individual MPs. Volodin's former position in the very core of the regime is key, as he clearly viewed his ostensible exile to the parliament in the best light possible.[82] Instead of merely holding the reins, he realized the benefits of leaning into a highly institutionalized legislative body, one endowed with significant nominal constitutional authority. The technocratic campaign would continue apace through multiple elections in the 2010s, regularizing membership and discipline internally while insisting on the legislature's right of technical review over decisions made by the government or the presidential administration.

We thus find the Russian State Duma stabilizing at the end of its second decade under Vladimir Putin's authoritarian regime. Without a return to the brief period when it formed a place of political contestation and opposition power, the legislature's current leadership has made a point to undo the atrophy of institutional powers and procedural muscle that had been lost over the course of the 2000s. Focused on strengthening once significant internal autonomy through a series of steps toward increasing insti-

---

81. Noble and Schulmann (2018).

82. Mark Galeotti (2019), "Russia's Security Council: Where Policy, Personality, and Process Meet," *Security Insights* 41.

tutionalization, the Duma shows us an example by which an authoritarian parliament can tread the waters of authoritarianism and emerge with some privileges and even pursue goals for heightened privileges and control over its own internal affairs. Linkage to society remains exceedingly low, and it is likely that with the lack of clear ties to public constituencies and without improved reputation, internal autonomy may be all that can be acquired by the legislature with mission autonomy remaining out of reach.

The Kuwaiti National Assembly:
The Dynamic Power of Linkage and Latent Power

If the evolution of the Russian State Duma provides insight into the way in which a de- and reinstitutionalization processes can have important ramifications for parliamentary autonomy, the Kuwaiti National Assembly (Majlis al-Umma) illustrates the vital relevance of *linkage* for authoritarian parliaments. Through this case, we observe that linkages—combined with modest and uneven, but real, levels of institutionalization—make possible not only a significant (if shifting) degree of internal autonomy but also an odd kind of mission autonomy. The assembly's mission, though keenly pursued, is one that is generally exercised negatively through obstructionism. This is because it is based on a strong sense of prerogative in the body and among individual members, which is however not supported by a coherent ideological majority or a clear and workable hierarchy within the institution.

In this section, we will see how the parliament came into being in 1963, based on short-term regime calculations regarding the parliament's usefulness but drawing on genuine historical antecedents. Were it not for the birth of the Kuwaiti parliament, those antecedents were sufficiently feeble that they would likely have been forgotten along with other odd structures of the period (such as councils that heard disputes among Kuwait's merchants with their far-flung commercial interests). But when these antecedents were given new life in the country's constitution, the result struck deep roots that made the assembly difficult to weed out later on, although the regime certainly tried.

The past became the present and the future through a series of steps—some taken by an improvising regime looking to find political partners; some by ruling family members taking advantage of the parliament's utility as a place to air family grievances; and some by parliamentarians themselves, whose personal ambitions, reformist beliefs, or policy goals found traction in moments of chaos and opportunity.

Public constituencies in Kuwaiti society—initially a group of long-standing, oligarchic merchant families but also tribal groups, the intelligentsia, and later the devoutly religious—have all found critical representation and opportunities for interest articulation within the institutional frame of the Kuwaiti parliament. This has been aided by strong formal prerogatives built into the constitutional position of the body. And it has been furthered by the consistent institutionalization of the procedures and rights of the parliament to intervene in Kuwaiti politics, ones that have led the parliament up to and past the brink of constitutional confrontation with the regime. The parliament has often lost battles while sometimes winning larger political wars. We thus find Kuwait to have a dynamic and empowered parliament—sometimes holding forth, sometimes standing back, sometimes suffering defeats, and sometimes temporarily hamstrung, but rarely out of public authoritarian politics for very long and never without a fight.

How Do You Solve a Problem Like the Majlis?

Kuwait's rulers—along with the Dow Chemical executives who saw share prices plunge in 2008 when a huge agreement they made with Kuwait's government foundered on parliamentary posturing they did not expect—would likely laugh at the idea that the parliament is functional for the regime.[83] The country's amirs have suspended it twice before bringing it back, have blustered when it seemed to meddle in family politics, have found that it paralyzes ambitious development programs, and have sought ways to stack its membership often successfully over the short term but only by whetting parliamentary appetites over time.[84] The parliament has

---

83. The material in this section is based in part on research conducted by one of the authors (Brown) in periodic visits to Kuwait between 1994 and 2013. In this regard, see Nathan J. Brown (1997), *The Rule of Law in the Arab World: Courts in Egypt and the Gulf* (New York: Cambridge University Press), chapter 6; Nathan J. Brown (2002), *Constitutions in a Nonconstitutional World: Arab Basic Laws and the Prospects for Accountable Government* (Albany: SUNY Press), chapter 4; Nathan J. Brown (2007), "Moving Out of Kuwait's Political Impasse," Carnegie Endowment for International Peace; and Nathan J. Brown (2008), "The Beginning of Real Politics in Kuwait?" Carnegie Endowment for International Peace.

84. Michael Herb (2014), *The Wages of Oil: Parliaments and Economic Development in Kuwait and the UAE* (Ithaca: Cornell University Press).

made elite coordination more difficult, rather than facilitating it, which provides a sharp and intriguing contrast to common functionalist explanations for legislative activity under authoritarianism. But despite all this, the assembly marches on, its dysfunctional effects now an accepted part of the Kuwaiti political scene.

Linkages have grown over time—beginning with fairly modest connections to a few leading families and the country's limited number of Western-educated intellectuals but growing so much that when strict security measures were taken to control entrance to the previously open parliament building in the early 2000s, it was constituents seeking favors or lobbying opportunities, not terrorists or assassins, who seemed to be the main concern.

While both *internal* and *mission autonomy* have waxed and waned over time, the strength of the institution has always been rooted in its ability to include key elements of broader Kuwaiti society within the legislative chamber. Despite persistent gerrymandering, changes to the actual size of the electorate, and significant pressure on voters from the ruling family and the executive, the Kuwaiti parliament has consistently been able to translate politically relevant public constituencies into seats in a parliamentary format since its inception. The continued foothold of these vertical linkages in the National Assembly has provided it with motivated political actors who seek to use their parliamentary privileges to the fullest— especially given the otherwise closed nature of technocratic ministries, some of which are directly led by members of the ruling family who also dominate the rest of the country's state apparatus. And when the parliament was shuttered in 1976 and then again in 1986, a broad web of public constituencies who were sometimes directly at odds with each other came together to successfully demand the parliament's return.

Reliance on these public constituencies, and in turn their reliance on the parliament to ensure access to formal political power, has buttressed the National Assembly's mission autonomy considerably. This is augmented by elements of significant legislative institutionalization that began with the 1962 Kuwaiti constitution promulgated by Amir Abdullah Al Sabah.[85] Empowered with notable interpellative powers, permissive in allowing small groups of MPs to force action, possessing strong influence over the budgetary and lawmaking processes, and able to attract public attention by holding raucous plenary debates, the Kuwaiti National Assembly has been a politically powerful institution.

---

85. Herb (2014).

The parliament over time has strongly institutionalized in two particular ways—though it lags specifically in another. First, the parliament is formally endowed with, and informally practices, considerable *adaptability*—mostly through the use of procedural tools that allow it to engage with crises and changing times more easily. The parliament's flexibility in using its structural and procedural powers to situate and arm itself during uncertain periods has been a key asset, allowing it to move with the punches it has been given by an unfriendly ruling family and a technocratic ministerial bureaucracy that does not welcome oversight. Second, this adaptability is reinforced by a degree of *coherence* among the membership, insofar as multiple generations of parliamentarians have internalized a specific understanding of the boundaries, privileges, and role that they inhabit—something passed down from older to younger MPs, despite the turnover of officeholders and changing factional standings. This coherence is sharply bounded, however. It creates a sense of entitlement for MPs given their official position, but does not entail any coordination among parliamentarians Indeed, the parliament has remained infamously fractious, and in this way thus limits its own possibilities for extending autonomy further.

The parliament's *complexity* is far less developed, with reviewing and scrutiny committees and research facilities less capable than government counterparts. Yet, where the parliament most clearly falls short in terms of institutionalization lies in its failure to assure clear *hierarchy* and to develop stable partisan divides or a majority "party" able to control the parliamentary agenda. The inability to form a "bloc of blocs"—an alliance to bring together smaller parliamentary groupings—or to stabilize and coordinate the political opposition means that both loyalist voting coalitions and alliances for obstruction are easily undermined. The parliament has thus defended its internal autonomy but has varied greatly in the degree to which it exercises mission autonomy over time.

The Kuwaiti parliament's varying autonomy is sometimes treated as a function of regime needs and ruler intentions. The movement toward the creation of a legislative body started in the early twentieth century, culminating in the Majlis movement that saw the birth of an obstreperous parliament lasting six months in 1938. However brief that body, the historical memory of it led Kuwait's leaders to revive it when seeking to forge a political community when the British protectorate came to an end in 1961 and Kuwait was on its own. A constituent assembly of ruling family members and elected delegates drafted a constitution that placed the parliament on a permanent basis.

There is much value to a functionalist narrative for the parliament—

especially in its origin and institutional predecessors—in a way that is analogous to how the growth of authoritarian parliaments in nineteenth-century monarchies followed a similar path of needed co-optation.[86] Yet, we also find strong trends of institutional stickiness and permanence that undermine a fully functionalist story. Kuwait's rulers clearly found the parliament dysfunctional enough to suspend it twice. But it was restored both times. Each closure of the parliament represented a period in which parliamentary overreach threatened the royal regime's core. And each reopening saw renewed active debate, new ministerial interpellations and anti-corruption scrutiny, and further usage of the same, previously existing parliamentary privileges and prerogatives to apply pressure on the cabinet and even the ruling family. This does not fit with an account that assumes reactive functioning to regime commands; quite the opposite—the parliament has continually tested the bounds of the permissible and regularly shifted the goalposts of interinstitutional norms. And since 1992, suspension has largely been taken off the table.

In fact, we find a significant ratchet effect over time as the National Assembly gathered ever more informal power and prestige between its founding decade and the current era. To take just one example from the early 1990s, writing on the Kuwait Investment Office (KIO) scandal investigated by parliament in the years following the First Gulf War, Baaklini, Denoeux, and Springborg find that "the NA's leading role in investigating and publicizing the KIO scandal was highly significant. Prior to the Iraqi invasion, such an action would have been regarded as an unacceptable parliamentary intrusion into matters that were the prerogative of the Al Sabah and the cabinet. . . . Instead, the NA this time was allowed to perform its constitutional role as a watchdog over public investments."[87] We find that this pattern is replete in the institution's history since the parliament's founding over a half century ago, in which the ambit of acceptable activity and interest expands far beyond what either the ruling family or the parliament's own initial founding intended.

This pattern has been long running. Linkages to critical societal and economic groups crystalized in the assembly as early as the mid-1960s, resulting in the assertion of the parliament's mission autonomy as an oversight body checking the amir, his family, and his formally unaccountable

---

86. Michael Herb (2004), "Princes and Parliaments in the Arab world," *Middle East Journal* 58 (3): 367–84.

87. Abdo I. Baaklini, Guilain Denoeux, and Robert Springborg (1999), *Legislative Politics in the Arab World: The Resurgence of Democratic Institutions* (Boulder: Lynne Rienner), 195.

Parliaments · 173

cabinet. This grew to parliamentary conduct so disorderly that it was shuttered more than a decade later, but economic crisis and mobilized social discontent would bring the parliament back—only for the same procedural tools and debating freedom to be used immediately upon its return.[88] Even when packed with nominally "pro-government" tribal deputies and conservative loyalists, the parliament proved more active than anticipated, and norms of scrutiny and self-importance show through even in years with strong royalist de facto majorities.[89] Although the disruption of membership turnover often limits the coherence of any legislative body, the thickening shared norms on proper legislative activity by Kuwaiti MPs have been sustained over multiple decades.

The permissive procedural powers of the National Assembly and the adaptive use and maintenance of them across many years have proved to be vital to its unusual activity and rambunctiousness. The low number of deputies needed to call for general debate on any topic and for requesting an interpellation (a session of formal questioning treated locally as something approaching impeachment) of a minister has been particularly critical, with downstream mechanisms to investigate and even call for ministerial resignation through no-confidence votes acting as key reserve powers when the body can get its act together.[90] Such legislative powers have been increasingly deployed, and they have created new, internal understandings of what the parliament's proper place is within the regime as a whole. Coupled with its semi-mythological self-justification as an institution of Kuwaiti nation building, the parliament has become a singular touchstone of societal influence on an otherwise distant monarchy.[91] Befitting our earlier discussion on trends of convergence toward institutional similarity among authoritarian parliaments, since the assembly's founding, its structure has remained broadly unchanged across decades of regime crisis and institutional interruption.

This strong linkage to public constituencies and growing institutionalization—themselves catalyzed by adaptable procedural powers and a coherent normative sense of parliamentarism—has kept the Kuwaiti National

---

88. Jill Crystal (1989), "Coalitions in Oil Monarchies: Kuwait and Qatar," *Comparative Politics* 21 (4): 427–43.

89. Sean Yom (2023), "Kuwait's Democratic Promise," *Journal of Democracy* 34 (3): 46–61.

90. Baaklini, Denoeux, and Springborg (1999). Michael Herb (2016), "The Origins of Kuwait's National Assembly," *London School of Economics and Political Science* 39:1–26.

91. Jill Crystal (1995), *Oil and Politics in the Gulf: Rulers and Merchants in Kuwait and Qatar*, vol. 24 (New York: Cambridge University Press), 58.

Assembly in the thick of politics, despite being formally subservient to the autocratic royal executive and often threatened with dissolution.

Convergent Pressures and the National Assembly's Founding

Kuwait's early history bears a clear family resemblance to our earlier discussion of the growth in parliamentary bodies across the authoritarian regimes of Europe's nineteenth century. While there are notable differences between Arab monarchies and the older European constitutional monarchies of the prior century, the antecedent institutions of the Kuwaiti National Assembly quite closely fit the mold.[92] Through the nineteenth century and into the twentieth, the Al Sabah ruler governed with the acquiescence of wealthy trading and merchant families tied to the pearl-diving industry and related commerce. The mobile capital of these families, allowing them to decamp for a different port if taxes were ever too high or the customs burden too onerous, provided a credible threat to ensure accommodation between the crown and the merchant elite. As with the rise of representative institutions elsewhere,[93] this led to informal social councils that enabled the local economic elite to air grievances in official forums that were in dialogue with—yet structurally differentiated in both position and identity from—Kuwait's ruler and surrounding regime elites.[94] Eventually, the merchant families pushed for a formalized institution to lock in a sociopolitical status that was under threat of being undermined by the twin dangers of (1) a ruling family with access to British imperial support and (2) rising oil revenues, which could potentially be used to build and mold a state apparatus with no meaningful separation from the amir.

There were a few such attempts, most either specialized or (if they had more general competences) fleeting, from a formalized Succession Council put together in 1921 to an Education Council in 1936. All navigated the relationship between Al Sabah rule, British oversight, and the merchant families' deep interest in maintaining their positions. New bureaucratization efforts of the underdeveloped Kuwaiti state proceeded at the time in the same direction, creating a "municipality" that oversaw health and social affairs but also was financed independently from the ruler and had an elected board. All of this formed the background and content of the so-called Majlis movement of regime liberalization and elite inclusion.[95]

---

92. Herb (2004).
93. Stasavage (2010).
94. Crystal (1995), 4.
95. Eran Segal (2012), "Political Participation in Kuwait: Dīwāniyya, Majlis and Parliament," *Journal of Arabian Studies* 2 (2): 131–32. Crystal (1995), 42–48.

The movement toward representative (but oligarchic) institutions culminated in a Legislative Assembly elected by 150 heads of the leading families. Lasting only six months, it claimed control over the budget and over justice and public security functions, as well as having the authority to deal with education and public works.[96] The ruler of the time was able to disband this outburst of parliamentarism.

This prehistory is relevant for two reasons. First, it underscores the fact that patterns found in European experiences of parliamentary assertion and supremacy can travel with some empirical detail to the twentieth century and well out of the European sample.[97] Second, this background suggests the existence of powerful public constituencies that would bolster the more sustained parliamentary successor. The experience of the Majlis movement brought the merchant families together in a political battle. Although losing the institutional fight of the 1930s, the merchant families would remain a potential challenge to the authority of the ruler, who in turn had to rely more heavily on his own family.[98]

The ruling Al Sabah family did try to forge a more amenable path for themselves that would allow for the bypassing of any meaningful structural differentiation between ruler, regime, and state apparatus at the country level. They pursued a series of purely administrative, conciliar institutional experiments in the 1950s, with the ruler first declaring a High Executive Committee staffed by family and loyalists, replaced by a Supreme Council of ten sheikhs that formed a proto-cabinet. The municipality administrative organ was changed to fully appointed status, and advisory committees of merchants attached to state departments were finally eliminated as well.[99] The remaining leverage that the merchant families had was systematically eliminated through debt buybacks, lowered shares of customs duties to the state budget, and continued resource rents from oil.

But this administrative expansion brought its own challenges, built as it often was on foreign workers and expertise. The inculcation of a sense of Kuwaiti identity—one that discouraged ideas of pan-Arabism that Egyptian, Palestinian, and other expatriate workers favored and counteracted any claim of neighboring Iraq to annexation of the city-state—suggested policies of separating nationals from expatriates, giving a measure of freedom and a dose of welfare benefits to the Kuwait citizenry. This in turn fostered a strong sense of entitlement even beyond the merchant families—

---

96. Crystal (1995), 48–50.
97. Herb (2004).
98. Crystal (1995), 63–70.
99. Crystal (1995), 70–73.

leading not only to a measure of co-optation but also to the emergence of critical voices in a somewhat permissive environment.

Formal independence came in 1961 and led the ruler to formalize the emerging arrangements in a constitutional text. A royally appointed Organizing Body oversaw the transition to an elected Constituent Assembly, which drew up a constitution that was approved by the amir with no alterations whatsoever. It ushered in a system that would have been quite familiar to many Europeans living a century earlier—an unaccountable hereditary head of state who appoints the cabinet regardless of parliamentary confidence, coupled with a National Assembly empowered with lawmaking, budget approval, ministerial interpellation, and no-confidence motion powers against that cabinet.[100]

In sum, Kuwait's rulers permitted a constitution not in a far-sighted act (the amir's successors showed great annoyance with what the amir of 1961 had allowed to emerge). They did so because of an institutional toolkit that was used to address a set of political problems—national identity, Iraqi threat, the challenges of state building in a newly independent state—that were pressing at the time but led to political choices that also proved difficult to reverse later on. This significant base of constitutional centrality, which was augmented by processes of institutionalization based in part by the increasingly isomorphic nature of parliaments throughout the world, led the current body to a level and kind of institutionalization that would have surprised members of earlier assemblies in the region. And institutionalization, in turn, rendered parliamentary powers active and well used. But far and above, we will see that it is the parliament's unusually strong linkages to society that have made it a particularly frustrating annoyance to the regime.

Public Constituencies, Mission Autonomy, and Parliamentary Resilience in Troubled Times

The empowered National Assembly was filled with its inaugural class in 1963, bringing in both merchant families and several other societal groups (such as educated professionals) that had been largely absent from previous Kuwaiti decision-making bodies. An Arab nationalist and leftist current emerged rooted in the modern professional classes. Almost immediately, this group took advantage of parliamentary procedure and constitutional provisions to prevent a new cabinet overweighted with merchants from

---

100. Herb (2014), 40–47. Herb (2016), 7.

taking its oath of office.[101] Although the challenge did not lead to a formal vote of no-confidence, this disruption actually supported efforts by some members of an often fractious ruling family, ultimately forcing the amir to put an end to the cabinet and install a new one made of technocrats.

Vocal criticism of state policy continued, so much so that the regime took recourse in gerrymandering the 1967 election. Such electoral tinkering represented an attempt to drown the leftist and nationalist voices with tribal deputies who could be co-opted with benefits rather than the policy concessions demanded by an emerging current of ideologically driven mission autonomy among sitting MPs. Enticing the hitherto marginalized Bedouin population of the desert with state housing, military service, and citizenship grants, the executive brought a new population into the electorate. Bedouins made up only 21 percent of the electorate in 1963 but 45 percent by 1975.[102]

This attempt to pack and silence the assembly provided a momentary respite from truly unwelcome activity. Despite a more pliable membership, new parliamentarians came to relish their status and found institutional tools in the parliament's structure to amplify their independent voices. With the enforcement of internal regulations about attendance and with a low quorum threshold, participation was high and debate was wideranging given the different personalities in the small, intimate chamber of fifty MPs.[103] The tripartite factional division of Bedouin royalists, merchant families, and the pan-Arab national leftist intelligentsia provided a shifting majority for the cabinet selected by the amir and the crown prince (who doubled as prime minister until the twenty-first century). At the same time, permissive and adaptable procedural rules meant that the National Assembly was in many ways a pivotal public forum that set the discursive agenda regarding some critical domestic issues—including oil policy and even international ties.[104]

Elections in 1975 brought a more emboldened pan-Arab leftist-nationalist alliance that moved from scrutiny and debate to active oversight of the ruling family and its expenditures. With the background of civil war in Lebanon and the increasingly obvious ties between opposition MPs and Palestinian, Bahraini, Omani, and Lebanese expatriates and governments, the situation proved intolerable for the executive. But while the MPs could make collective noise, they could not find a harmonious voice.

---

101. Crystal (1995), 87.
102. Crystal (1995), 88–89.
103. Baaklini, Denoeux, and Springborg (1999), 178.
104. Baaklini, Denoeux, and Springborg (1999), 179.

Financial policy split the left and the merchants, while leftist rhetoric (and tone) on a host of issues alienated socially conservative tribal deputies. The parliamentary effort to enhance MP prerogatives extended to higher pensions, making the body seem self-serving in the eyes of some constituents while furthering the goal of strengthening its own internal autonomy. The divided assembly was effectively demonstrating its own reflection of divisions within the society. In this respect, strong linkages fostered internal autonomy but undermined any coherent sense of mission autonomy, angered the regime, and illustrated divisions within its social support. After dissolving the National Assembly in 1976, the amir would have it sit empty for four years.

Prorogation rid the amir of a day-to-day nuisance but provided neither stability nor a more docile political elite. Informal mechanisms (such as the scattered, if vital, social institution of *diwaniyya*[105]) allowed Kuwaitis to discuss politics in smaller, like-minded fora. There was much to interest them: domestic issues (the influx of oil revenues and the provision of welfare benefits) and regional trends (an Islamist rise among Sunnis, tensions around support for the Palestinian cause, the Iranian Revolution) had many important domestic ramifications. Palpable divisions festering within the society seemed to make the regime feel that while it did not like life with the National Assembly it also did not like life without it. As with many authoritarian regimes, it moved for short-term reasons to manipulate the system in crude and somewhat clumsy ways.

In 1980, the amir moved to reconvene the National Assembly, hoping to make it more manageable perhaps through some constitutional changes, ones that it never settled on or secured. Instead of redesigning the political system, the regime fell back on further gerrymandering to diminish the influence of the groups that it was most concerned about—leftist nationalists and Shia Muslims who it thought might be overly influenced by neighboring Iran's attempt to build an Islamic republic. It got what it wanted but also found that the diminution of progressive and Shia influence was simply replaced by very strong Sunni religious representation. The public

---

105. A *diwaniyya* is a social gathering of male guests in a specific reception hall for socialization as well as for discussion of private business and public interest topics. In periods of parliamentary absence, it has functioned as a substitute that complements newspapers and other social club gatherings. While useful for exchanging information, developing or maintaining social trust, and ensuring group cohesiveness (among merchant families and the intelligentsia especially), it has no formal recourse to regime action and so functions at a less privileged level than formal parliamentary representation. For further information on these informal but crucial aspects of political participation in Kuwait, see Segal (2012).

constituencies into which the National Assembly tapped had grown in time from merchants, Bedouins, and urban pan-Arab/leftist intelligentsia to also include grassroots religious movements that now were appearing across the Kuwaiti electorate.

Urban progressives and religious conservatives would act as twin factional pillars for the next six years. A 1982 financial crisis—one that led to suspicions of official corruption, favoritism, and mismanagement—led parliament to revive its investigative and interpellative powers that it had previously been so happy to use. The 1985 election increased the pressure, raising the urban progressive[106] share while stimulating a cross-sectarian understanding between Sunni and Shia religious constituencies. Sunni Islamists also found common cause with tribal deputies over conservative social issues. The pattern of shifting alliances—ones that made the parliament a reliable host for opposition voices without giving the opposition voice any reliable stability—had returned.

And once more, this vocal and obstructionist parliament caused headaches for the regime. Successfully blocking some government bills, including ones that were meant to be bailout responses to the continued economic crisis, the parliament moved against certain ministers. Forcing the resignation of the Minister of Justice by threatening to call a no-confidence vote, the parliament then targeted Oil Minister Ali Khalifa. Both were leading members of the ruling family and key members of the cabinet.[107] This yet again proved intolerable for the amir, likely because it seemed a threat to Al Sabah dominance but also because the parliament's activism appeared to be magnifying rivalries within the ruling family. He dissolved the National Assembly almost exactly one decade after its previous prorogation.[108]

Amir Jaber Al Sabah, having already experienced the first parliamentary prorogation when he had been crown prince and prime minister, attempted to rule without the parliament—or at least without the parliament that Kuwait had known since independence. Former parliamentarians and other opposition voices began meeting again regularly in *diwaniyya*s, which through their informal character and nature as societally organized venues

---

106. Over the course of the 1970s and the early 1980s, the urban intelligentsia cohort of the Kuwaiti electorate became less pan-Arab nationalist, given the changing ideological contours of the broader region. Most MPs within that transitioning bloc could be largely classified as either leftist (in an older socialist sense) or progressive in the sense of reformist, constitutionalist, and suspicious of the dominant merchant families.

107. Crystal (1995), 104–5.

108. Baaklini, Denoeux, and Springborg (1999), 183.

remained insulated and structurally distinct from the ruling family even as it asserted itself and sought to expand its reach. The regime reacted not only by trying to shut down the *diwaniyya*s but also by trying to construct a new parliamentary body, stripped of most authority, to replace the old one. As that attempt was getting underway in 1990, however, Iraq invaded Kuwait and annexed it.

Meeting in exile, regime leaders and the opposition hammered out an agreement: Kuwaitis would stand united behind the amir, but the National Assembly would be restored in any postwar order. And that deal was honored, with the regime mindful not only that it needed full social support but also that a post-1990 American security guarantee provided a new-found international linkage that connected the National Assembly with the continued existence of Kuwait as a sovereign state (with the US government weighing in on the necessity of reconvening the parliament in 1992).

The postwar National Assembly was once more populated by a disparate assortment of progressive reformists, Islamists, merchants, and tribal members. Within these groups, the long-standing public constituencies of the merchant families, the intelligentsia, the Sunni and Shia religious, and the Bedouins all found their informal factional places. United by little other than the importance of parliament, the amir bowed and chose five elected MPs as ministers for the newly named cabinet, while the opposition merely complained about not having full responsibility for the cabinet but accepted the result. The previous speaker, an opposition firebrand, returned to his role, embodying continuity from the previous era and underlining the curious elements of notable institutionalization in the parliament. The survival of key figures in the parliamentarian old guard through to the new post-occupation body allowed the parliament as an institution to pass through its second dissolution without losing significant informal capacity and know-how.

The returned parliament brought the same patterns—and even deepened them. In earlier decades, the regime had broadened the franchise to include more tribal members from outlying areas, diluting the impact of urban progressives and other troublemakers. The MPs representing these areas were openly termed "service deputies" because their electoral success depended quite clearly on distributing benefits to constituents. This made them easy to fit into patronage politics—at first. Over time, their demands tended to grow, and some concluded that they could demonstrate their worth to constituents through public posturing as much as quiet cooperation.

The postwar parliament proved itself, as its predecessors had always been, fractious but ambitious. Elections tended to redistribute seats among a growing welter of factions (progressives, merchants, Sunni Islamists of various stripes, Shia of various stripes, regime loyalists, tribalists, and feminists) with membership in various blocs not mutually exclusive. Older MPs returning after 1992 also passed on their knowledge and skills in parliamentary norms and procedures into an increasingly institutionalized chamber.

Ratchet Effects and Authoritarian Parliamentarism

Recent decades of the Kuwaiti parliament suggest a need to restrict the scope of simplifying functionalist logics, which appear to hold less water for long-standing authoritarian legislatures than more short-lived bodies. Some parliaments may be created or systematically remolded to meet a short-term need but often outlive their creators. Kuwait's rulers seem to have given up on returning to the drawing board of institutional design. The two parliamentary closures in the 1970s and 1980s have not been replicated in the post-occupation period. Instead, the parliament has become a seemingly inevitable part of the institutional landscape of the Kuwait state. It even secured a victory in terms of political norms when the amir finally acquiesced to appointing a prime minister who, while a leading member of the Al Sabah, was not the crown prince. The effect was to make it far more conceivable that parliamentary pressure could play a role in bringing down a prime minister (as indeed happened subsequently) by making the figure less sacrosanct as a result of increasing the position's degree of separation from the highest ranks of the ruling family.

This, of course, does not mean that the National Assembly has been a bastion of normative liberalism, a pillar of representative government, or a body free from autocratic meddling—far from it. But it does mean that from a shaky grounding in a 1962 royally promulgated constitution and multiple fights with the executive, the institution has emerged as vital and with significant staying power.

The regime does manipulate the parliament—using gerrymandering and patronage politics at times—to obtain a more manageable body for periods (such as the late 1990s).[109] Yet even in that period, the parliament made use of the threat of engaging with a vote of no-confidence against a minister from the ruling family to induce the government to resign in

---

109. Herb (2016), 18.

1998, and MPs always held their interpellative powers in reserve as a tool to deny the cabinet total latitude.[110] Even moments of potential strong opposition power that might have usurped cabinet power—or forced another parliamentary closure—were undercut (as in 2000 and 2002) by the tactical defection of parts of the opposition to maintain the status quo.[111]

The pattern has been thus of a parliament that uses its autonomy in ways the regime finds annoying and obstructive but usually manageable. The parliament has sometimes veered close to being seen as an existential danger and has seemed on the brink of change three times in the last two decades—but each time it has turned back with the underlying dynamics shifting but unchanged.

The first came when the parliament seemed to have finally formed a coherent agenda. In 2005, a majority formed in the parliament that insisted—over government objections—on combining the country's tiny twenty-five districts into five, allotting each voter four votes (with the top ten vote getters in each district winning seats). The parliament claimed that this would produce an assembly more attuned to national needs than neighborhood demands; programmatic campaigns would replace the retail politics that had dominated parliamentary elections. Fearing the prospects of a more cohesive, party-based assembly, the amir went so far as to dissolve the parliament as it pressed for the electoral reform and to call for new elections. But he was ultimately forced to back down when reformers won an absolute majority in the new parliament.

The new electoral law passed when the parliament convened in 2006, and the long-standing, vague ideological tendencies formed as parliamentary blocs. And the triumphant blocs came together to form a "bloc of blocs"—a parliamentary majority that agreed on a legislative agenda that it hoped to impose on the system. For a moment, it seemed that the parliament had made significant progress in institutionalization through increasing coherence and promoting hierarchy. The effort, however, was forgotten within months as the "majority" proved that it could defend its common interests in reelection but could otherwise not find much common ground. When the opposition coalition crumbled, highly factionalized parliamentarians resumed their previous political posturing, now doing so in small groups in pursuit of no coherent agenda.

The second came shortly afterward with the royal succession crisis in

---

110. Herb (2004), 374.

111. Michael Herb (2002), "Democratization in the Arab World? Amirs and Parliaments in the Gulf," *Journal of Democracy* 13 (4): 41–47.

Parliaments · 183

2006. The parliament appeared forced to choose between asserting itself forcefully or accommodating the ruling family. It chose the second. Amir Jabir Al Sabah had died, but his elderly heir Sa`d was too ill to inherit any of the responsibilities and unable to speak the oath of office. The constitution formally empowered the National Assembly to approve the amir's choice of a crown prince; upon the amir's death, the crown prince was to take an oath before the body prior to ascending the throne. Sa`d's incapacity produced a regime crisis that necessitated a parliamentary role: it was the National Assembly where he was to be sworn in (and thus the question of nodding in response to someone else reading the oath for him was one of parliamentary procedure). In the end, the parliament as a body seemed not to wish to push its role too far—it allowed itself to be the setting where a compromise was worked out within the ruling family (Sa`d would nod, become amir, name a crown prince, and, following parliament's assent to the position, resign and be replaced).[112]

But while this moment saw parliament working hand in hand with the cabinet and ruling family to resolve a crisis, it hardly shifted ongoing patterns of conflict. The regime tried to forge a sustainable majority and failed, leading to seven elections in the years from 2006 to 2016. It sometimes was able to secure more favorable results, but only at the cost of electoral manipulation by individual members of the ruling family. Such intervention—often supplying leaked information or funds to favored politicians—not only drove wedges among parliamentarians but also among members of the Al Sabah, transforming ruling family rivalries and squabbles into public power struggles.

Third, in 2011, with waves of popular protest sweeping the Arab world, a Kuwaiti movement arose loosely gathering around demands for political reform, with political corruption a major theme. Coalescing around a demand that the prime minister be sacked, some parliamentarians forged independent linkages with the movement. A few firebrands addressed large public rallies (themselves an anomaly in Kuwait). When a group of demonstrators stormed the parliament building, some MPs seemed to endorse the step. The crowd withdrew; the prime minister was eventually replaced; and the crisis seemed defused. But the regime seemed to wish to move quickly beyond defusing the challenge to subduing its rivals. The most vocal MP was eventually charged for his role in the storming. His fellow deputies agreed to strip him of his immunity; the Constitutional Court (generally a

---

112. Segal (2012), 138.

body loathe to defy the regime) found a flaw in the electoral law and forced new elections and then repeated the ruling again, forcing yet another round of balloting. Those elections—which the regime attempted to mold by decreeing electoral changes and less public manipulation—prompted some boycotts and produced a slightly more pliable body. But the underlying dynamic—a fractious parliament that could not form its own agenda but swung unevenly and unpredictably between defying the regime and obstructing it—remained.

The linkages between individual MPs (and some parliamentary blocs, especially Islamist ones) and key public constituencies—Islamist social movements, urban liberal clubs, and tribal connections—were proving quite robust. And such linkages to supportive societal constituencies allowed the parliament to achieve an impressive degree of internal autonomy. At the same time, those linkages also pull parliamentarians in different direction and do not immunize the body from regime manipulation. So, it should be no surprise that efforts to institutionalize procedures that empowered the parliament to pursue a coherent policy or legislative agenda—and not merely to allow individual MPs to pursue their interests or shifting coalitions to obstruct regime initiatives—have floundered.

In the end, the parliament of Kuwait exemplifies several key aspects of modern authoritarian rule. To call its existence functional for the regime would come as a surprise to the Al Sabah, who seem to regard it on the best of days as a noisy and nettlesome nuisance. The National Assembly is strongly imbued with linkages to important economic and societal public constituencies, which have both emboldened and salvaged its pursuit of autonomy in the face of authoritarian governance and repression. It is endowed with considerable procedural powers, which have provided tools for ambitious MPs to hold the government to account and pressure the ruling family over many decades. It has institutionalized over time, with more coherent factions, adaptable legislative powers, and an increasingly stable cohort of leadership and old knowledge through multiple speakers and their relations.

The last has allowed for the parliament to survive multiple closings and has ensured that its knowledge base and potential capacity have only grown with time. Yet it remains deficient in establishing stable party or leadership hierarchies, and its coherence is often limited to a sense of corporate togetherness rather than legislative policy coordination. In many ways, the Kuwaiti National Assembly exemplifies the strong, authoritarian parliament of the modern era—utilizing together both linkage and institutionalization as a means to buttress its own internal autonomy and a sense of mission autonomy, though one that does not go beyond protecting its prerogatives to developing a positive political program.

Conclusion: The Complicated History of Parliaments and Authoritarianism

Authoritarian parliaments are state institutions often endowed with considerable latent power, but they have great difficulty sustaining the autonomy needed to exercise it regularly. Their historical development has granted them many privileges that can be successfully used to frustrate regimes or bring constituent interests into an otherwise unaccountable system of rule, but it is far easier for them to pursue forms of autonomy that are self-oriented or disruptive rather than a positive policy-oriented mission per se.

Through this chapter, we identified the historical pathway toward an isomorphic, yet often latent, parliamentary power in authoritarian regimes, causing their autonomy to now be expressed so distinctively today. We then showed the limits of institutional autonomy when linkages are consistently weak or lacking by looking at the Russian State Duma, which experienced only very brief moments of mission autonomy and a newfound, if moderate, internal autonomy dependent on the ambitions of its individual leadership and its investment in institutionalization. Finally, we looked to the Kuwaiti parliament to show the highs and lows of mission autonomy when strong linkages to different parts of society are well developed yet institutionalization is intermittent, providing institutional opportunities through permissive procedural rules but lacking the staying power afforded by more coherent and hierarchical structures.

Overall, we find that linkage to societal constituencies is far more important for authoritarian parliaments to exercise mission autonomy, while their internal autonomy requires enthusiastically grabbing onto a given parliament's preexisting powers and ensuring sufficient institutionalization to be able to exercise them.

These general findings—that long patterns of institutional evolution have converged on an oddly powerful latent structure for most authoritarian parliaments; that institutionalization is critical to holding internal autonomy and necessary for many of the tools that a more activist parliament uses; and that without societal linkage mission autonomy is largely impossible—provide us with new questions, distinct from the ones that top-down lines of investigation lead us toward.

Under what conditions do we see greater coherence within authoritarian parliaments that aspire to grab for a degree of mission autonomy? That is, when should we expect the chaotic, MP-oriented Kuwaiti experience, and when should we see more coordinated efforts by political parties—or by the parliamentary leadership—as has sometimes been the case during periods of authoritarian rule in places like Brazil and Mexico? What allows this coherency and hierarchical coordination to develop within authoritarian parliaments in some places but not others?

In a different vein, we might further question how parliaments of technocracy—those with some notable institutionalization but largely cowed and cut off from societal input—evolve and reproduce themselves over multiple electoral cycles. Do they maintain their institutionalization at the cost of bureaucratization and increasing integration with the state? Do they fall away over time and return to the pleasures of the rubber stamp? Or can they hold on, preparing the ground to assert further autonomy at opportune moments in future days? We have seen some effort for the latter in Russia, but a similarly bureaucratic parliament in Singapore has lived as such for far longer and has thus far failed to show much verve for change toward a more assertive direction.

These and many more questions lie in the future. And we believe our focus on linkages and institutionalization offers a significant advantage in raising new queries that may otherwise fall by the wayside under top-down investigations that focus most acutely on regime-centric and functionalist logics.

CHAPTER 5

Religious Establishments

Religion, too, is a weapon. What manner of weapon is religion
when it becomes the government?
  Frank Herbert, *Dune Messiah*

No, you couldn't blame these things on God. It was people, just
ordinary, regular people, who did this to each other. People ruined
other people's lives.
  Elizabeth Strout, *Amy and Isabelle*

Henry VIII of England, Emperor Constantine the Great of Rome, General
Secretary of the Communist Party Leonid Brezhnev of the Soviet Union,
President Xi Jinping of China, and Prime Minister António de Oliveira
Salazar of Portugal were all authoritarian rulers steering state apparatuses
that tread on religious turf—and indeed they each encountered religious
authority while striving to maintain their regimes. It should therefore
be no surprise that these powerful rulers shaped the nature of religious
authority in their countries. But their actions and intentions are hardly
enough to explain the way that religious establishments were structured,
how they operated, or what they did. State religious institutions were certainly affected by these rulers' activities, but the institutions were not constructed simply as a function of their needs.

In previous chapters, we saw that state institutions can forge linkages
and grow their own institutional capacity. They can, thus, acquire great
control over their own affairs even when they report to authoritarian
structures. In some circumstances, they even develop their own image of

the public good and pursue it. But such general clarity masks a lingering murkiness in the details of this explanation for how institutional autonomy emerges. What kind of linkages work best? What forms of institutionalization matter? Are either linkages or institutionalization independently sufficient, or must they work together to foster autonomy?

In this chapter, we seek not to give sweeping or categorical answers to such questions but to use them to explore linkages and institutionalization more thoroughly in a complex institutional setting: religious establishments under authoritarianism. Underlying this effort is a single question: When are religious establishments able to achieve autonomy from authoritarian regimes?

Again, we find that when institutionalization and linkages are low, religion can be more easily structured as a function of regime needs—but that for such complex and deeply rooted bodies, these conditions are quite restrictive. We also find that certain kinds of linkages matter; for instance, religious establishments whose social allies support the regime are more malleable and establish autonomy far less easily.

Admittedly, this is an unusual setting to consider the politics of authoritarianism. Religion is an infrequent focus of work on authoritarian regimes, a gap we explore below because this lacuna is itself quite odd. The problem is not that religion seems irrelevant to understanding authoritarianism. Just the opposite is most often the case. But, more profoundly, bringing "religious establishments" into research on authoritarian politics raises two difficult practical questions. First, is the venue of a "religious establishment" too amorphous for clear juxtapositions to be made across cases? Second, might religious establishments, to the extent we can generalize at all, best be viewed as institutions that can lie outside the state?

Our answer to both questions is yes, but not enough to stop us.

On the first question, the term "religious establishment" is indeed amorphous. We choose it deliberately because it allows us to include a wide array of cases that, while not homologous, are fruitful for comparison. Chapter 3 began with constitutional courts because they are clear and well-defined structures. Moving to parliaments in chapter 4 introduced overtly political bodies but also ones with increasingly isomorphic structures cross-nationally. That made each easy to compare, allowing us to home in on linkages and institutionalization as general factors that foster autonomy. This chapter seeks finer insights by leveraging the sheer heterogeneity in institutions that make up a "religious establishment" across authoritarian polities.

With respect to the second question, the disparate positioning of religious establishments will deepen our empirical analysis of how linkages impact autonomy. This is because religious establishments do not always lie wholly within the state but vary in how they are arranged between state and society. While we have treated linkages a bit indiscriminately in prior chapters, the variable positioning of religious establishments sets up a platform for investigating how linkages to different types of actors can vary in their effects.

Our first task in this chapter is to explain the significance of the religious terrain to the study of authoritarian institutions. We then proceed to specify what we mean when we use the term "religious establishment" and highlight its state-oriented parts. Next, we will turn to the empirical heart of the chapter—a series of historical explorations of religious establishments under authoritarianism in Germany, Egypt, Saudi Arabia, and Thailand.

These cases offer a strong test for our theory on the conditions that facilitate institutional autonomy under authoritarianism. In Germany, Egypt, Saudi Arabia, and Thailand, autocrats have actively—and, in some cases, quite aggressively—sought to control religious establishments and subordinate them to the service of regime ends. Shortly after the unification of Germany, Chancellor Otto von Bismarck presided over a six-year campaign to destroy the Catholic Church structure and subjugate it to Imperial control.[1] Half a century later, the German Nazi Party—which was "easily the most anti-clerical of Europe's fascist movements"[2]—launched its own campaign "to destroy the Church"[3] and to subjugate Germany's Protestant establishment. In mid-twentieth-century Egypt, President Gamal `Abd al-Nasir heavy-handedly restructured and purged the country's religious establishment, aiming to subordinate it to regime supervision and institutionalize top-down control of the clergy.[4] For Saudi Arabia, scholars often stress how the ruling House of Saud is broadly intolerant of auton-

---

1. Herbert Lepper (1982), "Widerstand gegen die Staatsgewalt," in *Lebensraum Bistum Aachen: Tradition-Aktualität-Zukunft*, ed. Philipp Boonen (Aachen: Einhard-Verlag), 124. Michael B. Gross (1997), "Kulturkampf and Unification: German Liberalism and the War against the Jesuits," *Central European History* 30 (4): 546.

2. Richard Steigmann-Gall (2007), "The Nazis' 'Positive Christianity': A Variety of 'Clerical Fascism'?" *Totalitarian Movements and Political Religions* 8 (2): 315.

3. Waldemar Gurian (1952), "Totalitarian Religions," *Review of Politics* 14 (1): 3.

4. Malika Zeghal (1996), *Gardiens de l'Islam: Les Oulemas d'Al Azhar dans l'Egypte Contmeporaine* (Paris: Presses de la Foundation Nationale des Sciences Politiques).

omy for the religious establishment,[5] controls key religious institutions,[6] and allows those institutions to exercise authority "only in accordance with the needs of purely political actors."[7] Last, Thailand's Buddhist Sangha establishment was initially designed—and sporadically restructured over time—to serve as a tool for effectuating absolutist rule (by the monarchy, the military, or both at different periods).[8] As a result, much research on Thailand's Buddhist establishment tends to describe it as being "subservient" to regime authority,[9] "captured by the state,"[10] or "the handmaiden of the Thai state."[11]

Thus, if we observe internal or mission autonomy for religious establishments in these four cases, it is unlikely to be a result of regime intentionality. Indeed, from a purely regime-centric perspective, we might hardly expect to observe any autonomy for these religious establishments at all. By making the intersection of religion and authoritarian politics focal in this chapter, we add nuance to such top-down views by showing that the dynamics of linkage and institutionalization play a critical role in explaining when religious establishments are—and are not—capable of attaining autonomy under authoritarian rule.

In each historical case study, we sharpen our theoretical framework by showing that differences in types of linkages and institutionalization produce disparate effects on the development of internal and mission autonomy. We will see how linkages to old regimes and different kinds of publics (e.g., organized vs. disorganized; nationalized vs. localized; oppositional vs. pro-state or neutral) shape the levels of autonomy that these institutions obtain. With respect to *institutionalization*, we chart the effects of *adaptability* (the capacity to adjust to new circumstances and challenges), *complexity*

---

5. Ayman Al-Yassini (1985), *Religion and State in the Kingdom of Saudi Arabia* (Boulder: Westview Press).

6. Nabil Mouline (2015), "Enforcing and Reinforcing the State's Islam: The Functioning of the Committee of Senior Scholars," in *Saudi Arabia in Transition: Insights on Social, Political, Economic and Religious Change*, ed. Bernard Haykel, Thomas Hegggammer, and Stéphane Lacroix (New York: Cambridge University Press).

7. Michele L. Kjorlien and Michele L. Michele (1994), "State and Religion in Saudi Arabia," *Arab Studies Journal* 2 (1): 42.

8. Yoneo Ishii (1986), *Sangha, State, and Society: Thai Buddhism in History* (Honolulu: University of Hawaii Press).

9. Somboon Suksamran (1982), *Buddhism and Politics in Thailand: A Study of Socio-Political Change and Political Activism of the Thai Sangha* (Singapore: Institute of Southeast Asian Studies), 29.

10. Duncan McCargo (2004), "Buddhism, Democracy and Identity in Thailand," *Democratization* 11 (4): 155.

11. McCargo (2004), 157.

Religion and Authoritarianism

(the scope and intricacy of a religious establishment's various structures and roles in social life), *coherence* (the degree to which various parts of the establishment act in concert), and *hierarchy* (the degree to which institutional authority is centralized in top levels) on the acquisition of autonomy by religious bodies. And we go a step further by tying linkages and institutionalization together. For linkages to facilitate autonomy, there must be a high degree of institutional coherence, so that the religious establishment and its constituencies can operate as a unified pressure group.

Religion and Authoritarianism

While most scholars of comparative politics overlook religion as a "peripheral subject matter,"[12] religious establishments can be a powerful force in politics. Religion has a strong and sustained impact on many believers' daily lives, and it can affect a vast range of policy issues: family and criminal law, education, citizenship, media censorship, property ownership, taxation, inheritance, and public comportment.

Because regimes and states encounter religious institutions in a multitude of policy areas, ruling political authorities often develop a strong interest in what religious establishments do. Fascist Italy reached a mutual, though far from complete, accommodation with the Catholic Church through the Lateran Pacts.[13] The Soviet Union and China under Communist rule opted for the outright repression of religious communities and organizations.[14] The modern Egyptian state inherited al-Azhar, an independent religious establishment founded in the tenth century, and worked to absorb it and co-opt its leadership.[15] Thailand's Chakri dynasty established its own royalist sect within the Buddhist monkhood. In Singapore, the constitution mandates that the state remain secular, while the law criminalizes actions that threaten "religious harmony."[16] Kemalist Turkey declared the

---

12. Anthony Gill (2001), "Religion and Comparative Politics," *Annual Review of Political Science* 4 (1): 117–38.

13. Mark Donovan (2003), "The Italian State: No Longer Catholic, No Longer Christian," *West European Politics* 26 (1): 95–116.

14. Richard Madsen (1998), *China's Catholics: Tragedy and Hope in an Emerging Civil Society* (Berkley: University of California Press). Karrie J. Koesel (2014), *Religion and Authoritarianism: Cooperation, Conflict and the Consequences* (New York: Cambridge University Press).

15. Jocelyne Cesari (2014), *The Awakening of Muslim Democracy: Religion, Modernity and the State* (New York: Cambridge University Press).

16. Jothie Rajah (2012), *Authoritarian Rule of Law: Legislation, Discourse and Legitimacy in Singapore* (New York: Cambridge University Press).

state secular while simultaneously nationalizing religious institutions. And in Saudi Arabia, the ruling House of Saud forged an interdependent partnership with the Wahhabi Muslim movement, which afforded significant political influence to the Wahhabi establishment.

Despite the range of cases where authoritarian regimes dabble in, penetrate, or clash with the religious sector, religious establishments are not a common setting for academic studies of authoritarian politics.[17] Perhaps this is because much of what they do seems a bit far afield from politics or because they often sit uncomfortably astride the boundary between state and society. Religious establishments appear to be overwhelmingly large and cumbersome, but they are also moving targets; they bounce among the spiritual, social, and political spheres, eluding many scholarly inquiries into authoritarian institutions in the process.

Religious bodies often jointly serve as government entities and as representatives of a country's religious population, and this dual role is analytically provocative. It will help us build out our account of linkages, specifically by foregrounding the effects that linkages to different types of actors have on the development of autonomy. Perhaps just as important for our purposes is the fact that religious establishments are institutionally complex; their administrative frameworks operate on the national and local levels, commonly subsuming houses of worship, courts, schools, endowments, and some segment—if not all—of the clergy. Such complexity presents a unique opportunity to probe different dimensions of institutionalization.

Because religion is such a powerful presence, it looms large for authoritarian regimes that attempt, as they do, to control the state and guide society. But autocrats rarely create religious establishments through acts of institutional design. Most religious spheres are populated by institutions and pious constituencies that predate the modern state and, thus, had space to fashion their own sense of purpose and place in society. Moreover, because religious officials often see themselves as pursuing higher, divine, or transcendent truths, the prospects for observing internal and mission autonomy would appear favorable—if highly variable.

These features of religious establishments motivate us to tread into the under-tended fields of religion and politics under authoritarian rule. After all, Juan Linz, the figure who helped introduce the concept of "authoritarianism" to political scientists, not only used religion to distinguish authori-

---

17. Gill 2001. See also Anna Gryzmala-Busse (2012), "Why Comparative Politics Should Take Religion (More) Seriously," *Annual Review of Political Science* 15:421–42.

tarianism from totalitarianism but also expressed regret that the relationship between religion and authoritarianism did not draw more attention.[18] It is time to follow Linz, however belatedly, because we see the religious field as one often organized in a way that forces states, regimes, and societies to collide.

This chapter will show that state religious institutions are sometimes, but not always, able to position themselves as autonomous actors within an authoritarian system and amass meaningful policymaking authority. This insight is hardly new to scholars of democratic systems, for whom it is often easier to identify how religious organizations lobby elites, affect voting behavior, align with political parties, and influence public policy over issues like welfare, reproduction, and education.[19]

In authoritarian systems, however, most scholarly energy has gone into understanding how religious institutions can either sustain authoritarian power or promote democratization.[20] Our aim is to instead cultivate a deeper understanding of the ongoing operation of religious institutions within authoritarian systems when regime change (or reproduction) is not the primary question at hand. When can a religious establishment successfully manage its own affairs, reject subordination, and independently affect policy?

This task raises an important question of identification: What does it look like when a religious establishment operates with internal and mission autonomy under authoritarian conditions? Much like with judiciaries, internal autonomy manifests when a religious institution controls its own budget, decides on its own internal procedures, appoints its own personnel, and monitors and disciplines employees for itself.

---

18. Juan Linz (2000), *Totalitarian and Authoritarian Regimes* (Boulder: Lynne Rienner), 22–23.

19. Grysmala-Busse (2012). Richard Rose and Derek Urwin (1969), "Social Cohesion, Political Parties and Strains in Regimes," *Comparative Political Studies* 2 (1): 7–67. Arend Lijphart (1979), "Religious vs. Linguistic vs. Class Voting: The Crucial Experiment of Comparing Belgium, Canada, South Africa and Switzerland," *American Political Science Review* 73 (2): 442–58. Stathis N. Kalyvas (1996), *The Rise of Christian Democracy in Europe* (Ithaca: Cornell University Press). John E. Roemer (1998), "Why the Poor Do Not Expropriate the Rich: An Old Argument in New Garb," *Journal of Public Economics* 70 (3): 399–424.

20. Anthony Gill (1998), *Rendering unto Caesar: The Catholic Church and the State in Latin America* (Chicago: University of Chicago Press). Sabrina P. Ramet (1998), *Nihil Obstat: Religion, Politics, and Social Change in East-Central Europe and Russia* (Durham: Duke University Press). Steven M. Fish (2002), "Islam and Authoritarianism," *World Politics* 55 (1): 4–37. Daniel Philpott (2004), "Christianity and Democracy: The Catholic Wave," *Journal of Democratization* 15 (2): 32–46. Samuel Huntington (1993), *The Third Wave: Democratization in the Late Twentieth Century* (Norman: University of Oklahoma Press).

Mission autonomy, on the other hand, is rooted in the religious establishment's sense that a transcendent purpose guides its activities. We observe this when religious institutions (1) are concerned with an a priori or divine truth as opposed to a politically filtered message; (2) manage their own activities in society, such as proselytizing, conducting rituals, or collecting alms; and (3) carve out roles for themselves in public policy—perhaps education, law, or welfare—and orient policy to align with their own religious mission.

Religious Establishments: A Very Motley Crew

Before turning to the empirical case studies, we must first clarify what we mean to probe when studying "religious establishments," a term not in common usage. One simple, and more common, way of describing our topic of inquiry might be how authoritarian regimes handle the relationship between church and state or between faith and politics. But such commonly used terms—as well as many alternatives—can be confounding, meaning different things in different contexts. So perhaps it would be more accurate to reiterate that it is the very complexity of describing the subject, not its simplicity, that draws us to it.

The basic vocabulary of "church" and "state" grows out of a specific historical experience; the structures and issues involved in that conceptualization sometimes travel well and sometimes quite badly. To refer to "church" in contradistinction to "state" presupposes not only Christianity but also a set of institutional arrangements that emerged out of the internecine conflicts of early modern Europe.

Occasionally substituting "mosque" or "temple" for "church" might be a healthy step to suggest openness and toleration, but it simply does not help the analysis. Even here, an overly (modern) Christian lens slips in to suggest simpler boundaries between the secular and the religious than are often warranted. Muslim religious authorities, for instance, generally do not fit into analogous "church/mosque" versus "state" categories; they might be scholars, judges, muftis (those who answer questions of religious law), ministers (as in members of the cabinet, not clergy), bureaucrats, or, even in some instances, heads of state. Those of non-Abrahamic faiths add further complexities to sort out, whether animist authorities undercut or reified by colonial law in sub-Saharan Africa; the congeries of overlapping yet distinct traditions within the Hindu pantheon; or the monastic institutional lives of the Buddhist world.

Yet, for readers most familiar with the history of Christianity in Europe, the term "religious establishment" likely has a distinctive meaning that implies religious structures specifically supported by the state. Indeed, the evolving relationship between church and state in Europe consistently implicated the question of whether religious institutions should be "established" (folded into the state) or "disestablished" (separated from the state). While we use the term "religious establishment" a bit more broadly, highlighting our divergence from this historically specific usage is necessary given how greatly the terminology on religion gets colored by experiences of European Christianity. Our use of the term "religious establishment" is intended to travel beyond Christian and European cases, indicating any sets of religious institutions in a society regardless of whether they are state bodies, non-state bodies, or something else in between.

What is considered "religious" varies from one creed and one society to another. Religions are not homologous or truly analogous, and what we include in the religious field will necessarily vary in different contexts. This variation brings us to the second part of the term, "establishments"—a word selected in order to encompass formal institutions while remaining agnostic on their precise nature or even their association with the state. They may be officially recognized or chartered, straddle the state-society divide, be a formal part of the state apparatus, provide strong support for a particular regime, or be some mixture of all these things. The Spanish Church in the Francoist period, for instance, was a pillar of support for the regime, took on many state-like functions, was financially supported by the state, and received legal protection and privileges. Spain was declared "Catholic" constitutionally. But the Church remained formally independent, and its status as a global organization was unaffected by its affiliation with the state and regime.

Thus, in order to be considered a "religious establishment," we require that an institution (or a set of multiple interrelated institutions) be active in the religious field (as defined in the terms of a particular society) and have some formal structure, bureaucracy, and authority. The precise relationship to the state and regime is *not* part of the definition because it is what we wish to investigate.

As the state's reach has grown, it has competed with, edged out, folded in, or blissfully ignored what religious establishments already do in society: register births, police morality, adjudicate disputes, administer land, or educate the public. Unlike parliaments, which emerge as a result of similar political battles (demands for taxation, redistribution, or widening the franchise), religious institutions vary a lot more in terms of the initial starting conditions that predate their actual formation.

Such variation in the seam between religion and politics is theoretically provocative, but it also presents inherent challenges of analytic clarity. We tackle these challenges in part by moving in our empirical case studies from the more familiar (for those readers whose historical knowledge is rooted primarily in the European and North American experiences) to the less familiar.

We begin with a well-studied tussle in Germany between a recognizable Church (the Catholic one) and a new authoritarian regime (the German Empire under Otto von Bismarck as chancellor), followed, after an interregnum, by a very different and much less accommodative authoritarian regime (the Nazi Third Reich). We then proceed to Egypt and Saudi Arabia, where the faith in question is different but organized in ways that evoke vaguely familiar structures and issues to those more comfortable with European history. Finally, we travel far out of the usual sample of well-trodden cases to Thailand, where the history and structures we encounter will be less analogous and, for that reason, provide us with exciting new constellations of interaction, domination, and cooperation between state and religious establishment.

The basic view of the politics of religious establishments in authoritarian systems that we develop in this chapter is one that portrays them as historically grounded in the period of state formation but not in immutable fashion. Regimes do use religious establishments, but not as they please. And the results of regime efforts at instrumentalizing religion are uneven—not just because the tools are clumsy but also because they are wielded for tactical reasons; their effects often outlast the motives for their original usage.

In order to understand when religious establishments realize internal and mission autonomy, then, we will see that what seems to matter is patterns of institutionalization based in the state-building period but reshaped by regimes along the way, and especially the linkages that religious establishments have with pious publics, ones that make the establishments more useful but also more unwieldy.

Germany

We begin our empirical assessment of religious establishments in authoritarian systems with two periods of church-state confrontation in

Germany—one during the 1870s under the authoritarian German Empire and a second in the era of the National Socialist dictatorship in the 1930s. In imperial Germany, a decade-long fight over the Catholic Church's role in that newly united polity led to a surprising regime defeat, setting the stage for significantly increased autonomy for the Catholic Church. Moving forward in time to Nazi Germany in the 1930s, our account will probe a shorter struggle, one that ended with the country's Protestant religious establishment subdued under the regime's heel with sharply reduced autonomy, while institutional Catholicism exchanged silence and arguable complicity with regime goals in return for retaining internal autonomy.

The first of these two historical accounts draws attention to the power of two converging forces: a religious establishment's strong linkages to society and its high degree of institutionalization. The nascent German Empire under the guidance of Chancellor Otto von Bismarck prosecuted its anti-Catholic Kulturkampf ("culture struggle") from 1871 to 1889, with the greatest period of attempted state coercion of the Church between 1872 and 1878. During this Kulturkampf era, tight and deep linkages with the believing Catholic mass public in many parts of the empire provided critical financial and activist support for the Church when it was on the backfoot against the state. This was coupled with the high degree of institutionalization that the Church had, particularly through (1) the strongly hierarchical nature of the Church organization present since the medieval period; (2) the effective coherence of the clerical class vis-à-vis this attack by the regime and its bureaucratic execution; and (3) the adaptability and complexity of Catholic organizations that performed a variety of state-like roles in education, health care, and social control. All these linkages and forms of institutionalization were actually invigorated by the state assault against the Church, allowing Catholicism to endure—even thrive—as an independent and societally legitimate institution during the Kulturkampf.

The second historical account draws our attention to entirely different conditions: a Protestant religious establishment with fraying linkages and a less institutionalized infrastructure. Over fifty years and two regime changes after the confrontation between the Church and Bismarck's state, the National Socialist dictatorship engaged in its own Kirchenkampf ("struggle of the churches") that led to a hostile takeover of the dominant confederal church association known collectively as the Protestant Evangelical Lutheran Church. For the fairly decentralized Protestant religious establishment that had developed over the eighteenth and nineteenth centuries, its subjugation to the Nazi regime can in part be explained in terms of its surprisingly weak linkages to Protestant German society in the 1930s. Widespread secularization among all classes, the decline of the Prussian Junker aristocracy as a key part of the elite, and the rise of explicitly atheist social democracy among the culturally Protestant working class of northern and eastern Germany undermined linkages that might have otherwise strengthened Protestant clerical leaders and the established Protestant churches in their fight against the Nazis. The Catholic Church's experience with the Nazis took a different course, with a highly institutionalized and (still) societally linked religious establishment taking great pains to find a means of cohabitation alongside the new dictatorial reality.

In what follows, these paired German cases will first shine light on the capacity for constituency-linked religious authorities to resist authoritarian encroachment—particularly when the religious establishment is entrenched in society and relied upon by the public to perform state-like functions. We also see an important caveat—that linkages to public constituencies are rendered less effective when those constituencies also actively support (or even ambivalently tolerate) the regime. Second, the German cases highlight the importance of the four dimensions of institutionalization: hierarchy, coherence, complexity, and adaptability.

Finally, the German cases illustrate that top-down efforts to subdue religious establishments and reconfigure them to suit regime functions have mixed success. When institutionalization is high and linkages strong, top-down functionalist logics explaining institutional autonomy as a function of regime needs have limited empirical traction because regimes are less capable of commanding or restricting the religious sphere from the outside. But when institutionalization is lacking and linkages to supportive constituencies become weak or unreliable, religious institutions' autonomy can be more fully understood by referencing regime interests and actions.

Bismarck's Reich, the Kulturkampf, and the Stubbornness of Institutional Catholicism

The modern German state was born during the fevered era of nineteenth-century national unification wars, crafted from a patchwork of primarily German-speaking monarchies and city-states once part of the decentralized Holy Roman Empire. Riven since the sixteenth century by confessional divides between Protestant Lutheran states in the north, center, and east and Roman Catholic lands in the south and along the Rhineland in the west, divergent religious institutions were long baked into regional identities and organizations.

By 1871, a mixture of lucky historical accidents and intentional action by the regime of the Kingdom of Prussia led to the creation of a semi-federalized, authoritarian order under the auspices of the Prussian king, now German emperor. Masterminded by Chancellor Otto von Bismarck, Protestant-dominated Prussia found itself leading a new state that included a grand swathe of German-speaking territories. The early decades of the empire would be taken up with the nationalization of imperial politics and concerted efforts at state building.[21] A strong anti-Catholic movement united secular German liberals, northern Protestants, and state-building Prussian elites ideologically and practically, with many seeing Catholicism as a cause of economic and social backwardness as well as confessional disunity.[22] The Catholic minority, roughly 35 percent of the empire's population at the time, found itself on the wrong side of the complementary nineteenth-century trends of liberalism, centralism, and nationalism.

The newly founded German state spent two decades fighting the institutional Roman Catholic Church, with the strongest efforts concentrated between 1872 and 1878. This Kulturkampf sought to undermine the Catholic establishment, transfer its authority in German society to the new state, and supplant the Church in its roles as a provider of education and health care, as an authority for civil registration (of births, deaths, and marriages), and as an organizer and legitimator of major life events for Catholic believers. The Church, however, proved to be a formidable foe.

The Catholic Church was (and remains) venerable, strongly hierarchical, and complex in the ways it was integrated into social life. The Church maintained strong vertical hierarchies of prelates with total nominal authority over lower institutional levels. And the Catholic Church as a broader religious establishment in Germany was highly complex, with a patchwork of monasteries, convents, religious hospitals, cathedral cities and property-holding bishoprics, confessional schools, and embedded village and town churches dotting a diocesan network that only partially matched political boundaries at the subnational or national level. Thus, the nineteenth-century Church in Germany inherited a high level of institutionalization; its legacy also included deep linkages with the large parts of society that were made up of confessional Catholics.

Unsurprisingly, this was all seen as a historic threat to the unity of the new empire and a thorn in the side of a centralizing and nationalizing regime built on liberal authoritarianism, cultural Protestantism, and

---

21. Jasper Heinzen (2017), *Making Prussians, Raising Germans: A Cultural History of Prussian State-Building after Civil War, 1866–1935* (New York: Cambridge University Press).

22. Gross (1997).

an aspiration to undercut preexisting levels of structural differentiation that allowed for boundaries to separate the executive leadership from state and societal institutions. For German elites and the bourgeois Protestants, liberal politicians, businessmen, and newspapermen who supported them, institutional Catholicism was an enemy of modernity, centralism, and national glory.

The most important forays against the Church came in the form of the so-called May Laws of 1873, which were designed to undermine the Church's extensive and empowered internal autonomy.[23] These laws forced clerical candidates for ordination to submit to state-controlled examinations, gave the Prussian state the right to veto Church appointments, restricted the Church's ability to discipline its members,[24] and simplified procedures allowing individuals to leave the Church.[25]

These laws were followed by legislation giving officials the power to strip citizenship of and exile clerics who did not comply with state laws—most importantly, those laws that had just restricted the Church's own autonomy. The Prussian state also purged Catholics from its own bureaucratic ranks to ensure compliance.

The Jesuit Order—seen as a prime institutional source of reviving and strengthening Catholicism—was banned in 1872.[26] In 1875, all monastic orders, convents, and religious congregations were suppressed and closed to further weaken the Church's institutional presence.[27] The Catholic press was censored, and all state funding for Catholic dioceses ceased by 1875. A further education decree was enacted in 1876 that prohibited priests remaining in the educational field from giving religious instruction.[28]

Finally, the state ambitiously sought to take over Catholic bishoprics directly by assigning state administrators in places where priests and bish-

---

23. It is relevant to note that this and other Kulturkampf laws were passed within the area of authority of the Prussian part of the empire, given the curious federal system that unification had required. This overlarge federal territory contained many Catholics in its western parts (the Rhineland) and far eastern parts (formerly Poland) and was mimicked to lesser degrees by liberals in the more explicitly Catholic federal kingdoms and duchies elsewhere in the west and south.

24. Most critically, interconfessional marriage, mandatory marriage in the Church, and divorce.

25. Ronald J. Ross (1984), "Enforcing the Kulturkampf in the Bismarckian State and the Limits of Coercion in Imperial Germany," *Journal of Modern History* 56 (3): 460.

26. Gross (1997), 546.

27. Ross (1984), 468–69.

28. Marjorie Lamberti (1986), "State, Church, and the Politics of School Reform during the Kulturkampf," *Central European History* 19 (1): 74–75.

ops had been imprisoned, were deceased, or had been stripped of office for violating any of the Kulturkampf laws. This also had the added benefit of expropriating Church property and denying non-state financial support to the Church.

The imperial state's wide-ranging assault on the Church aimed to undermine the Church's internal autonomy and connections with the believing masses. However, the Kulturkampf ultimately floundered on widespread noncompliance, shirking, and covert action by all levels of the Catholic Church's hierarchy. Importantly, the lower clergy, episcopal hierarchs, and the fraternal and sororal religious orders proved to be highly coherent and adaptable, allowing for sustained and concerted opposition against the anticlerical decrees over many years with very few defections to the demands of the Kulturkampf laws.

In most cases, laws that challenged the Church's control over its own members failed spectacularly. Benefitted by its tremendous degree of institutional complexity, the Catholic Church was able to adapt to the hostile environment created by the imperial state. Exiled bishops found proxies within the Church's sprawling diocesan system, and they surreptitiously began using agents known as "apostolic delegates" to continue de facto administrative control over their dioceses.[29] Exiled priests navigated the copious networks that connected the Church's various structures in German society in order to discretely find their way back to their parishes, or to nearby ones, and continue their ministries. On top of such skillful and creative forms of noncompliance, most religious orders actually ended up being exempted from closure or illegally tolerated, as they provided much of the hospital and educational capacity in the Catholic parts of the empire, and the state did not have the capacity to replace them in these roles.[30] Because the Catholic Church was highly institutionalized, performing a widespread and complex set of roles in German social life, the imperial state encountered great difficulty and costs in effectuating the Kulturkampf.

Significant public constituencies linked to the Catholic Church throughout the empire in Bavaria, Baden, Württemberg, and the Rhineland further mobilized in support of clerical noncompliance, first through

---

29. Ross (1984).

30. Ross (1984). As an aside in favor of taking deep roots of institutional stickiness seriously, it should be noted that this is not something held only to Germany's century-old past— even in today's era of secularism the largest employer in German social work and disaster relief is in the hands of the specifically confessional organizations Caritas (Catholic) and Diakonie (Evangelical Lutheran).

street protest and then via more powerful means over the 1870s. Making up roughly 37 percent of the empire's population in 1870,[31] Catholics flocked to the newly formed Center Party (Zentrumspartei)—a political organization that was specifically formed to defend Catholic interests and quickly built tight connections to both the Church hierarchy and the Catholic bourgeoisie and aristocracy. This channeled the natural constituency that the Catholic Church cultivated within the German public sphere into a coherent party vehicle that was more disciplined than the Prussian conservative elite. Here we see strong linkages and a high degree of institutionalization working in conjunction with one another, being jointly activated to fend off a determined assault on the Catholic Church's autonomy.

The tactic of party-based institutionalization of religious interest is a testament to the Catholic establishment's adaptability when confronting new challenges and a significantly reconfigured political environment. It was also facilitated by a general and macrolevel degree of structural differentiation in the federal system, whereby party and legislative organs operated as separate units that were meaningfully insulated from imperial elites and so offered viable tools for enterprising Catholics seeking to promote their Church's influence and autonomy. The move toward party politics proactively prevented further inroads by the anti-religious socialist movement, a growing concern that would undermine German Protestantism severely in the coming decades. The Center Party notably bundled a cross-class societal constituency in support of the Roman Catholic Church, its institutional prerogatives, and the legitimacy of Catholic confessional identity as a large minority group in the empire.[32]

The Center Party acted as the political means by which the Catholic Church could fight the active threats against its autonomy, and it thrived for decades as a powerful political opposition to the imperial and Prussian governments, becoming a kingmaker in legislative politics in the 1890s.[33] As late as 1903, 20 percent of the Center Party's parliamentarians in the imperial Reichstag were actual, frocked clergy.[34] Meanwhile, the parlia-

---

31. Manuel Baroutta (2003), "Enemies at the Gate: The Moabit Klostersturm and the Kulturkampf: Germany," in *Culture Wars: Secular-Catholic Conflict in Nineteenth-Century Europe*, ed. Christopher Clark and Wolfram Kaiser (New York: Cambridge University Press), 229.

32. Willfried Spohn (1980), "Religion and Working-Class Formation in Imperial Germany 1871–1914," *Politics and Society* 19 (1): 109–32. David Blackbourn (1980), *Class, Religion and Local Politics in Wilhelmine Germany: The Center Party in Württemberg before 1914* (New Haven: Yale University Press).

33. Blackbourn (1980).

34. Stanley Suval (1985), *Electoral Politics in Wilhelmine Germany* (Chapel Hill: University of North Carolina Press), 70.

ments of the majority-Catholic southern German federal state entities remained dominated by the Center Party well into the twentieth century.[35]

Linkages between Church and public were further strengthened in the crucible of the Kulturkampf.[36] Two-thirds of the ostensibly closed religious orders found ways to survive, while voluntary donations, fundraising drives, and a "clandestine system of ecclesiastical taxation"[37] more than replaced lost funds from state subventions. Of the four thousand Catholic priests in Prussia proper, only twenty-four complied with the Kulturkampf laws. By the end of the state's concerted efforts to undermine the Catholic Church in the empire, the network of strong, Church-supporting institutions included political parties, savings and credit associations, consumer cooperatives, journeymen's and artisans' clubs, organizations for religious and practical education, trade unions, and even a federation of bourgeois entrepreneurs and business owners.[38] Thus, top-down efforts to cripple the Catholic establishment and sever its linkages to German society ultimately had the opposite effect in practice.

In the end, the attempt by the imperial state to destroy the Catholic Church's authority failed due to the enduring hierarchical structure of authority, the coherence within the religious establishment, the complex network of linkages tying the Church to broader Catholic German society, and the adaptability that the Church displayed in response to the Kulturkampf. Of relevance to system-level—as opposed to institutional-level—factors, structural differentiation presented openings in the new empire's authoritarian structures that proved particularly useful in the Church's efforts to defend its internal autonomy and continue pursuing its holy mission. The existence of an elected parliament that in turn had some significant constitutional powers helped in giving the Church's political supporters sizeable institutional purchase within the regime's political apparatus and, moreover, allowed Catholic priests-cum-legislators to construe their religious mission into an overarching political platform that proved successful for decades. Despite the imperial regime's intentions, the Kulturkampf left the Church's internal autonomy unscathed, and it ended up strengthening its mission autonomy as an institution independent from the state, intertwined with huge sections of German society and active in political and parliamentary life.

---

35. Ian Farr (1983), "From Anti-Catholicism to Anticlericalism: Catholic Politics and the Peasantry in Bavaria, 1860–1900," *European Studies Review* 13 (2): 249–69.

36. Ross (1984), 474.

37. Ross (1984), 478.

38. Spohn (1991), 117–18.

Nazis at the Pulpit and Fights over the Flock: Protestantism and Catholicism under Hitler

Three generations after the Kulturkampf, Germany experienced a second period of far less qualified authoritarian rule. Under Adolf Hitler's National Socialist dictatorship, regime goals ultimately promoted whatever policy direction would denude religious institutions of independent value from the regime's totalizing ideology.[39] But even under Nazi rule, some of the aspects of the Catholic religious establishment that had protected its autonomy under the empire continued to operate, allowing a degree of internal autonomy to be preserved even under such hostile circumstances. The same was not to be for the Protestant religious establishment in Germany, however.

The thrust to subordinate independent religious institutions took two forms—one targeted against the German Evangelical Church Confederation (Deutscher Evangelischer Kirchenbund) and another against the Roman Catholic Church. The former was a confederation of Lutheran, Reformed, and United Protestant church bodies that acted as established state churches in twenty-eight of the Weimar Republic's legacy territorial jurisdictions—a long institutional holdover from Protestant victories in the religious wars of the sixteenth and seventeenth centuries. The latter remained the same basic religious institution that the imperial state had fought unsuccessfully sixty years before.

The Nazi regime struck first at the Protestant establishment's internal autonomy, seeking both to force an institutional centralization that would be more strongly tied to the German state and to infiltrate its ranks with members of a pro-Nazi church movement known as the German Christians (Deutsche Christen). Within a few months of Hitler's ascent to the chancellery, the German Evangelical Church Confederation's leadership agreed to Nazi requests to merge the confederal, region-based churches of Evangelical Lutheranism into a new, national church organization, the German Evangelical Church (Deutsche Evangelische Kirche), in April 1933. The initial process proved to be insufficiently controlled, and Hitler's handpicked man lost an internal vote to be the newly established church head (*Reichsbischof*). This caused a scandal and further regime agitation for the Protestant establishment to fall into line. By September of the same

---

39. John S. Conway (1968), *The Nazi Persecution of the Churches, 1933–1945* (Vancouver: Regent College Publishing).

year, the regime deployed such massive coercion and mobilized so many Nazi-friendly Protestant activists from the ideologically aligned Deutsche Christen movement that the national Protestant establishment saw no choice but to accede to all regime requests.[40]

The capture of the Protestant institutional apparatus in Nazi Germany was aided by several key weaknesses of the old German Evangelical Church Confederation. The regional Protestant churches' linkages to German society were significantly weaker than their Catholic counterparts, due to widespread secularization among the population and the close alignment of Protestantism with the German state. Even before the rise of the Third Reich, the Protestant establishment was known as a state-supporting institution, which meant that both clergy and lay members had already internalized a long-standing tradition of reconciling religious interest with state interest.[41]

Unfortunately for the Protestant clergy who vehemently opposed the Nazi regime, a far larger proportion of Protestants voted for the National Socialists than did Catholics.[42] The grassroots German Christian movement, which sought to "de-Judaize" Protestant Christianity and support Nazi principles of racial glorification and submission to the state, grew particularly popular among bourgeois Protestants.[43] The Protestant religious constituency thus developed its own authoritarian linkages to the Nazi regime, rendering it unreliable as a countervailing force against assaults on the Protestant establishment's autonomy.

Mission autonomy was entirely undermined by the Protestant establishment's subordination to the Nazi regime and its ideological goals, as the strong-arm tactics used in 1933 and 1934 were able to exploit the loose organizational structure of Protestantism; those who resisted fell back on an independent breakaway clerical network that only splintered the reli-

---

40. Richard Steigmann-Gall (2004), "Nazism and the Revival of Political Religion Theory," *Totalitarian Movements and Political Religions* 5 (3): 376–96.

41. Robert M. Bigler (1972), *The Politics of German Protestantism: The Rise of the Protestant Church Elite in Prussia, 1815–1848* (Berkley: University of California Press). Jonathan Sperber (1997), *The Kaiser's Votes: Electors and Elections in Imperial Germany* (New York: Cambridge University Press).

42. Hans Otto Frøland, Tor Georg Jakobsen, and Peder Berrefjord Osa (2019), "Two Germanys? Investigating the Religious and Social Base of the 1930 Nazi Electorate," *Social Science History* 43 (4): 765–84. Jörg L. Spenkuch and Philipp Tillmann (2018), "Elite Influence? Religion and the Electoral Success of the Nazis," *American Journal of Political Science* 62 (1): 19–36.

43. Doris L. Bergen (1996), *Twisted Cross: The German Christian Movement in the Third Reich* (Chapel Hill: University of North Carolina Press). Susannah Heschel (2008), *The Aryan Jesus: Christian Theologians and the Bible in Nazi Germany* (Princeton: Princeton University Press).

gious establishment further. While nominally illegal and never counting more than 20 percent of the Protestant clergy elite,[44] the anti-Nazi Confessing Church (Bekennende Kirche) acted as a counterbalance to the Nazi takeover. Confessing Church members attempted to reassert control over the national Protestant establishment several times over the course of the 1930s, although without success and experiencing increasingly deadly repression.

The Catholic experience was notably different under the National Socialist dictatorship. In general, the institutional Catholic Church was able to fend off threats against its internal autonomy, but at the significant cost of staying quiet as the Nazi regime systematically violated anything resembling Catholic ethical or moral teaching—thus largely denying expression of mission autonomy. Why was the Church only capable of salvaging its internal autonomy in this period, whereas it successfully asserted both internal and mission autonomy in the previous Kulturkampf era? One important factor producing these disparate outcomes is that the Catholic Church in Nazi Germany remained highly institutionalized—hierarchic, adaptable, complex, and coherent—but found that its linkages to societal constituencies in Germany were weakening and thus a less reliable source of political leverage. In this regard, the German case provides an instructive example where institutionalization on its own was sufficient to protect internal autonomy but, in the absence of dependable and mobilized societal constituencies, proved insufficient in the defense of mission autonomy.

The Catholic establishment's interest in finding a clear accommodation with the German political regime was partly spurred by increasing secularization and diversification among the Catholic population. While clerics could command truly profound electoral support even into the 1910s, the postwar disillusionment eventually undermined the Center Party's hold on the Catholic minority electorate. By the 1920s, only 60 percent of the German Catholic population voted for the Center Party, down from well over 80 percent in the 1890s.[45] The Catholic establishment maintained strong linkages with Catholic German society but was less assured of loyalty than before in the political realm. Catholic Nazis were relatively rare, but the National Socialist message of anti-liberalism and German nationalism resonated well in many Catholic constituencies.[46]

---

44. Mark Edward Ruff (2014), "The Critical Reception of John Conway's 'The Nazi Persecution of the Churches, 1933–1945.'" *Kirchliche Zeitgeschichte* 27 (1): 31–42.

45. Guenter Lewy (2009), *The Catholic Church in Nazi Germany* (Boston: Da Capo Press), 6.

46. Douglas J. Cremer (1999), "To Avoid a New Kulturkampf: The Catholic Workers'

Given its precarious position and the questionable reliability of supporting constituencies in society, the Roman Catholic Church was receptive to a regime olive branch. This resulted in the Reichskonkordat of July 1933, which safeguarded Church internal autonomy, with its first article recognizing "the right of the Catholic Church to regulate and manage her own affairs independently." Subsequent articles further ensured freedom of communication between all levels of the national and transnational Catholic hierarchy, exemptions from public obligations, guarantees of pastoral secrecy, and episcopal control over clergy engaging in state functions.[47]

In exchange for these guarantees of internal autonomy, two key concessions were extracted that very pointedly limited the Catholic establishment's mission autonomy. First, Catholic bishops were required to take loyalty oaths to the German government. Second, the Catholic Church was banned from membership in political parties and agitation in the political sphere. This eliminated the long-standing linkage between the Church and the confessional Center Party that had previously articulated Catholic political interests in both the German Empire and the Weimar Republic.[48]

For the Nazi regime, the Reichskonkordat was a sufficient concession as it effectively limited the Catholic Church's role in social and political life, even while the Church's internal autonomy persisted. In this sense, we find empirical purchase for a top-down functionalist account for the reconfiguration of the Catholic Church's role under the Third Reich. National Socialism was largely willing to acknowledge the claims of the Catholic Church over its own internal prerogatives, so long as those claims were prevented from competing with Nazi programs and ideology in German society.[49]

Nevertheless, the Reichskonkordat was a tactical victory for the Church that put it on a solid legal standing and slowed down the anti-Catholic tendencies of the Nazi regime, particularly in comparison to the wholesale takeover of the Protestant establishment taking place at the same time. Even though its social and political role was restricted, the Catholic Church succeeded in remaining operative as well as separate and autono-

---

Associations and National Socialism in Weimar-Era Bavaria," *Journal of Church and State* 41 (4): 740–47.

47. Pope Pius XI, "Concordat with Nazi Germany," cited in Sidney Z. Ehler and John B. Morrall, eds. (1954), *Church and State through the Centuries: A Collection of Historic Documents with Commentaries* (London: Burns and Oates).

48. Pope Pius XI, "Concordat with Nazi Germany."

49. Ernst Fraenkel (2017 [1941]), *The Dual State: A Contribution to the Theory of Dictatorship*, translated by Jens Meierhenrich (New York: Oxford University Press).

mous (at least internally) from the National Socialist regime. This success, of course, was no small matter given the totalitarian political context, in which the Third Reich sought to dominate and control all of society and eliminate any vestiges of structural differentiation that allowed state bodies and even non-state associations to operate as separate entities from the Nazi Party. After all, during the Nürnberg Party Congress of 1937, Adolf Hitler declared that "religions are only of value if they help to preserve the living substance of mankind."[50] Yet, the Catholic Church in Germany neither was fully abrogated by the Nazis for its perceived lack of value nor co-opted and repurposed in service of the Nazi regime's ruthless vision of what it meant to serve mankind.

But losing the means for institutionalized political influence still had profound effects on the Catholic Church's standing and mission autonomy.[51] Over the course of the 1930s, the Nazis began to shut down a plethora of Catholic civil society organizations; the clergy was increasingly intimidated by Nazi thugs; and its educational role was undermined. Even so, it was only in 1941 that all Catholic newspapers were finally banned by Joseph Goebbels. And in the face of such regime aggressions, the Pope spoke out in an unprecedented anti-Nazi encyclical, *Mit brennender Sorge* ("With Burning Concern"), which was read aloud in all Catholic pulpits throughout Germany on Passion Sunday and became a touchstone for bishops who sought to preserve internal autonomy by keeping their distance from the Nazi regime as the 1930s unfolded.[52]

Institutional Catholicism found itself cowed, under assault, and forced out of the political, social, and state administrative realms that the totalitarian regime claimed as its own. But it retained much more internal autonomy than the Protestant establishment, which was lacking both institutionalization and reliable linkages and thus easily and quite fully subordinated by the Nazi regime. Still, Catholic and Protestant public constituencies both proved weak in the face of National Socialist incursions—the former due to its adherents' general (though not universal) ambivalence to Nazi ideology as well as smaller, demographically minority presence in the Reich and the latter, more critically, through its members' more widespread support for the Nazi Party. As the course of

---

50. Fraenkel (1941), referencing transcripts published in *Deutsche Justiz* (1937), 873.

51. Anthony Rhodes (1973), *The Vatican in the Age of the Dictators, 1922–1945* (New York: Holt, Rinehart, and Winston). Ian Kershaw (2008), *Hitler, the Germans, and the Final Solution* (New Haven: Yale University Press).

52. Pius XI (1937), *Mit brennender Sorge* (Switzerland: St. Antonius-Verlag).

the Kirchenkampf suggests, institutional linkages to religious constituencies are less effective when believers are also regime supporters or otherwise linked to the regime in their own right.

Egypt and Saudi Arabia

When we turn from Europe to the Arab world, we initially encounter societies that seem very different in the way that they structure the relationship between religion and state. Aside from Lebanon, every Arab state declares Islam the official state religion, and most have ministries of religious affairs and court systems (generally for family law but sometimes for other issues) that adjudicate their cases on a clear religious basis. But the result may be less foreign to those coming with the European experience in mind. Indeed, Islam is an "established" religion in the European sense. And the particular institutional configurations—for family law, much charitable work, social service, and education where religious and state authority interact—should not be totally unfamiliar to those who know European history, even if the particular historical trajectory and structural basis differ.

Neither Egypt nor Saudi Arabia is a secular state. In dominant religious doctrine, Egypt currently positions itself as a beacon for "centrist" (*wasati*) Islam, while since its founding, Saudi Arabia has propounded "Wahhabism," a distinctive approach whose adherents prefer to eschew that label and instead present themselves as literalists hewing to original interpretations of religious teaching. Religious establishments in Egypt and Saudi Arabia are very much part of the state apparatus. They have had extensive presences in education, adjudication, charity, worship, and public morality. While they share an impressive reach, each also shows tremendous temporal variation within country as well as in comparison with one another.

Underlying this variation—indeed, substantiated by it—are some similar patterns. First, institutionalization arrived early and strong in Egypt; it has become notable more recently in Saudi Arabia. In both cases, institutionalization facilitated internal autonomy for the religious establishment, but only strong linkages allowed that internal autonomy to be augmented by a degree of mission autonomy. The strength of those linkages has varied over time. But just as important, the form of those linkages has also mattered considerably. In Egypt and Saudi Arabia, the most significant religious constituencies have generally been decentralized and diffuse groups (such as Egyptian alumni of al-Azhar or Saudi religious enthusiasts who sought to spread the Wahhabi message) actually coming together to the extent that they did in state-created and regulated spaces (mosques, universities, and even state agencies like the Saudi religious police). The effect has been to make an impressive degree of mission autonomy possible at times by steering policy from within the state but also to render that autonomy vulnerable to concerted regime countermeasures as its principal sources were derived from activity within state-regulated venues.

We probe the autonomy of Egyptian and Saudi religious establishments in two steps as part of a close, paired comparison. First, we begin by examining how religious establishments developed in relation to regime and state throughout the process of state building during the nineteenth and twentieth centuries. We will take a historical approach to charting the contrasting paths of state formation in each country, showing how the Saudi religious establishment exhibited slower institutionalization and greater linkages to diffuse constituencies within Saudi society. Each path resulted in a distinctive pattern for folding religious structures into the state, which produced divergent trajectories in the autonomy of Egyptian and Saudi religious establishments.

Second, we move to a fine-grained comparative analysis of the autonomy achieved by two critical structures within each country's religious establishment: (1) religious institutions for policing public morality and (2) religious leadership organs, called Councils of Senior Scholars. Starting with religious policing, we will show that the policing of public morality has been a widespread practice in many modern and premodern states and is thus less exotic than it may initially sound to an English-speaking audience. What is distinctive in the Egyptian and Saudi cases is the nature of the morality that is policed (based on Islamic legal understandings of permissible conduct) as well as the specific policing structures, their prominence as institutions unto themselves, and their capacity to achieve varying degrees of internal and mission autonomy over time.

We then proceed to examine an unfamiliar structure—the Council of Senior Scholars (Hay'at Kubar al-`Ulama)—that has come to sit atop the religious establishment in each country. The title and form of these councils may appear foreign, but anyone whose sense of a religious "establishment" comes from modern European history would sense their significance. In each case, these councils are populated by the country's most senior religious leadership, and their existence as an apex institution has allowed the regime to better control the religious establishment at times but also has enabled the religious leadership to develop a distinct and autonomous institutional will within the state—a bidirectional path that has caused considerable frustration to both regime and religious authorities alike.

Legacies of State Formation:
Linkages and Institutionalization in the Religious Sphere

Egyptian and Saudi "religious establishments," as we are using the term, evolved in the nineteenth and twentieth centuries alongside the construction of the modern state in a way that subsumed preexisting religious institutions (schools, courts, and even policing) within the state apparatus. But this process was distinct in each case, and three important historical forces produced a much higher degree of institutionalization in Egypt's religious establishment early on.

First, Egypt was a long-standing, if fitful, part of the Ottoman Empire, and its institutional development was deeply influenced by the Ottoman bureaucratization of Islam as a religion with systematized procedures and institutions. The Ottoman model of establishing structural differentiation between the regime and state bureaucracy, as well as its effort to cultivate institutionalization throughout the state apparatus, was thus passed on to the Egyptian state as the latter began to emerge as an autonomous, nearly sovereign, entity in the nineteenth century. The construction of key institutions—the Dar al-Ifta' (an official *fatwa*-giving institution), a ministry of religious endowments and religious affairs, and state regulation of mosques and religious education—often followed Ottoman models in which religious institutions became unambiguous parts of the state apparatus and were characterized by a notable degree of institutionalization, specifically in the forms of a strong and strict internal hierarchy and coherence.

The Saudi state, by contrast, was born in part through rebellion against Ottoman rule and emerged first in areas where Ottoman control was weak to non-existent. Thus, Saudi state building incorporated Ottoman structures only to a more limited extent, most notably in the region of the Hejaz, where Ottoman rule had been stronger and its imperial institutions had already taken some root. It generally allowed those structures to operate on a local level while it slowly built national institutions that absorbed or removed them.[53] And those national institutions, when built beginning in the 1940s, were constructed in part by creating an amorphous religious state within the broader administrative state, one that was staffed by devout personnel with training in Wahhabi Islam and notably less institutionalized than its Egyptian counterpart.

Second, European imperialism worked very different effects into each

---

53. David Commins (2015), *Islam in Saudi Arabia* (Ithaca: Cornell University Press).

country's religious establishment, with Egypt coming under direct British occupation in 1882. In Egypt, attempts to fend off imperialism, the capitulations (legal arrangements exempting Europeans from Egyptian law), the desire of British imperial rulers to avoid and contain the religious sector, and the efforts by Egypt's own leaders fostered an early arrangement that allowed religious structures to operate fairly autonomously in specific fields (personal status law, the educational sector, and mosque administration) but also sequestered those structures from other parts of the state apparatus. From the late nineteenth century forward, there was a distinct and autonomous set of schools, courts, and other institutions that could be identifiably labeled as "Islamic" striving to conduct their business in accordance with religious strictures. In this regard, a short-lived sense of mission autonomy existed during Egypt's state-building period, though it was isolated and confined to religious pockets carved out from the surrounding state bureaucracy that constructed alternate structures in many of these same areas (courts of general jurisdiction and state schools, for instance, that stood apart from the older religious structures and were not staffed by personnel with significant religious training, unlike the increasingly compartmentalized Islamic courts and schools).

Saudi Arabia, by contrast, developed institutions in the same areas—law and education most especially—that were not based on a separation between the religious and nonreligious parts of the state. Top religious officials in the mid-nineteenth century controlled a number of important posts within the Saudi state bureaucracy—president and vice president of the judiciary, director of the religious education system, general president of the girls' schools, and head of the "religious police," among others.[54] Imperialism played a less prominent role in shaping the contours of Saudi Arabia's religious sphere. And in the absence of foreign powers pushing the Saudi state to demarcate boundaries separating religious and nonreligious institutions, there was more fertile ground for overlapping horizontal state linkages between the two to take root.[55] The Wahhabi establishment, thus, found itself with access to important levers of power throughout the Saudi state. While this privileged status gave it a strong interest in supporting the Saudi royal family, the religious establishment also vigorously resisted

---

54. Steffen Hertog (2011), *Princes, Brokers and Bureaucrats: Oil and the State in Saudi Arabia* (Ithaca: Cornell University Press).

55. Bernard Haykel, Thomas Hegghammer, and Stephan LaCroix (2015), *Saudi Arabia in Transition: Insights on Social, Political, Economic and Religious Change* (New York: Cambridge University Press).

any state-building initiatives (including those sponsored by the royal family) that would restrict its extensive influence within the state. Wahhabi clerics' success in this regard is a testament to the degree of mission autonomy that the religious establishment asserted throughout the state-building period—one that helps explain some remarkable idiosyncrasies of state development in Saudi Arabia, such as the lack of codified law and the absence of secular courts.

Finally, Egypt's and Saudi Arabia's regimes built modern states in different ways after their clear emergence as sovereign political entities in the middle third of the twentieth century. The Egyptian state was built gradually in a manner that tended to maintain existing religious institutions but progressively move them under the clear and direct supervision of nonreligious officials and even regime leaders. Shortly into Gamal `Abd al-Nasir's presidency, religious schools, personal status courts, al-Azhar, and religious endowments supporting a great deal of charitable, religious, and educational activity were all centralized and brought under clearer oversight by senior state officials. Opposition groups, sometimes well organized, put pressure on state religious institutions as competitors, though in periods where regime control loosened, they also sometimes influenced and even infiltrated them.[56]

The reforms of al-Azhar under Gamal `Abd al-Nasir are particularly noteworthy, given the institution's status as the central node of Egypt's religious establishment; the institution traces its origin to a mosque constructed in the tenth century with a teaching institution attached that gradually gained in influence. Today, al-Azhar is a combination mosque, university, and theological research complex that is unambiguously part of the Egyptian state. It enjoyed considerable autonomy throughout much of the modern period even as ruling regimes have often tinkered with its institutional structure. In 1961, the regime undertook a more ambitious set of measures, placing it under presidential oversight and expanding its educational curriculum to include secular subjects (mathematics, engineering, natural sciences, medicine), thus diluting the religious content of the body.[57]

---

56. See Nathan J. Brown (2011), "Post-Revolutionary al-Azhar" (Washington, DC: Carnegie Endowment); (2013), "Islam and Politics in the New Egypt" (Washington, DC: Carnegie Endowment); and (2017), "Official Islam in the Arab World: The Struggle for Religious Authority" (Washington, DC: Carnegie Endowment).

57. Malika Zeghal (1999), "Religion and Politics in Egypt: The Ulema of al-Azhar, Radical Islam, and the State (1952–94)," *International Journal of Middle East Studies* 31 (3): 374.

These interventions in al-Azhar align with a top-down and functionalist account of institutional autonomy in the Egyptian case, at least in the short term. Al-Azhar was reconfigured during the presidency of `Abd al-Nasir to better serve the regime and neutralize a potential source of opposition. And through the 1960s, al-Azhar indeed promoted elite interests by delivering *fatwas* in support of regime programs. In the medium and long term, however, `Abd al-Nasir's reforms expanded al-Azhar's linkages throughout the Egyptian state and society and thus had the unintended effect of enhancing its capacity for mission autonomy. Through regime-led centralization, al-Azhar achieved a de facto monopoly over the authority to "confer religious legitimacy on the regime's political decisions," one that it exercised timidly under `Abd al-Nasir but with more assertiveness in later years.[58] And augmenting the secular curriculum helped expand al-Azhar's network of social linkages by equipping it to attract a diverse student body and place graduates in technical professions as well as the state bureaucracy.[59] Given this impressive reach in Egyptian society, the regime began to find itself accommodating al-Azhar as it relied on its support to confront an increasingly mobilized religious opposition from the 1970s onward. And al-Azhar used its influence to pursue its own sense of mission in social life, securing policy concessions from the regime over issues of education, medicine, media, divorce, birth control, and child custody.[60]

Saudi Arabia was similarly authoritarian in its development, but the state evolved into a far less coherent entity, shaped from the mid-1940s on, and especially since the mid-1970s, by the existence of oil revenues. With a fiscal basis that made hard choices unnecessary, leadership by a far-flung ruling family, and a privileged and somewhat autonomous religious sphere, Saudi state formation allowed fiefdoms to develop within the administrative state.[61] At the system level, structural differentiation between all state organs and the royal family was quite low as various princes claimed different segments of the state apparatus as their own. But the religious sector, even while being officially folded into the state and generally supportive of the Saudi dynasty, remained the most notable field in which sociopolitical authority was by no means dictated by—or, in practice, fused with—the House of Saud.

---

58. Zeghal (1999), 375.

59. Zeghal (1999), 378.

60. Meir Hatina (2003), "Historical Legacy and the Challenge of Modernity in the Middle East: The Case of al-Azhar in Egypt," *Muslim World* 93 (1): 63. Steven Barraclough (1998), "Al-Azhar: Between the Government and the Islamists," *Middle East Journal* 52 (2): 236–49.

61. Hertog (2011).

Criticism and opposition from religious actors could certainly be heard in Saudi Arabia, but it found space within state structures that stood partially co-opted but not fully subdued by the ruling House of Saud that cohabited many of those same sectors. In practice, this allowed an independent—though not fully uniform—sense of mission to persist within the Wahhabi establishment.

But that mission could hardly be negotiated and articulated into a coherent message that overtly challenged regime objectives, most principally because Wahhabi clerics themselves came together and interacted with one another only within a fragmented hodgepodge of state spaces that were subject to varying degrees of regime supervision. As a result, religious opposition in Saudi Arabia took less formal shape, ambiguously situating itself outside of official religious institutions while still incorporating a range of sympathetic establishment figures who occupied diverse positions throughout the state apparatus. Only toward the end of the twentieth century did distinct and identifiable religious movements arise, and even then the extent to which they represented organized movements remains a subject of controversy.[62]

By the late twentieth century, the result of state development in Egypt was a bifurcation between a set of highly institutionalized and hierarchical official religious structures and unofficial (and some even illegal), formally organized religious movements—that is, between the religious establishment of the state and religious social movements. In Saudi Arabia, by contrast, the religious establishment was significantly less institutionalized during this same period, with an unclear chain of command and divisions of responsibility that were informal and in constant flux. Moreover, Saudi religious institutions were not segregated from state organs or limited to a distinct religious sphere but instead continued to include a diverse array of state institutions (legal, bureaucratic, educational) that were all far from secular in their makeup. And these institutions were anchored in linkages to a broader religious public (regionally concentrated in al-Qasim, the heartland of the Wahhabi movement), which formed an imposing geographic and demographic constituency that the Saudi regime felt compelled to respect and represent in specific policy areas.

In the segmented Saudi state, this had the effect of assembling the religious establishment and its linked public constituencies within an expansive, but disparate, set of state locations. Officially empowered religious

---

62. Stéphane Lacroix, *Awakening Islam: The Politics of Religious Dissent in Contemporary Saudi Arabia* (Cambridge: Harvard University Press, 2011).

actors in Saudi Arabia exercised considerable authority and had the capacity to effectuate mission autonomy by operating the machinery of the state. But empowering Wahhabi scholars with state authority also gave the regime tools to rein in their autonomy and influence if it ever found the nerve to use them. Being increasingly dependent on such state institutions for organizing and reproducing itself, the Saudi religious establishment has quite recently found itself incapable of resisting such a determined reconfiguration of the state apparatus under the thumb of Crown Prince Muhammed Bin Salman.

This historical analysis of how religious establishments evolved alongside processes of state building illustrates, with broad strokes, divergent patterns of institutional development and autonomy in Egypt and Saudi Arabia. But because the religious establishment is intricate and sprawling in each case, broad strokes can provide a strong foundation while still blinding us to much of the finer-grained context. In the following sections, we add in some needed detail and enrich our depiction by delving deeper into the varying levels of autonomy achieved by two specific components of each country's religious establishment: (1) structures for religious policing and (2) religious leadership organs (Councils of Senior Scholars).

Policing Public Morality

When comparing the Egyptian and Saudi religious establishments, we can identify important variation in mission autonomy by probing differences in the extent to which religious actors and principles have historically been involved in policing public space and morality.

Islamic religious scholars generally agree that rulers should engage in "enjoining virtue and preventing vice"; more succinctly, this is the function of *hisba* (accountability). If not undertaken by the ruler directly (one rarely pursued option, which fused ruler and juridical-religious functions), structural differentiation would instead characterize the *hisba*'s enforcement, as this task was traditionally assigned to an appointed official known as the *muhtasib*. The function of *hisba* may seem initially exotic, but it was akin to policing as it was understood throughout most of the world until the nineteenth century. The word "police" in English—and its counterpart in European languages—has also evolved alongside the development of modern states: originally referring to providing public order (an order that entailed not merely personal security and property rights but also righteous social conduct), the word came to mean a professional law enforcement body only in the nineteenth century. The shift was subtle and initially

Religious Establishments · 217

slow, and it did not leave public morality completely behind, as could be discovered by bathers wearing revealing swimsuits in Spain in the 1970s, merchants in some American cities selling alcohol on Sundays in the 1960s, or people showing same-sex affection in many countries up to the present.

Much of the Arab world followed a similar process in which policing shifted from an emphasis on public morality to one that stressed security, but the importance of the former lives on quite strongly in many places. Indeed, one of the most distinctive elements of the Saudi state religious establishment has been the body often referred to in English as the "religious police" (a term not used in Arabic).

Egypt's Marginalized Moral Policing Legacy

The Saudi religious police are actually a bureaucratized form of the *muhtasib*, an office that very much existed in Egypt in earlier centuries—dating as far back as the founding of Cairo by the Fatimids in the tenth century.[63] The post disappeared in Egypt during the eighteenth-century Ottoman period,[64] though the doctrine of *hisba* still lives on in two notable areas of Egyptian law.[65] First, Egyptian courts are often pulled into matters of morality (artistic expression, sexual conduct, and so on), and they often regulate public order in a way that incorporates religious sensibilities—the issue arises most frequently in matters of apostasy and religious conversion.[66] Second, other official religiously based institutions wade into matters of public practice and moral conduct, sometimes doing so with enforcement authority. Egypt's al-Azhar in the 1990s, for instance, declared its own religious authority for censoring cultural productions, and it received support for this mission creep within the cultural sphere from the State Council, a judicial body with no formal religious functions.[67] Having found some purchase among a segment of State Council judges who "share its vision

---

63. Boaz Shoshan (1981), "Fatimid Grain Policy and the Post of the Muhtasib," *International Journal of Middle East Studies* 13 (2): 181–89.

64. Seven Ağır (2010), "Sacred Obligations, Precious Interests: Ottoman Grain Administration in Comparative Perspective," unpublished manuscript, Yale University Economic History Workshop.

65. On the position in general, see Kristin Stilt (2012), *Islamic Law in Action: Authority, Discretion, and Everyday Experiences in Mamluk Egypt* (New York: Oxford University Press). On current forms of *hisba*, see Hussein Agrama (2012), *Questioning Secularism: Islam Sovereignty, and the Rule of Law in Modern Egypt* (Chicago: University of Chicago Press).

66. Maurits S. Berger (2003), "Apostasy and Public Policy in Contemporary Egypt: An Evaluation of Recent Cases from Egypt's Highest Courts," *Human Rights Quarterly* 25:720–40.

67. Tamir Moustafa (2000), "Conflict and Cooperation between the State and Religious Institutions in Contemporary Egypt," *International Journal of Middle East Studies* 32 (1): 3–22.

of a more pious state and society,"[68] al-Azhar still today uses litigation as a method of asserting its religious mission to police public morality.[69]

Decentralized efforts to enforce the *hisba* continue to occur, both by state-oriented bodies in Egypt's religious establishment and by private religious actors within the pious public. But in the modern period, discretion over policing public morality is now centralized within the authority of secular legal officials, making linkages between the religious establishment and the state legal complex an integral component of enforcing religious morals in social life. Al-Azhar in particular has utilized such linkages with Egyptian judicial institutions to keep intermittently—and somewhat effectively—asserting a role in policing public morality from within the state. In this sense, Egypt's religious establishment continues to display signs of mission autonomy in creatively effectuating the *hisba* and regulating public virtue and vice. But at the end of the day, successfully pursuing this mission in practice requires support from secular state institutions that have the final say.

Saudi Arabia and the Hay'a

In Saudi Arabia, a public body, one straddling the division between state and society, seems to embody both the older and the newer meanings of the English term "police." Often referred to in English by the strange phrase "religious police," the Hay'at al-amr bi-l-ma`ruf wa-l-nahi `an al-munkir (most accurately if stiffly translated as the "Body for Enjoining Virtue and Prohibiting Vice") is staffed by pious enthusiasts (*mutatawwi`in*) who are actually part of a professional force that polices moral conduct in public places. Initially formed in the late 1920s, the Hay'a pursues its mission by disciplining those who engage in unfair retail transactions, violate the prohibition on alcohol, and associate with people of the opposite gender in ways that defy its interpretation of Islamic norms. While some measure of formal legal authority has come to guide its structure and functioning,[70] the Hay'a presents itself as authorized by the ruler to carry out his duties

---

68. Moustafa (2000), 14.

69. In 2017, al-Azhar won a lawsuit before the State Council seeking to force the Egyptian government to ban a television show that allegedly cast doubt on the pillars of Islam (as they are interpreted by al-Azhar itself). See *Daily News Egypt* (29 October 2017), "Court Approves Al-Azhar Lawsuit, Bans Islam El-Behiery TV Show," http://www.dailynewssegypt.com/2017/10/29/court-approves-al-azhar-lawsuit-bans-islam-el-behiery-tv-show/

70. The relevant structures and regulatory framework are posted on the Hay'a's website: https://www.pv.gov.sa/Pages/PVHome.aspx (accessed 4 February 2018).

to enforce sharia-based norms and behavior. But within the bounds of official directives, the Hay'a operates in accordance with its personnel's own understanding of what those norms are, and it can thus exhibit an important degree of self-defined mission autonomy.

The Saudi Hay'a seems to be a modern bureaucratization of a medieval institution, one that does not carve out a distinct sphere for religion but instead blends morality, ethics, law, and religion with considerable discretion. As an institution, the Hay'a tends to be staffed by those from areas of the country more connected to Wahhabi teachings. And its activities have varied considerably over time and place, not so much in response to written public directives as through unofficial guidance from senior Hay'a officials.

Just as we saw in the Kulturkampf era, discussed above, here too, this religious institution's unshakable linkages to society proved consequential for preserving its internal autonomy. At various points in Saudi history, most notably under King Faysal in the 1960s, the royal family considered asserting direct control over the Hay'a and its moral policing authority. But religious leaders in the Wahhabi establishment leveraged their weight among the pious public and within the state apparatus to deter such top-down efforts to claim religious policing as a regime prerogative.[71] Unofficial top-down guidance was a mutually agreeable—if sometimes tumultuous—arrangement, but sacrificing internal autonomy in favor of regime control over the Hay'a remained off the table throughout the twentieth century.

Protected by its standing among pious members of the public, and linked with the religious establishment (indeed, almost its enforcement wing), the Hay'a historically proved hard for the Saudi regime to control other than by quietly giving instructions to relax when its enthusiasm for enforcing its will provoked problems with key domestic or international audiences.

But in 2016, the regime finally went further with a very simple but drastic change that curtailed Hay'a mission autonomy while leaving its internal autonomy largely intact: rather than directly preventing vice itself, the Hay'a was obligated to refer moral infractions to the state police and public prosecution. The effect was dramatic but avoided confrontation. The Hay'a was still allowed to promote virtue as much as it liked; it was edged out of authority but not directly subordinated to regime control.

---

71. Nabil Mouline (2014), *The Clerics of Islam: Religious Authority and Political Power in Saudi Arabia* (New Haven: Yale University Press), 210.

This critical part of the religious establishment survived but was slowly marginalized; by 2019, the Saudi king issued a law on public decency that cited traditions and values but did not mention religion or Islamic law at all—and avoided reference to the Hay'a altogether. When probing the diminished mission autonomy enjoyed by the Saudi Hay'a in recent years, top-down accounts emphasizing regime actions, interests, and functions prove quite useful. But a longer historical perspective suggests that the utility of such functionalist logics is most principally limited to the contemporary period—a noteworthy point that we will return to below.

The Councils of Senior Scholars: Fraternal, Not Identical Twins

While the religious police are an important component of the religious establishment—particularly in Saudi Arabia—its members are rarely senior religious officials. Both countries currently place a Council of Senior Scholars at the apex of their religious establishments, and the coincidence in name is not accidental.

Egypt's Council of Senior Scholars: Disappearance and Return

An Egyptian council of the name emerged to lead the religious-educational institution of al-Azhar in the early twentieth century. That council presented itself as a collegial body of senior Islamic legal scholars who could give guidance on matters of Islamic teachings. But to the authoritarian and avowedly socialist regime that gained power in the 1960s, the existence of an autonomous religious leadership—and one that appeared overly conservative—seemed too much of an annoyance. The regime thus reorganized al-Azhar significantly in 1961, eliminating much of the autonomy that the institution had enjoyed, placing favored figures at its head, and abolishing its Council of Senior Scholars.

But with al-Azhar still something of a friendly zone for more pious members of the public, resentment against political control over the institution lived on. A social group calling itself the "al-Azhar Scholar's Front," for instance, emerged and demanded greater autonomy for the institution.[72] While suppressed by the regime, the front found that its message struck a responsive chord among some members of the institution who

---

72. Malka Zeghal (2007), "The 'Recentering' of Religious Knowledge and Discourse: The Case of Al-Azhar in Twentieth-Century Egypt," in *Schooling Islam*, ed. Robert W. Hefner and Muhammad Qasim Zaman (Princeton: Princeton University Press).

shared its goal of reinstating the Council of Senior Scholars, and it continued to operate informally. The Muslim Brotherhood—then tolerated but not legal—took up the cause, with differing reactions among scholars.

The opportunity to revive the Council of Senior Scholars suddenly emerged in Egypt with the uprising of 2011. During the uprising itself, those who had been involved in the front seized the moment to demand political reform—which for them meant freeing al-Azhar of political oversight and restoring a fuller measure of autonomy to the religious establishment. The interim military regime that took power in 2011, concerned with the erosion of credibility and viability in state institutions, saw an opportunity to enhance the legitimacy of the state religious apparatus and insulate it against the rising Muslim Brotherhood—fearing what might happen if a strong linkage between al-Azhar and the Brotherhood (or, worse, its subordination to the Brotherhood) did come to fruition. As a result, the regime proactively granted the sheikh of al-Azhar far more autonomy and allowed the recreation of the Council of Senior Scholars in 2012. This sudden change in autonomy and structure for the Egyptian religious establishment neatly illustrates how authoritarian regimes must grapple with a great deal of uncertainty and historical contingency when navigating relations even to their own state institutions. Self-interested regimes fixate on using what control they have to fend off short-term challenges and deal with what they perceive as the crisis du jour, but such tactical reactions by regimes can also have important—and often unforeseen—institutional consequences down the line.

Egypt's newly revived Council of Senior Scholars soon proved to be a thorn in the regime's side as contingency reentered the fray and tactical goals shifted focus. Members of this council, appointed by the leader of al-Azhar, were required to be consulted on top religious appointments (including the leader of al-Azhar, the head of Dar al-Ifta', and even any vacancies that opened in their own ranks), essentially making the official religious leadership a small, self-perpetuating cohort. The military certainly got what it wanted in the short term, with al-Azhar showing significant independence from the Muslim Brotherhood's civilian leadership that controlled the government in 2012–13. But when the military overthrew that leadership in 2013, it found itself grappling with the more consolidated and insulated religious hierarchy that it had created. The new regime clashed with al-Azhar's senior leadership on its harsh crackdown against the Muslim Brotherhood in 2013 and 2014 and its efforts to step up the patrolling of mosques and the policing of sermons. And the leader of al-Azhar was able to rely on the Council of Senior Scholars for support in more public confrontations, particularly over regime wishes to make changes in Egypt's family law.

While the reinstatement of the Egyptian Council of Senior Scholars in 2012 can be well understood as a short-term act of regime functionalism (one gladly embraced by the religious establishment from the inside), regime actions and interests prove insufficient in explaining the council's subsequent activity and turbulent relationship with the regime in the period after it was brought back into being. Indeed, the high level of al-Azhar's institutionalization and its linkages to broad, though ill-organized, public constituencies gave it and the attached Council of Senior Scholars a degree of internal and mission autonomy that regularly proved a headache for the regime. Periodic suggestions that the council's legal basis will be modified suggest its irksome nature in regime eyes; the failure to pursue those suggestions, tempting as they may be, simultaneously indicates that al-Azhar's extensive societal constituency makes it seem costly to target.

Saudi Arabia and Its Council of Senior Scholars: A Formidable Force

Saudi Arabia's rulers created a Council of Senior Scholars at the end of the decade when Egypt had abolished its own—and eventually discovered that they had a similar headache. In 1969, a longtime "grand mufti" (until then the chief religious official) died. In the words of Nabil Mouline, this "opened the way for the monarchy to directly intervene in the religious space."[73] It split up the mufti's authority among several state entities, including the newly created council, in an effort to make the religious establishment more manageable from the top down and less beholden to a single powerful religious personality steering its operation from within. But the regime eventually found that its efforts at fragmentation failed, given the significant adaptability of the religious establishment's leadership, which modified the newly created Council of Senior Scholars to suit its institutional needs.[74] Regime moves to depersonalize the Wahhabi establishment did not divide its ranks as intended but instead actually incited a new and surprising shift toward greater levels of institutionalization.

From the 1970s onward, the Saudi council became a centralized tool for the religious establishment within the state apparatus (rather than a vehicle

---

73. Mouline (2014), 149.
74. Mouline (2014), especially chapter 6.

for fragmentation) and one linked with a pious public looking to it as a guarantor that the state would be guided by the religious teachings of the Wahhabi movement. This more unified religious establishment was able to deepen linkages to courts, schools, universities, the religious police (Hay'a), and charities, creating a support network that safeguarded its authority and autonomy for decades.

And it was this powerful and institutionalized religious establishment that the Saudi regime finally decided to restrain after 2017, when Crown Prince Muhammad Bin Salman moved to limit the clergy's influence and rein in its constituency, claiming not to be launching in a new direction but returning to an old one that was more imagined than it was real: "We are simply reverting to what we followed—a moderate Islam open to the world and all religions."[75] The crown prince was not narrowly seeking to subdue the religious establishment in this period; more broadly, his move against the Wahhabi establishment was part of a much further-reaching effort to thwart all forms of structural differentiation that separated the Saudi ruler (de jure King Salman but de facto Muhammad Bin Salman), the regime (i.e., by strong-arming, arresting, and purging Saudi elites and even princes who previously enjoyed significant power), and the state apparatus (i.e., by extending Muhammad Bin Salman's authority to manage most state bodies directly).

As with the Hay'a, the regime initially balked at abolishing—or even frontally confronting—the powerful and highly institutionalized Council of Senior Scholars, linked as it was to other parts of the religious establishment and unorganized but strategically placed within societal constituencies. Throughout the twentieth century, the Saudi royal family was quite tepid in its efforts to influence religious leadership organs—intervening in some important cases, to be sure, but careful to back off when met with too much resistance. But the regime finally acted decisively in 2017, strong-arming a majority of the council to endorse its initiative allowing women to drive—a step that the body had fiercely resisted for years. It also used its power of appointments to bring dynastic loyalists into the council. And it winnowed away at its influence by establishing new state organs that diminished the centrality of the council and disrupted its linkages with other state institutions—creating a Ministry of Culture, for instance, in 2018, with a mission that said much about culture but little about religion,

75. "I Will Return Saudi Arabia to Moderate Islam, Says Crown Prince," *The Guardian*, 24 October 2017, https://www.theguardian.com/world/2017/oct/24/i-will-return-saudi-arabia-moderate-islam-crown-prince (accessed 19 December 2019).

a step toward the Egyptian model of containing religion within a specific sphere rather than having it permeate all aspects of political and public life.

Why has the Saudi regime taken steps that its Egyptian counterpart shrank from? One reason may be that the Saudi establishment's linkages with society, while strong, were with unorganized actors, many of whom were state employees (teachers, mosque employees, members of the "religious police"), while the Egyptian establishment counted many noncivil servants as supporters. But more significant was the fact that the Saudi establishment had progressively built a far more powerful place for itself within the state; the Egyptian counterpart dabbled in some important areas but left alone many issues of politics that the regime treated as critical. The Saudi religious establishment's leadership seems to have unwittingly demonstrated the adage that those who stick out their neck are more likely to have their head chopped off. Their mission autonomy had reached truly impressive heights, which Muhammad Bin Salman decided shortly after claiming de facto rulership of the kingdom that he would no longer ignore.

Intermixing State, Regime, and Religion in Egypt and Saudi Arabia

Narrating the stories of policing and senior scholars reveals some features directly and clearly, such as a high level of institutionalization for religious establishments in both countries (in which Saudi Arabia followed Egypt with some delay) and greater mission autonomy for religious institutions in the more segmented Saudi state. But these stories also show some subtle aspects about linkages that should be stated explicitly and explored briefly. Indeed, the divergent paths followed by Egypt and Saudi Arabia in terms of policing public morality and senior religious leadership are characteristic not of different understandings of religious doctrine but of different patterns and methods of state formation.

In both countries, broad religious publics existed that were closely linked to official religious institutions. Egypt's al-Azhar, for instance, oversees a separate school system, which today educates about one-twentieth of the school-age population—meaning that the institution has a constituency of alumni throughout Egyptian society who have had a connection with the religious sector from an early age. As far as horizontal links with other state institutions, there is some compartmentalization between religious and secular structures in the Egyptian state, but that has actually decreased over time. Egypt's religious institutions are now more active in cultivating linkages with other parts of the state apparatus, particularly legal and cultural institutions. These horizontal linkages have proven especially useful in enabling Egypt's religious establishment to assert and pursue mission autonomy in recent years, developing an assertive role for itself in matters like school curricula, cultural expression, and even state broadcasting.

In Saudi Arabia, a similar kind of religious public existed and found considerable purchase in state institutions. Outside of charitable work, however, there was no formal structure in society to allow them an organized, much less oppositional voice. Yet informality did not mean weakness. A decentralized and diffuse movement within the state protected the Saudi religious establishment as it institutionalized itself and developed impressive internal and mission autonomy over the course of the twentieth century. But the religious establishment was also left vulnerable, dependent as it was on state financial and legal empowerment. Historically, the regime used its latent power over the religious establishment gingerly, both because it generally enjoyed the establishment's support and because the evolved fusion of religious and state institutions meant that fully subduing the Saudi religious establishment would require a fundamental reordering of the state apparatus—through which flowed a vast network of mutually reinforcing linkages between religious actors, state agents, and the pious public.

Such a radical reordering is now unfolding today, as Muhammad Bin Salman has turned with surprising speed and zeal to subordinate the religious establishment, destroying its mission autonomy with a series of administrative, financial, legal, and ideological moves that left the establishment intact but subservient. Functionalist logics are now the key force reconfiguring relations between the new Saudi ruler and the Wahhabi religious establishment. But as our analysis has shown, this should be viewed as a powerful, yet quite idiosyncratic, achievement of the modern period—one that largely falters in its explanatory capacity when retroactively applied to the bulk of Saudi history.

Thailand: A Regime Creation with a Bit of a Life of Its Own . . . at Times

We turn now further afield, beyond the confines of Europe and the broadly defined Mediterranean Basin to Southeast Asia's Thailand, for a case that provides a great deal of insight into the working of religious establishments in authoritarian regimes. To facilitate cross-case comparison, we put the spotlight on an easily identifiable structure that has presided over Thailand's amorphous Buddhist establishment—the Sangha Administration, a state religious institution charged with managing Buddhist affairs and doctrine. This case exemplifies the ways in which linkage can be conceptualized not only as ties to groups in society but also as ties to coherent horizontal groups elsewhere within the elite. Furthermore, we illustrate how processes of institutionalization can become regularly interrupted by reform and counterreform efforts, which undermine broader goals of achieving autonomy due to their pernicious impact on patterns of institutionalized coherence and hierarchy within the religious establishment.

We show that the initial co-optation of the Sangha Administration by the Thai monarchy during the state-building period of the early 1900s resulted from the type of linkages that the Buddhist establishment maintained with society—namely, disorganized and highly localized ties between individual religious actors, monastic organizations, and their surrounding communities.

We further track how reforms of the Sangha Administration map onto instances of regime change throughout the twentieth century. The frequency of regime change in Thailand highlights the importance of a new type of vertical, even hierarchical linkage—enduring relationships between the religious establishment and elites from previously deposed regimes. And we find that new regimes meddling in the Buddhist establishment are themselves analytically useful, as many reforms have produced only further variations on the nature of its institutionalization.

Finally, we look to the modern period for a demonstration of the ways in which religious establishments lacking institutionalization are vulnerable to political subjugation. We illustrate how incoherence within Thailand's Buddhist establishment precludes the pursuit of internal and mission autonomy and, further, how the inability of Sangha elites to maintain hierarchic authority provokes regime intrusions into the religious sphere.

Legacies of State Formation:
The Functionalist Logic of the Early Sangha Administration

Thailand's modern Sangha Administration was created by the Chakri dynasty in 1902 to enable the monarchy to better control the religious sector.[76] The origins of this religious body can certainly be described as rooted in a functionalist logic—its structure and operation were clearly dictated

---

76. Duncan McCargo (2012), "The Changing Politics of Thailand's Buddhist Order," *Critical Asian Studies* 44 (4): 627–42. Ishii (1986).

by the royal family of that era to serve its immediate governance needs. Why were Chakri monarchs so successful in tailoring the Sangha Administration to suit their interests? Contrary to imperial Germany, Egypt, and Saudi Arabia, the long-ruling Chakri dynasty largely created this new religious establishment from the ground up in an environment utterly lacking structural differentiation between ruler, regime, and state at the system level. To the extent that other state institutions existed as entities separate from the Chakri royal family (which was indeed strikingly minimal, as this setting had a fundamental paucity of structural differentiation), they were too scattered and isolated to mount a meaningful defense against Chakri dominance as the Thai state took on modern trappings.

The Chakri dynasty has ruled Thailand since the 1780s, but its perspective on how to deal and interact with the dominant Buddhist tradition of the country has changed over the centuries. Thai Buddhism had long been typified by distinct, locally oriented, and parochially integrated monasteries with relatively little horizontal connection to each other but instead involved in specific, local-level aspects of the broader society. Linkages between Buddhist monastic actors and societal constituencies in the public sphere were long disorganized and highly localized, which rendered them ineffective in the contest over the shape of the religious sector taking place on the national level.[77] Individual monks and monasteries (wats) were intimately connected to their own community-based constituencies, being institutions involved in local education, village administration, health care, artistic and cultural production, and social welfare.[78] But Thai wats were only loosely connected to one another through informal teacher-student or parent-dependent monastic networks.[79] Because Thailand's broader religious sector remained divided among a sundry of localities that failed to work in concert, the Chakri monarchy had ample space to structure the relationship between Sangha and state as it saw fit.

A few rudimentary structures uniting the Buddhist monkhood did exist, but these were not national in scope, and they were all created by the Chakri monarchs over the course of the eighteenth and nineteenth centu-

---

77. The Lao principalities in the north and northeast, for instance, administered their own Sanghas until the late nineteenth century, while Sanghas in the south were more fully separated and more closely connected to Bangkok and its surrounding environs. And within these various—not yet unified—Buddhist Sanghas, the importance of local communal ties historically dwarfed that of broader regional ties connecting the monkhood in different localities.

78. Ishii (1986).

79. Somboon Suksamran (1979), "Buddhism and Politics: The Political Roles, Activities and Involvement of the Thai Sangha" (PhD diss., University of Hull), 116.

ries. As such, institutionalization of the Buddhist establishment both was remarkably weak and—when it did emerge at low levels—was nested solidly within the formal and informal ambit of the royal family. The post of Sangkharat (Supreme Patriarch)—the leader of the Buddhist establishment—was created by the monarchy in 1782, with appointment authority reserved as a royal prerogative. The Chakri prince, Mongkut (later King Rama IV), also created a parallel royalist sect within the long-standing yet amorphous Buddhist monkhood through the establishment of the Thammayut Order in 1833. Initially, the Thammayut Order was intended to be a political vehicle that served Mongkut's personal aspirations for expanded authority in an internal rivalry with his half brother, Nangklao (then King Rama III). But after Rama III died in 1851 and Mongkut took the throne as King Rama IV, the Thammayut Order of monks gradually evolved to acquire a broader pro-royalist—rather than purely personalist—legitimating role.

While dwarfed in numbers by the older and larger Mahanikay Order of monks, the Thammayut Order has enjoyed close linkages to the royal family—it has generally been led by a Chakri prince and has received a substantial royal patronage.[80] To the extent that Thailand's religious establishment possessed any coherence and hierarchy as a corporate entity in the nineteenth century, it was within pockets of the religious sphere that were most linked to, and controlled by, the authoritarian executive of the Chakri monarchy.

Such incoherence among the vast majority of Thai Buddhist organizations persisted into the dawn of the twentieth century. At that time, there were over 7,000 Buddhist monasteries spread throughout the lands of modern Thailand. Of these, only a small fraction (the 117 royal monasteries that were founded by Chakri monarchs) were unified as a part of any shared or meaningfully cohesive structure.[81] The vast majority of monastic institutions represented a fragmented array of "commoner monasteries [that] remained completely unorganized, surviving independently through the support of the provincial notables and people."[82]

Given the monkhood's own internal disunity, the initial structures that formed to relate Sangha, regime, and state were principally devised by Chakri monarchs and, thus, broadly reflected royal interests.[83] Between

---

80. Benjamin Schonthal (2017), "Formations of Buddhist Constitutionalism in Southeast Asia," *International Journal of Constitutional Law* 15 (3): 705–33.

81. Ishii (1986), 69.

82. Ishii (1986), 72.

83. Stanley Jeyaraja Tambiah (1976), *World Conqueror and World Renouncer: A Study of Bud-*

1782 and 1801, the first Chakri king (Rama I) issued "an unprecedented series of laws designed to give the Chakri court greater control over the Sangha."[84] Late nineteenth- and early twentieth-century laws banned monks from participating in politics,[85] which effectively depoliticized the monkhood. And with the 1902 Sangha Administration Act (SAA), the monarchy entirely absorbed the previously amorphous and disorganized Buddhist establishment into the state bureaucracy—creating a centralized federal Sangha Administration characterized by a rigid internal hierarchy that concentrated authority in eight elite monks sitting on the Sangha Council of Elders (Mahathera Samakhom).[86]

The 1902 SAA ensured formal royal dominance over the Buddhist establishment, placing institutional autonomy out of reach for the time being. It charged the Council of Elders with "executing His Majesty's command." It gave the king authority over ecclesiastical appointments, allowing Thammayut monks linked to the monarchy to be elevated to leadership posts despite their minority status among the Thai Buddhist monkhood. The law also produced a strict hierarchic chain of command within the Sangha Administration by punishing disobedience to superiors and rendering Council of Elders decisions unquestionable.[87] Making royal control of the Sangha even more apparent, the post of Sangkharat was originally kept vacant so the king could personally exercise the Supreme Patriarch's authority as preeminent leader of the Sangha.[88]

We can helpfully explain the emergence of bureaucratized, Buddhist religious institutions in early twentieth-century Thailand through simple appeals to functionalism in part because this was very much a period of novel institutional design. In contrast to the Catholic Church in Germany and al-Azhar in Egypt, Chakri rulers did not inherit a previously

---

dhism and Polity in Thailand against a Historical Background (New York: Cambridge University Press).

84. Patrick Jory (2002), "The Vessantara Jataka, Barami, and the Bodhisatta-Kings: The Origin and Spread of a Thai Concept of Power," *Crossroads: An Interdisciplinary Journal of Southeast Asian Studies* 16 (2): 58.

85. Siamese Law of 1897 on local government administration, amended in 1914 to prohibit monks from voting in local elections for the position of village headman. See Thomas Larsson (2016), "Keeping Monks in Their Place?" *Asian Journal of Law and Society* 3 (1): 18.

86. Charles F. Keyes (1971), "Buddhism and National Integration in Thailand," *Journal of Asian Studies* 30 (3): 551–67.

87. See Thailand's 1902 Act on the Administration of the Buddhist Order of Sangha. See also McCargo (2012).

88. Peter A. Jackson (1989), *Buddhism, Legitimation, and Conflict: The Political Functions of Urban Thai Buddhism* (Singapore: Institute of Southeast Asian Studies).

institutionalized religious establishment but rather only an authoritarian's playground of disorganized monastic bodies that were only later brought into hierarchical order by royal direction. Local resistance to Chakri dominance of the monkhood did occur in the northern Lao regions that were historically independent from central (Siamese) control, but such resistance (1) remained localized; (2) did not cohere into a national religious institution or movement even close to being on par with what we observed above with the Catholic Church or Islamic al-Azhar; and (3) was quickly brought to heel after the 1902 SAA removed all formal Sangha authority from monks in the previously independent north and northeast.[89] Thus, the varied Buddhist religious world of Thailand became easily subsumed within a state creation with very little autonomy at the turn of the twentieth century. Due to this marked absence of preexisting institutionalization and linkages, functionalist logics that emphasize the top-down interests of Chakri monarchs actually explain the early organization of Thailand's Sangha Administration quite well.

The Royalist Sangha after Modern Regime Change

In the wake of the Great Depression, disaffection with the royal family came to a climax in 1932 with a bloodless coup ending absolute monarchy in Thailand—though the office of monarch was not formally disbanded.[90] The incoming political regime, headed by the People's Party (Khana Ratsadon), quickly moved to rid Thailand of the institutional remnants of absolute monarchy.[91] How did the rise of an anti-royalist regime affect the Thai Sangha Administration—an institution that remained penetrated by, and linked to, the Chakri royal family?

The Sangha Administration's linkages to the defunct monarchy were certainly a source of vulnerability. To the new regime, it was at best an anachronistic vestige of the monarchic era and at worst a potential source of counterrevolution.[92] Nevertheless, regime change had only a delayed effect on the Sangha Administration's internal autonomy in that era. For six years

---

89. Katherine Bowie (2014), "The Saint with Indra's Sword: Khruuba Srivichai and Buddhist Millenarianism in Northern Thailand," *Comparative Studies in Society and History* 56 (3): 681–713.

90. Chris Baker (2016), "The 2014 Thai Coup and Some Roots of Authoritarianism," *Journal of Contemporary Asian Studies* 46 (3): 388–404.

91. Bruce Reynolds (2004), "Phibun Songkhram and Thai Nationalism in the Fascist Era," *European Journal of East Asian Studies* 3 (1): 103.

92. Jackson (1989), 30.

after the revolution, the Sangha Administration continued to be dominated by royally appointed Thammayut monks and led by a member of the Chakri royal family—Supreme Patriarch and Prince Chinaworasiriwat.[93]

The Sangha Administration of the 1930s proved difficult to reform due to three features of lingering institutionalization that endured even after the Chakri dynasty's end. First, the rigid institutional hierarchy produced by the 1902 SAA continued to bolster old religious elites. Second, efforts to disempower royalist monks were frustrated by the significant degree of coherence within the ranks of the royalist Thammayut Order. Third, the lack of a procedural mechanism for removing the Supreme Patriarch—which the monarchy did not require because the Supreme Patriarch himself was historically an extension of the royal family—hamstrung the new regime's ability to reconfigure the Sangha Administration to its liking.

While the People's Party had an interest in stripping authority from royalist Thammayuts in the Sangha Administration, accomplishing this goal in practice would have required a direct confrontation with the clergy. Thailand's Buddhist public was a disorganized religious constituency, but a political ousting of the Supreme Patriarch was still momentous enough to be viewed as crossing a so-called saffron line, which threatened significant and unpredictable popular backlash. Meanwhile, efforts at reforming the Sangha Administration from within also proved impossible so long as royalist Thammayut elites held its reins.

For instance, an emergent organization of monks called the Group to Restore the Religion advocated restructuring the Sangha Administration as a majoritarian monastic body as well as unifying the still distinct Thammayut and Mahanikay Orders. Both of these goals would have effectively shifted power toward the larger, but previously marginalized, Mahanikay Order. But the persistence of Thammayuts at the top of the Sangha hierarchy, and the legal prohibition on defying ecclesiastical elites, offered royalist monks a plethora of institutional tools for protecting the status quo. The Thammayut-controlled Council of Elders unified in defense of their minority order's institutional prerogatives. Using its monopoly of religious authority granted by the 1902 SAA, the council disrobed monastic members of the Group to Restore the Religion on the basis that its proposals constituted rebellion against the Supreme Patriarch.[94]

Thus, the post-Chakri era was characterized by a notable, though short-

---

93. Jackson (1989), 30.
94. Jackson (1989), 71.

lived, period of internal autonomy based in the previous era's institutionalization around a specific monastic elite of royal prominence. Thammayut linkages to the old monarchy placed the Sangha Administration in the new regime's crosshairs. Nevertheless, the privileged status of Thammayut monks at the apex of the Sangha hierarchy, combined with the absolute concentration of formal institutional authority in those highest tiers of the religious elite, allowed Thammayuts to forestall efforts to dislodge them from power.

Not Able to Have Nice Things:
The Sangha in the Regime Tumults of the 1940s and 1950s

The regime's non-interference in the Sangha Administration ended in 1938 after the death of the Thammayut Supreme Patriarch, Prince Chinaworasiriwat. This leadership change disrupted the coherent blocs that had formed among religious elites, as the new Supreme Patriarch and the Council of Elders were now drawn from rival orders of the broad Buddhist monkhood. And because the new Supreme Patriarch (a Mahanikay monk) was amenable to restructuring the Thai Sangha along majoritarian lines, the Sangha hierarchy no longer posed a significant obstacle to institutional reform.

In 1941, Field Marshal Plaek Phibun's military regime passed a new Sangha Administration Act that removed the institution's hierarchy and decentralized religious authority.[95] The Council of Elders was dissolved, and its powers were diffused throughout majoritarian bodies that sidelined the minority Thammayut Order. When Phibun's government crafted the 1941 SAA, little thought was given to designing an institution that would effectively manage religious policy or fulfill regime desires. In practice, the 1941 SAA simply replicated the organs of the post-1932 Thai state and added the adjective "religious" to them: the Religious Council of Ministers (for proposing religious decrees); the Religious Legislative Council (for voting on decrees); and the Religious Judiciary (for disciplining monks).[96]

Decentralizing authority within the Sangha Administration quickly led to disarray, as the 1941 SAA law eliminated the forms of institutionalization that had coalesced in previous decades. Hierarchy was replaced with turmoil, and coherence among religious elites slipped into parochial and

---

95. See Thailand's 1941 Act on the Administration of the Buddhist Order of Sangha.
96. Jackson (1989), 73.

debilitating monastic factionalism.[97] Within a few years, the Thammayut Order fully seceded from the Sangha Administration and established its own parallel religious bureaucracy at the provincial level.[98] While Thammayuts and Mahanikays reached a limited compromise in 1951, this did little more than solidify gridlock in the religious sphere by forbidding the Sangha Administration from acting on any issues where the two monastic orders disagreed.[99]

Thailand's 1941 SAA stripped power from royalist monks and undercut internal autonomy. But it did not craft a Sangha Administration that would faithfully promote regime interests in the religious sphere. In fact, the processes of deinstitutionalization incited by the 1941 act left the Sangha Administration unable to effectuate much religious policy at all.

More Short-Term Functionalism: Reversing Sangha Administration Reform

When Field Marshal Sarit Tharanat took power in a 1957 coup, he inherited a Sangha Administration that had grown profoundly ineffective through its deinstitutionalization, with a predictably negative impact on its ability to effectuate any level of autonomy, either internal or mission. Sarit, who once summarized Thailand's woes in famously authoritarian tones by stating "the garb of democracy was weighing down Thailand,"[100] viewed the majoritarian structure of the Sangha as the root of its decay—a morbid but notable endorsement of the perceived political importance of the Sangha Administration to Thai sociopolitical life. Sarit's vision for reform was simple: he would revive the Sangha Administration's rigid hierarchy and concentrate authority in religious elites who supported his regime's developmentalist and anti-communist ideology.[101]

Because the existing state Buddhist establishment was now severely incoherent—more focused on infighting than on unifying against regime interference—this made it all the easier for Sarit to conquer and subordinate on the pretext of protecting against a potential communist infiltration of the monkhood. Competing factions of monks became susceptible to co-optation in exchange for appointments to leadership posts at the expense of

---

97. Ishii (1986), 102.

98. Ishii (1986), 107.

99. Keyes (1971), 560.

100. Frank C. Darling (1960), "Marshal Sarit and Absolutist Rule in Thailand," *Pacific Affairs* 33 (4): 352.

101. Schonthal (2017).

their rivals. In 1960, the vacant position of Supreme Patriarch was filled by Plot Kittisophana, a Mahanikay monk who openly professed loyalty to the regime.[102] And a new Religious Council of Ministers was appointed, which quickly appeased Sarit by announcing its intention to purge communist infiltrators from the monkhood,[103] to disrobe monks who opposed government policies, and to "recentralize the monkhood's administration along the lines of the royalist act of 1902."[104] The last component of this plan materialized in 1962, when Sarit introduced a new Sangha Administration Act that was basically a modern replication of the original 1902 SAA. It transferred the bounds of religious legislative and judicial authority back to the Supreme Patriarch. It also reinstituted the Sangha Council of Elders and gave the Supreme Patriarch control over this body.[105]

New provisions were layered upon the basic framework of the 1902 SAA, with the purpose of more fully subjecting the Sangha Administration to state control. Ecclesiastical appointments required the Minister of Education's signature, state legislation could overturn patriarchal commands, the Supreme Patriarch himself could be dismissed by executive decree, and state judges and police officers were given authority to disrobe monks accused of crimes.[106] Consequently, the post-1962 Sangha Administration elevated regime loyalists, purged potential agitators, and subject the institution as a whole to heightened state oversight—concurrently reducing its internal autonomy with bureaucratic fiat and diminishing mission autonomy through subsuming it into the broader structures of regime loyalism.

Sarit's return to Chakri-era institutional design is perhaps understandable given his broader efforts to revive the monarchy as a source of symbolic legitimation—a notable shift to reviving a royalist-military linkage that had otherwise remained sundered since the military coup against the

---

102. Jackson (1989), 97. One prominent monk, Phra Phimonlatham, who was in line to become Supreme Patriarch notably came into the Sarit regime's crosshairs for opposing a rule that would bar communist sympathizers from entering the monkhood. Phimonlatham's resistance on this matter led to his later being disrobed and imprisoned on the basis of suspected communist sympathies and sexual misconduct. For a more detailed discussion here, see Phibul Choompolpaisal (2011), "Reassessing Modern Thai Political Buddhism: A Critical Studies of Sociological Literature from Weber to Keyes" (PhD diss., University of London, School of Oriental and African Studies), chap. 8.

103. Suksamran (1979), 212.

104. Eugene Ford (2017), *Cold War Monks: Buddhism and America's Secret Strategy in Southeast Asia* (New Haven: Yale University Press), 92.

105. Suksamran (1982).

106. See Thailand's 1962 Act on the Administration of the Buddhist Order of Sangha. See also Ishii (1986), 116–18.

royal family in 1932. The revival of Chakri Sangha structures in the Sarit period is also part of a trend that should draw our attention: promoting institutionalization through the establishment of strict administrative hierarchies seems attractive to rulers and regimes that first create (or re-create) religious establishments and can install compliant elites at the top. Conversely, institutionalized hierarchies that had formed outside the current regime's control can be quite frustrating for autocrats who inherit them—as we saw with the Catholic Church in Germany, al-Azhar in Egypt, and the Sangha Administration immediately following Thailand's 1932 revolution.

Institutional Incoherence, Scattered Linkages, and the Sundering of the Sangha Administration

In contrast to those of his predecessors, Sarit's interventions in the Sangha Administration in the 1960s were not limited to the goal of keeping the Buddhist establishment out of politics or undercutting its counterrevolutionary potential. By co-opting the Sangha hierarchy through the 1962 SAA, Sarit intended to deploy the monkhood to promote his political agenda.[107] Dhammic ambassadors, Buddhist studies centers, and wandering dhamma programs dispatched monks to strengthen villagers' ties to the central state, steer them away from communist ideology, and supply the government with information on local affairs.[108] For our purposes, Sarit's short-term politicization of the Buddhist establishment helps to shed light on long-term, often unintended, side effects of close regime concern over—and tinkering in—the religious sphere.

By using the Sangha as a policy tool, the regime reshaped the Buddhist establishment in two critical ways. First, it eroded the widespread norm of an apolitical clergy,[109] thereby normalizing monks acting within a sense of mission in politics. Second, it undermined the Sangha Administration's internal hierarchy and therefore the guidelines of its internal autonomy. While a formal structural hierarchy persisted, it grew to be disrespected and sometimes disregarded outright.

At the top echelons of the Sangha Administration, those packed with regime loyalists, monks perceived a duty to promote the regime's political mission. But rank-and-file monks in the villages, as well as younger

---

107. Suksamran (1979), 157.
108. Keyes (1971). Suksamran (1979).
109. David Ambuel (2001), "New Karma: Buddhist Democracy and the Rule of Law in Thailand," *American Asian Review* 19 (4): 131–62.

monks in Bangkok, were less enthusiastic. Some grievances were rooted in monks' desire to eschew any political mission and instead remain confined to the spiritual sphere. Perhaps more importantly, the general religious policy of the 1960s was objectionable to monks in rural communities, who viewed themselves as spiritual guides for local Buddhist constituencies and not agents of the central state.[110] Therefore, new fault lines formed within Thailand's Buddhist religious establishment, breeding institutional dissension through a particularly strong divide between the elite monastic corpus and rank-and-file monks.

In the early 1970s, a brief political opening following a new regime change from military rule allowed many monks to begin building independent linkages with new secular political groups, indicating that some facets of the monkhood began to identify their own sense of mission within ostensibly nonreligious aspects of the political realm.[111] As a testament to the institutional and hierarchical incoherence that plagued the broader Buddhist establishment, these missions remained scattered and never translated into any unified sense of mission autonomy for the state Sangha Administration, which itself only reluctantly tolerated, and sometimes even punished, monks who ventured into political life.[112] While linkages to suborned political constituencies proliferated, they also remained severely disorganized—tied to scattered segments of the monkhood across interest groups and disparate regions of Thailand but not the central Sangha Administration that governed it.

Yet, there were many monastic groups that sought to cultivate their own linkages to politically active segments of the Thai public and civil society. The Organization of Sangha Brotherhood appealed to Thailand's peasant class, arguing the merits of land redistribution. The Monks for Independence, Democracy, and Justice joined nationalist groups agitating against American military bases. Other monastic organizations focused their efforts on supporting labor unions. Buddhadasa Bhikku, Thailand's most famous Buddhist theologian between the 1950s and 1990s, gave lectures endorsing a leftist ideology of "Dhammic Socialism." And a movement of militant Buddhism aligned itself with right-wing radicals, deploying Buddhism to justify violence against communists.[113]

---

110. Somboon Suksamran (1981), "Religion Politics and Development: The Thai Sangha's Role in National Development and Integration," *Southeast Asian Journal of Social Science* 9(1/2): 58.

111. Suksamran (1978), 248.

112. McCargo (2004), 158.

113. Suksamran (1979), 248–73.

There was a simultaneous rise in deviant religious movements that rejected the traditional Buddhist establishment altogether. The Wat Phra Dhammakaya movement courted middle-class, urbanized, and consumerist-oriented Thais with its model of Buddhism for profit—which in many ways should seem familiar to the recent rise of megachurches and teachings of the so-called prosperity doctrine in other parts of the world.[114] And the Santi-Asoke movement of the 1970s onward, which purported a religious vision of anti-statism, anti-capitalism, and vegetarianism, formally seceded from the Sangha Administration.[115]

By the time the military reclaimed power in 1976, the monkhood was slipping outside the Sangha Administration's control. To make matters worse, the Sangha became embroiled in numerous financial and sexual scandals involving monks in the 1980s and 1990s.[116] As the Buddhist establishment fragmented into incoherent and often competing religious movements, the Sangha Administration was simultaneously criticized for its inability to enforce discipline and orthopraxy in the monkhood. Although the Sangha Administration lacked much internal autonomy, it also proved an unreliable tool for any regime seeking to control Thailand's increasing lively religious sphere. Institutional incoherence, combined with disjointed linkages between monks and Thai society, meant nobody (religious or regime elites) got what they wanted; the Sangha Administration had no unified constituency to mobilize in pursuit of internal autonomy, and its failure to unify the Buddhist public also rendered it ineffective as a tool for regime legitimation or social control.

Sangha Incoherence and the Defeat of Internal Autonomy

The chaotic and polarizing attempts at semi-democratic government in the early 2000s ultimately produced a populist party (the Thai Rak Thai) revolving around the personalist leader Thaksin Shinawatra. Many rank-and-file monks were folded into a constituency of Thaksin sympathizers, a linkage that later spurred the wholesale abrogation of internal autonomy for the Sangha Administration following Thaksin's removal from power.

---

114. Schonthal (2017), 20. Rachelle M. Scott (2006), "A New Buddhist Sect? The Dhammakāya Temple and the Politics of Religious Difference," *Religion* 36 (4): 215–30.

115. Rory Mackenzie (2007), *New Buddhist Movements in Thailand: Towards and Understanding of Wat Phra Dhammakaya and Santi Asoke* (Milton Park, UK: Routledge). Marja-Leena Heikkilä-Horn (2010), "Santi Asoke Buddhism and the Occupation of Bangkok International Airport," *ASEAS-Austrian Journal of South-East Asian Studies* 3 (1): 31–47. Frank Reynolds (1994), "Dhamma in Dispute: The Interactions of Religion and Law in Thailand," *Law and Society Review* 28 (3): 447.

116. McCargo (2004), 158.

Thaksin did much to alienate elites on the Sangha Council of Elders—once proposing to make it a purely ceremonial body and later bypassing its authority to nominate the Supreme Patriarch.[117] But Thaksin's brand of poverty-oriented populism cultivated a linkage between his party and Thailand's rank-and-file Buddhist clergy, most of whom had roots in the countryside and shared an affinity toward "the disadvantaged peoples from the North and Northeast," which constitute much of Thaksin's electoral base.[118] Thaksin also established strong linkages with the heterodox Wat Phra Dhammakaya movement, as its teaching of "Buddhism for profit" bore a marked similarity to Thaksin's own brand of "plutocracy for the poor."[119]

Given a pretext of anti-Thaksin protests in 2006, the military (itself alienated by and hostile to Thaksin and further backed by the monarchy, which had grown to reassert its influence in Thai politics) launched a coup removing him from power.[120] Nearly 80 percent of the Thai monkhood was sympathetic toward the "ideals of the pro-Thaksin redshirt movement," which denounced the coup as illegitimate.[121] Hundreds of monks participated in pro-Thaksin demonstrations conducted by his partisan Redshirts in 2010,[122] while the Wat Dhammakaya movement threatened to send its one hundred thousand novice monks to be human shields for Redshirt demonstrators.[123] Once again, linkages between the monkhood and a recently deposed regime put the Buddhist establishment in the crosshairs. Following the 2010 Redshirt protests, the military placed eleven senior monks on a surveillance watchlist, and it leaked that list to the media in a less than subtle display of antagonism toward the Sangha Administration's failure to police the boundary between religion and politics.[124]

---

117. McCargo (2012), 628 and 637.

118. McCargo (2012), 632.

119. Patchanee Malikhao (2017), *Culture and Communication in Thailand* (Singapore: Springer), 31.

120. Michael K. Connors (2009), "Liberalism, Authoritarianism and the Politics of Decisionism in Thailand," *Pacific Review* 22 (3): 366.

121. McCargo (2012), 632.

122. Jim Taylor (2012), "No Way Forward but Back? Re-emergent Thai Falangism, Democracy and the New 'Red Shirt' Social Movement," in *Bangkok May 2010: Perspectives on a Divided Thailand*, ed. Michael J. Montesano, Pavin Chachavalpongpun, and Aekapol Chongvilaivan (Singapore: ISEAS-Yusof Ishak Institute).

123. Ben Richardson (2017), "How Thailand's Monks Became Proxy Warriors," *Asia Times*, February 17, https://cms.ati.ms/2017/02/thailands-monks-became-proxy-warriors/ (accessed 10 February 2020).

124. McCargo (2012), 631.

Following Thailand's most recent coup in 2014, the current ruling junta clearly does not trust the Sangha Administration to police its own ranks. In 2016, the resurgent royalist-military linkage inspired the junta to amend the Sangha Act in a way that allowed the king to appoint the Supreme Patriarch directly. This move reestablished formal royalist control of the Sangha and staved off the junta's own fears that prodemocratic (or pro-Thaksin) forces might gain a foothold within the Buddhist establishment through any internal decision to appoint a heterodox Dhammakaya monk to the patriarchate. In 2017, the junta also revoked the Council of Elders' authority to nominate candidates for Supreme Patriarch. The 2017 constitution further expanded police and judicial authority to defrock monks and "prevent Buddhism from being undermined," ensuring that state officials—rather than clerics—were charged with monitoring and disciplining the monkhood.[125]

The junta also initiated a crackdown on corruption within the Sangha. The goal was not simply to eliminate dissent within the monkhood but also to break linkages between the Sangha and the Buddhist public by tarnishing its institutional legitimacy. In 2017, thousands of police officers besieged the Wat Dhammakaya Temple on politically motivated, if perhaps justified, charges of theft and money laundering.[126] In 2018, the junta even began targeting the Sangha Council of Elders, with two of its members arrested for corruption and another fleeing to Laos to avoid arrest.[127]

In recent years, the Sangha Administration, while lacking internal autonomy, has hardly been an instrument that serves regime interests or facilitates religious legitimation. Severe incoherence and the destabilization of hierarchy within Thailand's Buddhist establishment means that the regime cannot trust the Sangha to keep its own house in order and command monks' political complacency. As a result, the current military-royalist regime is now fundamentally intolerant of internal autonomy for Sangha Administration and willing to intrude in the religious sphere without hesitation. The Thai Sangha has now become a direct target of the new junta's repressive activities, serving as a pious site for the trumped-up

---

125. Schonthal (2017), 722.

126. George Styllis and Patthiya Tongfueng. "A Temple under Siege: Wat Phra Dhammakaya," *The Diplomat*, 23 March 2017, https://thediplomat.com/2017/03/a-temple-under-siege-wat-phra-dhammakaya/ (accessed 10 February 2020).

127. "Former Top Monk 'on the Run' in Laos," *Bangkok Post*, 2 June, 2018, https://www.bangkokpost.com/thailand/general/1477257/former-top-monk-on-the-run-in-laos (accessed 10 February 2018).

war against corruption that the regime is waging to discredit the pre-coup political order. There are certainly a few short-term political points to be scored in painting pious elites as corrupt and self-serving. But if that is as useful as the Sangha Administration gets, then we can hardly say that this institution's continued existence is "functional" for anyone—even though it will likely continue to exist long into the future.

Conclusion: What Matters Is Quality as Well as Quantity of Institutionalization and Linkages

In earlier chapters, we argued that internal autonomy and mission autonomy for authoritarian state institutions are best understood as functions of their institutionalization and the degree to which they have linkages to other state bodies and social constituencies—though rulers' interests and regime maintenance strategies can also have varying levels of impact.

In this chapter we used religious establishments as a prism to understand how those two factors—institutionalization and linkages—mattered and in what ways. Our findings are, as with all aspects of this book, designed to be more suggestive than definitive in their portrait of how state institutions work under authoritarianism. That modesty about the generalizability of our specific answers emboldens us to make sweeping if tentative suggestions of where and how to look for answers elsewhere. Based on what we have found in this diverse array of religious establishments, we expect that those who examine state institutions will find it helpful to pay attention to institutionalization and linkages in specific ways. We thus close this chapter with four sweeping, but only suggestive, observations.

First, the nature of institutionalization matters. In the German case, we observed a Catholic establishment that proved highly complex and adaptable, capable of reorienting itself to fend off regime attempts to undercut its autonomy—particularly when these forms of institutionalization coincided with strong linkages to reliable societal constituencies. But as we observed in Thailand, sometimes a "religious establishment" is less a single establishment operating in concert than a loose umbrella organization combining competing groups who seek to pull the establishment in different directions. In such weakly institutionalized settings, we should expect internal and mission autonomy to be further out of reach. Adding a further qualification to when we should expect institutionalization to matter, the Egyptian and Saudi cases showed that while institutionalization can indeed facilitate internal autonomy for religious establishments, strong linkages to state and societal actors are likely required to translate this into any meaningful level of mission autonomy.

Second, the nature of linkages matters. Linkages to societal constituencies are less effective in generating institutional autonomy when those constituencies are localized and disorganized (Thailand in the state-building period). By contrast, linkages to constituencies with a meaningful capacity for regional or national cooperation (Saudi Arabia and imperial Germany) strengthen religious establishments seeking to wrest internal and mission autonomy from the regime. We also found that linkages to societal constituencies that support the regime (German Protestants) are less useful, as supporters do not reliably place the religious establishment's interests above those of the regime. Moreover, we saw that linkages to deposed regimes are particularly threatening, as new elites may seek to purge the institution of its supposed counterrevolutionary potential (Thailand).

Third, institutionalization and linkages are related to each other. Some linkages, for instance, are institutionalized in a formal sense—they are based on formal ties between a state body and a formal non-state actor; a formal procedure or chain of command in which an action by the religious establishment is forwarded to another state body for implementation; or a legal requirement that personnel in a specific institution possess a degree from a specific religious institution or academy. Others are more diffuse and based on personal ties and networks, chains of social relationships or information, or similarities in life experiences or worldviews. Less coherent and hierarchical state institutions may lend themselves more to the second kind of linkages. This second set is powerful and can be harder for regimes to control, although they also seem less likely to provide firm guarantees of internal autonomy. But they might be especially helpful for developing a strong sense of mission autonomy—an internalized belief that the religious establishment has a higher, even transcendental and eternal, purpose that is not dictated by the regime's short-term political needs or instructions. And they are hardly immune to regime manipulation, particularly—as in the two Arab cases examined here—when the informal linkages are forged in institutions controlled and regulated by the state (such as state mosques and public universities).

Fourth and finally, the autonomy of state institutions is best understood historically. A focus on the regime's actions should not be lost but also should not edge out other broader and longer-term vantage points. Regime concerns are often expressed in short-term, reactive, or ad hoc measures—ones with lasting effects, to be sure, but not ones in which the line from tactical regime consideration to long-term outcome can be drawn automatically (as is evidenced in some detail, for instance, by both the German and Thai cases). This account has shifted much of the focus instead to long-term questions: when establishments were founded; how they evolved over time; whether they existed in political systems with high or lower overall degrees of structural differentiation; and how residues of past crises or conflicts remain long after the particular struggles have passed into memory. In a sense, such a historical focus allows us to understand the tactical nature of much decision-making while still being attentive to strategic outcomes.

CHAPTER 6

Does Authoritarianism Make a Difference?

No, but Democracy Does

PRESIDENT MUFFLEY: General Turgidson, I find this very difficult to understand. I was under the impression that I was the only one in authority to order the use of nuclear weapons.

GENERAL TURGIDSON: That's right, sir, you are the only person authorized to do so. And although I, uh, hate to judge before all the facts are in, it's beginning to look like, uh, General Ripper exceeded his authority.

—*Dr. Strangelove, Or: How I Learned to Stop Worrying and Love the Bomb*

When political scientists use the term "authoritarianism" today, they generally mean "nondemocracy," a capacious definition we have chosen to accept. But we still have resisted some of the assumptions that are often pirated into our conceptual set of tools when lumping such a diversity of regimes together. In doing so, we find that the phenomenon we have highlighted throughout this book—the surprising variation in state autonomy under widely different but thoroughly authoritarian conditions—actually holds useful lessons in application to how we view modern democracy.

A Reprise: Functional and Dysfunctional Authoritarianism

We began this study by probing what scholars mean when they use the term "authoritarianism"—and how this meaning has evolved in some fundamental but unnoticed ways. We traced etymology not for its own sake but to uncover conceptual fuzziness and also to understand its sources and implications. We argued that the dominant conception of authoritarianism that has evolved—and one that now prevails quite widely—is simultaneously, and anomalously, residual (by lumping together all nondemocracies) and specific, by tilting at varying degrees toward a functionalist image in which the structure and operation of authoritarian institutions are explained primarily by reference to regime needs.

We further observed an unfortunate tendency among specialists to collapse all ruler motivations to that of classical tyranny, skewing our assessments of actually existing regime decision-making and reducing much of politics to a regime-survival logic that is generally assumed rather than assessed. We argued that unconsciously conflating ruler, regime, and state, something scholarly writings often do but rarely acknowledge, furthers this functionalist logic—a logic that we do not fully reject but insist must be subjected to empirical verification rather than taken as a given.

Thus, while we accepted the capacious way that authoritarianism has recently come to be defined, we have challenged the way authoritarianism is too often understood as a political system in which the will and interests of the ruler and the regime map (and actively guide) the structure of the state closely, shoving distinctions among them out of view. We show that this vision of authoritarian politics sometimes holds well and sometimes does not—and that this variation needs to be explained.

In another sense, we identified the scope conditions that determine when functionalist approaches are most and least likely to be empirically fruitful: functionalism is most helpful in explaining policy outcomes in authoritarian systems when institutional autonomy is low. And while functionalism can sometimes lend itself well to explaining variation in institutional autonomy, it does so reliably only for those state institutions that have particularly weak levels of linkage and institutionalization, making them more prone to top-down direction.[1]

We have further noted how a basic question of regime type that motivated much comparative politics scholarship from its inception in the ancient world until quite recently—the purposes for which state power is

---

1. Robert Barros (2002), *Constitutionalism and Dictatorship: Pinochet, the Junta, and the 1980 Constitution* (New York: Cambridge University Press). Tom Ginsburg and Tamir Moustafa (2008), *Rule by Law: The Politics of Courts in Authoritarian Regimes* (New York: Cambridge University Press). Jennifer Gandhi and Adam Przeworski (2007), "Authoritarian Institutions and the Survival of Autocrats," *Comparative Political Studies* 40 (11): 1279–1301. Tamir Moustafa (2000), "Conflict and Cooperation between the State and Religious Institutions in Contemporary Egypt," *International Journal of Middle East Studies* 32 (1): 3–22.

Does Authoritarianism Make a Difference? · 245

used—has also partially disappeared from view. Instead, we cluster in favor of a limited vision of authoritarian politics understood primarily as the pursuit of power for its own sake.

The struggle for power can be a strong motivator unto itself, but so can a struggle over the purposes and ends for which state power is exercised. Sharp differences over policy, or even fundamental normative questions, do still exist in nondemocratic settings.[2] And the variation in the ability of official actors to develop their own understanding of the public good turns out to be quite significant for explaining political dynamism and the resurgence of institutional autonomy itself.

Our use of the historical institutionalist framework enabled us to take decades, and in some cases centuries, of institutional evolution seriously when explaining the emergence of autonomy and its decay. We were, of course, less than dogmatic in our use of the historical institutionalist approach—eschewing its standard definition of "institutions" as overbroad for our purposes, while also relaxing what can sometimes amount to a deterministic reliance on path dependence and increasing returns in our effort to remain alert to dynamics of historical contingency.[3] Yet our employment of a historical and institutionalist analysis—albeit a slightly modified one—allowed for a rich and nuanced explanation of institutional autonomy that accounts for long time horizons, critical junctures, contingent events, institutional accumulation, conversion, and drift.[4]

In developing this approach, we crafted the building blocks of our

---

2. Andrew F. March (2003), "From Leninism to Karimovism: Hegemony, Ideology, and Authoritarian Legitimation," *Post-Soviet Affairs* 19 (4): 307–36. Marianne Kneuer (2017), "Legitimation beyond Ideology: Authoritarian Regimes and the Construction of Cissions," *Zeitschrift für vergleichende Politikwissenschaft* 11 (2): 181–211. Christian Von Soest and Julia Grauvogel (2017), "Identity, Procedures and Performance: How Authoritarian Regimes Legitimize Their Rule." *Contemporary Politics* 23 (3): 287–305. Ben Ross Schneider (1992), *Politics within the State: Elite Bureaucrats and Industrial Policy in Authoritarian Brazil* (Pittsburgh: University of Pittsburgh Press). Vladimir Gel'man, and Andrey Starodubtsev (2016), "Opportunities and Constraints of Authoritarian Modernisation: Russian Policy Reforms in the 2000s," *Europe-Asia Studies* 68 (1): 97–117. Jessica Weeks (2014), *Dictators at War and Peace* (Ithaca: Cornell University Press).

3. Peter Hall and Rosemary Taylor (1996), "Political Science and the Three New Institutionalisms," *Political Studies* 44 (5): 936–57. Paul Pierson (2000), "Increasing Returns, Path Dependence, and the Study of Politics," *American Political Science Review* 94 (2): 251–67. Juliet Johnson (2001), "Path Contingency in Postcommunist Transformations," *Comparative Politics* 33 (3): 253–74. Ellen Immergut (2005), "Historical Institutionalism in Political Science and the Problem of Change," in *Understanding Change*, ed. Andreas Wimmer and Reinhart Kossler (Basingstoke: Palgrave).

4. James Mahoney and Kathleen Thelen, eds. (2009), *Explaining Institutional Change: Ambiguity, Agency, and Power* (New York: Cambridge University Press).

inquiry by suggesting that we can learn a great deal about authoritarian politics in practice by looking at the autonomy of the state institutions that operate it. We elaborated on the two dimensions by which state institutions achieve varying levels of autonomy: *internal autonomy*, or the extent to which state institutions are able to effectively control their own affairs and administration; and *mission autonomy*, or the capacity for state institutions to pursue their own senses of purpose in some areas of public policy or to exert decision-making influence.

Throughout this book, we have shown that understanding variation in these two forms of autonomy requires paying attention to the levels of *institutionalization* within a state body (structural hierarchy, coherence, complexity, and adaptability) and the strength of its *linkages* to supportive constituencies in society or allies elsewhere within the state apparatus. As such, autonomy can vary over time and place as well as from one institution to another. The endowments of the past can weigh heavily on the possibilities of the present, in this framing, yet also remain in a persistent push and pull vis-à-vis the regime core itself.

Over the course of three empirical chapters, we developed this explanation in detail. We did so not in a series of empirical tests so much as in a series of inductive explorations of what institutionalization and linkage look like in the day-to-day operation of state institutions and how they have changed over time. We sought not to resolve all questions but rather to show the considerable fruit in raising them and pursuing them without baked-in functionalist assumptions. We engaged this approach first in an unlikely place: constitutional courts, the exact kind of state body that would seem to be most easily sighted in the crosshairs of any micromanaging autocrat.[5]

Such courts are actually quite common cross-nationally, and we selected those of modern-day Egypt and Palestine for fine-grained case studies. These two courts are structurally very similar, with the law and organization of the latter based heavily on the former. By contrasting the establishment and historical evolution of these judicial bodies, we saw that institutionalization and linkages fostered varying levels of autonomy in the Egyptian Supreme Constitutional Court over time, whereas the absence of these factors has left the Palestinian Supreme Constitutional Court a fairly impotent body in which functionalist theorizing brings more explanatory value.

---

5. Tamir Moustafa (2014), "Law and Courts in Authoritarian Regimes," *Annual Review of Law and Social Science* 10:281–99. Peter H. Solomon Jr. (2015), "Law and Courts in Authoritarian States," *International Encyclopedia of the Social and Behavioral Sciences* 2:427–34.

Does Authoritarianism Make a Difference? · 247

Our second empirical probe focused on parliaments in authoritarian systems, beginning with a historical analysis of how these assembly chambers have evolved throughout the world. Unlike constitutional courts, they tended to have very diverse origins in terms of their longevity, organization, and even powers cross-nationally, but they have increasingly grown to resemble each other in their structure and formal authorities over time, especially from the mid-twentieth century onward.[6] The outcome of this growing isomorphism has been the development of a vast array of formal, though often latent, privileges and political potentialities that could be used to great chaos if they ever got the nerve: from legislative obstruction and ministerial interpolation to rights to initiate legislation, budgetary authority, cabinet responsibility, and even votes of no confidence.[7]

We studied the Russian State Duma and Kuwaiti Majlis al-Umma to assess if and when authoritarian parliaments actually ever use these powers that have accumulated over the centuries to pursue internal and mission autonomy in practice. And we found that institutionalization and linkages still had the expected connection with increasing degrees of autonomy in each case. We also saw, though, that the very centrality of parliamentary bodies as organs of explicit, constitutional political power made any effort at asserting their autonomy in practice more likely to lead them to obstructive behavior and generating political frustration rather than an ability to develop a coherent and positive sense of mission. In this way, parliaments allowed us to probe the meaning of institutional autonomy at a greater level of complexity—both in the degree to which it emerges but also when it expresses itself less by articulating a clear vision and more by obstructing the regime or forcing it to adapt.

Our empirical analysis then moved to a more wide-ranging investigation of religious establishments and state religious institutions in imperial and Nazi Germany, Saudi Arabia, Egypt, and Thailand. Against this multifarious backdrop, we explored how variation in linkages and institu-

---

6. Nelson W. Polsby (1975), "Legislatures," in *Handbook of Political Science*, ed. Fred I. Greenstein and Nelson W. Polsby (Boston: Addison-Wesley). Michael L. Mezey (1979), *Comparative Legislatures* (Durham: Duke University Press). Philip Norton (1990), "Parliaments: A Framework for Analysis," *West European Politics* 13 (3): 1–9.

7. Irina Khmelko, Rick Stapenhurst, and Michael L. Mezey, eds. (2020), *Legislative Decline in the 21st Century: A Comparative Perspective* (Milton Park, UK: Routledge). Steven M. Fish and Matthew Kroenig (2009), *The Handbook of National Legislatures: A Global Survey* (New York: Cambridge University Press). Svitlana Chernykh, David Doyle, and Timothy J. Power (2017), "Measuring Legislative Power: An Expert Reweighting of the Fish-Kroenig Parliamentary Powers Index," *Legislative Studies Quarterly* 42 (2): 295–320.

tionalization is a matter not merely of degree but also of kind. Institutionalization can operate with varying combinations of hierarchy, complexity, coherence, and adaptability, each with its own effect on autonomy.

Linkages matter not only for the overall strength of linked constituencies but also in terms of with whom different institutions associate and link—state actors, oppositional forces, old regime elements, or others. The German case highlighted a specific importance for institutionalization in the forms of hierarchy, coherence, and complexity and further showed that linkages to public constituencies become less effective when those constituencies were themselves supportive of the ruler or regime.

In Egypt and Saudi Arabia, we found that institutionalization and linkages to a broad population of believers facilitated religious establishments' pursuit of internal and mission autonomy. But we also observed an important distinction involving the extent to which linkages were either folded into the state or forced into networks of operation outside of the official sphere.

Finally, our analysis of the religious establishment in Thailand showed that linkages are less effective in promoting institutional autonomy when they are established primarily with disorganized and localized groups; that enduring linkages between a state religious establishment and a previously deposed regime often place internal autonomy in the crosshairs; and that institutional incoherence and the destabilization of institutional hierarchies tend to inhibit the pursuit of mission autonomy by religious establishments.

Throughout this book, we have described authoritarian systems as allowing a great degree of variation in which of their institutions are autonomous and how much. That is to be expected given that the range of authoritarian systems folded into the standard residual definition is so wide and heterogenous. But if there is so much variation, is there anything left that is uniquely distinctive about authoritarianism itself?

Not really.

That may be a surprising claim with which to conclude a book on authoritarianism. It is indeed deliberately dramatic. But rather than being simply provocative, we can answer the question more accurately and helpfully by bringing democracy back into the discussion. It turns out that asking about the nature of authoritarianism, especially when defined so broadly as a residual category, actually tells us something a bit unexpected and significant about the distinctiveness of democracy. The key outcome we have focused so much attention on explaining—the autonomy of state institutions—is typically very high across most democracies, especially those that most scholars tend to view as normatively proper democracies worthy of emulation.[8]

In other words, the countries that we call democracies today are distinctive due to much reduced variation at the institutional level—authoritarian systems show wildly different levels of institutional autonomy, but democracies find such institutional autonomy far more readily.[9] At least the ones that most scholars are confident that we can agree in calling democracies, which tend toward well-developed state structures and have a higher likelihood of long-standing institutional arrangements.[10]

Many democratic regimes share a high degree of structural differentiation between rulers and the state institutions they preside over. Democracies combine the unusual situation in which there is uncertainty over political outcomes at the highest level of the executive (through regular, competitive elections) but more certainty over the autonomy of the state institutions below them.[11] Authoritarian regimes, for all their diverse variations, reverse this. Indeed, they find mostly fixed political executives ruling over state institutions that cover a wide—and often fluctuating—range of potential autonomy across country cases and even across time periods within one country.

That is what we mean when we say that authoritarianism is not distinctive but democracy is. It turns out that treating authoritarianism as a residual category tells us something quite important about the nature of

---

8. Francis Fukuyama (2014), *Political Order and Political Decay: From the Industrial Revolution to the Globalization of Democracy* (New York: Macmillan). Francis Fukuyama (2011), *The Origins of Political Order: From Prehuman Times to the French Revolution* (New York: Farrar, Straus and Giroux).

9. Daniel Carpenter (2020), *The Forging of Bureaucratic Autonomy: Reputations, Networks, and Policy Innovation in Executive Agencies, 1862–1928* (Princeton: Princeton University Press). Steven J. Balla and William T. Gormley Jr. (2017), *Bureaucracy and Democracy: Accountability and Performance* (Washington, DC: CQ Press). Judith Gruber (2021), *Controlling Bureaucracies: Dilemmas in Democratic Governance* (Berkeley: University of California Press).

10. Staffan I. Lindberg, Michael Coppedge, John Gerring, and Jan Teorell (2014), "V-Dem: A New Way to Measure Democracy," *Journal of Democracy* 25 (3): 159–69. Michael Coppedge, Staffan Lindberg, Svend-Erik Skaaning, and Jan Teorell (2016), "Measuring High Level Democratic Principles Using the V-Dem Data," *International Political Science Review* 37 (5): 580–93. Vanessa A. Boese (2019), "How (Not) to Measure Democracy," *International Area Studies Review* 22 (2): 95–127.

11. Arend Lijphart and Carlos H. Waisman, eds. (2018), *Institutional Design in New Democracies: Eastern Europe and Latin America* (Milton Park, UK: Routledge). Steven Levitsky and María Victoria Murillo (2009), "Variation in Institutional Strength," *Annual Review of Political Science* 12:115–33.

modern democracy. It is by teasing out this unexpected insight that we conclude this book.

Talking Authoritarianism While Thinking about Democracy

We have defined authoritarianism as a political system in which executive authority is not in practice accountable, directly or indirectly, to any structure or process that is recognizably democratic in the modern, electoral, and representative sense. So, when we are talking about authoritarianism, we are still necessarily thinking about the more distinct (and the more precisely defined in a positive sense) oddity that is democracy: systems where there *is* electoral accountability of the executive through competitive voting with uncertain outcomes.

Since the word "democracy" was coined, analysts have probed and activists have poked, prodded, and tinkered around how democracy might undermine, support, or be molded to coexist with a number of fundamental, normative characteristics of political rule: the rule of law, political stability, the avoidance of violence, constitutionalism, the pursuit of public rather than private interests, and other various political outcomes deemed generally desirable at one time or another.[12]

Yet, this built-in assumption of normative governance must be understood as a patently modern development. In no sense did older thinkers intend to beg the question by wrapping such values into democracy by definition. The recent habit of defining "democracy," often implicitly though sometimes quite explicitly, as political systems that follow the rule of law, avoid violence, allow change only through peaceful means, or pursue a clear public interest would seem odd to earlier generation of analysts, waving away their concerns (e.g., that the rule of the people might undermine those values) as oxymoronic. And to treat authoritarianism as those regimes that eschew some or all of these things—and then to treat that

---

12. John Gerring, Carl Henrik Knutsen, and Jonas Berge (2022), "Does Democracy Matter?" *Annual Review of Political Science* 25:357–75. Kenneth Scheve and David Stasavage (2017), "Wealth Inequality and Democracy," *Annual Review of Political Science* 20:451–68. Alan M. Jacobs (2016), "Policy Making for the Long Term in Advanced Democracies," *Annual Review of Political Science* 19:433–54. Susan C. Stokes (1999), "Political Parties and Democracy," *Annual Review of Political Science* 2 (1): 243–67. Simone Chambers (2003), "Deliberative Democratic Theory," *Annual Review of Political Science* 6 (1): 307–26. José Antonio Cheibub (2007), *Presidentialism, Parliamentarism, and Democracy* (New York: Cambridge University Press). Cass R. Sunstein (2001), *Designing Democracy: What Constitutions Do* (New York: Oxford University Press).

absence as not merely the defining difference but also the most important factor for explaining political outcomes—would seem quite odd as well.

But in many senses that is exactly the trap that political scientists have walked into today. Thus, one recent work by leading scholars of authoritarianism implicitly defines democracy the same way we have here and includes all other systems in the residual category: "The absence of fair, reasonably competitive elections through which citizens choose those who make policies on their behalf defines autocracy or dictatorship."[13] But they then move to explain—in a matter that blends definition with claims that would seem to require analytical clarification and empirical verification—that "because dictatorships lack third-party enforcement of formal political rules, the kinds of formal political institutions that shape politics in democracies have less influence on the behavior of elites in dictatorships."[14]

If it is indeed the case that only democracies have mechanisms to enforce rules outside of executive fiat, that is a noteworthy claim indeed.[15] And it is not one that we accept—our book is premised on the idea that such a claim is a topic for empirical inquiry, not a definitional byproduct or sleight of hand assumption.

But a milder version of the claim has some value, and we can get at it better if we rephrase the question about the distinctiveness of authoritarianism: What does the absence of electoral accountability mean for governance? What difference does it truly make to be governed by an authoritarian regime? Do democracies enforce rules better, with less violence and more predictability?

Over the rest of this concluding chapter, we will explore those questions—and we will find that democracy can indeed make a difference. That means that there are good reasons—well, not so much good conceptual reasons as understandable empirical ones—why so many scholars slide quickly, if sometimes unconsciously, from minimal procedural definitions of democracy to assumptions about the inherent nature of authoritarian-

---

13. Barbara Geddes, Joseph Wright, and Erica Frantz (2018), *How Dictatorships Work* (New York: Cambridge University Press), 1.

14. Geddes, Wright, and Frantz (2018), 5.

15. For a recent research overview discussing elements of this issue, see, e.g., Anne Meng, Jack Paine, and Robert Powell (2023), "Authoritarian Power Sharing: Concepts, Mechanisms, and Strategies," *Annual Review of Political Science* 26. On whether democracies should be so characterized, see a variety of contrasting views, e.g., Barry R. Weingast (1997), "The Political Foundations of Democracy and the Rule of the Law," *American Political Science Review* 91 (2): 245–63. Manfred G. Schmidt (2002), "Political Performance and Types of Democracy: Findings from Comparative Studies," *European Journal of Political Research* 41 (1): 147–63.

ism being highly tyrannical and thus, by implication, the inherent nature of democracy as being its converse. They should be less quick to do so, we will see, but their hidden assumptions have a real, if shaky, basis.

In order to explore these questions, we will have to clear some conceptual thickets that have grown around the terms in ways that are rarely noticed. And in the process, we will indeed argue in favor of working less by slippery definitions and more through the guidance of careful empirical inquiry.

Avoiding Definitional Sleights of Hand

How essential is the difference—or, perhaps, what exactly is essential about the difference—between authoritarianism and democracy? Does it lie in the realm of procedural stability, lack of violence (or its leering shadow), or institutional autonomy? The answer to that question is currently taken to be all three, but we should pause and try to query why such an assumption would have seemed strange for many who lived in earlier eras, even those not so long ago.

As we noted in the first chapter, the term "authoritarianism" as a distinct type of political regime can be traced to diverse origins, but perhaps the most meaningful for the trajectory of political science since the mid-nineteenth century is Juan Linz's 1964 article on Spain.[16] Let us begin there to throw some of the current, fashionable assumptions about authoritarianism into question.

Unfortunately for these viewpoints, the Spanish regime was not nearly as unstable, violent (at least after its bloody birth, although regime founding through warfare is hardly the prerogative of authoritarian systems alone), or lawless as current images about the nature of authoritarianism often lead us to expect. In fact, the midcentury Spanish regime is a great example of what is lost when we assume too much about the universal nature of authoritarian regimes or the clarity of democratic difference.

The leader of that Spanish regime—Francisco Franco—would die only a decade after Linz's article, suffering from an illness so protracted that it became a standing joke on an American comedy television program. Upon hearing of Franco's 1975 death, Richard Nixon, a democratically elected president of the United States who had been forced to resign a year earlier over involvement in attempts to corrupt the American electoral process,

---

16. Juan J. Linz (1964), "An Authoritarian Regime: Spain," in *Transactions of the Westmarck Society, Volume X, Cleavages, Ideologies and Party Systems: Contributions to Comparative Political Sociology*, ed. Erik Allardt and Yrjo Littunen (Helsinki: Academic Bookstore).

Does Authoritarianism Make a Difference? · 253

released a statement that associated the late ruler with stability and justice: "General Franco was a loyal friend and ally of the United States. He earned worldwide respect for Spain through firmness and fairness."[17]

Nixon's judgment of Franco's fairness would be jarring to many; but firmness there was aplenty. Franco also left instructions for succession that unintentionally but clearly led Spain away from his legacy.[18] In fact, the system moved into a direction that seemed for a while to leave not only authoritarianism but stability behind. Franco was succeeded in a process designed years before his death—one that was generally peacefully followed, even by the many Spaniards who would have balked at describing him as fair. In the democratic United States, Nixon's departure also followed prearranged procedures, though arguably more tumultuous, as his successor survived two assassination attempts within a year of taking office.[19]

When Franco's successor guided the country toward a democratic transition, the country's political process followed legal channels with a redesign of the political system—and also into significant uncertainty as democratization unfolded. There was an outbreak of violence launched by the Basque ETA organization, which was unpersuaded that the democratic process offered an appropriate channel for those whose language and culture had been excluded from public life. This was followed by a coup attempt by army officers that nearly succeeded in 1981.[20]

A Spaniard living through these years (mindful of events in his own country but also of those in the United States) might be excused for concluding that authoritarianism brought stability while democracy brought not only uncertainty and disorder but also the potential for violence. Such thinking would not be the product of unique circumstances. Indeed, the post-Franco path would not have seemed anomalous whatsoever to those who first grappled with the idea of "authoritarianism" as a regime type. The coexistence of democracy with violence seemed less anomalous in that period.[21]

Back in 1964, when Linz was incubating the idea of "authoritarianism"

---

17. "Nixon Asserts Franco Won Respect for Spain," *New York Times*, 21 November 1975, https://www.nytimes.com/1975/11/21/archives/nixon-asserts-franco-won-respect-for-spain.html

18. Donald Share (1986), "The Franquist Regime and the Dilemma of Succession," *Review of Politics* 48 (4): 549–75.

19. Arthur M. Schlesinger (1974), "On the Presidential Succession," *Political Science Quarterly* 89 (3): 475–505.

20. Benny Pollack and Graham Hunter (1988), "Dictatorship, Democracy and Terrorism in Spain," in *The Threat of Terrorism*, ed. Juliet Lodge (Milton Park, UK: Routledge).

21. G. Bingham Powell (1982), *Contemporary Democracies: Participation, Stability, and Violence* (Cambridge, MA: Harvard University Press).

as a category of political regime, the Soviet Union's leader was ousted—through established procedures, when the politburo of the country's Communist Party voted to remove him based on his performance.[22] The country in which Linz had come to live, the United States, by contrast, had just lost its president to assassination. It was in the throes of a period of racial strife, upheaval, and a sometimes violent struggle concerning political rights—including electoral participation and democratic procedures—that had been carefully designed to exclude large parts of the population on racial lines.

Violence surrounding elections is hardly an American invention—it is an intermittent but striking part of elections that have been held under democratic conditions in places as diverse as India, Malaysia, Nigeria, France, Italy, and Germany. We do not need to hide behind claims of American exceptionalism to note the pattern, or rather the refutation of a pattern, for stability that is so often assumed to be a byproduct of democracy today.

It should therefore be no surprise that the same year that Linz wrote on Spain, two other leading political scientists wrote a book comparing the American and Soviet political systems, acknowledging their differences but also exploring areas of similarity.[23] While they eschewed the idea that the two systems were converging, a retrospective reading of their work would strike a political scientist today for its failure to stress the differences in regime type as more essential or significant than some similarities. One of the authors of that book, Samuel Huntington, later expanded the argument in ambitiousness and scope by opening his extremely influential monograph in exactly this stark way:

> The most important political distinction among countries concerns not their form of government but their degree of government. The differences between democracy and dictatorship are less than the differences between those countries whose politics embodies consensus, community, legitimacy, organization, effectiveness, stability, and those countries whose politics is deficient in these qualities.

---

22. William J. Tompson (1991), "The Fall of Nikita Khrushchev," *Soviet Studies* 43 (6): 1101–21. Joseph Torigian (2022), "'You Don't Know Khrushchev Well': The Ouster of the Soviet Leader as a Challenge to Recent Scholarship on Authoritarian Politics," *Journal of Cold War Studies* 24 (1): 78–115.

23. Zbigniew Brzezinski and Samuel P. Huntington (1964), *Political Power: USA/USSR* (New York: The Viking Press).

Communist totalitarian states and Western liberal states both belong generally in the category of effective rather than debile political systems. The United States, Great Britain, and the Soviet Union have different forms of government, but in all three systems the government governs.[24]

Such views are not simply outdated relics of the 1960s. Egyptians or Libyans in 2011 watching how their leaders were deposed (the first by military communique following mass demonstrations; the second by mass lynching) and what happened afterward might find Huntington rather prescient—with confusion and contentious rivalry among state and nonstate actors fostering the construction of a new, stable authoritarian regime in Egypt, while warlordism, civil war, and chaos reigned in Libya.

And such observers might wonder, if institutions are built under authoritarian rule as a function of the interests of the autocrat, why the institutional terrain happened to be so very different in the two pre-2011 autocratic systems. Elections took place in both countries after their authoritarian rulers were deposed, but the essential difference in trajectories and outcomes had much more to do with the strength of state institutions that were built in the pre-uprising period than with electoral outcomes.

We do not go as far as Huntington in asserting that institutional strength is the essential difference in explaining political outcomes or that institutionalization is the single most important variable. But we worry that large variations in institutional autonomy might be overlooked simply by definitional fiat or (as we have argued throughout the book) by an overly eager reliance on functionalist explanations for when institutions emerge and how they operate in authoritarian systems.

The association of democratic regimes with other political features—transparency, rule of law, controlled legal violence, and so on—is based on valid historical experiences; those who see democracy as distinctive in its relationship with these things have many examples they can cite. But the point is not to replace empirical political science with anecdotal experiences. And it is also better that we avoid declaring some experiences true by definition and others oxymoronic and puzzling by implication. Careful analysis and empirical inquiry rather than terminological sleight of hand should be the tools used to uncover answers to the questions that have laid

---

24. Samuel P. Huntington (1968), *Political Order in Changing Societies* (New Haven: Yale University Press), 1.

at the foundation of much political debate and inquiry for decades, centuries, and even millennia.

One does not have to go even as far back as the 1960s to find scholars who would find the elision among democracy, stability, rule of law, and rule-bound state institutions puzzling. The institutional turn in comparative politics generally did not fix regime type (especially in a binary authoritarian/democratic manner) at the center. When the state was "brought back in" through an interest in the autonomy of state structures—beginning perhaps with the interest in corporatism in the 1970s, as well as interest in O'Donnell's "bureaucratic authoritarianism" or Stepan's "organic statism"—there was no assumption that state structures were explained largely as a function of regime type or needs.[25] And when the autonomy of the state was addressed most explicitly, democracy and authoritarianism were sometimes not even mentioned. Theda Skocpol, for instance, used terms that would fit our current analysis very well:

> In short, "state autonomy" is not a fixed structural feature of any governmental system. It can come and go. This is true not only because crises may precipitate the formulation of official strategies and policies by elites or administrators who otherwise might not mobilize their own potentials for autonomous action. It is also true because the very structural potentials for autonomous state actions change over time, as the organizations of coercion and administration undergo transformations, both internally and in their relations to societal groups and to representative parts of government. Thus, although cross-national research can indicate in general terms whether a governmental system has "stronger" or "weaker" tendencies toward autonomous state action, the full potential of this concept can be realized only in truly historical studies that are sensitive to structural variations and conjunctural changes within given polities.[26]

---

25. Guillermo O'Donnell (1978), "Reflections on the Patterns of Change in the Bureaucratic-Authoritarian State," *Latin American Research Review* 13 (1): 3–38. Alfred C. Stepan (1978), *The State and Society: Peru in Comparative Perspective* (Princeton: Princeton University Press).

26. Theda Skocpol (1985), "Bringing the State Back In: Strategies of Analysis in Current Research," in *Bringing the State Back In*, ed. Peter B. Evens, Dietrich Rueschemeyer, and Theda Skocpol (New York: Cambridge University Press), 14.

When other scholars followed such approaches to examine specific polities and issue areas (with economic policy and social welfare taking center stage), regime type reared its head but did not dominate all of the explanation, nor were democracy and authoritarianism understood in such antithetical ways.

These ideas have begun to fade. A recent article by three leading scholars of authoritarianism asserts that "realistic models of authoritarian politics must recognize that institutional rules may be circumvented, that political conflicts may be resolved violently, and that information is often limited or asymmetric."[27] They go on to describe all nondemocratic politics by "the questionable relevance of formal institutions, the absence of a higher authority to enforce contracts, the prominent role of violence in the resolution of political conflicts, and pervasive asymmetries of information."[28]

These are just definitions to be sure, but we believe it would be a mistake to use them, not because we see them as always misleading but because they can still quite consequentially feed into a misleading and monolithic caricature of authoritarian politics. Variation in the nature of democracy and authoritarianism should be at the heart of our inquiries rather than obscured from our field of vision. We should not define away some of the most portentous questions human beings have grappled with regarding governance. Democracy and authoritarianism do indeed differ, but we can disassociate violence from democracy and associate it with all nondemocratic systems—and treat that as a key difference explaining political outcomes—only by erasing the historical record.

The relationships between regime type and institutional autonomy, violence, stability, secrecy, and other aspects of policy should be empirically investigated, not slipped into our understandings. The relationship among regime type and secrecy, for instance, does reveal some differences—but ones that display themselves more helpfully through careful analysis of how systems operate than through definitional fiat.[29] And states with strong traditions of the rule of law may seem uniquely democratic today, but both their pre-democratic predecessor regimes from the nineteenth century and the plethora of authoritarian outliers today would likely suggest caution at overinterpretation.

---

27. Scott Gehlbach, Konstantin Sonin, and Milan W. Svolik (2016), "Formal Models of Nondemocratic Politics," *Annual Review of Political Science* 19:566.

28. Gehlbach, Sonin, and Svolik (2016), 567.

29. Robert Barros (2016), "On the Outside Looking In: Secrecy and the Study of Authoritarian Regimes," *Social Science Quarterly* 97 (4): 953–73.

We can turn briefly to the example of religious establishments to illustrate the point in more concrete terms. In a recent work on the role of churches in national policy, Anna Grzymala-Busse has investigated a set of cases, all of which are electoral democracies for part of the period under examination.[30] She finds, however, that churches exert most political influence not through the democratic process but through moral power, whereby religion and the Church were tied to national identity when the latter was formed. This gave them an ability to pose as a speaker for higher truth and the public good rather than as a self-interested political actor.

In other words, the variation in religious authority is largely rooted in the past of the societies examined, not in the present regime type; patterns forged in old regimes (ones that were more authoritarian) survived into the democratic present. Most of this argument would travel seemingly well to currently authoritarian contexts. There is a democratic difference, to be sure: Grzymala-Busse's study finds that churches that do not enjoy such moral authority can still achieve a lesser level of political influence through electoral alliances, a path presumably open only to electoral democracies. In this sense, the democratic difference is not fundamental, but it can be found through empirical examination. Her finding does not rest on any definition requiring democracies to separate church and state but instead on a close examination of the historical record. Regime type turns out to matter sometimes, but the fundamental causal factors lie elsewhere.

This is a path we need to follow more often. And, actually, we have been following it throughout this book. Alert readers might have noted that when discussing the Russian parliament, the Saudi Council of Senior Religious Scholars, the Catholic Church in imperial Germany, or the Palestinian Supreme Constitutional Court, we described some authoritarian actions—but our explanation did not really seem to rely heavily on the point that the regime was authoritarian rather than democratic.

Limited democratic mechanisms in regimes that remained authoritarian (in that senior executive leaders could not plausibly be ejected through electoral means) did sometimes matter—the Center Party in Germany and shifts in Russian parliamentary balloting figured into our accounts; the elected Palestinian Legislative Council was an actor as well. But varying limits on electoral competition did not matter so much that we found ourselves drawn into an extended discussion of hybrid regimes. Lack of

---

30. Anna Grzymala-Busse (2015), *Nations under God: How Churches Use Moral Authority to Influence Policy* (Princeton: Princeton University Press).

democracy figured into our story but was not central to it. The diversity of the authoritarian experience suggests humility when we search for either pluralism or conformity.

Indeed, we presented most of our cases without constantly referring back to the presence or absence of electoral oversight of senior leaders. Maybe authoritarianism is not so distinct? Or, to phrase the question differently, might the same conclusions about institutional autonomy apply to democratic systems? Is authoritarianism a scope condition for our explanation to work? Do state institutions attain their degree of autonomy in a distinct matter in authoritarian systems?

Our short answer is probably not; we expect that our general argument on institutionalization and linkages would travel well to democratic systems. Our view here has echoes in scholarly writings on American political development (as noted in chapter 2) and in historical institutionalist approaches more broadly. When state institutions are structurally differentiated from the ruling regime (or administration, cabinet, "political officials," or "government," in varying democratic terminology); when they hold tight linkages to other powerful actors in society or within the state; and when they are more capable through high levels of institutionalization, we would expect greater institutional autonomy regardless of whether those institutions exist in democratic or authoritarian political systems.

Authoritarianism, which we have accepted as a residual category, is unsurprisingly not all that distinctive when viewed in this manner. Franz Kafka's burdened and inscrutable officials of a highly fictionalized Austrian Habsburg bureaucracy were not somehow fulfilling the autocratic writ of Emperor Franz Josef or his ministers. Joseph Heller's American military bureaucracy and the fictional permanent secretary Sir Humphrey Appleby in the UK's *Yes Minister* acted the way they did despite oddly common assumptions about regime type.

Describing a system as authoritarian turns out not to tell us that much about the way its institutions operate until we know something more about its history and its politics. But we come now back to our repeated claim: if authoritarianism does not seem to make a difference on its own, democracy *does*. We close our study by turning this ambiguous aphorism into a conceptually grounded argument about regime type and the modern administrative state.

Briefly, democratic systems—defined the way we have come to define them—see institutional autonomy emerging for the same reasons that it does in authoritarian systems. Institutionalization and linkages are as apropos to discussions of the autonomy of state institutions in democracy as to the varieties of authoritarianism we have surveyed. The same rules operate. Yet in democracies, the proclivities we have identified are much more richly found in the soil; the conditions that fertilize institutional autonomy are simply likely to be in greater supply than in nondemocratic systems. This is a probabilistic claim, not a definitional one.

And this critical aspect of democracy is not the one that is usually cited. Or perhaps, rather, it is one that is vaguely sensed and implicitly expressed but rarely spelled out. We therefore close by putting this vague sense into clearer words.

Defining Democracy Again

In order to understand why democracy is fertile soil for high levels of institutional autonomy, we will need to resume the definitional discussion that began our inquiry.

When "the rule of law" is considered to be a fundamental part of democracy, then some institutions will be autonomous by definition. The rule of law requires the autonomy of courts, judicial bureaucratic apparatuses, and law enforcement services, as well as the guardrailed "forbearance" of political bodies willing to allow for the insulation of state structures that may sometimes threaten (or at least annoy) them.[31]

But, of course, that is not what the term "democracy" has historically meant. It referred instead simply to rule by the people—and indeed such rule was often seen as being just as likely to undermine the rule of law as to support it. The warnings about mobocracy and majoritarian tyranny are as replete in the ancient sources as they now appear in the teeth gnashing about the dangers of electoral populism today.[32]

In chapter 1, we favored Adam Przeworski's more analytically precise definition of democracy as a system in which political parties lose elections. We noted that it partook of the classical conception of democracy by remaining agnostic about connecting it to the shopping list of political virtues and liberal values (e.g., free speech, individual rights, equality) that have come to be associated with the term both in everyday political speech and in scholarly discussions. Noting that Przeworski's definition

---

31. Steven Levitsky and Daniel Ziblatt (2018), *How Democracies Die* (New York: Broadway Books).

32. Gareth Jones (2020), *10% Less Democracy: Why You Should Trust Elites a Little More and the Masses a Little Less* (Stanford: Stanford University Press).

subtly folded in elements unknown to the classical view (which tended to view political authority exercised in a democracy either by the entire citizenry assembled or by individuals chosen by lot) by introducing elections, political parties, and representational structures, the definition adapts the classical conception to modern practice.

In many ways, the currently prevailing, and often normatively preferred, democratic system (often termed the "liberal democratic" model) is one that could only be poorly understood as a replication of a classical democracy.[33] If classical terminology were used, it would be better characterized as an Aristotelian "mixed" system, where representative democratic elements fit together with an admixture of aristocratic (judicial hierarchies, party elites, and perhaps even media oversight) and monarchic (executive rule by a president or parliamentary-approved prime minister, a coherent administrative state) components.[34]

And there is another subtle difference between classical and modern ideas as well, or one that is rarely expressed: modern conceptions of democracy (including even Przeworski's) seem to assume the existence of a modern administrative state without saying so.[35] Of course, it might be possible to apply modern definitions retroactively to all kinds of states that did not have extensive administrative structures and bureaucracies, and some have done so to interesting effect.[36] But it is the reach and the complexity of the modern state that makes older ideas of how democracy operates in practice—generally involving direct administration and decision-making by the people assembled (or individuals chosen by lot in a mass meeting of citizens)—seem so anachronistic.

When we find traces of those older forms of democracy, we attach a qualifying adjective and call it "direct democracy." The older idea lives on only in very particular pockets such as Swiss cantons or New England town meetings or in far from ubiquitous mechanisms such as popular referenda, juries, or deliberative polling.[37] The power of an administrative apparatus

---

33. Fukuyama (2014).

34. Aristotle (1998), *Politics*, translated by C. D. C. Reeve (Indianapolis: Hart).

35. Francis Fukuyama (2004), "The Imperative of State-Building," *Journal of Democracy* 15 (2): 17–31.

36. David Stasavage (2020), *The Decline and Rise of Democracy: A Global History from Antiquity to Today* (Princeton: Princeton University Press).

37. Frank M. Bryan (2010), *Real Democracy: The New England Town Meeting and How It Works* (Chicago: University of Chicago Press). Arthur Lupia and John G. Matsusaka (2004), "Direct Democracy: New Approaches to Old Questions," *Annual Review of Political Science* 7:463–82.

is furthest from these phenomena and thus renders such direct democratic tools as islands in our current, highly technocratic age.[38]

That is why we have come to see the ultimate, electoral accountability of the executive as the defining characteristic of democracy, given the context of the modern bureaucratic state. If we found a country with an Anglo-Saxon jury system and occasional plebiscites but no electoral oversight of the executive in any way, we would certainly not call it democracy. And, yet, if we found the reverse, such as an executive chosen as a result of competitive elections but no referenda or juries, we just as certainly would call it a democracy.

It is this modern conception of democracy, one that focuses on electoral accountability of those at the top of an extensive administrative state, that has led us to accept the spirit of Przeworski's definition while tinkering with it a little. The sine qua non of what we understand democracy to be today rests on uncertainty over the political choice of executive, ideally iterated at regular intervals, and essentially nothing else.

Uncertain Democracies, Certain Institutions, and (Ancient) Populism

The bounded uncertainty, present at the highest political levels, that is baked into the operation of modern democracies forms the key element that makes this political regime so distinctive—and it is thus the element that justifies bracketing it from the diverse authoritarian alternatives that have dominated much of human history. This becomes especially clear when looking at how the autonomy of state institutions survives within either the prescribed contours of modern democracy or the capacious variations of authoritarianism.

Political uncertainty is part of our understanding of democracy by definition: it must be possible to oust the holders of political power through an election. If those at the top cannot lose an election, the system is authoritarian, not democratic. So, in a democracy, it is not clear who will be at the apex of state authority five or ten years from now. Franco's Spain was authoritarian because he could not lose—there was *too much*, not too little, certainty.

But what is especially distinctive about democracy's special brand of uncertainty is that, given the modern administrative state, it applies to very

---

38. Yascha Mounk (2018), *The People vs. Democracy: Why Our Freedom Is in Danger and How to Save It* (Cambridge, MA: Harvard University Press).

specific offices *only* at the apex of the system. The definition says absolutely nothing about offices submerged within any given state institution below the preeminently political. Of course, patronage systems affecting the distribution of such offices have very much been part of some modern democratic states—but they are not an essential or even usual element and, when operating too extensively, are seen as corrosive to democracy proper.[39] We need only recall repeated efforts to professionalize bureaucracies or remove "spoils systems" and "cronyism" across the political histories of most modern democracies today. An impartial, meritocratic state administration in almost all cases means that democratic contestation is explicitly excluded from the job description.[40]

This leads to the curious specificity of modern democracies (in their most normative form) that we see today. While we like to consider models of democracy to be those that combine all good things against all bad things, such models sometimes run into problems. The virtue of institutional autonomy can turn into the vices of diminishing democratic accountability in favor of technocracy, party cartelization, or the hegemony of self-styled right-thinking elites convinced of their own capacity to divine and pursue the public good.[41]

But reaction against this—attempts to combat institutional autonomy and allow those who control the top to aggrandize greater discretion over state employees (eroding the state/regime distinction within the administrative apparatus)—often makes modern democrats nervous. This is sometimes the case in "delegative democracies" or in some forms of what is often termed "populist" rule, and it is certainly the case for ancient versions of "direct democracy." Democratic backsliding becomes a concern, though not necessarily an inevitability, precisely when elected officials move to erode preexisting features of structural differentiation that establish clear boundaries between rulers, regimes, and states.[42]

And democrats also worry when elections lose their uncertainty—because the same people will be at the top and start behaving as if such

---

39. Mark E. Warren (2004), "What Does Corruption Mean in a Democracy?" *American Journal of Political Science* 48 (2): 328–43.

40. Fukuyama (2014).

41. Mounk (2018). Richard S. Katz and Peter Mair (1995), "Changing Models of Party Organization and Party Democracy: The Emergence of the Cartel Party," *Party Politics* 1 (1): 5–28. Chantal Mouffe (2018), *For a Left Populism* (London: Verso Books).

42. Nancy Bermeo (2016), "On Democratic Backsliding," *Journal of Democracy* 27 (1): 5–19. David Waldner and Ellen Lust (2018), "Unwelcome Change: Coming to Terms with Democratic Backsliding," *Annual Review of Political Science* 21:93–113.

should be the normal condition. Every uncertain election is only as good as the next, after all. A hegemonic governing party in any democracy may be so eager to maintain and elongate its rule that, in fact, it undermines the broad set of virtues that democrats hope their preferred regime type will bring, from the rule of law, to liberal rights, to general governmental transparency. A "one man, one vote, one time" democracy is not a democracy in any modern sense of the word.

This insight is often perceived but rarely stated explicitly in the form we have just presented. But it frequently recurs, most forcefully in recent years with descriptions of "populism"—defined here perhaps best as a democracy with weak institutional autonomy, where a democratic leader (or we might even say a "regime") is able to use distinctively individualized ties to a subset of the public to fuse her rule with the entire state apparatus and undercut structural differentiation in the process. This slightly unorthodox depiction of populism does manage to square the circle of why commentators often refer to leaders as populists when they disrespect state institutions such as courts and broader judicial structures, promote vigorous rubber-stamp legislating in parliaments, or deemphasize traditional authorities in morality or justice from religious communities.

Fears about populism, as with older fears about "delegative democracy," do not simply amount to a concern that elections will become less competitive (although that might be the end result, as countries such as Turkey or Venezuela demonstrate). But there is something that worries normative liberals and democrats all along the way, regardless of actual, true authoritarianism: that formal institutions and liberal practices will be steadily crippled, sometimes explicitly through majoritarian and democratically accountable channels that are ostensibly the governing rules of democratic regimes.

A democracy where institutional autonomy is weakened and hollowed out from the inside is difficult to sustain and perhaps even more difficult to associate with good governance. Because the regime ideal of democracy and practiced state institutional autonomy are so easily and routinely conflated by contemporary social scientists, it is no coincidence that when democratic leaders erode the autonomy of state institutions, their critics typically accuse them of eroding democracy *itself*.

This is, at the same time, exactly what so many have historically feared that democratic regimes would allow, ever since the term was invented. The problem of executive uncertainty being solved by majoritarian certainty is part and parcel of premodern and early modern critiques of democracy;

indeed, it was taken as a truism in many circles until the twentieth century that popular democracy pulled in one direction and the guidance of legitimate expertise, the dominion of the rule of law, and true institutional autonomy for state bodies pulled in the opposite one.

Fears of populism revive this ancient concern but recast it as a *pathological* development rather than a *natural* tendency of democracy. They also insert such fears into a new and formidable context—the politics of an extensive bureaucratic state. And those denounced as populists often cast themselves as embodying the will of the people against the forces of that very same bureaucratic state, in a way that has become especially pronounced in contemporary rebukes of a pernicious yet amorphous and ever more abstruse "deep state" proper.

A state with strong and autonomous institutions may also be one in which those institutions edge out or act rather too independently of democratic structures. And perceptions of such a gap leave an opening to populists who claim to speak for the people rather than the bureaucrats. Some populists may indeed be enemies of democracy (as the term is understood today), but concerns about technocracy are not only the stuff of conspiracy theories, online trolling, and media manipulation.

Such problems can be real and deep, and ignoring them results in casting two key elements of what we understand democracy today to be into serious opposition. Institutional autonomy is not an unalloyed blessing, and an overly autonomous institution might over time be seen quite understandably as an enemy of popular government.

That democracies foster institutional autonomy does not mean that they have resolved political pathologies; sometimes this institutional feature of modern democracy is simply the starting place for politics and its problems. Thus, democracy holds the seeds of its own destabilization—by populism or majoritarian tyranny without and by unresponsive autonomous institutions within. In both sets of circumstances, democratic mechanisms may be a mask for authoritarian practices, either by a leader or regime that undermines democracy or by a "deep state" that ultimately determines the real governing political regime.

Structurally Differentiated Democracy

Democratic systems focus great attention on fixing the balance between the rule of law and the voicing of those elected by the people in ways that are sustainable over time. Democracies do fail in this task, and in many cases such democracies do not last long. We have explicitly *not* defined democracies as ones in which ruler, regime, and state are clearly distinct—yet in a modern administrative state, those that do not separate these clearly have some trouble remaining democracies qua democracies. Elections among competing parties that have uncertain outcomes are not always the first thing to go, but they almost always wind up disappearing when ruler, regime, and state become wholly indistinct at the system level.

This is one reason why democracies, as we have defined them, set within the powerful apparatus of modern administrative states, tend to look similar: they require competitive parties, some arrangements for democratic accountability of the executive, and various ways of combining such mechanisms to make sure they can be perpetuated over time. Regularizing uncertainty through fixed elections for a small set of offices has been part of the recipe for longevity, and definitionally a necessary ingredient, in democracy's fairly short modern life.

In such systems, our key explanatory variables, institutionalization and linkages, are especially likely to be found and, thus, to allow institutional autonomy to flourish. In fact, we are happy to make our argument plain for all of this. Within the subset of contemporary democracies, we expect that the structural differentiation of state and regime to be generically large, and we similarly expect relatively high institutionalization and linkage across state institutions—from constitutional courts and their interconnected nodes of juridical networks, to parliamentarians looking to engage and utilize their prerogatives, to religious bodies performing their societal roles in contest and concession to state desires.

In a sense, we are saying that stable democracies are ones where state, ruler, and regime (a term that it seems impolite to apply to democracy but here again meaning the senior leadership group) are easy to distinguish. Authoritarian regimes and autocratic executives, as we have seen, vary widely in the degree to which they are distinct from the state apparatus as a whole. And, indeed, because the separation of state and regime is itself clear and marked by a short menu of institutional configurations in stable democracies, we tend to avoid the term "regime" altogether but instead refer to "cabinet," "administration," or "government." Authoritarian systems are much more heterogeneous than democratic ones, so it is more necessary to find an often idiosyncratic and even impromptu term to refer to the central leadership group wherever it might be located (in a politburo, dynastic family, theocratic clergy, military high command, or military clique).

And it is not just state, ruler, and regime that tend to be distinct in a democracy. Politician and civil servant, as well as political party membership and official state position are generally distinguishable from each other. Again, democracies do not have a monopoly on such virtues (if virtues they are), but these distinctions are particularly likely to occur in modern democratic states. It might be possible to avoid them in a purely plebiscitary democracy, but we share a common scholarly feeling that such a system is unlikely to be democratic for long (because leaders will use their authority to devise ways to avoid losing elections).

Perhaps that is another reason why we seem to be in an age of concern for democrats everywhere, as parties in some Western states seem more cartelized and bureaucratized than ever,[43] while in other democracies official state office, boorish party clientelism, and the development of personalized courts of executive favorites seem increasingly plausible.[44] Distinctions between state, ruler, and regime are so deeply embedded in our conception of democracy in a modern polity that democrats become deeply concerned when they see that distinction eroding.

In this sense as well, the institution-level variables we found so important for understanding the nature and degree of institutional autonomy are likely to be in rich supply in modern administrative states with democratic systems. With such clear organizational roots, institutionalization would seem to find fertile ground. And with parties losing (and winning) elections, linkages also seem relatively easy to form. Parties that cannot forge links between social constituencies, organized civil society, and parliamentary bodies (and perhaps many other state structures as well) will not be parties as we recognize them in a democratic setting.

Again, none of this is necessarily true by definition. The overlap among various quantitative means of measuring democratic political systems—whether V-Dem, Polity, or Freedom House—as well as the unconscious elision often made between democratic and liberal political systems may be conceptually awkward. But it rests on a likely empirical reality: the distinctive ways in which democracies in modern administrative states have to operate to meet and sustain the narrow, procedural definition.

But this means that it is not authoritarian systems that are distinctive; they vary considerably. *It is democracies that are distinctive.*

---

43. Peter Mair (2013), *Ruling the Void: The Hollowing of Western Democracy* (New York: Verso Books).

44. Robert C. Lieberman, Suzanne Mettler, Thomas B. Pepinsky, Kenneth M. Roberts, and Richard Valelly (2019), "The Trump Presidency and American Democracy: A Historical and Comparative Analysis," *Perspectives on Politics* 17 (2): 470–79.

Where leaders of administrative states are chosen in elections with uncertain outcomes, that feature of politics is generally associated with greater institutional autonomy and structural differentiation at the system level. Removing uncertain elections will not necessarily remove the possibility for institutional autonomy and structural differentiation to emerge or endure; and that is precisely why institutional autonomy under authoritarian conditions can range so widely. The absence of institutional autonomy *might* undermine democracy—but *providing* institutional autonomy does not guarantee democracy.

And realizing this will help us untangle the conceptual knots that defining authoritarianism residually has created. Political scientists after Huntington have drawn back from his insistence, quoted earlier, that "the most important political distinction among countries concerns not their form of government but their degree of government."[45] They have likely recoiled on normative grounds against the extreme stress on political order that seems so . . . well, it sounds authoritarian.[46] They have also gravitated (partly on normative grounds as well) toward insisting that forms do matter and that democracy is substantially different from authoritarian rule. We agree, but we do not wish that statement to lead us into the empirical dead end of viewing the form and operation of state institutions in authoritarianism *only*, or even primarily, as functions of dictators' needs.

After all of this, defining authoritarianism as nondemocracy (a standard practice that we have accepted) ends up telling us quite a bit about what authoritarian systems are not but very little about what they are. As a residual category, "authoritarianism" includes a capacious and variegated set of political systems—some that differ more among one another than they do from democracies. And this differentiation extends across both space and time, as we more truly grasp the multifaceted nature of authoritarian rule that has dominated much of our common human history. To that end,

---

45. Huntington (1968), 1.

46. The implicit elision among democracy, justice, and order is powerful but so recent that older ideas that disentangle them persist in locales (including popular culture and literature) that retain influence. It was, after all, Sauron's unceasing desire for order and harmony that drove him to become the tyrannically Dark Lord that would eventually seek to conquer all of Middle Earth. Even so, we should not forget that the "virtuous" alternative for the Free Peoples of Middle Earth was itself a patently authoritarian system of restoring order through the revived Kingship of Aragorn, Isildur's heir. Thus, the choice of order to promote the common good against order to promote tyranny may have little to do with democracy at all, at least in certain framings. See J. R. R. Tolkien (1994), *The Lord of the Rings* (New York: Houghton Mifflin).

Does Authoritarianism Make a Difference? · 269

we can say quite explicitly: *There is no single, common factor that unites authoritarian countries and makes their politics distinctive*.

Such diversity can be hidden by the conceit of those living in—or aspiring to join—the world of liberal democracy (or those who treat the ideal of liberal democracy as a natural or existing system). Studying systems that fall far short of those ideas should lead us to varied terrain indeed in which the shared absence of liberal democracy does not even provide a clear map. Authoritarianism is a far-distant concept that is in fact quite regular and normal for human civilization; it is only our curious luxury to avoid it being an ever-present reality in our daily, bureaucratic, and political lives.

Efforts to find any sense of coherence, or even worse to bask in untested assurance, are apt to obscure just as much variation as they explain by subtly taking the residual and repackaging it as something specific. Even those who embrace the diversity in authoritarian systems and parse it into neat regime typologies (single party, military, personalist, monarchy) may find themselves falling into this trap—by assuming that power is similarly and functionally exercised from the top down across all authoritarian systems, such that it is both appropriate and useful to categorize them according to who is on top. Yet, by investigating the autonomy of authoritarian state institutions, we have shown that this assumption is valid in some cases but can also be exceptionally misleading in others.

We began this book voicing a concern that much variation across authoritarian systems was getting paved over by a growing, though often implicit, tendency to treat authoritarianism as something much more specific than it actually is—both conceptually and empirically. Our goal was to uncover that variation and offer a fruitful, but not definitive, approach for grappling with it that could be applied to a wide variety of cases. If this investigation has raised more questions about the nature of authoritarian and democratic systems than it has answered, we hope that readers will forgive us in considering that to be an achievement rather than a shortcoming.

Bibliography

Abdel Fattah, Nabil. (2008). "The Political Role of the Egyptian Judiciary." In *Judges and Political Reform in Egypt*, ed. Nathalie Bernard-Maugiron. Cairo: American University of Cairo Press.

Abramson, Scott F., and Carles Boix. (2019). "Endogenous Parliaments: The Domestic and International Roots of Long-Term Economic Growth and Executive Constraints in Europe." *International Organization* 73 (4): 793–837.

Acemoglu, Daron, and James A. Robinson. (2006). *Economic Origins of Dictatorship and Democracy*. New York: Cambridge University Press.

Adorno, Theodore W., Else Frenkel-Brunswik, Daniel J. Levinson, and R. Nevitt Sanford. (1950). *The Authoritarian Personality*. New York: Harper and Brothers.

Ağır, Seven. (2010). "Sacred Obligations, Precious Interests: Ottoman Grain Administration in Comparative Perspective." Unpublished manuscript. Yale University Economic History Workshop.

Agrama, Hussein. (2012). *Questioning Secularism: Islam Sovereignty, and the Rule of Law in Modern Egypt*. Chicago: University of Chicago Press.

Ahmed, Zahid Shahab, and Maria J. Stephan. (2010). "Fighting for the Rule of Law: Civil Resistance and the Lawyer's Movement in Pakistan." *Democratization* 17 (3): 492–513.

Albertus, Michael, and Victor Menaldo. (2012). "Dictators as Founding Fathers: The Role of Constitutions under Autocracy." *Economics and Politics* 24 (3): 279–306.

Al-Yassini, Ayman. (1985). *Religion and State in the Kingdom of Saudi Arabia*. Boulder: Westview Press.

Ambrosio, Thomas, and Jakob Tolstrup. (2019). "How Do We Tell Authoritarian Diffusion from Illusion? Exploring Methodological Issues of Qualitative Research on Authoritarian Diffusion." *Quality and Quantity* 53 (6): 2741–63.

Ambuel, David. (2001). "New Karma: Buddhist Democracy and the Rule of Law in Thailand." *American Asian Review* 19 (4): 131–62.

Arendt, Hannah. (2005). *The Promise of Politics*. New York: Schocken.

272 · Bibliography

Aristotle. (1998). *Politics.* Translated by C. D. C. Reeve. Indianapolis: Hackett.

Arrington, Celeste L. (2019). "Hiding in Plain Sight: Pseudonymity and Participation in Legal Mobilization." *Comparative Political Studies* 52 (2): 310–41.

Baaklini, Abdo I., Guilain Denoeux, and Robert Springborg. (1999). *Legislative Politics in the Arab World: The Resurgence of Democratic Institutions.* Boulder: Lynne Rienner.

Baker, Chris. (2016). "The 2014 Thai Coup and Some Roots of Authoritarianism." *Journal of Contemporary Asian Studies* 46 (3): 388–404.

Bakiner, Onur. (2020). "Endogenous Sources of Judicial Power: Parapolitics and the Supreme Court of Colombia." *Comparative Politics* 52 (4): 603–24.

Balla, Steven J., and William T. Gormley Jr. (2017). *Bureaucracy and Democracy: Accountability and Performance.* Washington, DC: CQ Press.

Barnett, Michael, and Martha Finnemore. (1999). "The Politics, Power and Pathologies of International Organizations." *International Organization* 53 (4): 699–732.

Baroutta, Manuel. (2003). "Enemies at the Gate: The Moabit Klostersturm and the Kulturkampf: Germany." In *Culture Wars: Secular-Catholic Conflict in Nineteenth-Century Europe*, ed. Christopher Clark and Wolfram Kaiser. New York: Cambridge University Press.

Barraclough, Steven. (1998). "Al-Azhar: Between the Government and the Islamists." *Middle East Journal* 52 (2): 236–49.

Barros, Robert. (2002). *Constitutionalism and Dictatorship. Pinochet, the Junta, and the 1980 Constitution.* New York: Cambridge University Press.

Barros, Robert. (2016). "On the Outside Looking In: Secrecy and the Study of Authoritarian Regimes." *Social Science Quarterly* 97 (4): 953–73.

Bartels, Brandon L., and Eric Kramon. (2020). "Does Public Support for Judicial Power Depend on Who Is in Power? Testing a Theory of Partisan Alignment in Africa." *American Journal of Political Science* 114 (1): 144–63.

Bates, Clifford A., Jr. (2002). *Aristotle's "Best Regime": Kingship, Democracy, and the Rule of Law.* Baton Rouge: LSU Press.

Beck, Nathaniel, Jonathan N. Katz, and Richard Tucker. (1998). "Taking Time Seriously: Time-Series-Cross-Sectional Analysis with a Binary Dependent Variable." *American Journal of Political Science* 42 (4): 1260–88.

Bell, Lauren C. (2018). "Obstruction in Parliaments: A Cross-National Perspective." *Journal of Legislative Studies* 24 (4): 499–525.

Bellin, Eva. (2004). "The Robustness of Authoritarianism in the Middle East: Exceptionalism in Comparative Perspective." *Comparative Politics* 36 (2): 139–57.

Bergen, Doris L. (1996). *Twisted Cross: The German Christian Movement in the Third Reich.* Chapel Hill: University of North Carolina Press.

Berger, Maurits S. (2003). "Apostasy and Public Policy in Contemporary Egypt: An Evaluation of Recent Cases from Egypt's Highest Courts." *Human Rights Quarterly* 25:720–40.

Bermeo, Nancy. (2016). "On Democratic Backsliding." *Journal of Democracy* 27 (1): 5–19.

Bernard-Maugiron, Nathalie. (2008). *Judges and Political Reform in Egypt.* Cairo: American University in Cairo Press.

Bigler, Robert M. (1972). *The Politics of German Protestantism: The Rise of the Protestant Church Elite in Prussia, 1815–1848.* Berkley: University of California Press.

Blackbourn, David. (1980). *Class, Religion and Local Politics in Wilhelmine Germany: The Center Party in Württemberg before 1914.* New Haven: Yale University Press.

Blaydes, Lisa. (2010). *Elections and Distributive Politics in Mubarak's Egypt.* New York: Cambridge University Press.

Blockmans, Wim P. (1978). "A Typology of Representative Institutions in Late Medieval Europe." *Journal of Medieval History* 4 (2): 189–215.

Boesche, Roger. (1993). "Aristotle's 'Science' of Tyranny." *History of Political Thought* 14 (1): 1–25.

Boese, Vanessa A. (2019). "How (Not) to Measure Democracy." *International Area Studies Review* 22 (2): 95–127.

Boix, Carles, Michael K. Miller, and Sebastian Rosato. (2013). "A Complete Data Set of Political Regimes, 1800–2007." *Comparative Political Studies* 46 (12): 1523–53.

Boix, Carles, and Milan Svolik. (2013). "The Foundations of Limited Authoritarian Government: Institutions, Commitment, and Power-Sharing in Dictatorships." *Journal of Politics* 75 (2): 300–316.

Bonvecchi, Alejandro, and Emilia Simison. (2017). "Legislative Institutions and Performance in Authoritarian Regimes." *Comparative Politics* 49 (4): 521–44.

Bowie, Katherine. (2014). "The Saint with Indra's Sword: Khruuba Srivichai and Buddhist Millenarianism in Northern Thailand." *Comparative Studies in Society and History* 56 (3): 681–713.

Boyle, Kevin, and Abdel Omar Sherif, eds. (1996). *Human Rights and Democracy: The Role of the Supreme Constitutional Court of Egypt.* London: Kluwer Law International.

Brancati, Dawn. (2014). "Democratic Authoritarianism: Origins and Effects." *Annual Review of Political Science* 17:313–26.

Brown, Nathan J. (1997). *The Rule of Law in the Arab World: Courts in Egypt and the Gulf.* New York: Cambridge University Press.

Brown, Nathan J. (2002). *Constitutions in a Nonconstitutional World: Arab Basic Laws and the Prospects for Accountable Government.* Albany: SUNY Press.

Brown, Nathan J. (2003). *Palestinian Politics after the Oslo Accords: Resuming Arab Palestine.* Berkeley: University of California Press.

Brown, Nathan J. (2007). "Moving Out of Kuwait's Political Impasse." Carnegie Endowment for International Peace.

Brown, Nathan J. (2008). "The Beginning of Real Politics in Kuwait?" Carnegie Endowment for International Peace.

Brown, Nathan J. (2011). "Post-Revolutionary al-Azhar." Washington, DC: Carnegie Endowment.

Brown, Nathan J. (2012). *When Victory Is Not an Option: Islamist Movements in Arab Politics.* Ithaca: Cornell University Press.

Brown, Nathan J. (2013). "Islam and Politics in the New Egypt." Washington, DC: Carnegie Endowment.

Brown, Nathan J. (2016). *Arguing Islam after the Revival of Arab Politics.* New York: Oxford University Press.

274 · *Bibliography*

Brown, Nathan J. (2017). "Official Islam in the Arab World: The Struggle for Religious Authority." Washington, DC: Carnegie Endowment.

Brown, Nathan J., and Julian G. Waller. (2016). "Constitutional Courts and Political Uncertainty: Constitutional Ruptures and the Rule of Judges." *International Journal of Constitutional Law* 14 (4): 817–50.

Bryan, Frank M. (2010). *Real Democracy: The New England Town Meeting and How It Works*. Chicago: University of Chicago Press.

Brzezinski, Zbigniew, and Samuel P. Huntington. (1964). *Political Power: USA/USSR*. New York: Viking Press.

Bueno de Mesquita, Bruce, Alastair Smith, Randolph M. Siverson, and James D. Morrow. (2003). *The Logic of Political Survival*. Cambridge, MA: MIT Press.

Bury, John Bagnell. (2014). *The Constitution of the Later Roman Empire*. New York: Cambridge University Press.

Capoccia, Giovanni. (2016). "When Do Institutions 'Bite'? Historical Institutionalism and the Politics of Institutional Change." *Comparative Political Studies* 49 (8): 1095–1127.

Carpenter, Daniel. (2020). *The Forging of Bureaucratic Autonomy: Reputations, Networks, and Policy Innovation in Executive Agencies, 1862–1928*. Princeton: Princeton University Press.

Casula, Philipp. (2013). "Sovereign Democracy, Populism, and Depoliticization in Russia: Power and Discourse during Putin's First Presidency." *Problems of Post-Communism* 60 (3): 3–15.

Cesari, Jocelyne. (2014). *The Awakening of Muslim Democracy: Religion, Modernity and the State*. New York: Cambridge University Press.

Chambers, Simone. (2003). "Deliberative Democratic Theory." *Annual Review of Political Science* 6 (1): 307–26.

Cheeseman, Nick. (2015). *Opposing the Rule of Law: How Myanmar's Courts Make Law and Order*. New York: Cambridge University Press.

Chehabi, Houchang E., and Juan Linz. (1998). *Sultanistic Regimes*. Baltimore: Johns Hopkins University Press.

Cheibub, José Antonio. (2007). *Presidentialism, Parliamentarism, and Democracy*. New York: Cambridge University Press.

Chernykh, Svitlana, David Doyle, and Timothy J. Power. (2017). "Measuring Legislative Power: An Expert Reweighting of the Fish-Kroenig Parliamentary Powers Index." *Legislative Studies Quarterly* 42 (2): 295–320.

Cherry, Kevin M. (2009). "The Problem of Polity: Political Participation and Aristotle's Best Regime." *Journal of Politics* 71 (4): 1406–21.

Choompolpaisal, Phibul. (2011). "Reassessing Modern Thai Political Buddhism: A Critical Studies of Sociological Literature from Weber to Keyes." PhD diss., University of London, School of Oriental and African Studies.

Chua, Lynette, and Stacia L. Haynie. (2016). "Judicial Review of Executive Power in the Singaporean Context, 1965–2012." *Journal of Law and Courts* 4 (1): 43–64.

Clark, Janine A. (2006). "The Conditions of Islamist Moderation: Unpacking Cross-Ideological Cooperation in Jordan." *International Journal of Middle East Studies* 38 (4): 539–60.

Clemens, Elizabeth, and James Cook. (1999). "Politics and Institutionalism: Explaining Durability and Change." *Annual Review of Sociology* 24 (1): 441–66.

Collier, David, and Fernando H. Cardoso, eds. (1979). *The New Authoritarianism in Latin America*. Princeton: Princeton University Press.

Collier, David, and Steven Levitksy. (1997). "Democracy with Adjectives: Conceptual Innovation in Comparative Research." *World Politics* 49 (3): 430–51.

Collord, Michaela. (2021). "Pressuring MPs to Act: Parliament, Organized Interests and Policymaking in Uganda and Tanzania." *Democratization* 28 (4): 723–41.

Commins, David. (2015). *Islam in Saudi Arabia*. Ithaca: Cornell University Press.

Connors, Michael K. (2009). "Liberalism, Authoritarianism and the Politics of Decisionism in Thailand." *Pacific Review* 22 (3): 355–73.

Conway, John S. (1968). *The Nazi Persecution of the Churches, 1933–1945*. Vancouver: Regent College Publishing.

Coppedge, Michael, John Gerring, Carl Henrik Knutsen, Staffan I. Lindberg, Jan Teorell, David Altman, Michael Bernhard, Agnes Cornell, M. Steven Fish, Lisa Gastaldi, Haakon Gjerløw, Adam Glynn, Sandra Grahn, Allen Hicken, Katrin Kinzelbach, Kyle L. Marquardt, Kelly McMann, Valeriya Mechkova, Pamela Paxton, Daniel Pemstein, Johannes von Römer, Brigitte Seim, Rachel Sigman, Svend-Erik Skaaning, Jeffrey Staton, Eitan Tzelgov, Luca Uberti, Yi-ting Wang, Tore Wig, and Daniel Ziblatt. (2022). "V-Dem Codebook v12." *Varieties of Democracy (V-Dem) Project*.

Coppedge, Michael, Staffan Lindberg, Svend-Erik Skaaning, and Jan Teorell. (2016). "Measuring High Level Democratic Principles Using the V-Dem Data." *International Political Science Review* 37 (5): 580–93.

Cox, Gary W. (2017). "Political Institutions, Economic Liberty, and the Great Divergence." *Journal of Economic History* 77 (3): 724–55.

Cremer, Douglas J. (1999). "To Avoid a New Kulturkampf: The Catholic Workers' Associations and National Socialism in Weimar-Era Bavaria." *Journal of Church and State* 41 (4): 740–47.

Crouch, Melissa. (2020). "Pre-Emptive Constitution Making: Authoritarian Constitutionalism and the Military in Myanmar." *Law and Society Review* 54 (2): 487–515.

Crystal, Jill. (1989). "Coalitions in Oil Monarchies: Kuwait and Qatar." *Comparative Politics* 21 (4): 427–43.

Crystal, Jill. (1995). *Oil and Politics in the Gulf: Rulers and Merchants in Kuwait and Qatar*. Vol. 24. New York: Cambridge University Press.

Dahl, Robert A. (1971). *Polyarchy: Participation and Opposition*. New Haven: Yale University Press.

Darling, Frank C. (1960). "Marshal Sarit and Absolutist Rule in Thailand." *Pacific Affairs* 33 (4): 347–60.

David, Paul A. (2001). "Path Dependence, Its Critics and the Quest for 'h=Historical Economics.'" In *Evolution and Path Dependence in Economic Ideas: Past and Present*, ed. Pierre Garrouste and Stavros Ioannides. Cheltenham: Edward Elgar.

De Grand, Alexander. (1991). "Cracks in the Facade: The Failure of Fascist Totalitarianism in Italy 1935–9." *European History Quarterly* 21 (4): 515–35.

Desposato, Scott W. (2001). "Legislative Politics in Authoritarian Brazil." *Legislative Studies Quarterly* 26 (2): 287–317.

Diamond, Larry. (2002). "Elections without Democracy: Thinking about Hybrid Regimes." *Journal of Democracy* 13 (2): 21–35.

Diefenbach, Thomas. (2013). *Hierarchy and Organisation: Toward a General Theory of Hierarchical Social Systems*. Milton Park: Routledge.

Ding, Iza, and Jeffrey Javed. (2021). "The Autocrat's Moral-Legal Dilemma: Popular Morality and Legal Institutions in China." *Comparative Political Studies* 54 (6): 989–1022.

Donovan, Mark. (2003). "The Italian State: No Longer Catholic, No Longer Christian." *West European Politics* 26 (1): 95–116.

Dundee, Angelo, and Bert Sugar. (2008). *My View from the Corner: A Life in Boxing*. New York: McGraw Hill.

Ehler, Sidney Z., and John B. Morrall, eds. (1954). *Church and State through the Centuries: A Collection of Historic Documents with Commentaries*. London: Burns and Oates.

El-Ghobashy, Mona. (2006). "Taming Leviathan: Constitutionalist Contention in Contemporary Egypt." PhD diss., Columbia University.

Elkins, Zachary, Tom Ginsburg, and James Melton. (2009). *The Endurance of National Constitutions*. New York: Cambridge University Press.

Epperly, Brad. (2016). "Political Competition and De Facto Judicial Independence in Non-Democracies." *European Journal of Political Research* 56 (2): 279–300.

Farr, Ian. (1983). "From Anti-Catholicism to Anticlericalism: Catholic Politics and the Peasantry in Bavaria, 1860–1900." *European Studies Review* 13 (2): 249–69.

Ferejohn, John. (2002). "Judicializing Politics, Politicizing Law." *Law and Contemporary Problems* 65 (3): 41–68.

Ferejohn, John, and Pasquale Pasquino. (2004). "The Law of the Exception: A Typology of Emergency Powers." *International Journal of Constitutional Law* 2 (2): 210–39.

Finkel, Jodi. (2008). *Judicial Reform as Political Insurance: Argentina, Peru and Mexico in the 1990s*. Notre Dame: University of Notre Dame Press.

Finnemore, Martha. (1996). "Norms, Culture, and World Politics: Insights from Sociology's Institutionalism." *International Organization* 50 (2): 325–47.

Fish, Steven M. (2002). "Islam and Authoritarianism." *World Politics* 55 (1): 4–37.

Fish, Steven M. (2017). "The Kremlin Emboldened: What Is Putinism?" *Journal of Democracy* 28 (4): 61–75.

Fish, Steven M., and Matthew Kroenig. (2009). *The Handbook of National Legislatures: A Global Survey*. New York: Cambridge University Press.

Ford, Eugene. (2017). *Cold War Monks: Buddhism and America's Secret Strategy in Southeast Asia*. New Haven: Yale University Press.

Foschi, Martha. (1997). "On Scope Conditions." *Small Group Research* 28 (4): 535–55.

Fraenkel, Ernst. (2017). *The Dual State: A Contribution to the Theory of Dictatorship*. First published 1941. New York: Oxford University Press.

Frøland, Hans Otto, Tor Georg Jakobsen, and Peder Berrefjord Osa. (2019). "Two

Germanys? Investigating the Religious and Social Base of the 1930 Nazi Electorate." *Social Science History* 43 (4): 765–84.

Fukuyama, Francis. (2004). "The Imperative of State-Building." *Journal of Democracy* 15 (2): 17–31.

Fukuyama, Francis. (2011). *The Origins of Political Order: From Prehuman Times to the French Revolution*. New York: Farrar, Straus and Giroux.

Fukuyama, Francis. (2014). *Political Order and Political Decay: From the Industrial Revolution to the Globalization of Democracy*. New York: Macmillan.

Galeotti, Mark. (2019). "Russia's Security Council: Where Policy, Personality, and Process Meet." *Security Insights* 41.

Gallagher, Mary E. (2017). *Authoritarian Legality in China: Law, Workers, and the State*. New York: Cambridge University Press.

Gandhi, Jennifer. (2008). "Dictatorial Institutions and Their Impact on Economic Growth." *European Journal of Sociology* 49 (1): 3–30.

Gandhi, Jennifer. (2008). *Political Institutions under Dictatorship*. New York: Cambridge University Press.

Gandhi, Jennifer, Ben Noble, and Milan Svolik. (2020). "Legislatures and Legislative Politics without Democracy." *Comparative Political Studies* 53 (9): 1359–79.

Gandhi, Jennifer, and Adam Przeworski. (2007). "Authoritarian Institutions and the Survival of Autocrats." *Comparative Political Studies* 40 (11): 1279–1301.

Garud, Raghu, Arun Kumaraswamy, and Peter Karnøe. (2010). "Path Dependence or Path Creation?" *Journal of Management Studies* 47 (4): 760–74.

Geddes, Barbara. (1999). "Authoritarian Breakdown: Empirical Test of a Game Theoretic Argument." Paper presented at the annual meeting of the American Political Science Association, Atlanta.

Geddes, Barbara. (1999). "What Do We Know about Democratization after Twenty Years?" *Annual Review of Political Science* 2 (1): 115–44.

Geddes, Barbara. (2003). *Paradigms and Sand Castles: Theory Building and Research Design in Comparative Politics*. Ann Arbor: University of Michigan Press.

Geddes, Barbara, Joseph Wright, and Erica Frantz. (2014). "Autocratic Breakdown and Regime Transitions: A New Data Set." *Perspectives on Politics* 12 (2): 313–31.

Geddes, Barbara, Joseph Wright, and Erica Frantz. (2018). *How Dictatorships Work: Power, Personalization and Collapse*. New York: Cambridge University Press.

Gehlbach, Scott, Konstantin Sonin, and Milan W. Svolik. (2016). "Formal Models of Nondemocratic Politics." *Annual Review of Political Science* 19:565–84.

Gel'man, Vladimir. (2005). "Political Opposition in Russia: A Dying Species?" *Post-Soviet Affairs* 21 (3): 226–46.

Gel'man, Vladimir. (2008). "Party Politics in Russia: From Competition to Hierarchy." *Europe-Asia Studies* 60 (6): 913–30.

Gel'man, Vladimir, and Andrey Starodubtsev. (2016). "Opportunities and Constraints of Authoritarian Modernisation: Russian Policy Reforms in the 2000s." *Europe-Asia Studies* 68 (1): 97–117.

Gerring, John, Carl Henrik Knutsen, and Jonas Berge. (2022). "Does Democracy Matter?" *Annual Review of Political Science* 25:357–75.

Getty, J. Arch. (1991). "State and Society under Stalin: Constitutions and Elections in the 1930s." *Slavic Review* 50 (1): 18–35.

278 · *Bibliography*

Gilbert, Leah, and Payman Mohseni. (2011). "Beyond Authoritarianism: The Conceptualization of Hybrid Regimes." *Studies in Comparative International Development* 46 (3): 270–97.

Gill, Anthony. (1998). *Rendering unto Caesar: The Catholic Church and the State in Latin America*. Chicago: University of Chicago Press.

Gill, Anthony. (2001). "Religion and Comparative Politics." *Annual Review of Political Science* 4 (1): 117–38.

Gill, Graeme. (2012). "The Decline of a Dominant Party and the Destabilization of Electoral Authoritarianism?" *Post-Soviet Affairs* 28 (4): 449–71.

Gilley, Bruce. (2010). "Democratic Enclaves in Authoritarian Regimes." *Democratization* 17 (3): 389–415.

Ginsburg, Tom. (2003). *Judicial Review in New Democracies: Constitutional Courts in Asian Cases*. Cambridge: Cambridge University Press.

Ginsburg, Tom. (2008). "Administrative Law and the Judicial Control of Agents." In *Rule by Law: The Politics of Courts in Authoritarian Regimes*, ed. Tom Ginsburg and Tamir Moustafa. New York: Cambridge University Press.

Ginsburg, Tom, and Tamir Moustafa, eds. (2008). *Rule by Law: The Politics of Courts in Authoritarian Regimes*. New York: Cambridge University Press.

Ginsburg, Tom, and Alberto Simpser. (2014). "Introduction." In *Constitutions in Authoritarian Regimes*, ed. Tom Ginsburg and Alberto Simpser. New York: Cambridge University Press.

Gisselquist, Rachel M. (2014). "Paired Comparison and Theory Development: Considerations for Case Selection." *PS: Political Science and Politics* 47 (2): 477–84.

Golosov, Grigorii V. (2012). "The 2012 Political Reform in Russia: The Interplay of Liberalizing Concessions and Authoritarian Corrections." *Problems of Post-Communism* 59 (6): 3–14.

Graves, Michael. (2014). *The Parliaments of Early Modern Europe: 1400–1700*. Milton Park: Routledge.

Green, December, and Laura Luehrmann. (2016). *Contentious Politics in Brazil and China: Beyond Regime Change*. Boulder: Westview Press.

Gross, Michael B. (1997). "Kulturkampf and Unification: German Liberalism and the War against the Jesuits." *Central European History* 30 (4): 545–66.

Gruber, Judith. (2021). *Controlling Bureaucracies: Dilemmas in Democratic Governance*. Berkley: University of California Press.

Gryzmala-Busse, Anna. (2012). "Why Comparative Politics Should Take Religion (More) Seriously." *Annual Review of Political Science* 15:421–42.

Grzymala-Busse, Anna. (2015). *Nations under God: How Churches Use Moral Authority to Influence Policy*. Princeton: Princeton University Press.

Gurian, Waldemar. (1952). "Totalitarian Religions." *Review of Politics* 14 (1): 3–14.

Hadenius, Axel, and Jan Teorell. (2007). "Pathways from Authoritarianism." *Journal of Democracy* 18 (1): 143–57.

Hale, Henry E. (2005). *Why Not Parties in Russia? Democracy, Federalism, and the State*. New York: Cambridge University Press.

Hall, John R. (2007). "Historicity and Sociohistorical." *The Sage Handbook of Social Science Methodology*, ed. William Outhwaite and Stephen P. Turner. Thousand Oaks, CA: Sage.

Bibliography · 279

Hall, Peter. (2010). "Historical Institutionalism in Rationalist and Sociological Perspective." In *Explaining Institutional Change: Ambiguity, Agency, and Power*, ed. James Mahoney and Kathleen Thelen. New York: Cambridge University Press.

Hall, Peter, and Rosemary Taylor. (1996). "Political Science and the Three New Institutionalisms." *Political Studies* 44 (5): 936–57.

Halliday, Terence C., and Lucien Karpik. (1997). *Lawyers and the Rise of Western Political Liberalism: Europe and North America from the Eighteenth to Twentieth Centuries*. New York: Oxford University Press.

Hardy, Duncan. (2018). *Associative Political Culture in the Holy Roman Empire: Upper Germany, 1346–1521*. New York: Oxford University Press.

Haspel, Moshe, Thomas F. Remington, and Steven S. Smith. (1998). "Electoral Institutions and Party Cohesion in the Russian Duma." *Journal of Politics* 60 (2): 417–39.

Hatina, Meir. (2003). "Historical Legacy and the Challenge of Modernity in the Middle East: The Case of al-Azhar in Egypt." *Muslim World* 93 (1): 51–68.

Haykel, Bernard, Thomas Hegghammer, and Stephan LaCroix (2015). *Saudi Arabia in Transition: Insights on Social, Political, Economic and Religious Change*. New York: Cambridge University Press.

Heikkilä-Horn, Marja-Leena. (2010). "Santi Asoke Buddhism and the Occupation of Bangkok International Airport." *ASEAS-Austrian Journal of South-East Asian Studies* 3 (1): 31–47.

Heinzen, Jasper. (2017). *Making Prussians, Raising Germans: A Cultural History of Prussian State-Building after Civil War, 1866–1935*. New York: Cambridge University Press.

Hekster, Olivier. (2015). *Emperors and Ancestors: Roman Rulers and the Constraints of Tradition*. New York: Oxford University Press.

Helmke, Gretchen. (2002). "The Logic of Strategic Defection: Court-Executive Relations in Argentina under Dictatorship and Democracy." *American Political Science Review* 96 (2): 291–303.

Herb, Michael. (2002). "Democratization in the Arab World? Amirs and Parliaments in the Gulf." *Journal of Democracy* 13 (4): 41–47.

Herb, Michael. (2004). "Princes and Parliaments in the Arab World." *Middle East Journal* 58 (3): 367–84.

Herb, Michael. (2014). *The Wages of Oil: Parliaments and Economic Development in Kuwait and the UAE*. Ithaca: Cornell University Press.

Herb, Michael. (2016). "The Origins of Kuwait's National Assembly." *London School of Economics and Political Science* 39:1–26.

Hertog, Steffen. (2011). *Princes, Brokers and Bureaucrats: Oil and the State in Saudi Arabia*. Ithaca: Cornell University Press.

Heschel, Susannah. (2008). *The Aryan Jesus: Christian Theologians and the Bible in Nazi Germany*. Princeton: Princeton University Press.

Hewison, Kevin. (2007). "Constitutions, Regimes and Power in Thailand." *Democratization* 14 (5): 928–45.

Hilbink, Lisa. (2007). *Judges beyond Politics in Democracy and Dictatorship: Lessons from Chile*. New York: Cambridge University Press.

Hilbink, Lisa. (2012). "The Origins of Positive Judicial Independence." *World Politics* 64 (4): 587–621.

280 · Bibliography

Hirschl, Ran. (2008). "The Judicialization of Mega-Politics and the Rise of Political Courts." *Annual Review of Political Science* 11:93–118.

Höbelt, Lothar A. (1986). "The Delegations: Preliminary Sketch of a Semi-Parliamentary Institution." *Parliaments, Estates and Representation* 6 (2): 149–54.

Hölkeskamp, Karl J. (2010). *Reconstructing the Roman Republic: An Ancient Political Culture and Modern Research*. Princeton: Princeton University Press.

Hopkins, Raymond F. (1979). "The Influence of the Legislature on Development Strategy: The Case of Kenya and Tanzania." In *Legislatures and Development*, ed. Joel Smith and Lloyd D. Musolf. Durham: Duke University Press.

Huntington, Samuel P. (1965). "Political Development and Political Decay." *World Politics* 17 (3): 386–430.

Huntington, Samuel P. (1966). "Political Modernization: America vs. Europe." *World Politics* 18 (3): 378–414.

Huntington, Samuel P. (1968). *Political Order in Changing Societies*. New Haven: Yale University Press.

Huntington, Samuel. (1993). *The Third Wave: Democratization in the Late Twentieth Century*. Norman: University of Oklahoma Press.

Huntington, Samuel P., and Clement Moore. (1970). "Conclusion: Authoritarianism, Democracy, and One-Party Politics." In *Authoritarian Politics in Modern Society: The Dynamics of Established One-Party Systems*, ed. Samuel Huntington and Clement Moore. New York: Basic Books.

Imam, `Abd Allah. (1976). *Madbahat al-qada* [The Massacre of the Judiciary]. Cairo: Maktabat Madbuli.

Immergut, Ellen. (2005). "Historical Institutionalism in Political Science and the Problem of Change." In *Understanding Change*, ed. Andreas Wimmer and Reinhart Kossler. Basingstoke: Palgrave.

Ipsen, Annabel. (2020). "Repeat Players, the Law, and Social Change: Redefining the Boundaries of Environmental and Labor Governance through Preemptive and Authoritarian Legality." *Law and Society Review* 54 (2): 201–32.

Ishiguro, Kazuo. (1989). *The Remains of the Day*. New York: Random House.

Ishii, Yoneo. (1986). *Sangha, State, and Society: Thai Buddhism in History*. Honolulu: University of Hawaii Press.

Jackson, Peter A. (1989). *Buddhism, Legitimation, and Conflict: The Political Functions of Urban Thai Buddhism*. Pasir Panjang: Institute of Southeast Asian Studies.

Jacobs, Alan M. (2016). "Policy Making for the Long Term in Advanced Democracies." *Annual Review of Political Science* 19:433–54.

Jensen, Nathan M., Edmund Malesky, and Stephen Weymouth. (2014). "Unbundling the Relationship between Authoritarian Legislatures and Political Risk." *British Journal of Political Science* 44 (3): 655–84.

Johnson, Juliet. (2001). "Path Contingency in Postcommunist Transformations." *Comparative Politics* 33 (3): 253–74.

Johnson, Paul. (2015). "Making Unjust Law: The Parliament of Uganda and the Anti-Homosexuality Act 2014." *Parliamentary Affairs* 68 (4): 709–36.

Jones, Gareth. (2020). *10% Less Democracy: Why You Should Trust Elites a Little More and the Masses a Little Less*. Stanford: Stanford University Press.

Bibliography · 281

Jory, Patrick. (2002). "The Vessantara Jataka, Barami, and the Bodhisatta-Kings: The Origin and Spread of a Thai Concept of Power." *Crossroads: An Interdisciplinary Journal of Southeast Asian Studies* 16 (2): 36–78.

Judge, David. (1998). "Parliament and Interest Representation." In *Parliament and Pressure Politics*, ed. Michael Rush. New York: Oxford University Press.

Kalyvas, Stathis N. (1996). *The Rise of Christian Democracy in Europe*. Ithaca: Cornell University Press.

Katz, Richard S., and Peter Mair. (1995). "Changing Models of Party Organization and Party Democracy: The Emergence of the Cartel Party." *Party Politics* 1 (1): 5–28.

Kellow, Geoffrey C., and Neven Leddy. (2016). *On Civic Republicanism: Ancient Lessons for Global Politics*. Toronto: University of Toronto Press.

Kelsen, Hans. (1942). "Judicial Review of Legislation: A Comparative Study of the Austrian and the American Constitution." *Journal of Politics* 4 (2): 183–200.

Kerrouche, Eric. (2006). "The French Assemblée Nationale: The Case of a Weak Legislature?" *Journal of Legislative Studies* 12 (3–4): 336–65.

Kershaw, Ian. (2008). *Hitler, the Germans, and the Final Solution*. New Haven: Yale University Press.

Keyes, Charles F. (1971). "Buddhism and National Integration in Thailand." *Journal of Asian Studies* 30 (3): 551–67.

Khmelko, Irina, Rick Stapenhurst, and Michael L. Mezey, eds. (2020). *Legislative Decline in the 21st Century: A Comparative Perspective*. Milton Park, UK: Routledge.

Kim, Nam Kyu, and Jun Koga Sudduth. (2021). "Political Institutions and Coups in Dictatorships." *Comparative Political Studies* 54 (9): 1597–1628.

Kjorlien, Michele L., and Michele L. Michele. (1994). "State and Religion in Saudi Arabia." *Arab Studies Journal* 2 (1): 36–64.

Kneuer, Marianne. (2017). "Legitimation beyond Ideology: Authoritarian Regimes and the Construction of Cissions." *Zeitschrift für vergleichende Politikwissenschaft* 11 (2): 181–211.

Koesel, Karrie J. (2014). *Religion and Authoritarianism: Cooperation, Conflict and the Consequences*. New York: Cambridge University Press.

Köker, Philipp. (2020). "Why Dictators Veto: Legislation, Legitimation, and Control in Kazakhstan and Russia." *Democratization* 27 (2): 204–23.

Kolkowicz, Roman. (1985). *The Soviet Military and the Communist Party*. Boulder: Westview Press.

Krol, Gerrit. (2021). "Amending Legislatures in Authoritarian Regimes: Power Sharing in Post-Soviet Eurasia." *Democratization* 28 (3): 562–82.

Kunicova, Jana, and Thomas Frederick Remington. (2008). "Mandates, Parties and Dissent: Effect of Electoral Rules on Parliamentary Party Cohesion in the Russian State Duma, 1994–2003." *Party Politics* 14 (5): 555–74.

Kureshi, Yasser. (2021). "When Judges Defy Dictators: An Audience-Based Framework to Explain the Emergence of Judicial Assertiveness against Authoritarian Regimes." *Comparative Politics* 53 (2): 233–57.

Lamberti, Marjorie. (1986). "State, Church, and the Politics of School Reform during the Kulturkampf." *Central European History* 19 (1): 74–75.

282 · Bibliography

Landau, David. (2018). "Courts and Support Structures: Beyond the Classic Narrative." In *Comparative Judicial Review*, ed. Erin F. Delaney and Rosalind Dixon. Cheltenham: Edward Elgar.

Larsson, Thomas. (2016). "Keeping Monks in Their Place?" *Asian Journal of Law and Society* 3 (1): 17–28.

Laruelle, Marlene. (2013). "Conservatism as the Kremlin's New Toolkit: An Ideology at the Lowest Cost." *Russian Analytical Digest* 138 (8): 2–4.

Law, David, and Mila Versteeg. (2014). "Constitutional Variation among Strains of Authoritarianism." In *Constitutions in Authoritarian Regimes*, ed. Tom Ginsburg and Alberto Simpser. New York: Cambridge University Press.

Lepper, Herbert. (1982). "Widerstand gegen die Staatsgewalt." In *Lebensraum Bistum Aachen: Tradition-Aktualität-Zukunft*, ed. Philipp Boonen. Aachen: Einhard-Verlag.

Levitsky, Steven, and María Victoria Murillo. (2009). "Variation in Institutional Strength." *Annual Review of Political Science* 12:115–33.

Levitsky, Steven, and Lucan A. Way. (2010). *Competitive Authoritarianism: Hybrid Regimes after the Cold War*. New York: Cambridge University Press.

Levitsky, Steven, and Daniel Ziblatt. (2018). *How Democracies Die*. New York: Broadway Books.

Lewy, Guenter. (2009). *The Catholic Church in Nazi Germany*. Boston: Da Capo Press.

Lieberman, Robert C., Suzanne Mettler, Thomas B. Pepinsky, Kenneth M. Roberts, and Richard Valelly. (2019). "The Trump Presidency and American Democracy: A Historical and Comparative Analysis." *Perspectives on Politics* 17 (2): 470–79.

Lieberthal, Kenneth, and Michel Oksenberg. (1988). *Policy Making in China: Leaders, Structures and Processes*. Princeton: Princeton University Press.

Lijphart, Arend. (1979). "Religious vs. Linguistic vs. Class Voting: The Crucial Experiment of Comparing Belgium, Canada, South Africa and Switzerland." *American Political Science Review* 73 (2): 442–58.

Lijphart, Arend, and Carlos H. Waisman, eds. (2018). *Institutional Design in New Democracies: Eastern Europe and Latin America*. Milton Park, UK: Routledge.

Lindberg, Staffan I., Michael Coppedge, John Gerring, and Jan Teorell. (2014). "V-Dem: A New Way to Measure Democracy." *Journal of Democracy* 25 (3): 159–69.

Linz, Juan José. (1964). "An Authoritarian Regime: Spain." In *Transactions of the Westmarck Society, Volume X, Cleavages, Ideologies and Party Systems: Contributions to Comparative Political Sociology*, ed. Erik Allardt and Yrjo Littunen. Helsinki: Academic Bookstore.

Linz, Juan José. (2000). *Totalitarian and Authoritarian Regimes*. Boulder: Lynne Rienner.

Lü, Xiabo, Mingxing Liu, and Feiyue Li. (2020). "Policy Coalition Building in an Authoritarian Legislature: Evidence from China's National Assemblies (1983–2007)." *Comparative Political Studies* 53 (9): 1380–1416.

Lupia, Arthur, and John G. Matsusaka. (2004). "Direct Democracy: New Approaches to Old Questions." *Annual Review of Political Science* 7:463–82.

Lupu, Yonatan. (2015). "Legislative Veto Players and the Effects on International Human Rights Agreements." *American Journal of Political Science* 59 (3): 578–94.

Lust-Okar, Ellen. (2006). "Elections under Authoritarianism: Preliminary Lessons from Jordan." *Democratization* 13 (3): 456–71.

Mackenzie, Rory. (2007). *New Buddhist Movements in Thailand: Towards an Understanding of Wat Phra Dhammakaya and Santi Asoke*. Milton Park, UK: Routledge.

Madsen, Richard. (1998). *China's Catholics: Tragedy and Hope in an Emerging Civil Society*. Berkley: University of California Press.

Magaloni, Beatriz. (2006). *Voting for Autocracy: Hegemonic Party Survival and Its Demise in Mexico*. New York: Cambridge University Press.

Magaloni, Beatriz, and Ruth Kricheli. (2010). "Political Order and One-Party Rule." *Annual Review of Political Science* 13:123–43.

Mahoney, James, and Kathleen Thelen, eds. (2009). *Explaining Institutional Change: Ambiguity, Agency, and Power*. New York: Cambridge University Press.

Mainwaring, Scott. (1998). "Party Systems in the Third Wave." *Journal of Democracy* 9 (3): 67–81.

Mair, Peter. (2013). *Ruling the Void: The Hollowing of Western Democracy*. New York: Verso Books.

Malesky, Edmund, and Paul Schuler. (2010). "Nodding or Needling: Analyzing Delegate Responsiveness in an Authoritarian Parliament." *American Political Science Review* 104 (3): 482–502.

Malikhao, Patchanee. (2017). *Culture and Communication in Thailand*. Singapore: Springer.

Manin, Bernard. (1997). *The Principles of Representative Government*. Cambridge: Cambridge University Press.

March, Andrew F. (2003). "From Leninism to Karimovism: Hegemony, Ideology, and Authoritarian Legitimation." *Post-Soviet Affairs* 19 (4): 307–36.

Marshall, Monty G., and Ted Robert Gurr. (2020). "Polity V: Political Regime Characteristics and Transitions, 1800–2018." *The Polity Project*.

McCargo, Duncan. (2004). "Buddhism, Democracy and Identity in Thailand." *Democratization* 11 (4): 155–70.

McCargo, Duncan. (2012). "The Changing Politics of Thailand's Buddhist Order." *Critical Asian Studies* 44 (4): 627–42.

McCubbins, Mathew D., and Thomas Schwartz. (1984). "Congressional Oversight Overlooked: Police Patrols versus Fire Alarms." *American Journal of Political Science* 28 (1): 165–79.

McFaul, Michael, and Kathryn Stoner-Weiss. (2008). "The Myth of the Authoritarian Model-How Putin's Crackdown Holds Russia Back." *Foreign Affairs* 87:68–84.

Meng, Anne, Jack Paine, and Robert Powell. (2023). "Authoritarian Power Sharing: Concepts, Mechanisms, and Strategies." *Annual Review of Political Science* 26:153–73.

Mezey, Michael L. (1979). *Comparative Legislatures*. Durham: Duke University Press.

Mezey, Michael L. (1983). "The Functions of Legislatures in the Third World." *Legislative Studies Quarterly* 8 (4): 511–50.

284 · *Bibliography*

Miller, Michael K. (2011). "Democratic Pieces: Hybrid Regimes, Electoral Authoritarianism, and Disaggregated Democracy." PhD diss., Princeton University.

Moe, Terry. (1990). "Political Institutions: The Neglected Side of the Story." *Journal of Law, Economics and Organization* 6:213–54.

Morgenbesser, Lee. (2016). *Behind the Façade: Elections under Authoritarianism in Southeast Asia.* Albany: SUNY Press.

Morlino, Leonardo. (2009). "Are There Hybrid Regimes? Or Are They Just an Optical Illusion?" *European Political Science Review* 1 (2): 273–96.

Mouffe, Chantal. (2018). *For a Left Populism.* London: Verso Books.

Mouline, Nabil. (2014). *The Clerics of Islam: Religious Authority and Political Power in Saudi Arabia.* New Haven: Yale University Press.

Mouline, Nabil. (2015). "Enforcing and Reinforcing the State's Islam: The Functioning of the Committee of Senior Scholars." In *Saudi Arabia in Transition: Insights on Social, Political, Economic and Religious Change,* ed. Bernard Haykel, Thomas Hegggammer, and Stéphane Lacroix. New York: Cambridge University Press.

Mounk, Yascha. (2018). *The People vs. Democracy: Why Our Freedom Is in Danger and How to Save It.* Cambridge, MA: Harvard University Press.

Moustafa, Tamir. (2000). "Conflict and Cooperation between the State and Religious Institutions in Contemporary Egypt." *International Journal of Middle East Studies* 32 (1): 3–22.

Moustafa, Tamir. (2007). "Mobilizing the Law in an Authoritarian State: The Legal Complex in Contemporary Egypt." In *Fighting for Political Freedom: Comparative Studies of the Legal Complex and Political Liberalism,* ed. Terence C. Halliday, Lucien Karpik, and Malcom Feeley. London: Bloomsbury.

Moustafa, Tamir. (2007). *The Struggle for Constitutional Power: Law, Politics, and Economic Development in Egypt.* New York: Cambridge University Press.

Moustafa, Tamir. (2014). "Law and Courts in Authoritarian Regimes." *Annual Review of Law and Social Science* 10:281–99.

Nicgorski, Walter. (1991). "Cicero's Focus: From the Best Regime to the Model Statesman." *Political Theory* 19 (2): 230–51.

Noble, Ben. (2019). "Volodin's Duma: Cabinet 2.0." *RIDDLE Russia.*

Noble, Ben. (2020). "Authoritarian Amendments: Legislative Institutions as Intra-Executive Constraints in Post-Soviet Russia." *Comparative Political Studies* 53 (9): 1417–54.

Noble, Ben, and Ekaterina Schulmann. (2018). "Not Just a Rubber Stamp: Parliament and Lawmaking." In *The New Autocracy: Information, Politics, and Policy in Putin's Russia,* ed. Daniel Triesman. Washington, DC: Brookings Institution Press.

North, Douglass C. (1990). *Institutions, Institutional Change and Economic Performance.* New York: Cambridge University Press.

North, Douglass C. (1994). "Economic Performance through Time." *American Economic Review* 84 (3): 359–68.

North, Douglass C., and Barry R. Weingast. (1989). "Constitutions and Commitment: The Evolution of Institutions Governing Public Choice in Seventeenth-Century England." *Journal of Economic History* 49 (4): 803–32.

Norton, Philip. (1990). "Parliaments: A Framework for Analysis." *West European Politics* 13 (3): 1–9.

O'Brien, Kevin J., and Lianjiang Li. (2006). *Rightful Resistance in Rural China*. New York: Cambridge University Press.

Ochieng'Opalo, Ken. (2019). *Legislative Development in Africa: Politics and Postcolonial Legacies*. New York: Cambridge University Press.

O'Donnell, Guillermo. (1978). "Reflections on the Patterns of Change in the Bureaucratic-Authoritarian State." *Latin American Research Review* 13 (1): 3–38.

Ogushi, Atsushi. (2017). "Weakened Machine Politics and the Consolidation of a Populist Regime: Contextualization of the 2016 Duma Election." *Russian Politics* 2 (3): 287–306.

Oliveira, Richard Romeiro. (2019). "The Aristotelian Theory of Regimes and the Problem of Kingship in Politics III." *Trans/Form/Ação* 42 (2): 31–58.

Oneal, John R., and Bruce Russett. (1997). "The Classical Liberals Were Right: Democracy, Interdependence, and Conflict, 1950–1985." *International Studies Quarterly* 41 (2): 267–93.

Orlin, Eric M. (2002). *Temples, Religion, and Politics in the Roman Republic*. Leiden, Netherlands: Brill.

Ortmann, Stephan, and Mark R. Thompson. (2016). "China and the 'Singapore Model.'" *Journal of Democracy* 27 (1): 39–48.

Parker, Christopher Sebastian, and Christopher C. Towler. (2019). "Race and Authoritarianism in American Politics." *Annual Review of Political Science* 22:503–19.

Peerenboom, Randall. (2002). *China's Long March to the Rule of Law*. New York: Cambridge University Press.

Pepinsky, Thomas. (2013). "The Institutional Turn in Comparative Authoritarianism." *British Journal of Political Science* 44 (3): 631–53.

Pereira, Anthony W. (2005). *Political (In)justice: Authoritarianism and the Rule of Law in Brazil, Chile, and Argentina*. Pittsburgh: University of Pittsburgh Press.

Philpott, Daniel. (2004). "Christianity and Democracy: The Catholic Wave." *Journal of Democratization* 15 (2): 32–46.

Pierson, Paul. (2000). "Increasing Returns, Path Dependence, and the Study of Politics." *American Political Science Review* 94 (2): 251–67.

Pinto, António Costa, ed. (2017). *Corporatism and Fascism: The Corporatist Wave in Europe*. Milton Park, UK: Taylor & Francis.

Plato. (1943). *Plato's The Republic*. New York: Basic Books.

Pollack, Benny, and Graham Hunter. (1988). "Dictatorship, Democracy and Terrorism in Spain." In *The Threat of Terrorism*, ed. Juliet Lodge. Milton Park, UK: Routledge.

Polsby, Nelson W. (1975). "Legislatures." In *Handbook of Political Science*, ed. Fred I. Greenstein and Nelson W. Polsby. Boston: Addison-Wesley.

Powell, G. Bingham. (1982). *Contemporary Democracies: Participation, Stability, and Violence*. Cambridge, MA: Harvard University Press.

Przeworski, Adam. (1991). *Democracy and the Market: Political and Economic Reforms in Eastern Europe and Latin America*. New York: Cambridge University Press.

Przeworski, Adam, Michael E. Alvarez, José Antonio Cheibub, and Fernando Li-mongi. (2000). *Democracy and Development: Political Institutions and Well-Being in the World, 1950–1990*. New York: Cambridge University Press.

Rajah, Jothie. (2011). "Punishing Bodies, Securing the Nation: How Rule of Law Can Legitimate the Urbane Authoritarian State." *Law and Social Inquiry* 36 (4): 945–70.

Rajah, Jothie. (2012). *Authoritarian Rule of Law: Legislation, Discourse and Legitimacy in Singapore*. New York: Cambridge University Press.

Ramet, Sabrina P. (1998). *Nihil Obstat: Religion, Politics, and Social Change in East-Central Europe and Russia*. Durham: Duke University Press.

Ramos, Francisco. (2006). "The Establishment of Constitutional Courts: A Study of 128 Democratic Constitutions." *Review of Law and Economics* 2 (1): 103–35.

Remington, Thomas F. (2006). "Presidential Support in the Russian State Duma." *Legislative Studies Quarterly* 31 (1): 5–32.

Remington, Thomas F., and Steven S. Smith. (1998). "Theories of Legislative Insti-tutions and the Organization of the Russian Duma." *American Journal of Political Science* 42 (2): 545–72.

Reuter, Ora John. (2017). *The Origins of Dominant Parties: Building Authoritarian Institutions in Post-Soviet Russia*. New York: Cambridge University Press.

Reuter, Ora John, and Graeme B. Robertson. (2015). "Legislatures, Cooptation, and Social Protest in Contemporary Authoritarian Regimes." *Journal of Politics* 77 (1): 235–48.

Reynolds, Bruce. (2004). "Phibun Songkhram and Thai Nationalism in the Fascist Era." *European Journal of East Asian Studies* 3 (1): 99–134.

Reynolds, Frank. (1994). "Dhamma in Dispute: The Interactions of Religion and Law in Thailand." *Law and Society Review* 28 (3): 433–51.

Rhodes, Anthony. (1973). *The Vatican in the Age of the Dictators, 1922–1945*. New York: Holt, Rinehart, and Winston.

Roberts, Tyson L. (2015). "The Durability of Presidential and Parliament-Based Dictatorships." *Comparative Political Studies* 48 (7): 915–48.

Roemer, John E. (1998). "Why the Poor Do Not Expropriate the Rich: An Old Argument in New Garb." *Journal of Public Economics* 70 (3): 399–424.

Rosberg, James. (1995). "The Rise of an Independent Judiciary in Egypt." PhD diss., Massachusetts Institute of Technology.

Rose, Richard, and Derek Urwin. (1969). "Social Cohesion, Political Parties and Strains in Regimes." *Comparative Political Studies* 2 (1): 7–67.

Ross, Ronald J. (1984). "Enforcing the Kulturkampf in the Bismarckian State and the Limits of Coercion in Imperial Germany." *Journal of Modern History* 56 (3): 456–82.

Roth, Guenther. (1968). "Personal Rulership, Patrimonialism, and Empire-Building in the New States." *World Politics* 20 (2): 194–206.

Ruedin, Didier. (2009). "Ethnic Group Representation in a Cross-National Com-parison." *Journal of Legislative Studies* 15 (4): 335–54.

Ruff, Mark Edward. (2014). "The Critical Reception of John Conway's 'The Nazi Persecution of the Churches, 1933–1945.'" *Kirchliche Zeitgeschichte* 27 (1): 31–42.

Bibliography · 287

Rutherford, Bruce K. (1999). *The Struggle for Constitutionalism in Egypt: Understanding the Obstacles to Democratic Transition in the Arab World*. New Haven: Yale University Press.

Sakwa, Richard. (2010). *The Crisis of Russian Democracy: The Dual State, Factionalism and the Medvedev Succession*. New York: Cambridge University Press.

Sassoon, Joseph. (2016). *Anatomy of Authoritarianism in the Arab Republics*. New York: Cambridge University Press.

Scarrow, Susan. (2006). "The Nineteenth-Century Origins of Modern Political Parties: The Unwanted Emergence of Party-Based Politics." In *Handbook of Party Politics*, ed. Richard S. Katz and William Crotty. Thousand Oaks: Sage.

Schaaf, Steven D. (2021). "Contentious Politics in the Courthouse: Law as a Tool for Resisting Authoritarian States in the Middle East." *Law and Society Review* 55 (1): 139–76.

Schaaf, Steven D. (2022). "When Do Courts Constrain the Authoritarian State? Judicial Decision-Making in Jordan and Palestine." *Comparative Politics* 54 (2): 375–99.

Schedler, Andreas. (2006). *Electoral Authoritarianism: The Dynamics of Unfree Competition*. Boulder: Lynne Rienner.

Schedler, Andreas. (2013). *The Politics of Uncertainty: Sustaining and Subverting Electoral Authoritarianism*. Oxford: Oxford University Press.

Scheidel, Walter. (2019). *Escape from Rome: The Failure of Empire and the Road to Prosperity*. Princeton: Princeton University Press.

Scheve, Kenneth, and David Stasavage. (2017). "Wealth Inequality and Democracy." *Annual Review of Political Science* 20:451–68.

Schlesinger, Arthur M. (1974). "On the Presidential Succession." *Political Science Quarterly* 89 (3): 475–505.

Schmidt, Manfred G. (2002). "Political Performance and Types of Democracy: Findings from Comparative Studies." *European Journal of Political Research* 41 (1): 147–63.

Schmitt, Carl. (1926). *Die geistesgeschichtliche Lage des heutigen Parlamentarismus*. München and Leipzig: Duncker & Humblot.

Schmitter, Philippe C., and Terry Lynn Karl. (1991). "What Democracy Is . . . and Is Not." *Journal of Democracy* 2 (3): 75–88.

Schneider, Ben Ross. (1992). *Politics within the State: Elite Bureaucrats and Industrial Policy in Authoritarian Brazil*. Pittsburgh: University of Pittsburgh Press.

Schonthal, Benjamin. (2017). "Formations of Buddhist Constitutionalism in Southeast Asia." *International Journal of Constitutional Law* 15 (3): 705–33.

Schuler, Paul. (2020). "Position Taking or Position Ducking? A Theory of Public Debate in Single Party Legislatures." *Comparative Political Studies* 53 (9): 1493–1524.

Schulmann, Ekaterina. (2014). "Legislation as a Political Process." PhD diss., Russian Presidential Academy of National Economy and Public Administration.

Scott, Rachelle M. (2006). "A New Buddhist Sect? The Dhammakāya Temple and the Politics of Religious Difference." *Religion* 36 (4): 215–30.

Seawright, Jason, and John Gerring. (2008). "Case Selection Techniques in Case Study Research: A Menu of Qualitative and Quantitative Options." *Political Research Quarterly* 61 (2): 294–308.

Sebők, Miklós, Csaba Molnár, and Bálint György Kubik. (2017). "Exercising Control and Gathering Information: The Functions of Interpellations in Hungary (1990–2014)." *Journal of Legislative Studies* 23 (4): 465–83.

Segal, Eran. (2012). "Political Participation in Kuwait: Dīwāniyya, Majlis and Parliament." *Journal of Arabian Studies* 2 (2): 127–41.

Selinger, William. (2019). *Parliamentarism: From Burke to Weber.* New York: Cambridge University Press.

Semenova, Elena. (2012). "Patterns of Parliamentary Representation and Careers in Ukraine: 1990–2007." *East European Politics and Societies* 26 (3): 538–60.

Shalaby, Marwa, and Abdullah Aydogan. (2020). "Elite-Citizen Linkages and Issue Congruency under Competitive Authoritarianism." *Parliamentary Affairs* 73 (1): 66–88.

Shapiro, Martin. (1981). *Courts: A Comparative and Political Analysis.* Chicago: University of Chicago Press.

Share, Donald. (1986). "The Franquist Regime and the Dilemma of Succession." *Review of Politics* 48 (4): 549–75.

Sharma, B. S. (1965). "Parliamentary Government in Uganda." *International Studies* 7 (3): 448–56.

Shen-Bay, Fiona. (2018). "Strategies of Repression: Judicial and Extrajudicial Methods of Autocratic Survival." *World Politics* 70 (3): 321–57.

Shevchenko, Iulia, and Grigorii V. Golosov. (2001). "Legislative Activism of Russian Duma Deputies, 1996–1999." *Europe-Asia Studies* 53 (2): 239–61.

Shirikov, Anton. (2021). "Who Gets Ahead in Authoritarian Parliaments? The Case of the Russian State Duma." *Journal of Legislative Studies* 28 (4): 554–77.

Shoshan, Boaz. (1981). "Fatimid Grain Policy and the Post of the Muhtasib." *International Journal of Middle East Studies* 13 (2): 181–89.

Sievert, Jaqueline M. (2018). "The Case for Courts: Resolving Information Problems in Authoritarian Regimes." *Journal of Peace Research* 55 (6): 774–86.

Skilling, Harold G., and Franklyn Griffiths. (1971). *Interest Groups in Soviet Politics.* Princeton: Princeton University Press.

Skocpol, Theda. (1985). "Bringing the State Back In: Strategies of Analysis in Current Research." In *Bringing the State Back In,* ed. Peter B. Evens, Dietrich Rueschemeyer, and Theda Skocpol. New York: Cambridge University Press.

Slater, Dan. (2003). "Iron Cage in an Iron Fist: Authoritarian Institutions and the Personalization of Power in Malaysia." *Comparative Politics* 36 (1): 81–101.

Slater, Dan, and Sofia Fenner. (2011). "State Power and Staying Power: Infrastructural Mechanisms and Authoritarian Durability." *Journal of International Affairs* 65 (1): 15–29.

Smith, Steven S., and Thomas F. Remington. (2001). *The Politics of Institutional Choice: The Formation of the Russian State Duma.* Princeton: Princeton University Press.

Smyth, Regina. (2014). "The Putin Factor: Personalism, Protest, and Regime Stability in Russia." *Politics and Policy* 42 (4): 567–92.

Smyth, Regine, William Bianco, and Kwan Nok Chan. (2019). "Legislative Rules in Electoral Authoritarian Regimes: The Case of Hong Kong's Legislative Council." *Journal of Politics* 81 (3): 892–905.

Bibliography · 289

Smyth, Regina, Anna Lowry, and Brandon Wilkening. (2007). "Engineering Victory: Institutional Reform, Informal Institutions, and the Formation of a Hegemonic Party Regime in the Russian Federation." *Post-Soviet Affairs* 23 (2): 118–37.

Solomon, Peter H., Jr. (2010). "Authoritarian Legality and Informal Practices: Judges, Lawyers, and the State in Russia and China." *Communist and Post-Communist Studies* 43 (4): 351–62.

Solomon, Peter H., Jr. (2015). "Law and Courts in Authoritarian States." *International Encyclopedia of the Social and Behavioral Sciences* 2:427–34.

Somfalvy, Esther. (2020). *Parliamentary Representation in Central Asia: MPs Between Representing Their Voters and Serving an Authoritarian Regime.* Milton Park, UK: Routledge.

Spenkuch, Jörg L., and Philipp Tillmann. (2018). "Elite Influence? Religion and the Electoral Success of the Nazis." *American Journal of Political Science* 62 (1): 19–36.

Sperber, Jonathan. (1997). *The Kaiser's Votes: Electors and Elections in Imperial Germany.* New York: Cambridge University Press.

Spohn, Willfried. (1980). "Religion and Working-Class Formation in Imperial Germany 1871–1914." *Politics and Society* 19 (1): 109–32.

Stasavage, David. (2010). "When Distance Mattered: Geographic Scale and the Development of European Representative Assemblies." *American Political Science Review* 104 (4): 625–43.

Stasavage, David. (2020). *The Decline and Rise of Democracy: A Global History from Antiquity to Today.* Princeton: Princeton University Press.

Steigmann-Gall, Richard. (2004). "Nazism and the Revival of Political Religion Theory." *Totalitarian Movements and Political Religions* 5 (3): 376–96.

Steigmann-Gall, Richard. (2007). "The Nazis' 'Positive Christianity': A Variety of 'Clerical Fascism'?" *Totalitarian Movements and Political Religions* 8 (2): 315–27.

Steinmo, Sven. (2008). "Historical Institutionalism." In *Approaches and Methodologies in the Social Sciences: A Pluralist Perspective*, ed. Donatella Della Porta and Michael Keating. New York: Cambridge University Press.

Stepan, Alfred. (1978). *The State and Society: Peru in Comparative Perspective.* Princeton: Princeton University Press.

Stilt, Kristin. (2012). *Islamic Law in Action: Authority, Discretion, and Everyday Experiences in Mamluk Egypt.* New York: Oxford University Press.

Stokes, Susan C. (1999). "Political Parties and Democracy." *Annual Review of Political Science* 2 (1): 243–67.

Suksamran, Somboon. (1979). "Buddhism and Politics: The Political Roles, Activities and Involvement of the Thai Sangha." PhD diss., University of Hull.

Suksamran, Somboon. (1981). "Religion Politics and Development: The Thai Sangha's Role in National Development and Integration." *Southeast Asian Journal of Social Science* 9 (1/2): 54–73.

Suksamran, Somboon. (1982). *Buddhism and Politics in Thailand: A Study of Socio-Political Change and Political Activism of the Thai Sangha.* Pasir Panjang: Institute of Southeast Asian Studies.

290 · *Bibliography*

Sunstein, Cass R. (2001). *Designing Democracy: What Constitutions Do*. New York: Oxford University Press.

Suval, Stanley. (1985). *Electoral Politics in Wilhelmine Germany*. Chapel Hill: University of North Carolina Press.

Svolik, Milan W. (2012). *The Politics of Authoritarian Rule*. New York: Cambridge University Press.

Szakonyi, David. (2017). "New Rules, New Members, Same Results? A Look at the New Russian Duma." *Kennan Cable* 22.

Taagepera, Rein. (1974). "Civic Culture and Authoritarianism in the Baltic States, 1930–1940." *East European Quarterly* 7 (4): 407–12.

Tambiah, Stanley Jeyaraja. (1976). *World Conqueror and World Renouncer: A Study of Buddhism and Polity in Thailand against a Historical Background*. New York: Cambridge University Press.

Tarrow, Sidney. (2010). "The Strategy of Paired Comparison: Toward a Theory of Practice." *Comparative Political Studies* 43 (2): 230–59.

Taylor, Jim. (2012). "No Way Forward but Back? Re-emergent Thai Falangism, Democracy and the New 'Red Shirt' Social Movement." In *Bangkok May 2010: Perspectives on a Divided Thailand*, ed. Michael J. Montesano, Pavin Chachavalpongpun, and Aekapol Chongvilaivan. Pasir Panjang: ISEAS-Yusof Ishak Institute.

Thames, Frank C., Jr. (2001). "Legislative Voting Behaviour in the Russian Duma: Understanding the Effect of Mandate." *Europe-Asia Studies* 53 (6): 869–84.

Thelen, Kathleen. (1999). "Historical Institutionalism in Comparative Politics." *Annual Review of Political Science* 2 (1): 369–404.

Timoneda, Joan. (2020). "Institutions and Signals: How Dictators Consolidate Power in Times of Crisis." *Comparative Politics* 53 (1): 49–68.

Toharia, Jose J. (1975). "Judicial Independence in an Authoritarian Regime: The Case of Contemporary Spain." *Law and Society Review* 9 (3): 475–96.

Tolkien, J. R. R. (1994). *The Lord of the Rings*. New York: Houghton Mifflin.

Tompson, William J. (1991). "The Fall of Nikita Khrushchev." *Soviet Studies* 43 (6): 1101–21.

Torigian, Joseph. (2022). "'You Don't Know Khrushchev Well': The Ouster of the Soviet Leader as a Challenge to Recent Scholarship on Authoritarian Politics." *Journal of Cold War Studies* 24 (1): 78–115.

Trochev, Alexei, and Rachel Ellett. (2014). "Judges and Their Allies: Rethinking Judicial Autonomy through the Prism of Off-Bench Resistance." *Journal of Law and Courts* 2 (1): 67–91.

Trochev, Alexei, and Peter H. Solomon. (2018). "Authoritarian Constitutionalism in Putin's Russia: A Pragmatic Constitutional Court in a Dual State." *Communist and Post-Communist Studies* 51 (3): 201–14.

Troxel, Tiffany A. (2003). *Parliamentary Power in Russia, 1994–2001*. London: Palgrave Macmillan.

Truex, Rory. (2016). *Making Autocracy Work: Representation and Responsiveness in Modern China*. New York: Cambridge University Press.

Treux, Rory. (2020). "Authoritarian Gridlock? Understanding Delay in the Chinese Legislative System." *Comparative Political Studies* 53 (9): 1455–92.

Tsebelis, George. (1995). "Decision Making in Political Systems: Veto Players in Presidentialism, Parliamentarism, Multicameralism and Multipartyism." *British Journal of Political Science* 25 (3): 289–325.

Vallinder, Torbjörn. (1994). "The Judicialization of Politics—A World-Wide Phenomenon: Introduction." *International Political Science Review* 15 (2): 91–99.

Vanberg, Georg. (2008). "Establishing and Maintaining Judicial Independence." In *The Oxford Handbook of Law and Politics*, ed. Gregory A. Caldiera, R. Daniel Kelemen, and Keith E. Whittington. New York: Oxford University Press.

Van Evera, Stephen. (2015). *Guide to Methods for Students of Political Science*. Ithaca: Cornell University Press.

Van Zanden, Jan Luiten, Eltjo Buringh, and Maarten Bosker. (2012). "The Rise and Decline of European Parliaments, 1188–1789." *Economic History Review* 65 (3): 835–61.

Vardys, Vytas Stanley. (1974). "The Baltic States in Search of Their Own Political Systems." *East European Quarterly* 7 (4): 399–406.

Von Soest, Christian, and Julia Grauvogel. (2017). "Identity, Procedures and Performance: How Authoritarian Regimes Legitimize Their Rule." *Contemporary Politics* 23 (3): 287–305.

Waldner, David, and Ellen Lust. (2018). "Unwelcome Change: Coming to Terms with Democratic Backsliding." *Annual Review of Political Science* 21:93–113.

Waller, Julian G. (2021). "Elites and Institutions in the Russian Thermidor: Regime Instrumentalism, Entrepreneurial Signaling, and Inherent Illiberalism." *Journal of Illiberalism Studies* 1 (1): 1–23.

Waller, Julian G. (2022). "Beyond the Rubber-Stamp: Essays on Parliamentary Bodies Under Authoritarianism." PhD diss., George Washington University.

Waller, Julian G. (2023). "Mimicking the Mad Printer: Legislating Illiberalism in Post-Soviet Eurasia." *Problems of Post-Communism* 70 (3): 225–40.

Wang, Yuhua. (2018). "Relative Capture: Quasi-Experimental Evidence from the Chinese Judiciary." *Comparative Political Studies* 51 (8): 1012–41.

Warren, Mark E. (2004). "What Does Corruption Mean in a Democracy?" *American Journal of Political Science* 48 (2): 328–43.

Wawro, Gregory J., and Eric Schickler. (2010). "Legislative Obstructionism." *Annual Review of Political Science* 13:297–319.

Webb, Leicester C. (1958). *Church and State in Italy 1947–1957*. Victoria: Melbourne University Press.

Weber, Max. (1978). *Economy and Society: An Outline of Interpretive Sociology*. Berkeley: University of California Press.

Weeks, Jessica. (2012). "Strongmen and Straw Men: Authoritarian Regimes and the Initiation of International Conflict." *American Political Science Review* 106 (2): 326–47.

Weeks, Jessica. (2014). *Dictators at War and Peace*. Ithaca: Cornell University Press.

Wehner, Joachim. (2006). "Assessing the Power of the Purse: An Index of Legislative Budget Institutions." *Political Studies* 54 (6): 767–85.

Weingast, Barry R. (1997). "The Political Foundations of Democracy and the Rule of the Law." *American Political Science Review* 91 (2): 245–63.

Whiting, Susan. (2017). "Authoritarian 'Rule of Law' and Regime Legitimacy." *Comparative Political Studies* 50 (14): 1907–40.

Wiberg, Matti. (1995). "Parliamentary Questioning: Control by Communication." In *Parliaments and Majority Rule in Western Europe*, ed. Herbert Döring. Frankfurt: Campus.

Wickham, Chris. (2017). "Consensus and Assemblies in the Romano-Germanic Kingdoms: A Comparative Approach." *Vorträge und Forschungen* 82:389–426.

Wiebrecht, Felix. (2021). "Between Elites and Opposition: Legislatures' Strength in Authoritarian Regimes." *Democratization* 28 (6): 1075–94.

Wigley, Simon. (2003). "Parliamentary Immunity: Protecting Democracy or Protecting Corruption?" *Journal of Political Philosophy* 11 (1): 23–40.

Williamson, Scott. (2021). "Elections, Legitimacy, and Compliance in Authoritarian Regimes: Evidence from the Arab World." *Democratization* 28 (8): 1483–1504.

Williamson, Scott, and Beatriz Magaloni. (2020). "Legislatures and Policy Making in Authoritarian Regimes." *Comparative Political Studies* 53 (9): 1525–43.

Woo, Ae Sil, and Courtenay R. Conrad. (2019). "The Differential Effects of 'Democratic' Institutions on Dissent in Dictatorships." *Journal of Politics* 81 (2): 456–70.

Wright, Joseph. (2008). "Do Authoritarian Institutions Constrain? How Legislatures Affect Economic Growth and Investment." *American Journal of Political Science* 52 (2): 322–43.

Wright, Joseph, and Abel Escribà-Folch. (2012). "Authoritarian Institutions and Regime Survival: Transitions to Democracy and Subsequent Autocracy." *British Journal of Political Science* 42 (2): 283–309.

Xu, Jian. (2020). "The Role of Corporate Political Connections in Commercial Lawsuits: Evidence from Chinese Courts." *Comparative Political Studies* 53 (14): 2321–58.

Xydis, Stephen G. (1974). "Coups and Countercoups in Greece, 1967–1973 (with postscript)." *Political Science Quarterly* 89 (3): 507–38.

Yakobson, Alexander. (2010). "Traditional Political Culture and the People's Role in the Roman Republic." *Historia: Zeitschrift für Alte Geschichte* 59 (3): 282–302.

Yakobson, Alexander. (2012). "Political Rhetoric in China and in Imperial Rome: The Persuader, the Ruler, the Audience." *Extrême-Orient Extrême-Occident* 34:195–204.

Yamamoto, Hironori. (2007). *Tools for Parliamentary Oversight: A Comparative Study of 88 National Parliaments*. Geneva: Inter-Parliamentary Union.

Yan, Huang-Ting. (2020). "Does the Constitution Matter? Semi-Presidentialism and the Origin of Hegemonic Personalist Regimes." *International Political Science Review* 41 (3): 365–84.

Yom, Sean. (2023). "Kuwait's Democratic Promise." *Journal of Democracy* 34 (3): 46–61.

Young, Andrew T. (2015). "From Caesar to Tacitus: Changes in Early Germanic Governance circa 50 BC–50 AD." *Public Choice* 164 (3–4): 357–78.

Zeghal, Malika. (1996). *Gardiens de l'Islam: Les Oulemas d'Al Azhar dans l'Egypte Contmeporaine*. Paris: Presses de la Foundation Nationale des Sciences Politiques.

Zeghal, Malika. (1999). "Religion and Politics in Egypt: The Ulema of al-Azhar, Radical Islam, and the State (1952–94)." *International Journal of Middle East Studies* 31 (3): 371–99.

Zeghal, Malka. (2007). "The 'Recentering' of Religious Knowledge and Discourse: The Case of Al-Azhar in Twentieth-Century Egypt." In *Schooling Islam*, ed. Robert W. Hefner and Muhammad Qasim Zaman. Princeton: Princeton University Press.

Index

Abbas, Mahmoud: amendments by, 121–22, 123, 125; Arafat replaced by, 120; constitutional court law revived by, 125; against Dahlan, 128–29; Decree 16/2019 by, 131; Decree 17/2019 by, 131; judges chosen by, 126, 133; judges purged by, 131; law-making authority claimed by, 124; against Palestinian SCC autonomy, 122; Palestinian SCC supporting, 128–29; petitions by, 130; with PLC, 122–23; second draft bill signed by, 121; undermining of, 125

`Abd al-Nasir, Gamal, 104, 213–14

adaptability: in institutionalization, 76, 78, 190; of Kuwaiti National Assembly, 171; in religious establishments, 190

administration, 19, 40, 48

Adorno, Theodor, 17n19

Africa, 139; Kenya, 61–62; Libya, 46, 255; Morocco, 140; Uganda, 63, 143–44; Zimbabwe, 139–40. *See also* Egypt

Alvarez, Michael E., 10

Arafat, Yasser, 118, 120

Arendt, Hannah, 18

Argentina, 49

aristocracy, 33n76, 35

Aristotle, 34

Austria, 93

authoritarianism, 1–2; ambiguities and contradictory claims in, 24; authori-tarian institutions as oxymoron in, 23–24; authoritarian personality and, 17, 17n19, 21, 21n30; avoiding definitional sleights of hand with, 252–60; blurry view on, 21, 21n28; bottom-up approach to, 3; Chinese, 29–30; classical views on, 32–33, 33n73; classic attributes of, 23; classification of, 22–23; day-to-day life in, 60; definition of and why it matters, 10–13; democratic account-ability lacking in, 37, 37n82, 88; as functional or dysfunctional, 243–50; how it works for those who work it, 5–10; hybrid, 24–25, 24n36; inside out approach to, 4–5; institutional analysis of, 4, 10, 17–27, 245; insti-tutions opposite of, 5; intentionality in, 8; legal-rational authority and, 40–41; limited pluralism in, 42; Linzian view on, 20–21; lost mean-ings in, 32–37; as mattering, 88; as nondemocracy, 10–11, 19–20, 243; parliaments, untenable assumptions and, 138–41; parliaments coexisting with, 149–52, 149n44; persistence of, 28; as personality type, 17–18, 17n19; policymaking with, 39, 39n86; as political system, 18; politi-cal writings on, 32; regime survival in, 11–12; religion and, 191–94; as residual, 25, 48, 244, 259; as seen from above, 17–27; simplification of,

296 · Index

authoritarianism (*continued*)
12–13; structural diversity of, 9–10;
subtypes of, 23; systems in, 19–20,
49–50; thinking about Democracy
and, 250–52; top-down approach to,
3, 5–6, 8, 11–12, 23, 27, 244; totalitarianism *vs.*, 18, 27; tyranny *vs.*, 18,
24, 26, 29, 35, 43; ubiquity of, 11;
variation in, 6–7, 22, 31, 48–49, 51,
59, 245, 248, 257, 268–69
authoritarian personality, 17, 17n19,
21, 21n30
autocracy, 18; daily life of, 56–57
autocrats, 3–4; autonomy benefiting,
81; can't always get what they want,
27–32; constitutional courts created
by, 91–92; intentions of, 5; religious
establishments and, 192; as self-interested, 27–28; state institutions
and, 30–31, 55–58, 82–83; survival
of, 29. *See also* rulers
autonomy, 2–3; bounds of, 83–84;
of constitutional courts, 93–94;
meaning of, 61; of parliaments, 53,
141–45; of religious institutions,
54; as self-reinforcing, 79; of state
institutions, 59, 63–64, 66; of states,
256; in unlikely setting, 132–34. *See
also* institutional autonomy; internal
autonomy; mission autonomy
al-Azhar, 191, 213–14, 217–18, 218n69,
220–22, 224
al-Azhar Scholar's Front, 220–21
al-Azhar University, 30

Baaklini, Abdo I., 172
Barnett, Michael, 16
Basic Law (Palestine, 2002), 101, 118,
124, 126, 128, 130
Bedouin, 177, 179, 180
Bellin, Eva, 75–76
Bin Salman, Muhammed, 216, 223–24,
225
Bismarck, Otto von, 189, 196, 197, 199
bottom-up approach, 3

Brazil, 31, 63
Brezhnev, Leonid, 187
Brown, Nathan J., 24n38, 30n65,
31n70, 93n9, 94n13, 101n32,
104n34, 109, 109n37, 113n44,
130n60, 169n83, 213n56
Buddhadasa Bhikku, 236
Buddhism, 227–28, 227n77, 231, 236.
See also Sangha Administration
budgetary authority, 52
bureaucracy, 58–59
bureaucratic authoritarianism, 33n73,
105–6, 256
bureaucratic state, 36
bureaucrats, 5, 27, 31, 46

cabinet responsibility, 52
cabinets, 15, 49
Caesarism, 147
Canada, 47
Cardoso, Fernando, 47
Catholic Church, 30, 72, 87, 189,
191, 196; Bismarck's Reich, Kulturkampf and, 198–203; in Germany,
197; hierarchy in, 199, 201, 203;
under Hitler, 204–9; hospital and
educational work by, 201, 201n30;
institutionalization and, 202, 206;
laws against, 200–201, 200nn23–
24; linkages with, 206–7; mission
autonomy of, 203, 208; Nazis and,
198; priests exiled from, 200–201;
public constituencies linked to,
201–2; Reichskonkordat of July 1933
for, 207
Chamber of Fasces and Corporations,
151n50
Chehabi, Houchang E., 41
Cheibub, José Antonio, 19
chief justices, 46
Chile, 65
China, 29–30, 31, 46, 64, 140
Chinaworasiriwat, 231, 232
coherence: in institutionalization, 77,
78, 133, 191; of Kuwaiti National

Assembly, 171, 182, 184; in parliaments, 144, 185–86; in religious establishments, 191
Collier, David, 47
Communism: Buddhists against, 236; in China, 31, 46; parliaments and, 152; religious establishments and, 191; Soviet, 30
complexity: in institutionalization, 76–77, 78, 133, 190–91; of Kuwaiti National Assembly, 171; in religious establishments, 190–91, 192
Confessing Church, 206
Constantine the Great, 187
constitutional courts, 52, 57, 64; assumptions about, 95; in Austria, 93; as autonomous, 93–94; case studies for, 60; creation of, 93, 96; functionalist logics for, 92–95; functions of, 91–92, 94–95; institutionalization and, 89–90, 95, 132; internal autonomy in, 85–86, 98; Kuwaiti National Assembly and, 183–84; linkages, institutionalization, and judicial autonomy in, 96–98; linkages and, 89–90, 95, 132; mission autonomy in, 85–86, 97–98; organizational structure of, 68; as specific, 87; structural differentiation and, 96–97; in Uganda, 63; as useful tools, 89; as vulnerable, 93. *See also* Egypt; Palestine
constitutional order, 49–50
constitutions, 57
Council of Senior Scholars, 210; in Egypt, 220–22; in Saudi Arabia, 222–24
countries: institutionalization of, 83; state apparatus of, 83–84
coup, 47, 64, 230, 233, 238, 239

Dahlan, Mohammad, 125, 128–29
democracy: accountability in, 37, 37n82; associations with, 255–56; avoiding definitional sleights of hand

with, 252–60; certain institutions, ancient populism, and uncertain, 262–65; classical views of, 33–34, 260–61; competitive elections in, 37–38, 37n82; defining again, 260–62; definition of, 37–38, 251; delegative, 263–64; differences within, 37–41; direct, 261–62, 263; distinctiveness of, 248–49, 266–67; election uncertainty in, 263–64; electoral accountability in, 262; executive uncertainty in, 264–65; institutional autonomy in, 249, 259–60, 263, 264–65; institutionalization in, 41, 266; linkages in, 266; modern structures of, 38–39; negative connotations for, 34; normative governance and, 250–51; normative preference for, 34–35; as old term, 17; parliaments *vs.*, 149, 149n46; policymaking in, 39, 39n86; political uncertainty in, 40, 262–63; populism and, 263–64, 265; preconceptions of, 54; regimes in, 47; religious establishments and, 258; representatives elected in, 32–33; requirements in, 38; rule of law in, 260, 265; separation within, 54; specificity of, 263, 266; state, ruler, and regime distinct in, 266–67; state institutions in, 40, 248–49, 265; as structural differentiation, 249; as structurally differentiated, 265–69; talking authoritarianism and, 250–52; tyranny and, 34; variation in, 249, 257; violence and, 253
Denoeux, Guilain, 172
dictators, 2, 5, 6, 12
dictatorships: differences in, 23; essence of, 25; meaning interchangeable for, 18–19; as old term, 17; *vs.* tyranny, 33
diwaniyyas, 178, 178n105, 179–80
Draft Law (Palestine, 2003), 90, 116, 118–19, 119n47
Duma. *See* Russian State Duma

Egypt, 139–40; al-Azhar in, 191; bureaucratic authoritarianism in, 105–6; centrist Islam in, 209; constitution (1971) in, 105–6, 108, 109; Council of Senior Scholars in, 220–22; Dar al-Ifta' in, 211, 221; European imperialism influencing, 211–12; *hisba* in, 217–18; institutionalization in, 209; intermixing state, regime, and religion in, 224–25; junta in, 112; leaders deposed in, 255; linkages and institutionalization as legacies of state formation in, 211–16; linkages in, 209; marginalized moral policing legacy in, 217–18; *muhtasib* in, 217; Muslim Brotherhood in, 112–13; NGOs in, 108, 110, 114; Ottoman Empire influencing, 211; policing public morality in, 216–17; religious establishment in, 189, 196; Saudi Arabia, religious establishments and, 209–25; socialism in, 104–5, 107, 109; State Council in, 217–18; structural differentiation in, 112; uprising of 2011 in, 211

Egyptian Supreme Constitutional Court (SCC), 2, 30, 53–54, 64, 246; authoritarian measures by, 103–4; boldness of, 108; chief justice in, 108–9, 111, 114; endurance of, 115–16; establishment of, 85, 90–91, 100–102, 104; functionalist logic and, 101–2, 104; goal of, 92; informal norms in, 108–9; institutional autonomy seized and lost by, 108–16; institutionalization in, 52, 91, 102–3, 107, 115, 133; internal autonomy of, 96, 107, 109, 112, 115; Judges Club for, 103–4; judges in, 75, 91, 103; "Judicial families" in, 103; law 48 of 1979 by, 107–8; linkages of, 52, 91, 110, 115, 132–33; "massacre of the judiciary" in, 104; mission autonomy in, 86, 96, 107, 108, 109–10, 112;

Muslim Brotherhood against, 112–13; Palestinian court compared with, 98–101; against parliamentary election laws, 108; on property rights, 106, 106n36; religious establishment in, 58; restructuring of, 106; roots of, 99; as self-perpetuating, 109, 112; from short-term solution to part of ecosystem, 102–8; Socialist Public Prosecutor in, 106; structural differentiation and, 108, 132; unlikely autonomy in, 132–34

elections, 25, 28–29; in authoritarian systems, 15n16; competitive, 37–38, 37n82; in Middle East, 31; regime intentions and, 31; of representatives, 32–33; violence surrounding, 254–55

electoral authoritarianism, 23

elite coordination, 81

England, 6

Europe: assemblies in, 147–48; classes in, 150; dysfunction in, 150–51; parliamentarism rising in, 149–50, 149n44, 149n46

fascism, 151, 151n50

Fenner, Sofia, 44

Finnemore, Martha, 16

France, 48, 49n104

Franco, Francisco: Nixon on, 252–53; regime of, 49, 61, 87, 262; successor to, 253

Freedom House, 43

French Revolution, 149

functionalism: constitutional courts and, 92–95; definition of, 6; differentiation lacking with, 42; limits of, 16; linkages and institutionalization in, 80–83; power of, 9; of state institutions, 7, 14, 55; top-down, 80–81; use of, 7

functionalist logic, 3–4, 6–7, 9, 11, 16, 68, 244; for constitutional courts, 92–95; Duma and, 156, 158–59; of early Sangha Administration, 226–30; Egyptian SCC and, 101–2, 104; Kuwaiti National Assembly and, 181, 186; linkages and institutionalization as scope conditions for, 80–83; Palestinian SCC and, 116–17, 121, 127; in parliaments, 151; religious establishments and, 198, 220, 225; utility of, 127–32

Gandhi, Jennifer, 18, 27–28
Gaza, 100, 122, 124
Geddes, Barbara, 23, 48, 74
Gehlbach, Scott, 18–19, 24–25
George I (King), 6
German Evangelical Church Confederation, 204–5
German Nazi Party, 189
Germany, 147; Bismarck's Reich, Kulturkampf, and institutional Catholicism in, 198–203; Catholic Church in, 197; Center Party in, 202–3, 206; Confessing Church in, 206; German Empire in, 197; institutionalization in, 197–98; Kirchenkampf in, 197–98; Kulturkampf era in, 197; linkages in, 197, 202, 203; May Laws of 1873 in, 200, 200nn23–24; modern state of, 198; Nazi regime in, 197–98; Nürnberg Party Congress of 1937 in, 208; Protestantism and Catholicism under Hitler in, 204–9; Protestant religious establishment in, 197–98; Reichskonkordat of July 1933 in, 207; religious establishments in, 189, 196–209; structural differentiation in, 202
Goebbels, Joseph, 208
government: competitive elections in, 48; method of selection of, 47
Great Britain, 149
Greece, 147
Group to Restore the Religion, 231
Gryzlov, Boris, 162
Grzymala-Busse, Anna, 258

Hamas, 132; elections won by, 117, 123; Gaza controlled by, 124; opposition to, 122–24, 133
Heller, Joseph, 259
Henry VIII, 187
hierarchy: in institutionalization, 77–78, 191; in Kuwaiti National Assembly, 171, 182; in religious establishments, 191; in Russian State Duma, 161
Hilbink, Lisa, 65
hisba, 216, 217–18
historical institutionalism, 7–8, 14–15, 66, 88
Hitler, Adolf: in Nürnberg Party Congress of 1937, 208; Protestantism and Catholicism under, 204–9
House of Saud, 189–90, 192, 214–15
Huntington, Samuel: on degree of government, 254–55; on democracy, 38; on institutionalization, 75–76, 78; on single-party authoritarianism, 35n78; on structural differentiation, 42n94

independent courts, 26, 28
inside out approach, 4–5, 13
institutional autonomy, 2, 7, 9, 13, 27, 42–43; achieving of, 67; actions defining, 79; backlash against, 98; in democracy, 249, 259–60, 263, 264–65; of Egyptian SCC, 108–16; emergence of, 188; factors in, 60, 69, 71; forms of, 51–52; institutionalization and, 70; linkages and, 70; meaning of, 60–69; parliaments and, 185; problems in, 55–56; of religious organizations, 54; top-down functionalism and, 80–81; variation in, 80–81, 83. *See also* internal autonomy; mission autonomy
institutionalization, 9, 246; adaptability in, 76, 78, 190; autonomy facilitated by, 79–80; autonomy separate from, 79; Catholic Church and, 202, 206; coherence in, 77, 78, 133,

institutionalization (*continued*)
191; complexity in, 76–77, 78, 133,
190–91; conceptualizing of, 74–80;
constitutional courts and, 89–91,
95, 132; of countries, 83; definitions
of, 74–76; in democracy, 41, 266; in
Duma, 154, 155–68, 185; in Egypt,
209; in Egyptian SCC, 52, 91, 102–3,
107, 115, 133; general level of, 83;
in Germany, 197–98; as gradational, 82; hierarchy in, 77–78, 191;
institutional autonomy and, 70; in
judiciary, 97–98; of Kuwaiti National
Assembly, 138, 155, 170–71; leaders
in, 78; linkages, judicial autonomy,
constitutional courts and, 96–98;
linkages and, 69–71, 78–79; as low,
82; Palestinian SCC lacking, 91, 117,
127–28, 132, 134; in parliaments, 68,
136–37, 144–45, 154, 185; in political science, 74; quality and quantity
of, 240–42; as regime consolidation,
74, 78; religious establishments and,
188, 190–91, 196, 211–16; in Saudi
Arabia, 209; as scope condition, 80–
83; technocracy and, 186
Institutional Revolutionary Party,
29n62
institutions, 4; authoritarian institutions as oxymoron for, 23–24;
authoritarianism opposite to, 5; as
authoritarian or democratic, 88;
democratic requirements for, 38;
development of, 67, 70; elites in, 78;
evolution of, 8, 70–71; as heterogeneous, 4, 21, 61, 87, 266; historical, 7–8, 14–15, 67–68; horizontal
linkages with, 71; individual, 42–43;
lacking specificity, 44; old-fashioned
conceptualization of, 13–17; organizations *vs.*, 16; political, 15, 15n16;
power of, 17; profit from, 6; rationalist perspectives on, 14; as ruler, 46;
rulers using, 80–81; sociological, 15;
top-down view of, 6; usage of, 13.

See also religious institutions; state
institutions
internal autonomy, 246; in constitutional courts, 85–86, 98; definition
of, 59; of Duma, 154, 156–57, 158,
166–68, 185; in Egyptian SCC, 96,
107, 109, 112, 115; factors for, 52; in
Kenya, 61–62; of Kuwaiti National
Assembly, 170, 171, 178; linkages
facilitating, 73; low in Palestinian
SCC, 117, 122; mission autonomy
predicated on, 65–66; of parliaments,
136, 141, 185; of religious establishments, 54, 190, 193; in Sangha
Administration, 237–40; for state
institutions, 9, 51, 62; in Thailand,
232; as variable, 66; variation in, 61
international organizations, 16
Iraq, 180
Islam, 209
Israel, 100
Italy, 47, 191. *See also* Mussolini, Benito

Japan, 47
Jordan, 75, 140
judges, 5, 6, 27, 36; culture of, 64; in
Egyptian SCC, 75, 91, 103; horizontal linkages with, 71; linkages for, 97;
in Palestinian SCC, 126, 127
junta, 42, 112, 152, 239
A Just Russia, 165

Karl, Terry Lynn, 10, 45
Kenya, 61–62
Khalifa, Ali, 179
Khrushchev, Nikita, 63
KIO. *See* Kuwait Investment Office
Kittisophana, Plot, 234
Kricheli, Ruth, 29, 29n62
Kuwait, 53, 86–87; administrative
expansion in, 175–76; Bedouin in,
177, 179, 180; Constituent Assembly
in, 176; constitution (1962) in, 170,
181; convergent pressures in, 174–
76; divisions in, 178; *diwaniyyas* in,

178, 178n105, 179–80; early history
of, 174–75; elections (1975) in, 177;
elections (1985) in, 179; electorate
in, 178–79, 179n106; financial crisis
(1982) in, 179; formal independence
in, 176; Iraq invasion of, 180; Legislative Assembly in, 175; merchant
families in, 174–75; monarchy in,
154; national identity in, 175–76;
political reform movement in, 183–
84; public constituencies in, 169,
175, 180; structural differentiation
in, 174; urban progressives in, 179,
179n106. *See also* Al Sabah, Amir
Abdullah
Kuwaiti National Assembly, 53, 247;
adaptability of, 171; America and,
180; antecedents to, 168, 174;
"bloc of blocs" in, 171, 182; cabinet of, 176–77, 180; coherence of,
171, 182, 184; complexity of, 171;
Constitutional Court and, 183–84;
convergent pressures and founding
of, 174–76; creation of, 168–69, 171;
criticism of, 177; decent decades of,
181; as divided, 177–78; dynamic
power of linkage and latent power
in, 168–85; as dysfunctional, 169–70;
functionalist logic and, 181, 186;
functionalist narrative for, 171–72;
gerrymandering by, 177, 178, 181;
hierarchy in, 171, 182; institutionalization of, 138, 155, 170–71; internal
autonomy of, 170, 171, 178; interpellation in, 143; on KIO scandal, 172;
linkages with, 138, 154–55, 170,
178, 184–85; Majlis as problem to
solve in, 169–74; mission autonomy
of, 138, 155, 168, 170, 172–73, 185;
postwar, 180–81; powers of, 154,
170, 172, 173, 184; public constituencies, mission autonomy, and resil-
ience in, 176–81; public constituencies in, 169, 170, 173–74; ratchet
effects and authoritarian parliamen-

tarism in, 181–85; recent decades
of, 181; royal succession crisis and,
182–83; strength of, 170; structure
of, 173; suspension of, 154, 169, 170,
172, 173, 178, 179, 181, 182, 184
Kuwait Investment Office (KIO), 172

Lateran Pacts, 30, 191
Latin America, 139
Law of the Judicial Authority (Palestine, 2002), 125, 131
legislative obstruction, 52
legislatures, 146–47
liberalism, 34–35
Libya, 46, 255
Limongi, Fernando, 19
linkages, 9, 246, 248; autonomy facilitated by, 73, 79–80; autonomy separate from, 79; with Catholic Church,
206–7; conceptualizing of, 71–74;
constitutional courts and, 89–91, 95,
132; in democracy, 266; deterrence
through, 73; Duma lacking, 137, 154,
155–56, 159, 162, 163, 168; in Egypt,
209; of Egyptian SCC, 52, 91, 110,
115, 132–33; as formal, 73; forming
of, 72–73; in Germany, 197, 202,
203; as gradational, 82; horizontal,
71, 115, 144; institutional autonomy
and, 70; institutionalization and,
69–71, 78–79; international, 71–72;
for judges, 97; judicial autonomy,
institutionalization, constitutional
courts and, 96–98; Kuwaiti National
Assembly, power and, 168–85; with
Kuwaiti National Assembly, 178,
184–85; Kuwaiti National Assembly with, 138, 154–55, 170; lacking,
82; levels of, 71–72; mobilization
through, 73; with Palestinian SCC,
117, 127, 133; Palestinian SCC
lacking, 91, 116, 132, 134; in parliaments, 68, 72, 136–37, 144–45, 151,
154; with PLC, 117, 123; quality and
quantity of, 240–42; with religious

linkages (*continued*)
    establishments, 188, 190–91, 192,
    211–16; in religious institutions,
    72–73; of Sangha Administration,
    235–37; in Saudi Arabia, 209; as
    scope condition, 80–83; with state
    institutions, 187–88; structural dif-
    ferentiation and, 96–97; transforma-
    tion through, 73–74; types of, 96–97;
    vertical, 71, 110, 115, 145
Linz, Juan, 10, 253–54; on authoritar-
    ian *vs.* totalitarianism, 18, 21; on
    limited pluralism, 42; on nuance in
    authoritarianism, 20–21; on religious
    institutions, 87, 192–93, 252; on
    specificity of political institutions,
    44; on sultanism, 41

Magaloni, Beatriz, 29, 29n62
Mainwaring, Scott, 75
Majlis. *See* Kuwaiti National Assembly
Majlis al-Umma. *See* Kuwaiti National
    Assembly
Malaysia, 139–40, 143
Malenkov, Georgy, 63
May Laws (Germany, 1873), 200,
    200nn23–24
Medvedev, Dmitri, 49, 163
Mexico, 29n62, 47
militaries, 5
military regimes, 23
ministerial interpolation, 52
mission autonomy, 246; in Brazil, 63;
    of Catholic Church, 203, 208; in
    constitutional courts, 85–86, 97–98;
    definition of, 59, 62; of Duma, 155–
    56, 158, 162, 163, 185; in Egyptian
    SCC, 86, 96, 107, 108, 109–10, 112;
    factors for, 52; forms of, 64–65; of
    Hay'a, 219–20; in Kuwaiti National
    Assembly, 138, 155, 168, 170, 172–
    73, 176–81, 185; linkages facilitating,
    73; Palestinian SCC lacking, 117,
    122, 127; in parliaments, 136–37,
    142, 143, 185; as predicated on
    internal autonomy, 65–66; Protes-

tant establishment lacking, 205–6;
    in religious establishments, 54, 190,
    194; for state institutions, 9, 52, 62,
    65; in Uganda, 63; as variable, 66
monarchies, 23, 35n79; *vs.* aristocracy,
    33n76; contemporary views on, 35
Mongkut, 228
Monks for Independence, Democracy,
    and Justice, 236
Moore, Clement, 38
Morocco, 140
al-Morr, Awad, 111
Morsi, Muhammad, 113
Mouline, Nabil, 222
Moustafa, Tamir, 101–2
Mubarak, Hosni, 105, 112
muhtasib, 216, 217
multiparty legislatures, 25, 28
Museveni, Yoweri, 63
Muslim Brotherhood, 104, 112–13, 221
Mussolini, Benito, 30, 151n50

National People's Congress (NPC), 29
Nazi Germany, 48, 53–54, 197
Nazi Third Reich, 196
neo-institutionalist political science, 66
neo-patrimonial rule, 42
NGO. *See* nongovernmental
    organization
Nixon, Richard, 252–53
nongovernmental organization
    (NGO), 108, 110, 114
normative concerns, 34–35
North, Douglass, 14
NPC. *See* National People's Congress
Nürnberg Party Congress of 1937, 208

O'Donnell, Guillermo, 256
oligarchies, 35
one-party regimes, 23
Opalo, Ken, 61–62
Organization of Sangha Brotherhood,
    236
Ottoman Empire, 211

PA. *See* Palestinian Authority

Palestine: Basic Law (2002) in, 101, 118, 124, 126, 128, 130; challenges in, 116; civil war in, 124; deinstitutionalization in, 124–27; Fatah in, 100, 118, 122–23, 124–26, 128–29, 132; High Court in, 125, 128–30, 131; institution building in, 118; liberal court created in, 118–24; prime minister in, 120. *See also* Hamas

Palestinian Authority (PA), 118, 124–25

Palestinian Legislative Council (PLC): Abbas with, 122–23; constitutional court interest by, 118; discrepancy in, 121; dissolution of, 130–31; farewell session of, 123–24; first draft bill (2003) of, 118–19, 119n47; linkages with, 117, 123; second draft bill (2006) of, 119–22, 119n48

Palestinian Liberation Organization (PLO), 118, 132

Palestinian National Authority (PNA), 99–100, 119, 120

Palestinian Supreme Constitutional Court (SCC), 52, 85–86, 96, 246; on Decree 16/2019, 131; on Decree 17/2019, 131; deinstitutionalization and eventual establishment of, 124–27; Draft Law (2003) for, 90, 116, 118–19, 119n47; Egyptian court compared with, 98–101; Egyptian SCC influencing, 90–91, 116; establishment of, 90–91, 99–101, 116, 133; functionalist logic and, 116–17, 121, 127; history of, 116–17, 118; institutionalization lacking in, 91, 117, 127–28, 132, 134; internal autonomy low in, 117, 122; judges in, 126, 127; laws borrowed by, 90, 90n1, 98–99; linkages lacking in, 91, 116, 132, 134; linkages with, 117, 127, 133; mission autonomy low in, 117, 122, 127; outcome of, 92; on parliamentary immunity, 128–29; PLC dissolution ordered by, 130; president supported by, 128–29; roots of, 99; on short leash, 127–32;

societal opposition to, 126; unlikely autonomy in, 132–34

parliaments, 2–3; active amendment or law proposition in, 143; assemblies, diets, and, 145–55; assumptions about, 138–40; authoritarianism, untenable assumptions and, 138–41; authoritarianism coexisting with, 149–52, 149n44; autonomy of, 53, 141–45; bill dismissal or veto in, 144; case studies for, 60; coherence in, 144, 185–86; communist regimes and, 152; complicated history of, 185–86; constituent elements of, 153; democracy *vs.*, 149, 149n46; deputies in, 136; duration of, 7; dysfunction of, 137, 141, 146, 150–51; format of, 153; functionalist logic in, 151; historical analysis of, 145–55; history of, 137, 145; horizontal linkages with, 71; as inherited, 53, 139–40; institutional autonomy and, 185; institutionalization in, 68, 136–37, 144–45, 154, 185; internal autonomy of, 136, 141, 185; interpellation in, 142–43; juntas and, 152; juxtaposition in, 86; legislatures *vs.*, 146–47; linkages in, 68, 72, 136–37, 144–45, 151, 154; marginalization of, 153; mission autonomy in, 136–37, 142, 143, 185; modern, 152–54; new, same as old, 146–49; as old, 57, 139; origin of, 93; political parties influencing, 136; powers of, 52, 135, 142, 185; procedural obstruction in, 143; purpose of, 29, 64, 138–39; regime supported by, 135–36, 140–41; religious establishments *vs.*, 195–96; rise of, 149, 149n44; as rubber stamps, 135–36, 151, 152; as similar, 87; specific cases of, 154–55; structural differentiation and, 137; of technocracy, 186; tolerance of, 5–6; vertical linkages with, 71; work of, 141. *See also* Kuwaiti National Assembly; Russian State Duma

party systems, 75
patrimonialism, 23, 33n73, 41, 50
personalist regimes, 23
Phibun, Plaek, 232
Phimonlatham, Phra, 234n102
PLC. *See* Palestinian Legislative
    Council
PLO. *See* Palestinian Liberation
    Organization
PNA. *See* Palestinian National
    Authority
policing, 216–17
policymaking, 4, 8, 39, 39n86, 58
political community, 36n80
Political Order in Changing Societies
    (Huntington), 75
politicians, 27, 46
polity. *See* democracy
Polity Project, 43
popular assemblies, 57, 147–48
populism, 263–64, 265
Portugal, 49
procedural obstruction, 143
Protestant religious establishment, 189;
    in Germany, 197–98; under Hitler,
    204–9; mission autonomy lacking in,
    205–6
Przeworski, Adam, 18–19, 37–38,
    260–61
Putin, Vladimir, 2; election (2012) of,
    164; loyalty to, 155–56

al-Qadhdhafi, Mu`ammar, 46

Rama III, 228
Rama IV, 228
regime change, 2
regime legitimation, 81
regimes: bureaucracy and, 58–59; clas-
    sical terms for, 35–36, 36nn80–81;
    classification of, 34–35; communist,
    152; as conceptually slippery, 44–46;
    definitions of, 45, 47–50; in democ-
    racy, 47; democratic mechanisms in,
    258–59; distinguishing rulers, states

and, 41–51; history influencing, 80;
hybrid, 25–26; intentions of, 31–32;
naming of, 49; operations of, 35;
parliaments supporting, 135–36,
140–41; ruler, state, and meaning
of, 46–50; rules in, 47; secrecy and,
257; state distinct from, 51; survival
of, 11–12; tactical thinking in, 86;
types of, 10, 39, 47; word choice of,
19, 19n26
religious establishments, 2, 13, 15–
16, 15n16, 53–54, 87; adaptability
in, 190; as amorphous, 188, 194;
authoritarianism and, 191–94; autocrats and, 192; case studies for, 60,
189–90, 192, 196; coherence in, 191;
Communism and, 191; complexity
in, 190–91, 192; democracies and,
258; disparate positioning of, 189;
dual role of, 192; in Egypt, 189; in
Egypt and Saudi Arabia, 209–25;
functionalist logic and, 198, 220,
225; functions of, 195–96; in Germany, 189; hierarchy in, 191; historical explorations of, 189; horizontal
linkages with, 71; identification of,
193; institutionalization and, 188,
190–91, 196; institutions and, 195;
intermixing state, regime, and religion in, 224–25; internal autonomy
for, 190, 193; linkages and institutionalization as legacies of state
formation and, 211–16; linkages
with, 73, 188, 190–91, 192; mission
autonomy for, 190, 194; moral power
in, 258; as motley crew, 194–96; old
and new in, 57; origin of, 93; parliaments *vs.*, 195–96; policing public
morality by, 216–17; political impact
of, 191; publics and, 190; quality and
quantity of institutionalization and
linkages in, 240–42; rulers and, 187;
in Saudi Arabia, 189–90; as structurally complex, 87; terminology in,
194–95; in Thailand, 189–90, 225–

40; variations in, 194–96; vertical linkages with, 71. *See also* Council of Senior Scholars

religious institutions, 36–37, 53–54; autonomy of, 54, 193; international linkages with, 72; linkages cultivated in, 72–73; policing public morality by, 210; policymaking by, 58, 193; totalitarianism *vs.*, 87

representation, 47

rights to bill initiative, 52

rulers: can't always get what they want, 27–32; changing of, 49; definition of, 46, 50; distinguishing regimes, states and, 41–51; elected *vs.* unelected, 41; *hisba* for, 216; institutions used by, 80–81; loyalty of, 78; number of, 32; officers as, 32–33; religious establishments and, 187; state, regime meaning and, 46–50; state institutions as extension of, 50; types of, 27; virtue and, 35, 35n78. *See also* autocrats

Russia, 51, 53, 86, 137; Committee on Family, Women, and Children's Affairs in, 165; conservative turn in, 164–65; constitutional crisis in, 157–58; as nondemocratic, 157; protests in, 163–64; religious institutions in, 58; structural differentiation lacking in, 155–56, 157–58, 161; technocracy in, 186. *See also* Putin, Vladimir; Russian State Duma; United Russia

Russian State Duma, 53, 135, 137–38, 247; consolidation of, 158–59; creation of, 157; decay, sclerosis, and bureaucratizing institutionalization, 155–68; Duma Apparat in, 167; Duma Council in, 159–61; electoral system shift in, 162; functionalist logic and, 156, 158–59; hierarchy in, 161; homosexual propaganda legislation by, 165; institutionalization in, 154, 159, 185; internal autonomy of, 154, 156–57, 158, 166–68, 185; linkage lacking with, 137, 154, 155–56,

159, 162, 163, 168; as "Mad Printer," 165–66; ministries and, 167; mission autonomy of, 155–56, 158, 162, 163, 185; moral laws passed by, 165–66; opposition parties in, 163–64, 165; as placeholder parliament, 157–62; powers of, 157, 159; procedural obstruction in, 143; regime reconsolidation and bureaucratic institutionalization in, 164–68; reputation of, 162; revving parliament and reviving authoritarianism, 163–64; rubber-stamping role of, 161–62, 166; stabilizing of, 167–68; turf wars in, 166–67

al-Ruwayni, Salah, 114

SAA. *See* Sangha Administration Act

Al Sabah, Amir Abdullah, 170, 172, 174–75, 179, 183, 184

Al-Sabah, Sa`d Al-Salim, 183

al-Sadat, Anwar, 105

Salazar, António de Oliveira, 49, 187

Sangha Administration, 190, 191, 225; Council of Elders in, 229, 232, 238, 239; early, 226–30; functionalist logic of, 226–30; incoherence and defeat of internal autonomy in, 237–40; institutional incoherence, scattered linkages, and sundering of, 235–37; after modern regime change, 230–32; in regime tumults of 1940s and 1950s, 232–33; reversing reform of, 233–35

Sangha Administration Act (SAA): of 1902, 229–31, 234; of 1941, 232–33; of 1962, 235; of 2014, 239

Santi-Asoke movement, 237

Sarit Tharanat, 233–34, 235

Saudi Arabia, 30, 53–54, 64, 192; Council of Senior Scholars in, 222–24; Egypt, religious establishments and, 209–25; Hay'a and, 218–20; House of Saud in, 189–90, 192, 214–15; institutionalization in,

Saudi Arabia (*continued*)
209; intermixing state, regime, and religion in, 224–25; linkages and institutionalization as legacies of state formation in, 211–16; linkages in, 209; Ministry of Culture in, 223–24; *muhtasib* in, 216, 217; against Ottoman Empire, 211; policing public morality in, 216–17; religious establishment in, 189–90, 196; religious police in, 217, 218; structural differentiation in, 214, 223; Wahhabi establishment in, 209, 211, 212–13, 215–16, 222–23

SCAF. *See* Supreme Council of the Armed Forces

SCC. *See* Egyptian Supreme Constitutional Court; Palestinian Supreme Constitutional Court

Schedler, Andreas, 21n28

Schmitt, Carl, 149, 149n46

Schmitter, Philippe C., 10, 45

scope conditions, 9; application of, 81–82; definition of, 81; linkages and institutionalization as, 81–83

selectorate, 19n26

selectorate theory, 48

Siamese Law (Thailand, 1897), 229n85

Singapore, 186, 191

al-Sisi, `Abd al-Fattah, 1–2, 30, 113–14

Skocpol, Theda, 256

Slater, Dan, 44

Socialism, 104–5, 107, 109

sociological institutionalism, 15

Sonin, Konstantin, 18–19, 24–25

Soviet Union: America and, 254–55; military of, 30, 31, 63

Spain, 61, 87, 195, 252–53. *See also* Franco, Francisco

Springborg, Robert, 172

state institutions, 2, 4; autocrats and, 30–31, 55–58, 82–83; autonomy of, 43, 59, 63–64, 66; as concrete, 13–14; courts under, 55; in democracy, 40, 248–49, 265; dictators controlling,

12; explanations implausible for, 56; as extension of ruler, 50; founding of, 57; functionalism of, 7, 14; functionalist accounts of, 55; functionalist view of, 7; hybrid, 25–26; individual, 69–71; as inherited, 44; institutionalization of, 9; internal autonomy for, 9, 51, 62; linkages with, 9, 187–88; as malleable, 56; mission autonomy for, 9, 52, 62, 65; narrowing of, 15–16; organizations *vs.*, 16; problems in, 55–56; regime in, 46; restructuring of, 82; selecting of, 85–87; simplifying assumptions of, 55–56; social constituencies and, 8; structural differentiation in, 46, 259; subordination of, 42; as umbrella category, 15n16; variation in, 39–40. *See also* institutions

states: autonomy of, 256; definition of, 46–47, 50; distinguishing rulers, regimes and, 41–51; modern, 47; regimes distinct from, 51; ruler, regime meaning and, 46–50; as system of institutions, 44

Stepan, Alfred, 74, 78, 256

structural differentiation: autonomy's bounds in, 83–84; constitutional courts and, 96–97; definition of, 41–42, 42n94; in democracy, 249, 265–69; in Egypt, 112; Egyptian SCC and, 108, 132; in empirical analysis, 42; of entire system, 43, 69; in Germany, 202; *hisba* in, 216; in Kuwait, 174; as lacking, 42n94; levels in, 83–84; linkages and, 96–97; parliaments and, 137; as present, 43; Russia lacking, 155–56, 157–58, 161; in Saudi Arabia, 214, 223; in state institutions, 46, 259; at systemic level, 43; variation in, 44–46

sultanism, 10, 21, 41, 42, 50

Supreme Constitutional Court. *See* Egyptian Supreme Constitutional Court; Palestinian Supreme Constitutional Court

Supreme Council of the Armed Forces (SCAF), 112
Surkov, Vladislav, 160
Svolik, Milan W., 18–19, 22, 25
Syria, 58

technical ministries, 72
technocracy, 186
Thailand, 53–54, 64, 140, 191, 248; Buddhism in, 227–28, 227n77, 231; Chakri dynasty in, 226–31; coup in, 230, 233, 238, 239; early Sangha Administration in, 226–30; Group to Restore the Religion in, 231; institutional incoherence, scattered linkages, and sundering of Sangha Administration in, 235–37; internal autonomy in, 232; junta in, 239; monks banned from politics in, 229, 229n85; People's Party in, 230–31; Redshirt protests in, 238; regime creation in, 225–40; religious establishments in, 189–90, 196; reversing Sangha Administration reform in, 233–35; royalist Sangha after modern regime change in, 230–32; Sangha incoherence and defeat of internal autonomy in, 237–40; Sangha in regime tumults of 1940s and 1950s in, 232–33; Santi-Asoke movement in, 237; Siamese Law of 1897 in, 229n85; Thammayut Order in, 228, 231, 233; Wat Phra Dhammakaya movement in, 237, 238, 239. *See also* Sangha Administration; Sangha Administration Act (SAA)
Thaksin Shinawatra, 237–38
Third Reich, 48
totalitarianism, 18, 21, 27, 193;

religious institutions *vs.*, 87; state institutions in, 50
totalitarian regimes, 10
Truex, Rory, 29
Trump, Donald, 21n30
Turkey, 191–92
tyranny, 31; authoritarianism *vs.*, 18, 24, 26, 29, 35, 43; classical democracy and, 34; classical meaning of, 33; dictatorship *vs.*, 33

Uganda, 63, 143–44
Ukrainian parliament, 143
United Russia: consolidation into, 159; Duma dominated by, 161–62; protests against, 163; as supermajority, 160, 166

Varieties of Democracy, 43
Venezuela, 58, 144
veto players, 79
Vichy regime, 48, 49n104
Vietnam, 140
Volodin, Vyacheslav, 166–67
votes of no confidence, 52

Wahhabi Muslim movement, 192
Wat Phra Dhammakaya movement, 237, 238, 239
Weber, Max, 14, 33n73, 75–76
Weimar Republic, 48
West Bank, 100, 122, 124, 132

Xi Jinping, 187

Yanukovych, Viktor, 143

Zedong, Mao, 46
Zimbabwe, 139–40
Zoroastrian Mehestan Assemblies, 148